# The Pillar of Volozhin

Rabbi Naftali Ẓvi Yehuda Berlin and the World of Nineteenth-Century Lithuanian Torah Scholarship

STUDIES IN ORTHODOX JUDAISM

# The Pillar of Volozhin

Rabbi Naftali Ẓvi Yehuda Berlin and the World of Nineteenth-Century Lithuanian Torah Scholarship

GIL S. PERL

*Boston 2013*

Library of Congress Cataloging-in-Publication Data:
A catalog record for this title is available from the Library of Congress.


ISBN 978-1-936235-70-4 (hardcover)
ISBN 978-1-618113-01-6 (paperback)

Book design by Adell Medovoy

Published by Academic Studies Press in 2012, paperback edition 2013.
28 Montfern Avenue
Brighton, MA 02135, USA

press@academicstudiespress.com
www.academicstudiespress.com

## Table of Contents


| | |
|---|---|
| Acknowledgements | 7 |
| Preface | 9 |
| The Life and Times of Neẓiv | 11 |
| *'Emek ha-Neẓiv*: A Window into his World | 19 |
| Method and Approach | 23 |
| Note on Transliteration | 26 |
| **CHAPTER I:** The Text of *'Emek ha-Neẓiv* | 27 |
| Dating the Printed Text | 28 |
| The Manuscript | 32 |
| Censorship | 36 |
| The End of *'Emek ha-Neẓiv* | 38 |
| Conclusions | 40 |
| **CHAPTER II:** Neẓiv as an Early Nineteenth-Century Midrash Commentator | 42 |
| Midrash Commentary Prior to the Vilna Ga'on | 42 |
| The "Vilna Circle" | 43 |
| The "Volozhin Circle" | 54 |
| The Influence of Radal on the Young Neẓiv | 57 |
| **CHAPTER III:** *'Emek ha-Neẓiv*: An Early Nineteenth-Century Midrash Commentary | 61 |
| Straightforward Interpretation | 61 |
| Textual Emendation | 66 |
| Intellectual Breadth | 83 |
| The Selection of *Sifre* | 90 |
| Dual Commentary | 91 |
| Poetic Adornments | 94 |
| **CHAPTER IV:** The Young Neẓiv and the Ancient Rabbis | 97 |
| Rabbinic Methodology | 97 |
| Identification of *'Asmakhta'* | 101 |
| De' Rossian Hermeneutics | 105 |
| Explicit Use of *Me'or 'Einayim* in *'Emek ha-Neẓiv* | 111 |
| The Unattributed Influence of de' Rossi | 120 |
| **CHAPTER V:** *Emek ha-Neẓiv* in its Cultural Context | 127 |
| The Influence of the Vilna Ga'on | 127 |
| The Vilna Ga'on in *Emek ha-Neẓiv* | 137 |

The "Halakhic" Progression of Torah Commentary 142
The Lithuanian *Maggid* 146
Hebrew Print and the Study of Midrash 149
Neẓiv's Use of Newly Available Books 160

**CHAPTER VI:** From *'Emek ha-Neẓiv* to *Ha'amek Davar* 167
From *'Emek ha-Neẓiv* to *Ha'amek She'elah* 167
Dating *Ha'amek Davar* 169
*'Emek ha-Neẓiv* as the Foundation for *Ha'amek Davar* 171
Exegetical Positions Rooted in *Sifre* 180
*Ha'amek Davar* as Nineteenth-Century Midrash 182

**CHAPTER VII:** The Polemics of *Ha'amek Davar* 190
Literal Aggadah in *Ha'amek Davar* 192
Hermeneutics of a Rosh Yeshivah 193
The Antiquity of *Pilpulah Shel Torah* 196
The Salvific Power of Torah Study 202
Citation in *Ha'amek Davar* 206
The Hermeneutics of Traditionalism 208
The 1840s: Tension without Fissure 209
The 1860s: A Splintered Society 216
Lithuaniam Torah Scholarship Responds 220
*Maskilim* in *Ha'amek Davar* 229

Afterword: Avenues for Further Research 239

Appendices
Appendix A: The Unattributed Influence of Radal on *Ha'amek Davar* 242
Appendix B: Emendations to *Sifre 'Ekev* According to the Ga'on and Neẓiv 246
Appendix C: Selections from Ḥayyim Berln's "Letter on Education, 1902" 257
Appendix D: *Birkat ha-Neẓiv* and the Question of Genre 262

Bibliography 269

# Acknowledgements

This book began as my doctoral thesis for Harvard's Department of Near Eastern Languages and Civilizations under the direction of Professor Jay Harris. His passion for both the textual world of *midrash halakhah* and the intellectual world of eighteenth- and nineteenth-century Jewish Europe are clearly reflected in this work. My decision to pursue the study of modern Jewish history at Harvard owes much to the inspiration I received from Professor David Ruderman as an undergraduate at the University of Pennsylvania and the encouragement I received, and continue to receive, from Rabbi Dr. Jacob J. Schacter of Yeshiva University's Center for the Jewish Future. As will be discussed at the beginning of the first chapter, though I had the privilege of studying with Professor Haym Soloveitchik for only one semester, the methodology and critical approach to rabbinic texts I learned from him were formative in my own development as a student of rabbinic texts.

The transformation of my dissertation into the present work results from the efforts and support of quite a few individuals. First and foremost is Professor Shaul Stampfer. The world's leading scholar in the area of nineteenth-century Lithuanian *yeshivot*, he honored me with an unsolicited email praising my work and encouraging me to publish it. This was the push I needed to make this project happen.

I am grateful for the support I have received from the lay leadership of the Margolin Hebrew Academy in Memphis, Tennessee, who have allowed me to keep a foot in the academic world while also serving as dean of their elementary and high schools for the past four years. During that time my connection to the Neẓiv has only grown, in large part due to the weekly class I give to a wonderful group of highly motivated and keenly insightful women. Watching them grow in their appreciation for the Neẓiv and his work consistently stoked my desire to share the world of the Neẓiv with an even larger audience.

I am indebted to Dr. Marc Shapiro, editor of the Studies in Orthodox Judaism series, for inviting me to submit my manuscript to Academic Studies Press for inclusion in this series. His efforts, as well as those of Sharona Vedol, have made the process of publication both pleasant and professional. I am also deeply grateful to Rabbi Avraham Leiberman and to Ms. Erica Stoltz for their help in editing the manuscript.

Above all, though, there are two individuals without whom this book would not have come to fruition. While both of my parents have supported me in this endeavor every step of the way, my father, Dr. Harold Perl, has played a special role. From acting as my Neẓiv study partner while I was doing my research to his role as the constant voice in my ear encouraging, pushing, and prodding me first to complete the dissertation and then to publish it, he, more than anyone, made sure that I saw this project to completion. Doing so, however, required not only years of work on my part, but similar dedication and devotion to the cause by my partner in life, Melissa. An exceptional mother to Shmuel Meir, Racheli, Binny, and Eitan, she is also a gifted teacher and an excellent scholar in her own right. Over the past decade she has willingly and lovingly relegated her own dissertation, along with many other potential pursuits, to the back burner so as to enable me to complete this work. For this and all she does for our family, my gratitude and appreciation know no bounds.

Gil Perl

*April, 2011*
*Memphis, TN*

# Preface

The traditional historiographical account of Lithuanian Torah scholarship most often begins with a portrait of the unrivaled intellectual prowess and fierce communal polemics of Eliyahu ben Shelomoh (1720-1797), commonly referred to as the Vilna Ga'on. With the Ga'on's death in 1797, the story refocuses on his outstanding student, Ḥayyim of Volozhin (1749-1821), and his pioneering efforts in establishing the first of the great Lithuanian yeshivot in 1803 as well as the path he blazed in the world of Jewish ideas with the publication of his *Nefesh ha-Ḥayyim*. From his Eẓ Ḥayyim Yeshivah in Volozhin, historians generally shift their gaze toward the subsequent establishment of similar yeshivot, its progeny, throughout Lithuania. The story then proceeds to the rise of Yisrael Salanter's (1810-1883) *Mussar* movement in the middle of the nineteenth century, which acts as both an heir and a corrective to the world of Torah learning born in Volozhin, and then to the innovative method of study introduced by Ḥayyim Soloveitchik (1853-1918) of Brisk and his disciples as the nineteenth century draws to a close. This new method, by all accounts, served as a catalyst for the growth of traditional Lithuanian Torah scholarship well into the twentieth century.

The unspoken assumption of this historiographical account is that once Volozhin appears on the scene in 1803, yeshivot immediately become the center of intellectual activity for the rabbinic scholars of Lithuania's traditional Jewish community. Yet there is no question that, during the first few decades of the nineteenth century at the very least, the great minds of traditional Jewish Lithuania were not to be found in the large yeshivot. They were, much as they had been in the centuries before, the rabbis of communities and the heads of rabbinical courts, privately funded scholars and communally funded preachers. And, whereas the rise of the yeshivah, with its standardized curriculum and the ensuing social pressure to master it, gradually narrowed the focus of Lithuanian Torah scholarship to the proverbial four cubits of Talmud study, the Lithuanian intellectuals of the earlier decades of the nineteenth century knew no such bounds. To date, however, these scholars and their scholarship have been lost in the exaggerated shadow of the Lithuanian yeshivot.

This book focuses on the work of a man who is best known for having served at the helm of the yeshivah in Volozhin as it reached its pinnacle of success and eventual decline in the second half of the nineteenth century. As such, one is apt to view his scholarly work against the backdrop of the yeshivah world and its particular ideological and intellectual proclivities, but, as we shall see, when viewed against such a backdrop Naftali Ẓvi Yehudah Berlin (Neẓiv; 1816-1893) emerges as a cultural oddity. His work is not confined within the curricular boundaries of traditional Talmud study and he is not interested in the conceptual underpinnings of halakhic reasoning, nor is he preoccupied with the drawing of legal distinctions between seemingly similar instances of Jewish case law, as are most of the great works of Torah scholarship which were produced in the yeshivot of the late nineteenth and early twentieth centuries.[1] However, when one dims the lights shining on the yeshivot of the late nineteenth century and recognizes that during the formative years of Neẓiv's intellectual development the world of the yeshivah was still in its infancy, a very different understanding of his scholarship comes into focus. It is one which recognizes that while Neẓiv's early years were spent in the physical space of the Volozhin yeshivah, the cultural and ideological forces which later came to dominate the world of the yeshivot had yet to take shape. Therefore, the intellectual interests and methodology of the young Neẓiv and his associates in Volozhin were rooted in the vibrant world of early nineteenth-century Lithuanian Torah scholarship, still unconstrained by the distinctive mold of the modern yeshivah.[2]

---

1 See, for example, the works authored by and attributed to Ḥayyim Soloveitchik (1853-1918), Shimon Shkop (1860-1940), Moshe Mordecai Epstein (1866-1934), Baruch Ber Lebowitz (1870-1940), Issar Zalman Meltzer (1870-1953), and Elhanan Wasserman (1875-1941), amongst others.

2 I do not mean to suggest that all Lithuanian rabbinic scholars of the late nineteenth and early twentieth centuries were, in fact, constrained by such a mold. There were indeed preeminent Lithuanian scholars such as Meir Simḥah of Dvinsk (1843-1926) and later Avraham Yeshayahu Karelitz (1878-1953) who rose to prominence without spending time in the famous yeshivot, and whose scholarship is, therefore, of a different character. Likewise, there were rabbinic scholars such as Yosef Rosen (1858-1936) and Avraham Yiẓḥak Kook (1864-1935) who, though having spent time in the world of the mitnagdic yeshivot, were also clearly influenced by intellectual worlds well beyond it. Neẓiv, however, is unique in that he spent his entire adolescence and adult life, from the age of fourteen to the age of seventy-six, within the confines of Lithuania's leading yeshivah. It is this fact that leads one to view him as a cultural oddity rather than a late product of a cultural mainstream which was eventually eclipsed by the rise of the Brisker school.

## *The Life and Times of Neẓiv*

Naftali Ẓvi Yehudah Berlin, today known by the acronym Neẓiv,[3] was born on the eve of Rosh Ḥodesh Kislev in the Jewish year of 5577 (November 20, 1816)[4] to a prominent family in the small Lithuanian town of Mir.[5] Mir, along with much of the eastern regions of what was once the Polish-Lithuanian Commonwealth, was appropriated by Imperial Russia during the second partition of Poland in 1793. By 1795, the remaining areas of Lithuania and much of Poland came under Russian rule as well. Along with Polish-Lithuanian territory the Russian Tsars inherited its Jewish population, which is believed to have numbered close to one million at the end of the eighteenth century. While Catherine the Great, the architect of Russia's conquest of Poland, fashioned herself as an Enlightened Absolutist and thus a friend of her new Jewish subjects, the policies initiated during the reign of her son Paul (1796-1801) were characterized by his fear that the Jewish community might shift its allegiance to parties opposed to Imperial rule and his consequent desire to pull this large, cohesive, and culturally distinct population into mainstream Russian society. Alexander I (1801-1825), who succeeded Paul, began his rule by adopting a stance toward the Jewish population akin to that of his grandmother Catherine, as evidenced by his opening of state educational institutions to Jewish students. This too, however, was a failed attempt to facilitate the Russification of the Jewish population, and his seemingly progressive posture became far more oppressive and reactionary when he feared the development of a Jewish allegiance to

3 Traditional parlance tends to treat rabbinic acronyms as common nouns, and they are thus preceded by the word "the" as in "the Rambam" or "the Neẓiv," whereas academic literature treats them as proper nouns, thus obviating the need to precede the acronym with the word "the." In the case at hand, however, the acronym for Rabbi Berlin spells the Hebrew word *naẓiv*, meaning pillar. When referring to Berlin as "ha-naziv," therefore, the Hebrew speaker hears both the letters of Berlin's name and a reference to "The Pillar." While the preservation of this double entendre justifies reference to Berlin as "the Neẓiv," my work will defer to the general preference of the academy and thus refer to him simply as Neẓiv.

4 Barukh ha-Levi Epstein, *Mekor Barukh* (IV: 1678); Meir Bar-Ilan, *Rabban Shel Yisrael* (New York: Histadrut ha-Mizrahi beAmerikah, 1943), 131. The year of Neẓiv's birth is often misstated as 1817.

5 In what is today Belarus. The region referred to as cultural Lithuania by the nineteenth-century Jewish community is an expansive territory which generally corresponds to the territories which once comprised the Grand Duchy of Lithuania and includes modern-day Latvia, Lithuania, Belarus, parts of north eastern Poland, and parts of the western-most areas of modern Russia.

Napoleon during the invasion of 1812.

Naftali was nine years old when Nicholas I (1825-1855) crushed the Decembrist Uprising of 1825 and with it the liberal ambitions of its protagonists, thereby securing his place as successor to Alexander I on the Russian throne. What followed were decades of oppressive legislation that sought to curtail Jewish cultural activity and forcibly bring the Jewish population into line with Nicholas' imperial vision of "orthodoxy, autocracy, and nationality."[6] As a result of the consistent failure of these policies to encourage widespread acculturation, combined with the general sense of political stability brought about by the iron fist of Nicholas' lengthy reign, Jewish intellectual life during this period not only survived but flourished in an unprecedented manner.

Indeed, many of the movements which came to characterize Lithuanian Jewish society by the end of the nineteenth century emerged from the thirty years of Nicholas' reign. As noted above, the subsequent decades of the nineteenth century saw bastions of traditional Torah learning, following in the footsteps of the talmudic academy founded by Ḥayyim of Volozhin in 1803, rising throughout Lithuania, forming the foundation of the modern yeshivah movement.[7] Following the publication of Isaac Baer Levinsohn's *Te'udah be-Yisrael* in 1828, calls for Jewish educational reform coalesced into the movement for the general enlightenment of Russian Jewry known as the Haskalah.[8] The 1840s witnessed the creation of a movement, following the charismatic lead of Yisrael Salanter (1810-1883), that championed the study and practice of ethical behavior known as the *Mussar* movement.[9] It is in this world

---

6 For a general history of the period, see Nicholas Riasanovsky, *Nicholas I and Official Nationality in Russia* (Berkeley: University of California Press, 1959) and W. Bruce Lincoln, *Nicholas I: Emperor and Autocrat of All the Russias* (DeKalb: Northern Illinois University Press, 1989). For a social and political history of the Jewish community under Nicholas' rule, see Michael Stanislawski, *Tsar Nicholas I and the Jews: The Transformation of Jewish Society in Russia, 1825-1855* (Philadelphia: JPS, 1983).

7 See Shaul Stampfer, *Shalosh Yeshivot Lita'iyot bi-Me'ah ha-Tesha-'Esreh* (PhD dissertation, Hebrew University, 1981) and idem., *ha-Yeshivah ha-Lita'it be-Hithavutah ba-Me'ah ha-Tesh'a-'Esreh* (Jerusalem: The Zalman Shazar Center, 1995).

8 See Immanuel Etkes, *Te'udah be-Yisrael* (Jerusalem, 1977), introduction to photographic reprint; and Mordekhai Zalkin, *Ba-'a lot Ha-Shaḥar: ha-haskalah ha-yehudit be-'imperiah ha-rusit be-me'ah ha-tish'a 'esreh* (Jerusalem: Magnes Press, 2000). The term Haskalah here refers particularly to the movement for Jewish enlightenment in Eastern Europe and should be differentiated from the related movement which began decades earlier amongst a small circle of Jewish intellectuals in Western Europe.

9 On Yisrael Salanter and the early *Mussar* movement, see Immanuel Etkes, *Rabbi Israel*

of political oppression and intellectual vibrancy that the young Naftali Berlin comes of age.

Naftali's father, Ya'akov Berlin, a learned descendant of a German rabbinic family, earned a living as a moderately successful wool and flax merchant.[10] His mother, Batya Mirel, was a member of the Eisenstadt family, which took its name from Meir of Eisenstadt (1670-1744), the author of the highly respected work of halakhic responsa entitled *Panim Me'irot* (Amsterdam, 1715). The Eisenstadt family also included Yosef David Eisenstadt (1760-1846) and his son Moshe Avraham, who served as the communal rabbis of Mir for the first half of the nineteenth century, thus solidifying the position of the Berlin family amongst the upper echelons of their local community.[11]

In keeping with the aristocratic nature of Lithuanian Jewish society,[12] the children of Ya'akov and Batya Mirel Berlin generally assumed positions of prominence in the Jewish community as well. Avraham Meir Berlin lived in Pinsk, worked in Warsaw, and devoted much of his time to assisting in the publication of the work of the Vilna Ga'on. Eliezer Lipman (Lipah) Berlin lived first in Moghilev before leaving for the Land of Israel, and authored commentaries on the Talmud. Netanel Berlin was appointed to the rabbinate of the small town of Mileitzitz near Brest-Litovsk but died at a young age. Ḥayyim Berlin was considered amongst the lay leaders of the Vilna community and was actively involved in the early Zionist organization Hovevei Zion.[13]

Naftali's sisters found their way into the social elite through the mar-

---

*Salanter and the Mussar Movement: Seeking the Torah of Truth* (Philadelphia: JPS, 1993). See also Menahem G. Glenn, *Israel Salanter, Religious-Ethical Thinker: The Story of a Religious-Ethical Current in Nineteenth-century Judaism* (New York: Bloch Publishing, 1953); Dov Katz, *Rabbi Yisrael mi-Salant* (Jerusalem: ha-Histadrut ha-Tsiyonit ha-Olamit, 1974); Hillel Goldberg, *Israel Salanter: Text, Structure, and Idea* (New York: Ktav Publishing House, 1982); Rivka Horowitz, *Controversies Surrounding the Life, Work and Legacy of Rabbi Yisrael Salanter* (MA thesis, Touro College, 1993); Smadar Sharlo, *Polmos ha-Mussar ha-Sheni: Ben Shitat ha-Mussar Shel ha-Rav Kook le-Shitato Shel R. Yisra'el mi-Salant* (MA thesis, Touro College, 1996).

10 Epstein (IV: 942).

11 On the Jewish community of Mir, see *Sefer Mir*, ed. Nachman Blumenthal (Jerusalem: Encyclopedia of the Diaspora, 1962).

12 See Immanuel Etkes, "Marriage and Torah Study among the Lomdim in Lithuania in the Nineteenth Century," in *The Jewish Family: Metaphor and Memory*, ed. David Kraemer (Oxford: Oxford University Press, 1989), 153-178.

13 Bar-Ilan, 15. See also Ḥayyim Berlin, *Nishmat Ḥayyim: Ma'amarim u-Mikhtavim* (Jerusalem, 2003), 326. I have not been able to determine reliable dates of birth and death for Neẓiv's siblings.

riages which Ya'akov Berlin secured for them. Lipshah Berlin married Ḥayyim Leib Shaḥor, scion of a wealthy rabbinic family whose position in Lithuanian Jewish society is indicated by the fact that he was referred to as Ḥayyim Leib *ha-Naggid*, Ḥayyim Leib the Dignitary.[14] Miḥlah Berlin married Yeḥiel Mikhel Epstein (1829-1907), best known for his massive and highly regarded halakhic code and commentary entitled *'Arukh ha-Shulḥan*.[15]

In 1829, as a boy of but thirteen and a half years old, Naftali Berlin had an aristocratic marriage arranged for him as well. A year later he was married to Rayna Batya, the thirteen-year-old daughter of Isaac of Volozhin (1780-1849) and, at the age of fourteen and a half, left his parents' home in Mir for that of his in-laws in Volozhin.[16]

Nothing is known of the formal education given to the young Neẓiv prior to his arrival in Volozhin, but one can presume that both his learned father and the Eisenstadt family of Mir played a crucial role in his development. Barukh ha-Levi Epstein writes in a line that subsequently found its way into the popular imagination of the contemporary heirs of the Lithuanian Jewish community that his uncle,[17] Neẓiv, was a boy of "average intelligence" who rose to the greatest of heights through his "extraordinary diligence."[18] The available evidence, however, suggests otherwise.

To begin, it is rather unlikely that Isaac of Volozhin, popularly known

---

14 Epstein (II: 950).

15 The fate of Rivkah Berlin, another of Ya'akov and Batyah Mirel's children, is unclear. Bar-Ilan (*Rabban*, 15) writes that she married a man named Haslovitz but provides no further details. Contemporary members of the Bar-Ilan and Shaḥor families related to me that Rivkah was baptized and married a general of the Russian army, with whom she lived in the Belarussian town of Mstislavl (Amtchislav in Yiddish).

16 Bar-Ilan, 16-18. According to Eliezer Leoni, Neẓiv was taken by his father to Volozhin at age eleven, and was married to Rayna Batya when he was thirteen and a half. See his *Sifra shel ha'Ir ve-Shel Yeshivat "Eẓ Ḥayyim"* (Tel Aviv: ha-Irgun shel bene Volozin be-Medinat Yisrael uve-Artsot ha-Berit, 1970), 112.

17 Neẓiv was Barukh ha-Levi Epstein's uncle by virtue of the marriage of Yeḥiel Mikhel ha-Levi Epstein to Neẓiv's sister, Mihlah Berlin. After the death of his first wife, Rayna Batya, Neẓiv married his own niece, Batya Mirl Epstein, the daughter of his brother-in-law Yehiel Michel Epstein and his sister Mihlah. Batya Mirl is also the sister of Barukh ha-Levi Epstein, and thus as a result of Neẓiv's second marriage, Barukh Epstien becomes Neẓiv's brother-in-law in addition to being his nephew.

18 Epstein (IV: 1678). Tanhum Frank writes, "And henceforth for almost twenty years he isolated himself in his room, worked at his tasks with modesty and complete silence, to the point that even his relatives—and even his father-in-law—did not know of his greatness." See Tanhum Frank, *Toldot Bet ha-Shem be-Volozhin* (Jerusalem, 2001) 60.

as Reb 'Iẓele, would have chosen a boy of "average intelligence" to marry his daughter. As the son of Ḥayyim of Volozhin, who founded the Eẓ Ḥayyim Yeshivah in Volozhin, authored the highly influential *Nefesh Ha-Ḥayyim*,[19] and was widely viewed as the preeminent student of the Vilna Ga'on,[20] Reb 'Iẓele's family was more distinguished than all but a few families in the Jewish world. Although not the innovator that his father was, Reb 'Iẓele succeeded his father as head of the yeshivah in Volozhin and was widely recognized as one of the preeminent communal and intellectual leaders of Russian Jewry. As such, it is rather unlikely that he would have chosen a husband for his daughter who did not exhibit promise as a budding Torah scholar.

Furthermore, in recounting a meeting he had with Reb 'Iẓele in 1841, Max Lilienthal (1815-1882) writes that he was received by his "son-in-law Rabbi Lebele,[21] a man of some 30 years and one of the most celebrated Talmudists in Russia."[22] In truth, Neẓiv was only twenty-five years old at the time. The fact that Lilienthal's statement was first published in the late 1850s,[23] prior to the publication of any of Neẓiv's works, and the reasonable assumption that it was composed before Neẓiv was appointed head of the yeshivah in 1853, suggests that Lilienthal's tangential comment is an authentic reflection of Neẓiv's reputation in 1841 rather than a retrospective perception of a Rosh Yeshiva's youth. Therefore, either Epstein's 20th century characterization of the young Neẓiv as a boy of "average intelligence" is incorrect, or the perception of Neẓiv underwent a remarkable transformation from a boy of "average intelligence" to "one of the most celebrated Talmudists in Russia" over the course of only ten years.[24]

---

19 See Norman Lamm, *Torah Lishmah: Torah for Torah Sake in the Works of Rabbi Ḥayyim of Volozhin and his Contemporaries* (New York: Yeshiva University Press, 1989).

20 A claim which Ḥayyim of Volozhin denied in the letter which he circulated to garner support for his new yeshivah. A copy of the letter can be found in Tanhum Frank, *Toldot Bet Hashem be-Volozhin* (Jerusalem, 2001), 8.

21 Hirsch Leib is the Yiddish equivalent of Ẓvi Yehudah, thus the reference here is to Neẓiv, Naftali Zv. Yehuda, Berlin.

22 Max Lilienthal, *Max Lilienthal, American Rabbi: Life and Writings*, ed. David Philipson (New York: Bloch Publishing, 1915), 344.

23 1855-57 in *The Israelite of Cincinnati.*

24 If Epstein's characterization is incorrect, the misperception probably results from two different factors. The first is Neẓiv's own humility, to which his writings clearly attest (for example, see *MD* 1: 32; *MD* 1: 36; *MD* 2: 91; *MD* 4: 24). The second is the longstanding tradition stemming from the 1856 dispute between Neẓiv and Yosef Baer Soloveitchik over who would lead the yeshivah in Volozhin, in which the learning style of Neẓiv was

While there may be debate over the distinction of Neẓiv's earliest years, the lengthy career of the mature Neẓiv was incontrovertibly distinguished. The letter of appointment by which Neẓiv would officially become Rosh Yeshivah in Volozhin notes that he had already begun giving *shiurim* during the lifetime of Reb 'Iẓele.[25] Lilienthal notes that as early as 1841 Reb 'Iẓele had told him that due to his old age, his son-in-law Neẓiv had replaced him in giving the daily *shiur* at the yeshivah in Volozhin.[26] Upon the death of Reb 'Iẓele in 1849, his older son-in-law, Eliezer Isaac Fried, replaced him as the yeshivah's head, and Neẓiv was appointed as his assistant. When Fried died prematurely in 1853, Neẓiv, at the age of thirty-six, was appointed Rosh Yeshivah.

Neẓiv's tenure as head of the yeshivah began in a rather tumultuous manner with a series of challenges posed by descendants of Ḥayyim of Volozhin, who were thought by some to be more qualified than Neẓiv for

---

characterized by sweeping breadth and that of the Soloveitchik family was characterized by incisive depth. The genius and charisma of Ḥayyim Soloveitchik, son of Yosef Baer and son-in-law of Neẓiv's daughter, firmly cemented the incisive method as the intellectually superior mode of study in the imagination of Lithuanian rabbinic circles in the early twentieth century. As a result, it became perfectly plausible that, when viewed from the perspective of the proponents of Soloveitchik's methods, Neẓiv would be viewed as someone of "average intelligence," whose rise to prominence must have been due to the inordinate amount of time he devoted to acquiring his exceptionally broad knowledge base. While Epstein was indeed a member of Berlin's family, his high esteem for the Soloveitchik family (as evidenced by the fact that he sought rabbinic ordination from Yosef Baer Soloveitchik in addition to that granted by Neẓiv, as related in Chapter 38 of the fourth volume of his *Mekor Barukh*), the fact that his own method of study does not resemble that of Neẓiv, and the fact that his reconstruction of the Neẓiv's early years takes place in the 1920s, well after the death of Neẓiv and the rise of the Brisker school to prominence, makes Epstein's adoption of a Soloveitchik perspective on Neẓiv's youth all the more plausible.

25 *Volozhin; Sefer Shel ha-Ir-Shel Yeshivat "Eẓ Ḥayyim,"* ed. Eliezer Leoni (Tel-Aviv: 1970), 112.

26 Lilienthal, 348. The fact that Neẓiv started giving a daily shiur during the lifetime of Reb 'Iẓele is corroborated by his son Meir Bar-Ilan (*Rabban*, 25). Bar-Ilan (*ibid.*) and Epstein, (vol. IV, 1680) record differing accounts of Neẓiv's sudden public emergence as a first-rate Torah scholar. Bar-Ilan writes that Reb 'Iẓele happened upon a letter from David Luria (1798-1856) to Neẓiv in which Luria, a rabbinic scholar of considerable renown in Lithuanian circles, shows considerable respect for the erudition of Neẓiv. At that moment, writes Bar-Ilan, Reb 'Iẓele recognized that his son-in-law was a formidable scholar and asked him to begin delivering a *shiur* in the yeshivah. According to Epstein's account (vol. IV, 1680), and that of Moshe Shmuel Shapira, *Ha-Rav Moshe Shmuel ve-Doro* (New York, 1964), 51, it is Reb 'Iẓele's random discovery of Neẓiv's commentary on *Sifre* that opened his eyes to the erudition of his son-in-law. Both versions, however, are built on the assumption that Neẓiv's intellectual prowess was unknown prior to the random and fateful discovery by Reb 'Iẓele. Considering the weakness of the latter assumption, the difference in the two accounts, and the similarity between both accounts and those of typical hagiographic tales of the emergence of unknown heroes, there is good reason to suspect the authenticity of them both.

the position of Rosh Yeshivah.[27] In each case, however, Neẓiv mounted a successful defense, and for the next forty years he stood at the helm of the world's most prestigious institution of traditional Torah study, the Eẓ Ḥayyim Yeshivah in Volozhin. During that time he taught, advised, and guided thousands of Jewish boys and young men,[28] many of whom went on to offer their own significant contributions to the world of Jewish ideas both within the sphere of traditional Jewish learning and well beyond. From Ḥayyim Ozer Grodzenski (1863-1940),[29] Moshe Mordekhai Epstein (1866-1933),[30] Shimon Shkop (1860-1939),[31] and Avraham Yiẓḥak Kook (1865-1935),[32] to Avraham Harkavy (1839-1919),[33] Mikhah Yosef Berdyczewski (1865-1921),[34] and Ḥayyim Naḥman Bialik (1873-1934),[35] countless leading minds of the late nineteenth century and early twentieth century were cultivated under his tutelage. In 1892 Neẓiv was forced to close his famed yeshivah,[36] and he died in Warsaw a year later.

In addition to the minds he impacted through direct contact, Neẓiv penned numerous commentaries, some of which remain staples of the traditional Jewish library to the present day. From 1861 to 1867, he published a massive commentary on the geonic halakhic compendium *She'iltot de-Rav Aḥai Ga'on* entitled *Ha'amek She'elah*,[37] with an extensive

27 See Epstein (IV: 1691-1702); Bar-Ilan (Rabban, 27-28); and Leoni (Volozhin, 131). See also Ḥayyim Karlinski, *Ha-Rishon Le-Shoshelet Brisk* (Jerusalem: Mekhon Yerushalayim, 1984)

28 According to Bar-Ilan (*Rabban*, 137), at its height the yeshivah boasted an enrollment of over 500 students per annum. Others place the number closer to 400.

29 Rabbi in Vilna and leader of traditional Lithuanian Jewry.

30 Head of the yeshivah in Slobodka.

31 Head of the yeshivah in Telz and Grodno.

32 First Ashkenazic Chief Rabbi of modern Palestine.

33 Historian and librarian at the Imperial Library in St. Petersburg.

34 Secular Hebrew, Yiddish, and German author.

35 Hebrew poet.

36 On the exact circumstances surrounding its closing, see Jacob J. Schacter, "Haskalah, Secular Studies and the Close of the Yeshiva in Volozhin in 1892," *Torah u-Madda Journal* 2 (1990): 76-133, and the forthcoming work of Shaul Stampfer.

37 Professor Bernard Septimus pointed out to me that the correct pronounciation of this title might be *Ha'amek She'alah* based on the verse in Isaiah 7: 11 and the commentaries ad loc. All Neẓiv tells us of the title's origin is that his son Chaim Berlin is the one who devised it (HS KH p.12). However, given the fact that the work was published thirty years prior to Neẓiv's death, one would imagine that in Volozhin Neẓiv would have insisted that it be pronounced correctly and that some oral tradition would have developed within the world of the yeshivot, refering to the work as *Ha'amek She'alah.* However, to the best of my knowledge no such tradition exists. Also, if the pronounciation in Isaiah was intended by Neẓiv, the title would mean "sink to the depths," the "depths" (from the word *she'ol*) being a reference to the netherworld or Hell—a rather strange title for a work of halakhic commentary. In all likelihood, therefore, Neẓiv intended his title as a play on those words

and only tangentially related introduction entitled *Kidmat Ha-'Emek.*[38] *Ha'amek She'elah* is distinguished by Neẓiv's interest in drawing heretofore relatively obscure works of *halakhah,* such as the works of halakhic midrash, the Talmud Yerushalmi, and the works of the Ge'onim, into the mainstream of halakhic discourse, and by his focus on textual inaccuracies and anomalies in the *She'iltot,* the Talmud, and other halakhic texts. *Kidmat Ha-'Emek* is a lengthy excursus in three parts which presents Neẓiv's understanding of the nature of Torah study and its historical development.

From 1879 to 1880 Neẓiv published a commentary on the entire Pentateuch entitled *Ha'amek Davar,*[39] which was based heavily on the daily lectures he gave in the yeshivah in Volozhin on the weekly Torah portion. This commentary is marked by a unique blend of sensitivity to Hebrew grammar and syntax and an unwavering commitment to the method and content of rabbinic halakhic exegesis. While *Ha'amek Davar* displays a significant degree of intellectual independence and creativity on the part of Neẓiv, its repeated emphasis on the theological significance of Torah study reflects its strong connection to the ideological world of nineteenth-century mitnagdic society.[40]

In 1883 Neẓiv published *Rinah Shel Torah,* which included a commentary on Song of Songs and a lengthy essay on the roots of anti-Semitism.[41] Once again, his interpretation of the Song as a metaphor

---

from Isaiah pronounced *Ha'amek She'elah,* meaning "delve into the question" or perhaps "delve into the *She'ilta'.*" In fact, he plays on the phrase even further by transforming the imperitive verb *ha'amek* of the title, meaning "delve into," into the noun *ha-'emek,* meaning "the valley," in entitling his introduction *Kidmat ha-'Emek.* Therefore, in the absence of any further evidence to the contrary, we will continue to refer to this work as *Ha'amek She'elah.*

38 First edition (Vilna, 1861-1867). Most recently Naftali Ẓvi Yehudah Berlin, *Ha'amek She'elah* (Jerusalem: Mosad Harav Kook, 1999). The Neẓiv's lengthy introduction to *Ha'amek She'elah* was recently translated and published as an independent work. See Naftali Tzvi Yehuda Berlin, *The Path of Torah: The Introduction to Ha'amek She'elah,* Rabbi Elchanan Greenman trans. and ed. (Jerusalem: Urim Publications, 2009).

39 First edition (Vilna: 1879-1880). Most recently published with Neẓiv's later additions in Naftali Ẓvi Yehudah Berlin, *Ha'amek Davar* (Jerusalem: Yeshivat Volozhin, 1999).

40 The term mitnagdic referes to the highly intellectual and emotionally sober culture of Lituanian Jews which developed in response to the rapid spread of Hasidism in the second half of the eighteenth century. See Allan Nadler, *The Faith of the Mithnagdim: Rabbinic Responses to Hasidic Rapture* (Baltimore: Johns Hopkins Press, 1997)

41 Published recently as the sixth volume of Naftali Ẓvi Yehudah Berlin, *Ha'amek Davar* (Jerusalem: Yeshivat Volozhin, 1999). Some version of this text had been composed long before its publication, as evidenced by Neẓiv's references to it, which can be found in the 1861 edition of his *Ha'amek She'elah.* An English translation of the essay on anti-Semitism appears in Howard Joseph, *Why Anti-Semitism: A Translation of "The Remnant of Israel"*

for the relationship created between man and God through the study of Torah reflects the centrality of Lithuanian mitnagdic ideology to Neẓiv's work.

Throughout his career Neẓiv corresponded with leaders and laymen in the extended Jewish community on issues of halakhic and communal importance. With his reluctant approval, some of these letters were collected in the final years of his life and then published posthumously under the title *Meshiv Davar*.[42] Recently, a collection of his letters, taken largely from the Abraham Schwadron Collection at the Jewish National and University Library of The Hebrew University of Jerusalem, along with approbations he gave to the works of his students and contemporaries, was published under the title *Iggrot ha-Neẓiv*.[43]

Neẓiv also composed a commentary on the Passover Haggadah entitled *'Imre Shefer*, which has been published numerous times on its own and has been incorporated into larger anthologies of Haggadah commentaries as well.[44] From the 1950s to the 1970s his commentary on Talmud, *Meromei Sadeh*,[45] his commentary on *Sifre*, known as *'Emek ha-Neẓiv*,[46] a commentary on *Mekhilta'* and notes to *Torat Kohanim*[47] were also brought to press.

### 'Emek ha-Neẓiv: *A Window into his World*

This book proposes that unique insights into the creative and highly influential mind of Naftali Ẓvi Yehudah Berlin can be derived from an analysis of his earliest intellectual product, a commentary on the rabbinic compilation of halakhic midrash known as *Sifre*, posthumously published (1958) under the name *'Emek ha-Neẓiv*. Specifically, it argues that Neẓiv's earliest work belongs to the intellectually vibrant, yet heretofore unstudied, world of early nineteenth-century midrash commentary. Viewing it in such context allows one to see the significant impact which

(New Jersey: Jason Aronson, 1996).

42 Published recently with additions in Naftali Ẓvi Yehudah Berlin, *Meshiv Davar* (Jerusalem: 1993).

43 *Iggerot ha-Neẓiv* (Jerusalem: 2003).

44 It was first published in Warsaw in 1889.

45 Naftali Ẓvi Yehudah Berlin, *Meromei Sadeh* (Jerusalem: 1953-1959).

46 Naftali Ẓvi Yehudah Berlin, *'Emek ha-Neẓiv* (Jerusalem: *Va'ad le-Hoẓa'at Kitve ha-Neẓiv*, 1959-1961).

47 Printed most recently at the end of *Birkat ha-Neẓiv* (Jerusalem: Yeshivat Volozhin, 1997).

the methods and interests of this world had upon the intellectual development and literary endeavors of Neẓiv. Furthermore, grounding Neẓiv in his early nineteenth-century context serves to highlight the instances in which his later work diverges from his earlier intellectual roots, which, we shall argue, directly reflects the ways in which the Lithuanian Jewish society of his adult years differed from that of his youth.

While biographical accounts of Neẓiv's life abound, none has focused on *'Emek ha-Neẓiv*, and most are severely lacking in academic rigor. The accounts of his contemporaries, while offering invaluable pearls of information, are generally brief and represent the heavily biased views of his students and family members.[48] There are three works that treat much of the life of Neẓiv that were written after his death as well.[49] Since, however, their authors were, respectively, Neẓiv's son, Meir Bar-Ilan, who was only thirteen years old when his father died, and Neẓiv's nephew, Barukh ha-Levi Epstein, they too suffer from the biased perspective of close family members and from a heavy reliance on undocumented oral and often hagiographic evidence as documented above.[50] Furthermore, the biographical narrative in all of the literature to date covers the twenty-three years between Neẓiv's arrival in Volozhin

48 Mikha Yosef Berdyczewski, "*Toldot Yeshivat Eẓ HaḤayyim*," *He-Assif* (1887): 231-242; Mikha Yosef Berdyczewski, "'*Megilat Shir HaShirim' shel ha-Neẓiv*," *Ha-Ẓefirah* (25 Tevet 5648 [1888]); Hayim Nahman Bialik, *Igrot Ḥayim Naḥman Bialik* (Tel Aviv: Devir, 1937-39); Zalman Epstein, *Kitve Zalman Epshtayn* (St. Petersburg: Joseph Luria, 1904); Avraham Yiẓḥak Kook, "*Rosh Yeshivat Eẓ Ḥayyim*," *Kenesset Yisrael*, ed. S.J Finn (Warsaw, 1888), 138-147 [also in *Ma'amarei HaRe'iyah* (Jerusalem, 1984), 123-126]; Avraham Yiẓḥak Kook, "*Ẓvi La-Ẓadik*," *Maḥzike Ha-Das* 8 (1886); *Sefer Turov*, eds. Isaac Zilbershlag and Yohanan Twerski (Boston: Bet ha-Midrash le-Morim, 1938); Joseph Litvin, "Naphtali Tzevi Berlin (the Neẓiv)," *Men of the Spirit*, Leo Jung, ed. (New York: Kymson Publishing Co., 1964); Simḥah Assaf, *Mekorot le-toldot ha-ḥinukh be-Yisrael* (New York: Bet ha-Midrash le-Rabbanim be-Amerikah, 2001). Bits of biographical information can also be gleaned from the writings of his son Ḥayyim Berlin, recently collected in the work of Ya'akov Kosovsky-Shahor under the name *Nishmat Ḥayyim: Ma'amarim u-Mikhtavim* (Jerusalem, 2003). While sparse on detail, the information provided is possibly more accurate than that given by Meir Bar-Ilan, as Ḥayyim Berlin was born when Neẓiv was a mere sixteen years old and served as a lifelong confidant, while Bar-Ilan, his half-brother, born to Neẓiv at age sixty-four, only knew his father in the final years of his life.

49 Meir Bar-Ilan, *Fun Volozhin biz Yerushalayim* (New York: Oryom Press, 1933); Meir Bar-Ilan, *Rabban Shel Yisrael* (New York: Histadrut ha-Mizrahi beAmerikah, 1943); Barukh ha-Levi Epstein, *Mekor Barukh*, vol. IV (Vilna, 1928). Other smaller works of note are: Meir Bar-Ilan, "Introduction to *Ha'amek Davar*," *Ha'amek Davar*, ed. Hillel Cooperman (Jerusalem: 1981); Moshe Ẓvi Neriah, *Toldot* ha-Neẓiv (1942 / 1943); Moshe Shmuel Shapira, *Ha-Rav Moshe Shmuel ve-Doro* (New York, 1964).

50 See note 26 above.

as a boy of fourteen and his appointment as the yeshivah's head in but a few sentences, which simply state that he spent those years engrossed in diligent solitary study and offer no further detail.

There are also a number of studies which focus on Neẓiv's intellectual activity, the most significant being Shelomoh Yosef Zevin's portrayal of Neẓiv in his *Ishim ve-Shitot* (1952), Hanah Kats's *Mishnat ha-Neẓiv* (1990) and Nissim Eliakim's *Ha'amek Davar la-Neẓiv* (2003).[51] None of these works, however, treats *'Emek ha-Neẓiv* in any depth, nor do they adequately place *Ha'amek Davar* within the historical context of nineteenth-century Lithuania or the intellectual context of Neẓiv's other writings, as this book proposes to do.

Considerable attention is also given to Neẓiv in Shaul Stampfer's seminal work on the Lithuanian Yeshivot. The information presented by Stampfer, however, focuses on Neẓiv's role as Rosh Yeshivah in his later years and reveals little of his personal development or intellectual endeavors.[52] The same is true of the considerable memoir literature stemming from Volozhin, much of which has recently been collected by Immanuel Etkes.[53] To date, then, there is no published work which explores the formative years of Neẓiv's life or provides an adequate contextual analysis of his intellectual work. This book proposes to do both.

---

51 Shelomoh Yosef Zevin, *Ishim Ve-Shitot* (Tel Aviv: Bitan Ha-sefer, 1952); A.R. Malakhi, "*Pa'alo ha-Safruti shel R. Naftali Ẓvi Yehudah Berlin*," *Jewish Book Annual* 25 (1967-68): 233-238; Hannah Kats, *Mishnat* ha-Neẓiv (1989/1990); Y. Hager-Lau, *Ha-Ḥayyil ve-ha-Ḥosen: Ẓava u-Milḥamah be-Ha'amek Davar u-ve- Meshekh Ḥokhmah* (Mercaz Shapiro, 1989); M. Bar-Ilan, "*Peirush 'Ha'amek Davar le-ha-Neẓiv z"l*," *Afikei Neḥalim* III (1971): 119-125; M. Isaacs, "*ha-Ẓava ve-ha-Milḥamah be-Mishnat ha-Neẓiv*," *MiZohar LaZohar* (1984) 9-21; Shubert Spero, "The Neẓiv of Volozhin and the Mission of Israel," *Morasha* 2: 2 (1986): 1-14; A. Eisenthal, "*Mishnat ha-Neẓiv*," *Ereẓ Ẓvi* (1989), 71-89; H. Lifshitz, "*ha-Neẓiv ve-Yeḥuso l'Yeshuv Ereẓ Yisrael*," *Kotleinu* 13 (1990): 559-563; Y. Kupman, "*Et Milḥamah li'umat Et Shalom al pi ha-Neẓiv*," *Merhavim* 1 (1990): 285-297; Z.A. Neugroschel, "*Beḥirat Am Yisrael be-Mishnat ha-Neẓiv MiVolozhin*," *Talelei Orot* 6 (1995): 144-156; B.Z. Rosenfeld, "*Ben Ish le-Ishto al pi Peirush ha-Neẓiv BiParhsat Isaac ve-Rivkah*," *Talelei Orot* 6 (1995): 216-236; Y. Weiner, "*Mavet Moḥi – Da'at ha-Neẓiv MiVolozhin*" *Asya* 13: 3-4 (1996); Howard Joseph, "'As Swords Thrust Through the Body': Neẓiv's Rejection of Separatism," *Edah Journal* 1: 1 (2000); Henry Adler Sosland, "Discovering the Neẓiv and his 'Ha'amaik Davar'" *Judaism* 51: 3 (2002): 315-327; Nissim Eliakim, *Ha'amek Davar la-Neẓiv* (Moreshet Ya'akov, 2003).

52 Shaul Stampfer, *Shalosh Yeshivot Lita'iyot be-Me'ah ha-Tesha-'Esreh* (PhD dissertation, Hebrew University, 1981); idem., *Ha-Yeshivah ha-Litait be-hithavutah ba-me'ah ha-tesha'-'esreh* (Jerusalem: The Zalman Shazar Center, 1995). Mordechai Breuer's recent work on yeshivot also describes Volozhin and Neẓiv's role therein. See Mordechai Breuer, *Ohole Torah: ha-Yeshivah, Tavnitah ve-Toldoteha* (Jerusalem: The Zalman Shazar Center, 2003).

53 *Yeshivot Lita: Pirkei Zikhronot*, eds. Immanuel Etkes and Shlomo Tikochinsky (Jerusalem: The Zalman Shazar Center, 2004).

The social and political conditions under which Neẓiv developed as a young man have been amply described in Michael Stanislawski's work on the reign of Tsar Nicholas.[54] The intellectual history of the same period, however, tends toward an examination of the posthumous influence of the Vilna Ga'on and Ḥayyim of Volozhin on early nineteenth-century Lithuanian scholarship[55] or a retrospective analysis that seeks to locate the roots of the Eastern European Haskalah movement in the work of late eighteenth- and early nineteenth-century Jewish intellectuals.[56] While Jay Harris describes a few of the intellectual products of this era, he does so with the intent of portraying their role in the fragmentation of modern Judaism and, therefore, does not explore the larger indigenously Lithuanian intellectual context from which they arise. A serious study of the dominant intellectual trends in Lithuanian scholarship during the first half of the nineteenth century, then, remains a desideratum.[57]

This book, then, will offer three contributions to the current scholarship. It will describe the intellectual forays of the heretofore unstudied formative years of Neẓiv's life. It will examine the most famous book of Neẓiv's literary oeuvre, his *Ha'amek Davar*, against the backdrop of his

54 Michael Stanislawski, *Tsar Nicholas I and the Jews: The Transformation of Jewish Society in Russia, 1825-1855* (Philadelphia: JPS, 1983).

55 Ḥayyim Hillel Ben-Sasson, "*Ishiyuto shel HaGRA ve-Hashpa'ato Ha-Historit*," *Ẓion* 31 (1966); Norman Lamm, *Torah Lishmah: Torah for Torah's Sake in the Works of Rabbi Ḥayyim of Volozhin and His Contemporaries* (New York, NY: Yeshiva University Press, 1989); Immanuel Etkes, *The Ga'on of Vilna: The Man and His Image*, trans. Jeffrey M. Green (Berkeley: University of California Press, 2002); *ha-GRA u-Bet Midrasho*, eds. Moshe Halamish, et al. (Ramat Gan: Bar-Ilan University Press, 2003).

56 Michael Stanislawski, *For Whom Do I Toil?: Judah Leib Gordon and The Crisis of Russian Jewry* (New York: Oxford University Press, 1988); Mordekhai Zalkin, *Haskalat Vilna* (Jerusalem: Hebrew University, 1992); *Ha-Dat Ve-ha-Ḥayyim: Tenu'at ha-Haskalah be-Mizrah Eiropa*, ed. Immanuel Etkes (Jerusalem: The Zalman Shazar Center, 1993); Immanuel Etkes, "*Le-She'elat Mevasrei ha-Haskalah be-Mizraḥ Europah*," *Tarbiẓ* 57 (1987): 95-114 [reprinted in *Ha-Dat ve-ha-Ḥayyim: Tenu'at ha-Haskalah ha-Yehudit be-Mizraḥ Eropah*, ed. Immanuel Etkes (Jerusalem, 1993), 25-44]; David E. Fishman, *Russia's First Modern Jews: The Jews of Shklov* (New York: New York University Press, 1995); Mordechai Zalkin, *Ba-'a lot ha-Shaḥar: ha-Haskalah ha-Yehudit be-Imperiah ha-Rusit be-Meah ha-Tish'a 'Esreh* (Jerusalem: Magnes Press, 2000).

57 The paucity of material which has come down to us regarding the early years of Volozhin and its circle of scholars is recognized even in more traditionalist works of history and historiography. After offering a relatively sparse list of exceptional scholars known to have studied in Volozhin under Reb 'Iẓele, Tanhum Frank writes in his *Toldot Bet ha-Shem be-Volozhin* (Jerusalem, 2001) that, "It goes without saying that during the 28 years of Reb 'Iẓele's service, many more great [students] learned there. But in those times who would [care to] write down words of history?" (46).

earlier work. Finally, it will sketch a preliminary portrait of the world of nineteenth-century Lithuanian midrash study, to which *'Emek ha-Neẓiv* belongs, and the significant cultural factors which gave it rise.

### *Method and Approach*

The proposition that unique insight into the intellectual development of Naftali Ẓvi Yehudah Berlin can be derived from an analysis of his earliest intellectual product, *'Emek ha-Neẓiv,* relies on two basic assumptions regarding the text of that work. The first is that the printed text of *'Emek ha-Neẓiv* is an accurate representation of Neẓiv's commentary on *Sifre,* and the second is that Neẓiv's commentary on *Sifre* does, indeed, date from the earliest period of his literary career. As such, these two issues will be the first ones addressed. Through an analysis of textual clues and information gleaned from an examination of Neẓiv's manuscript, credible evidence will be offered in support of the validity of both assumptions.

Once we have established *'Emek ha-Neẓiv* as the earliest product of Neẓiv's prolific pen, and have shown that most of its content dates to the 1830s and 1840s, we will then proceed to place the commentary in the context of early nineteenth-century midrash study. We will first describe three generations of interconnected Lithuanian Torah scholars for whom the study and explication of midrashic texts was of paramount importance.

Our exploration of this intellectual coterie and Neẓiv's place therein will bring into focus an intriguing intellectual milieu at the very heart of traditional Jewish society, which was characterized by the unapologetic use of a broad array of literary sources, a keen sensitivity to textual errors and variant readings, and a desire to present only a close and straightforward reading of rabbinic texts. The young Neẓiv and the work he produced, we shall argue, are directly connected to that world. We will further demonstrate that the cultural elements which gave rise to this intellectual milieu, namely the influence of the Vilna Ga'on, the role of the Lithuanian Maggid, and the rise of Hebrew print, are clearly manifest in the pages of *'Emek ha-Neẓiv.*

Armed with an understanding of Neẓiv's earliest intellectual endeavors, we will then examine his later work against the backdrop of *'Emek ha-Neẓiv*. Doing so will demonstrate that much of Neẓiv's later commentarial endeavors are natural outgrowths of his early work and his formative experiences in the world of early nineteenth-century midrash study. At the same time, we will demonstrate that setting his later work against his earlier endeavors helps to highlight limited, yet critical, points where Neẓiv's *Ha'amek Davar* diverges significantly from the exegetical path he took in *'Emek ha-Neẓiv*. Much of this divergence will be attributed to the impact of a Jewish society which had greatly changed over the course of Neẓiv's life. Specific attention will be given to the rise of the Haskalah and the rabbinic reaction thereto, as well as to the growth of the ideology of Torah study which Neẓiv, after four decades in the study hall of Volozhin, seems to have accepted. These changes in society confronted the Lithuanian rabbinic establishment with an altered set of norms, expectations, and fears, many of which are reflected in Neẓiv's *Ha'amek Davar*. Thus our exploration of Neẓiv's later work offers important insight into the intellectual and religious development of Neẓiv, as well as into the history of nineteenth-century Jewish Lithuania as a whole.

The different components of this study require the employment of differing methods of historical study. A source-critical study of *'Emek ha-Neẓiv* and *Birkat ha-Neẓiv* (Neẓiv's *Mekhilta'* commentary) reveals evidence of multiple recensions in the printed text of both commentaries. I rely on historical references found within these texts, as well as references to their composition in other writings of Neẓiv, to establish approximate dates of composition of their core texts.

I am fortunate to have had a working relationship with the Shapira family of Jerusalem, who are the heirs, editors, and publishers of Neẓiv's manuscripts.[58] As members of contemporary Israeli ultra-Orthodox society, however, they are understandably skeptical of me and my work. To date, they have granted me limited access to the manuscript of *'Emek ha-Neẓiv*, under their constant supervision. My requests for unencumbered and unlimited study of the manuscripts have been declined. However, I have gained considerable insight into the text from my limited study of it, which has been incorporated into Chapter One.

Bibliographic methods also factor prominently into this study.[59] Over four hundred citations found in *'Emek ha-Neẓiv*, generally given in ab-

58 Theirs are the only known extant copies of Neẓiv's manuscripts.

59 Basic bibliographic information was ascertained through the use of the Institute for Hebrew Bibliography's software entitled "The Bibliography of the Hebrew Book 1473-1960," accessed via https://yulib002.mc.yu.edu:8443/login?url=http://www.hebrew-bibliography.com/search/.

breviated or acronymic form, are identified in an effort to reconstruct the library which influenced the young Neẓiv.[60] Additionally, the section of Chapter Five which examines the rise of print in Lithuania as a significant cultural factor in bringing about the move toward midrash study also draws heavily on bibliographic records.[61]

The literary analysis of *'Emek ha-Neẓiv* found in Chapters Three and Four identifies the most common characteristics of the commentary in an effort to reconstruct Neẓiv's objectives in writing the work and the means he employed in pursuing them. However, the comparative analysis of *'Emek ha-Neẓiv* with *Ha'amek Davar* in Chapter Six does not focus on Neẓiv's exegetical technique. As the purpose of this book is to describe not *Ha'amek Davar's* place in the history of Bible commentary[62] but its relationship to the larger corpus of Neẓiv's writing and the society from which it emerged, emphasis is placed instead on literary style, statements of purpose, and the content of the commentary, which seems to be in conversation with contemporary events and trends.

This book is not intended as the definitive work on Neẓiv. Its intent is rather to begin providing an intellectual and historical context for his voluminous writings and to open the vibrant, yet heretofore neglected, world of Lithuanian Torah scholarship in the first half of the nineteenth-century to further critical study and exploration. And, by noting the eclipse of that world by the more traditionalist elements of Lithuanian Jewish society, it intends to extend the questions of the origins of Orthodoxy which Jacob Katz, Moshe Samet, Michael Silber, and others have asked in regard to the Jewish community of Hungary to the Jewish community of late nineteenth-century Lithuania. It is, in the language of the Talmud, a means of stating *ta' shema'*: come and listen, come and learn, come and study the world of nineteenth-century Lithuanian Torah scholarship.

---

60 After accounting for multiple citations of the same source, *'Emek ha-Neẓiv* contains references to approximately 150 different works.

61 Basic biographical information will be drawn from the following sources: S. J. Fuenn, *Keneset Yisrael* (Warsaw, 1886); Aryeh Loeb Feinstein, *'Ir Tehilah: Ha-Lorot le-'Adat Yisrael she-bi-'Ir Brisk* (Warsaw, 1886); Moshe Reines, *Sefer Dor ve-Ḥokhamav*. (Cracow: Fischer, 1890); Hillel Noah Maggid Steinschneider, *' Ir Vilna,* vol. I (Vilna, 1900), vol. II (Jerusalem, 2002); *Jewish Encyclopedia* (1901-1906); S.J. Fuenn, *Kiriah Ne'emanah* (Vilna, 1915); Jacob Mark, *Gedoylim fun unzer Tsayt: Monografyes, Karaktershrikhen un Zikhroynes* (New York: 687 [1927]); Israel Cohen, *Vilna,* 2nd ed. (Philadelphia: JPS, 1992).

62 For an overview of Neziv's exegetical technique in *Ha'amek Davar*, see Nissim Eliakim, *Ha'amek Davar la-Neẓiv* (Moreshet Ya'akov, 2003).

*Note on Transliteration*

As the book includes significant Hebrew transliteration, the following system has been employed throughout:

| | |
|---|---|
| א | *’* |
| בּ | *b* |
| ב | *v* |
| ג | *g* |
| ד | *d* |
| ה | *h* |
| ו | *v* |
| ז | *z* |
| ח | *ḥ* |
| ט | *t* |
| י | *y* |
| כּ | *k* |
| כ | *kh* |
| ל | *l* |
| מ | *m* |
| נ | *n* |
| ס | *s* |
| ע | *‘* |
| פּ | *p* |
| פ | *f* |
| צ | *ẓ* |
| ק | *k* |
| ר | *r* |
| שׁ | *sh* |
| שׂ | *s* |
| תּ | *t* |
| ת | *t* |

# CHAPTER ONE:
## The Text of *'Emek ha-Neẓiv*

A historical analysis of the text and context of a printed work must always begin with an investigation as to the authenticity of the printed work. More specifically, the historian must always ask whether the work printed between the covers of a modern book is, in fact, what it purports to be.[1]

The printed edition of *'Emek ha-Neẓiv*, which was first published some sixty years after Neziv's death, opens with a short introduction from the publishers offering a brief historical description of the commentary. The second paragraph of their introduction reads as follows:

> And these are the beautiful words[2] which the honored Ga'on, the author, may the name of the righteous be a blessing, wrote himself in his gilded language in the *Kidmat Ha-'Emek* of the *She'iltot*, 1:17,[3] **regarding this book**:[4]
>
> And I, of meager stature (*he-'ani*), in my innocence pursued during my youth an investigation of the exegesis of our Rabbis of Blessed Memory which are scattered amongst the Talmud [and] which are not understood upon first glance at the Bible. And I poured over the *Mekhilta'* and *Torat Kohanim,* the primary books of source material, and from there explained positions of the sages of the Talmud, who are the true warriors, until I discovered explanations with the help of He Who Grants [Knowledge] even to the unworthy. And I wrote in a book

---

1 I am indebted to Professor Haym Soloveitchik who first sensitized me to these critical questions during his tenure as a visiting professor at the University of Pennsylvania (1998).

2 A word play on the title given to Neẓiv's commentary on the Passover Seder *'Imrei Shefer*. The following passage is one of a few places in *Kidmat Ha-'Emek* in which Neẓiv writes in rhyming prose. The awkwardness of the translation can be attributed to the poetic flourishes which he employs.

3 *HS*, vol 1, 11.

4 Emphasis added.

> a composition on *Sifre Midrash Bamidbar* and *ve-'Eleh ha-Devarim*, in which the ways of the Tanna' are brief, and from there explained some *beraiytot* in *Mekhilta'* and *Torat Kohanim*, which have not been addressed by the commentators. Yet, it[5] is hidden with me until I find the time, with the help of He who formed the luminaries, to bring it to press and to distribute it (*le-hakhnis le-she'arim*).[6]

The task at hand, then, is to determine whether the printed text of *'Emek ha-Neẓiv* is, in fact, an accurate rendition of the commentary which Neẓiv penned in his youth and to which he refers in the above-cited passage. This question can be further broken down into two component parts. First, we must question whether Neẓiv himself edited, revised, or rewrote his original work on *Sifre* in the years following the publication of the above passage. Second, we must determine whether the text posthumously brought to press under the name *'Emek ha-Neẓiv* veers in any significant manner from the text actually written by Neẓiv over a century earlier.

The significance of these questions to the larger project at hand should be quite clear. In order to use the text of *'Emek ha-Neẓiv* as a window into the early years of Neẓiv's intellectual development, one must first determine that the text does, in fact, accurately represent the thoughts of Neẓiv during the 1830s and 1840s.

### *Dating the Printed Text*

In the passage from *Kidmat Ha-'Emek* cited above, Neẓiv mentions his commentary on *Sifre* as a product of his youth[7] and laments having been forced to bring the *She'iltot* commentary to press prior to his commentary on *Sifre*.[8] From these statements one can conclude that a text worthy of being called a "composition"[9] and in the pre-publication stage was extant well before the 1861 publication of *Ha'amek She'elah*. In fact, Neẓiv most definitely had composed at least part of a commentary on *Sifre* as early

5 The *Sifre* commentary.
6 *EH*, *'Im Ha-Sefer*, introduction.
7 *Ha'amek She'elah*, vol. 1 (Jerusalem: Mosad Harav Kook, 1999), 11.
8 Ibid., 12.
9 See citation above.

as 1846, as evidenced by his letter written to Ḥayyim Yehudah Agus[10] in the fall of that year, in which he states that, "More than this I have expounded with the help of God on the *Sifre*, Torah portion *Ḥukat*, and this is not the place [to go into further detail]."[11]

The date of the *Sifre* commentary's composition can be pushed back even further through an analysis of Neẓiv's work on *Torat Kohanim*. The edition of this work printed at the end of the 1997 edition of *Birkat ha-Neẓiv* opens with "The year 5602[12] with the help of God." This date suggests that the printed work does reflect, at least in large part, the work on *Torat Kohanim* mentioned by Neẓiv as a product of his youth in the *Ha'amek She'elah* passage. While this brief collection of notes to the halakhic midrashim of Leviticus clearly contains lines and references added later than 1842,[13] the frequency with which this text refers to Neẓiv's commentary on *Sifre*—over fifty times in the span of forty pages of commentary—makes it difficult to believe that all such references represent later additions. Furthermore, many of the references to the commentary on *Sifre* found in the notes to *Torat Kohanim* bear the imprint of Neẓiv's original composition, rather than later authorial or editorial insertions. Thus, for example, in the middle of his comments on *Tazri'a* 1:3 (24) Neẓiv cites a passage from the beginning of *Sifre Naso* and writes mid-sentence, "...And I explained there with the help of God that..."[14] Were this comment, and the others like it, to be located at the end of a passage, one might well assume that they were added later, when Neẓiv returned to his *Torat Kohanim* commentary after having composed his commentary on *Sifre*. The placement of these comments in the middle of several passages, however, suggests that the *Sifre* commentary, or at least parts thereof, had been composed prior to the composition of his work on *Torat Kohanim*, and, thus, prior to 1842. As such, Neẓiv's work on *Torat Kohanim* also seems to suggest

---

10 For more on Agus, see Hillel Noah Maggid Steinschneider, *'Ir Vilna*, vol. II, ed. Mordechai Zalkin (Jerusalem: Magnes Press, 2003), 172, n. 1.

11 *Meshiv Davar* (II: 96) (Jerusalem: 1993).

12 1841 or 1842.

13 See Chapter 8.

14 Similarly, see *Shemini Mekhilta' de-milu'im* 30 (18), "*Ve-'ayyen mah she-katav be-Sifre* Pinḥas *be-siyyata' de-shmaya;*" *Shemini Mekhilta' de-milu'im* 1: 2: 12 (20) "*ve-'ayyen mah shekatav be-ta'ameh de-ḥanina'be-siyyata' dishmaya' be-Sifre parashat* Matot *piska'* 5; " *Aḥare Mot* 5: 3 (30) "*Sifre* Ḥukat...*u-kimo shekatavti sham be-siyyata dishmaya;* " *Kedoshim* 4: 1 (p.33) "*Pirashti be-Sifre parhsah* Shoftim *piska' 5 be-siyyata' de-shmaya';*" *Kedoshim* 4: 18 (33) "*be-Sifre parashat* Teẓeh *'al ha-pasuk lo' tilbash sha'atnez bi'arti da'at Rashi 'al ha-nakhon be-siyyata' dishmaya'*" *Emor* 17: 12 "*Sifre parashat* Re'eh *piska' 33 u-mah she-katavti sham be-siyyata dishmaya.*"

that the composition of his commentary on *Sifre* commenced in the 1830s, while he was in his late teens and early twenties.

The question remains, however, as to whether the text later printed with the title *'Emek ha-Neẓiv* is, in fact, the text referred to by Neẓiv in 1846.

From his statements in the introduction to *Ha'amek She'elah* it is clear that Neẓiv intended to publish his *Sifre* commentary. Nonetheless, the work did not appear in print during his lifetime. In fact, it remained unpublished until 1958 when it was edited and printed by the Shapira family (descendants of Neẓiv's son-in-law Raphael Shapira) under the aegis of the *Va'ad le-Hoẓa'at Kitve ha-Neẓiv* (Committee for the Publication of the Works of Neẓiv ). In 1977 the 1958 edition was reprinted with minor editorial corrections.

Given the fact that nearly a century elapsed between the composition of the work referred to in the 1861 edition of *Ha'amek She'elah* and the 1958 publication of *'Emek ha-Neẓiv,* one cannot assume that the printed text is identical to that which Neẓiv was preparing for publication in 1861. Thus, even though his commentary on *Sifre* is, in theory, his earliest literary product, assigning a date to the work reflected in the printed text, on which this book is based, requires further investigation.

The earliest textual clue to the work's date of composition is found in Neẓiv's comments on *Naso* where the printed text reads "the book *'Emek Halakhah* was newly printed after having written [this]."[15] The book to which he is referring, Zev Wolf ben Yehudah Ha-Levi's *'Emek Halakhah,* was first printed in Vilna in 1845.[16] As such, the comments directly preceding this statement in the printed text can be dated prior to 1845.

A similar conclusion can be drawn regarding passages in *Shelaḥ* and *Be-ha'alotekha* in which Neẓiv cites his father-in-law, Reb 'Iẓele, and follows his name with the word *"she-yiḥyeh,"* "may he live," which is a customary blessing of long life appended to the name of noted personalities who are still alive. The printed text follows the word *"she-yiḥyeh"* with brackets containing the acronym "*ZaẒaL,*" "may the memory of the righteous one be a blessing," a clear addition to the text, by the Neẓiv or by a later editor, following Reb 'Iẓele's death.[17] Since the original *"she-yiḥyeh"*

15 *EH* Naso 49 (I: 181) "*'aḥar kotvi yaẓah me-ḥadash sefer 'emek halakhah.*"

16 There is a printing error in the pagination in the 1845 Vilna edition of *'Emek Halakhah* and Neẓiv's citation refers to what should be (32) but is printed as (30).

17 *EH be-Ha'alotekha* 37 (I: 297) "*ḥotni she-yiḥyeh [zaẓal]*"; *EH* Shelaḥ 1 (II: 10) [*u-piresh ḥotni ha-*

is preserved in the printed text one can unequivocally date these texts prior to Reb 'Iẓele's death in 1849. Thus, there is further evidence that at least part of the text printed in 1958 was written in the 1840s or earlier.

However, the printed text also contains sufficient evidence to convince the reader that the commentary on *Sifre* referred to in the introduction to *Ha'amek She'elah* might not be identical to the one found in the printed text of *'Emek ha-Neẓiv*. After all, throughout the printed text of *'Emek ha-Neẓiv*, Neẓiv refers the reader to his commentary on *She'iltot*, *Ha'amek She'elah*, for further treatment of the topic under discussion.[18] As noted above, however, Neẓiv specifically writes in the introduction to *Ha'amek She'elah* that his commentary on *Sifre* was written before his commentary on *She'iltot* and that he intended to publish the *Sifre* commentary first as well.[19] While it is possible that an author may refer to a work that has not yet been published,[20] the quantity of citations to *Ha'amek She'elah* and the precise manner with which he refers to the location of the passage in *Ha'amek She'elah* suggest that these references found in *'Emek ha-Neẓiv* were added after the 1861 publication of *Ha'amek She'elah*.

---

*Ga'on she-yiḥyeh (zaẓal)...*]

18 E.g., Naso 2 (1: 18) – *'ayyen 'od...163: 8...bs"d* ; Naso 3 (I: 21) – *'ayyen...bs"d 150: 12...*; Naso 7 (I: 43) – *kimo she-hokhahti...120: 3;* Naso 15 (I: 65) – *ve-'ayyen...95: 8;* Naso 16 (I: 69) – *ve-'ayyen...derashah de-purim;* Naso 23 (I: 93) – *ve-'ayyen...100: 6 b"sd;* ; Naso 23 (I: 94) – *ve-'ayyen ...123: 1 bs"d;* Naso 39 (I: 154) – *u-be-bi'ur ha-she'iltot 4: 7...bs"d* ; Be-ha'alotekha 1 (I: 192) – *ve-'ayyen...be-bi'ur ha-she'iltot 26: 31 bs"d;* Be-ha'alotekha 34 (I: 291) – *ve-'ayyen ...51: 1;* (I: 292) – *ve-'ayyen 'od...140: 1;* Shelaḥ 9 (II: 70) – *ve-'ayyen...'Ekev : 21...bs"d;* Koraḥ 1 (hagah) (II: 79) – *ve-'ayyen...4: 1. bs"d* ; Ḥukat 1 (II: 147) *ve-'ayyen. be-bi'ur ha-she'iltot...*'Ekev *145: 3* ; Balak 1 (II: 204) *ve-'ayyen be-bi'ure ha-she'iltot ha'azinu 162.1* ; Balak 1- (II: 207) *ve-yashavti bs"d be-ḥiburi 'al ha- she'iltot derasha de-ḥanukah* ; Pinḥas 3 (II: 223) *ve-'ayyen... 'aḥare 95: 2 b"sd* ; Matot 1 (II: 285) – *ve-'ayyen ...136: 6* ; Shoftim 1 (III: 174) – interlinear addition in mss: *ve-'ayyen... be-bi'ur ha-she'iltot reish parashat* Shoftim; Shoftim 1 (III: 174) – interlinear addition in mss: *ve-'ayyen...bi'ur ha-she'iltot parashat* Shoftim *149: 3;* Shoftim 21 (III: 193) – *ve-'ayyen...be-bi'ur ha-she'iltot parashat ḥayye;* Shoftim 45 (III: 207) – *ve-'ayyen bi'ur ha-she'iltot parashat noaḥ 4: 9* ; Teẓeh 6 (III: 237) – *ve-'ayyen 'od...be-bi'uri 'al ha-she'iltot* 87; Teẓeh 36 (III: 288) – *ve-'ayyen 'od be-she'iltot parashat 'aḥarei 95: 4;* Teẓeh 37 (III: 290) – *ve-'ayyen...be-she'iltot 105: 1* ; Teẓeh 38 (III: 292) – *u-be-she'iltot parashat* Teẓeh *152...ve-'ayyen...be-bi'ur ot 4;* Matot 6 (III: 309) – *ve-'ayyen* ...Matot...*'ot 5 bs"d;* Matot 6 (III: 310) – *Ve-'ayyen...*[Matot]*...'ot 17.*

19 *HS,* vol 1, 12. An accident in which a copy of the manuscript of *Ha'amek She'elah* was lost prompted him to bring the text to print lest someone else obtain the lost copy and attempt to publish it under their own name. Ideally, though, he had hoped to publish his commentary on *Sifre* first. See the introduction to *HS.*

20 In fact, Neẓiv does so when he refers to his comments on *Torat Kohanim* [Naso 17 (I: 72), first published (Jerusalem, 1970)] and his commentaries on Talmud [Naso 44 (I: 174) and Shelaḥ 5 (II: 41) (first published Jerusalem, 1955-1959)]. Neẓiv is careful in those instances, though, to merely state that a greater elaboration can be found in these works, whereas in the citations of *Ha'amek She'elah* he generally employs the word "*'ayyen*" suggesting that the reader look up the citation for themselves. See note 11 above.

The suggestion that the references in the printed edition of *'Emek ha-Neẓiv* to *Ha'amek She'elah* were added after 1861 is bolstered by two other passages which could not have been written prior to 1861. The first is a reference to the fourth volume of Yehosef Schwarz's, *Divre Yosef*, published in Jerusalem in 1862.[21] The second provides unequivocal evidence that the printed text of *'Emek ha-Neẓiv* contains passages added as late as 1867: Neẓiv refers the reader to the column entitled *Ẓofeh* in the 28th edition of the 10th publication year of the Hebrew newspaper *ha-Maggid*.[22] That edition of *ha-Maggid* was printed on July 17th, 1867.

Thus, one is led to believe that the text of *'Emek ha-Neẓiv* printed in 1958 reflects a composite text whose core layer was written in the 1840s or earlier and to which numerous additions were made over the span of thirty subsequent years, if not more. This conclusion is supported by the manuscript from which the printed edition was taken.

### *The Manuscript*

The manuscript of *'Emek ha-Neẓiv* remains in the possession of the Shapira family and there are no additional extant copies. The family are prominent members of a staunchly traditionalist *Ḥaredi* community in the Geulah neighborhood of Jerusalem. Members of this community generally oppose sustained contact with Western culture and its representative institutions, including universities of any type. The Shapira family seems to harbor additional skepticism toward those researching Neẓiv, due to the fact that his relative openness to certain aspects of non-traditional culture has made him a controversial figure in some ultra-Orthodox communities.[23] These facts, combined with the sheer

21 *EH* Pinḥas 12 (II: 248).

22 *EH* Naso 45 (I: 177).

23 In recent years, certain circles in the ultra-Orthodox community recommended that Moshe Dombey and N.T. Erline's adaptation of Barukh Ha-Levi Epstein's *Mekor Barukh*, entitled *My Uncle the Neẓiv* (Brooklyn, N.Y.: Mesorah Publications, 1988), not be read due to its portrayal of Neẓiv as one who did not share all of the values of the contemporary ultra-Orthodox community. See Jacob J. Schacter, "Haskalah, Secular Studies, and the Close of the Yeshiva in Volozhin in 1892," *Torah u-Madda Journal* 1 (1989): 76-133; Don Seeman, "The Silence of Rayna Batya: Torah, Suffering, and Rabbi Barukh Epstein's Wisdom of Women'," *Torah u-Madda Journal* 6 (1995-1996): 91-128; Don Seeman and Rebecca Kobrin, "'Like One of the Whole Men': Learning, Gender and Autobiography in R. Barukh Epstein's Mekor Barukh," *Nashim* 2 (1999): 52-94; Brenda Bacon, "Reflections on the Suffering of Rayna Batya and the Success of the Daughters of Zelophehad," *Nashim* 3 (2000): 249-256; Dan Rabinowitz, "Rayna Batya and Other Learned Women: A Reevaluation of Rabbi Barukh

value of their manuscript collection,[24] make the family understandably guarded about allowing access to the materials they possess. However, with the assistance of Rabbi Zevulun Charlop, Dean of the Rabbi Isaac Elchanan Theological Seminary in New York City and a cousin of the Shapira family,[25] I was able to secure brief and accompanied access to the manuscript from which *'Emek ha-Neẓiv* was taken.[26]

The manuscript is handwritten in three volumes, corresponding to the three volumes of the printed text. The first two volumes were bound, but the binding has completely deteriorated and sections of each volume easily separate from one another. The third volume seems never to have been bound. The pages of all three volumes are severely frayed at the edges.

As suspected, the manuscript contains a core text with countless interlinear and marginal additions as well as words and entire lines that have been crossed out.

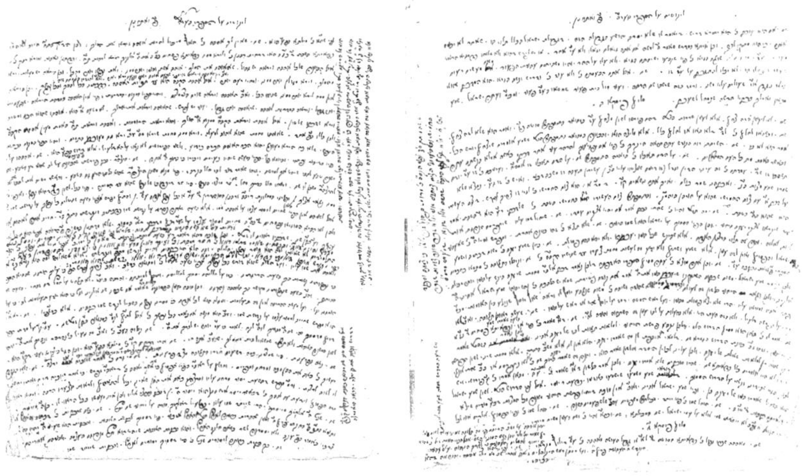

Halevi Epstein's Sources," *Tradition* 35: 1 (Summer 2001): 55-69. This position toward Neẓiv, however, was already espoused a century earlier when a series of articles appeared in the Galician newspaper *Maḥzike Ha-Da'at* (volumes 16, 17, and 18) warning traditionalist Jews to stay away from Neẓiv's Bible commentary, *Ha'amek Davar,* due to its modern stance toward the authority of the Talmudic Sages. A similar sentiment is reflected in the fact that many ultra-Orthodox houses of study have refused, and continue to refuse, to include *Ha'amek Davar* in their libraries.

24 A value which stands in stark contrast to the overwhelming poverty of most of Geulah's inhabitants.

25 See Neil Rosenstein, *The Unbroken Chain*. (New York: CIS Publishers, 1990), 433-440.

26 My examination of the manuscript took place in July of 2004 with the assistance of a Summer Travel Grant awarded by the Center for Jewish Studies at Harvard University.

It is important to note that the brackets and parenthesis which appear throughout the printed text do not correspond to these additions. Rather, they correspond to places in which Neẓiv placed parenthesis or brackets around his own words both in the core text and in the additions. The additions and the notes he appended to the end of the manuscript (referred to by the Neziv as *hashmatot* )[27] were incorporated without indication into the printed text.

The script of the core text through the first two volumes and half of the third is a fairly consistent narrowly-spaced brown cursive[28] written with a fairly wide-tipped pen. In the second half of the third volume the script of the core text changes to a blacker, wider-spaced cursive seemingly done with a thinner-tipped pen. The script of the later marginal and interlinear additions varies.

The notes which appear scattered throughout the printed text (referred to by the Neziv as *hagahot*) were written at the same time as the core text,[29] as evidenced by the identical script used and the intentional indentations left in the text of the core commentary in order to create space for the *hagahot*. The *hagahot* also contain marginal additions. A typical page in the manuscript containing *hagahot*, then, is represented in the following diagram:

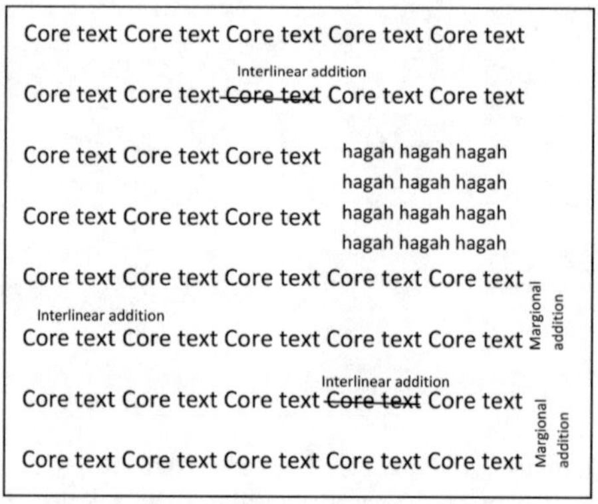


27 The *hashmatot* probably represent additions to the text which Neẓiv could not fit in the margins of the page of the core text due to lack of space.

28 The letters are in cursive form, but Neẓiv generally did not attach his letters to each other. The brown color was probably black when originally applied but has lost its vibrance with the passage of time.

29 The *hagahot* seem to have been intended as tangential footnotes to the main commentary in a manner similar to the way in which Neẓiv's *Harḥev Davar* was intended to supplement his *Ha'amek Davar* on the Bible. This format was typical of Lithuanian Torah commentary, for reasons which will be explained in Chapter Three below.

The reference to the newly printed book *'Emek Halakhah* mentioned above appears as an interlinear addition to the core text, thus implying that for that particular section of the commentary on *Naso*, the core text was written prior to 1845 and the addition was included after 1845. The references to Reb 'Iẓele are also found in the core text with the word "*she-yiḥyeh*," which dates those passages of the core text to the years prior to 1849 as well.[30]

The orderly progression of chapters in the core text, which begin at varying places on the physical page of the manuscript, indicates that Neẓiv wrote down his comments in this manuscript in proper sequence, following the order of *Sifre*.[31] That is, one can safely assume that in this particular copy of the manuscript, the core text of Neẓiv's comments on *Parashat Bamidbar* were committed to writing before those of *Parashat Naso*, and his comments on *pesikta' aleph* were committed to writing prior to those of *pesikta' bet*.[32] If the core text of the manuscript was written sequentially, and the core text of *EH Naso* 49 (I:181) was necessarily written prior to the publication of Zev Wolf ben Yehudah Ha-Levi's 1845 publication of *'Emek Halakhah*, one can deduce that, at the very least, the entire core text until that point was also committed to writing prior to 1845. Likewise, from the appearance of the word "*she-yiḥyeh*" in the core text of *Be-ha'alotekha* and *Shelaḥ*[33] one can assume that the text up to that point was written prior to Reb 'Iẓele's death in 1849. If we then add that the handwriting remains rather constant in the core text until the second half of the third volume, we have reason to believe that all of the core text until that shift in appearance was committed to writing prior to 1849.

Thus, one can safely conclude that a good portion of the printed

---

30 I had hoped to demarcate the beginning and end of each addition in my own printed text along with a description of the script used in each addition. The Shapira family, however, was not willing to grant me the sustained access to the manuscript required for such an endeavor.

31 If it had not been written in order, one would expect to find empty spaces on the bottom of a page where a particular chapter or section ended and new sections beginning on the top of new pages. Instead the end of each section in the manuscript is followed immediately by the beginning of the next section, indicating that they were written sequentially.

32 There is reason to believe that this manuscript itself is a later recension of an earlier edition. The family showed me what they said were the few extant leaves of an earlier version of the commentary written by Neẓiv which predates the manuscript used for the printed text, but I was not allowed to study them at length. As such, the above analysis does not suggest that Neẓiv actually composed his commentary according to the sequence of the *Sifre* text, but simply that the transcription of the core text of the commentary into the manuscript at hand was done in sequential order.

33 See note 17 above.

edition of *'Emek ha-Neẓiv* was indeed written while Neẓiv was a young man in his twenties and thirties. As such, the general character and main attributes of the work must be seen as a product of the cultural and intellectual atmosphere of Lithuanian Jewish society in the 1830s and 1840s. At the same time, given the large number of later additions and the lack of any demarcation in the printed text, one can not firmly ascribe a date to any specific passage found in it, with the exception of those which contain explicit or implicit references to the time of composition.

### *Censorship*

The process of preparing *'Emek ha-Neẓiv* for publication was painstakingly performed by the Shapira family over the course of many years, and thus the printed text seems to be relatively free of printing errors. However, there are two hints in the printed text which suggest the possibility of editorial censorship.

As noted above, Neẓiv's relative openness to sources of information beyond the pale of the current traditionalist canon is a character trait which is at odds with the values of the contemporary ultra-Orthodox community. As we will describe at length in the pages that follow, *'Emek ha-Neẓiv* is filled with citations and references to such sources of information. On two such occasions the reference found in the printed text appears to be intentionally altered so as to prevent proper identification of the source. In his comments on *'Ekev*, Neẓiv writes that for further study one should consult the book called "thirty-two Middot of [*sic*] in Vilna."[34] In all probability Neẓiv is referring to the book published in 1822 called *Netivot Olam: Beraita de-32 Middot* with the commentary of Ẓvi Hirsch Katzenellenbogen. Katzenellenbogen is known to have been a member of Vilna's more "enlightened" circles.[35] As such, the possibility exists that the publisher intentionally left out Katzenellenbogen's name. This prospect is bolstered by the fact that the manuscript contains a name in the standard acronymic form where the printed edition has a blank space. When I asked to look at this reference in the manuscript, it was reviewed by two members of the Shapira family and I was denied permission to look at it. Nonetheless, I did manage to see what seemed like a legible

34 *EH* 'Ekev 4 (III: 52).
35 See Chapter 2 below.

acronym ending in the letter *qof*.[36] Although it is possible that the editor could not discern the letters of the acronym, if such had been the case one would expect a bracketed editorial note, such as those which appear on several occasions in the printed text where the manuscript is illegible due to stains or frayed edges.[37]

The second possible instance of editorial censorship concerns a passage in Neẓiv's commentary on *Shoftim* which refers the reader to *"hakdamat ḥumash besau*[38] *ve-'tav"alef'."*[39] The most common referent for the initials *tav"alef* in the context of Torah commentary is *Targum Onkelos*, the ancient Aramaic translation of the Bible. However, if the *bet* of the word "besau" is replaced with a *daled* so as to read "desau" we might suggest that the *tav"alef* stands for *targum Ashkenaz*, German translation, rather than *Targum Onkelos*. As such, the citation would be of the well-known introduction to Moses Mendelssohn's Torah commentary, which was printed in Dessau and contains a German translation of the biblical text. The fact that the subject matter under discussion in this passage of Neẓiv's commentary correlates to subject matter discussed by Mendelssohn in the introduction to his Bible commentary supports the latter suggestion.

We might raise the question, then, as to whether the printed text was intentionally manipulated so as to prevent easy identification of Mendelssohn's work or whether the *daled* of Dessau was simply mistaken as a *bet* by the printsetter.[40] The fact that this particular citation was underlined in pink pencil in the manuscript bolsters the suspicion that the publishers of *'Emek ha-Neẓiv* were sensitive to the potential controversy the citation of Mendelssohn might have caused in the ultra-Orthodox community and that they therefore intentionally altered the printed text.[41]

---

36 My access to the manuscript was always limited to sitting next to a member of the Shapira family, who would turn to the page I wished to check and look at the specific textual anomaly before deciding whether to let me look as well. In this case I was able to peer over his shoulder and attempt to decipher the acronym. The exact response this member of the Shapira family gave to this particular request was, "Suffice it to say, it is not a *siman* in *Shulḥan Arukh*."

37 E.g., *EH* Naso 42 (I: 162); *EH* Naso 44 (I: 173); *EH* Matot 1 (II: 279); *EH* Matot 'Ekev (III: 45); *EH* Re'eh 9 (III: 92).

38 *Bet-ayyin-samekh-vav.*

39 *EH* Shoftim 16 (III: 189).

40 In cursive Hebrew writing the *bet* and *daled* look quite similar.

41 A glaring example of this type of censorship recently appeared in a photo-offset of the 1926 Frankfurt edition of David Ẓvi Hoffmann's responsa, *Melamed le-Ho'il*, published by the Lebovitz-Kest foundation. In Responsa #56 in the original printing (II: 50), Hoffmann

Both of the above instances of possible censorship beg the question as to why the references were included altogether if the printers wished them to remain unidentified. Furthermore, as will be discussed below, the printed text of *'Emek ha-Neẓiv* contains references to numerous other works that lie well beyond the traditional contemporary ultra-Orthodox canon which were not censored. As such, the evidence for editorial censorship cannot be considered conclusive. Nonetheless, these two passages do raise the possibility that other parts of the text were more cleverly censored or that other citations were completely deleted.

### *The End of* 'Emek ha-Neẓiv

The end of Neẓiv's commentary on *Sifre,* as it appears in the printed edition of *'Emek ha-Neẓiv,* is also an issue of concern to the critical reader. The commentary in both the printed edition and the manuscript comes to an abrupt halt halfway through the *parashah* of *Ki Teẓeh*[42] and well before the end of the text of *Sifre* itself. One is therefore led to question whether Neẓiv truly ended his commentary there, or whether there was more to the commentary that does not appear in the printed text.

Several factors indicate that Neẓiv's commentary did, in fact, extend beyond *piska'* 27 of *Parashat Ki Teẓeh.*[43] To begin, Neẓiv starts his commentary at the beginning of *Sifre* with an introductory double couplet, and thus one would expect a similar poetic composition at the end of the work, but none appears in the printed text or in the manuscript. Furthermore, a statement of completion marks the close of each *parashah* throughout the text, but none appears at the end of *Parashat Ki Teẓeh.* Likewise, the

gives his approval, in exigent cases, for an Orthodox Jew to swear before a civil court without a head covering. In the context of his piece, Hoffmann also attests to the fact that Samson Raphael Hirsch instructed the students in the Frankfurt Orthodox school which he founded to cover their heads only for Judaic studies and allowed them to remain bareheaded for their secular studies. The recent photo-offset contains an introduction by a grandson of Hoffmann, David Ẓvi ben Natan Naftali Hoffmann, which gives the reader the impression that the grandson belongs to the ultra-Orthodox community of Jerusalem. Responsa #56, however, permits a practice clearly anathema to that community. Hence, when one turns to page fifty in the off-set, in place of what was earlier Responsa #56, one finds a blank space. I thank Rabbi Moshe Schapiro, librarian at the Mendel Gottesman Library of Yeshiva University, for bringing this example to my attention.

42 *EH* Teẓeh (III: 296).

43 Note that the *piska'ot* of Neẓiv do not correspond to those of the *Sifre* text with which the commentary is printed. In the text of *Sifre* the last *piska'* for which there is continuous commentary is 43, and it then resumes in 54. See Chapter 5.

completion of the Book of Numbers is marked by two rhyming stanzas of nine lines each,[44] while Deuteronomy, and the commentary as a whole, has no formal conclusion at all.

One must entertain the possibility that the abrupt ending of the work suggests not that the final portion of the commentary is missing from the printed text but that Neẓiv never completed the commentary. This theory might be supported by the fact that the statements of conclusion which follow every *parashah* are in poetic form in the first two volumes, whereas in the third volume, which consists of the Book of Deuteronomy, the statements consist of nothing more than "*Piska'* 8 is complete and [so too] the entire portion of *ve-'Etḥ anan*."[45] One might interpret this phenomenon as suggesting that the final touches, such as the transformation of abrupt closing statements into clever couplets, were never applied to the third volume of the work.

Such a conclusion seems unlikely, however, when one considers the numerous revisions and recensions to which Neẓiv subjected the rest of the commentary. One generally does not spend the time editing, expanding, and re-copying a work that one has yet to complete. Furthermore, in his introduction to *Ha'amek She'elah* Neẓiv regrets that he has not yet brought his commentary on *Sifre* to press, but he makes no mention of not having completed writing the text. Similarly, in a comment found in his *Harḥev Davar*, published along with his *Ha'amek Davar* in 1878, Neẓiv writes that while he has not elaborated on a particular point in this work, he will do so at length when God grants him the merit of "publishing the commentary on *Sifre*."[46] Here too, Neẓiv does not ask for God's help in finishing the work, but in bringing it to press. Likewise, Avraham Yiẓḥak Kook, one of the outstanding students of Neẓiv, publically called upon his teacher to publish his *Sifre* commentary in a footnote to a biographical article on Neẓiv published in 1888.[47] He too seems to suggest that the work was complete.

The physical form of the third volume of the manuscript makes the possibility of missing material rather plausible as well. The printed text contains commentary to every *piska'* in *Sifre* up until *piska'* 27 of *Parashat*

---

44 *EH* Mas'ai (II: 334).

45 *EH* Ve-'Etḥanan (III: 43).

46 *HrD* Num. 6: 19.

47 Avraham Yiẓḥak Kook, "*Rosh Yeshivat Eẓ Ḥayyim*," *Kenesset Yisrael*, ed. S.J Finn (Warsaw, 1888), 138-147. Also in *Ma'amarei HaRe'iyah* (Jerusalem, 1984), 123-126.

*Ki Teẓeh.*[48] There is no commentary on *piska'ot* 27-54, but the text resumes with brief comments on *piska'* 54[49] and then ends completely. In the manuscript, *piska'* 27 ends at the bottom of a page, which raises the possibility that further commentary followed on subsequent pages which are now lost. The brief comments to *piska'* 54 appear on the reverse side of comments labeled as *hashmatot*; therefore, they may well represent *hashmatot* to a core commentary, now lost, on the end of Deuteronomy.[50] When one considers the fact that, unlike the first two volumes, the third volume of the manuscript is not bound and does not appear to ever have been bound, the notion that pages from the end of the commentary were lost must be seriously considered.[51]

## *Conclusions*

The conclusion one must draw from the above investigation of the text of *'Emek ha-Neẓiv* is that a historical analysis of the content found in the printed text must be made with caution. The possibility of the text being incomplete must always be considered both in regard to possible editorial censorship and in regard to the possibility that the text originally contained additional chapters that are currently lost. Whereas the core text of the commentary prior to *Shelaḥ*[52] can be rather definitively dated prior to 1849, the printed text makes no distinction between the core text and later additions. As such, with the exception of a few passages which include embedded historical evidence, no single passage in the printed text can conclusively be dated to the 1830s or 1840s. Nonetheless, there is sufficient evidence, both in Neẓiv's own testimony with which this chapter began and in the clues offered by the text and corroborated by the manuscript, to conclude that the bulk of the commentary does in-

48 *EH* Teẓeh (III: 296). *Piska'ot* here are according to Neẓiv's division. For more on Neẓiv's method of dividing *piska'ot* see Chapter 3 below.

49 *EH* Teẓeh (III: 299). In the absence of Neẓiv's commentary, *piska'ot* here refer to the division found in the standard Sulzbach edition.

50 When I asked the Shapira family about the strange ending of work, they too suggested that there might have been more that was lost. When I asked them who had possession of the manuscript prior to them, they declined to give me any names and replied instead, "Suffice it say, it has been handed down, son after son."

51 The existence of commentary on the latter parts of Deuteronomy could have been conclusively proven had Neẓiv included a reference to it in his other writings. I have found no such reference, but no conclusions can be drawn from silence.

52 *EH* Shelaḥ 1 (II: 10).

deed reflect a project with which Neẓiv was engrossed in his early years. Thus, trends which can be identified throughout the printed text and which comprise its general character must indeed be seen as a product of the intellectual currents of Lithuanian Jewish culture in the 1830s and 1840s.

# CHAPTER TWO:
## Neẓiv as an Early Nineteenth-Century Midrash Commentator

As demonstrated in the previous chapter, the young Neẓiv devoted much of his intellectual energy to the examination and explication of midrashic texts in general, and *Sifre* in particular. This scholarly passion, though, was not unique to Neẓiv. In fact, the study of midrashic texts, and the composition of commentaries thereon, was a salient feature of the intellectual milieu of early nineteenth-century Lithuanian Torah scholarship. It is against this backdrop, and in light of these influences, that *'Emek ha-Neẓiv* must be viewed.

### *Midrash Commentary Prior to the Ga'on*

While the volumes of halakhic and homiletic exegesis traditionally attributed to tanaitic and amoraic authors and referred to generally as midrash served as important sources for medieval rabbinic Bible commentators, Talmud commentators and halakhists, little intellectual energy was devoted by medieval authors to systematic studies of midrashic works in and of themselves. For example, while Rashi's Bible commentary is filled with references, paraphrases, and citations of midrashic literature, and while Maimonides consistently mined the halakhic midrashim in formulating his famous halakhic code,[1] neither of them sought to pen a commentary on a work of midrash per se.[2]

Compared to Bible and Talmud commentary, the canon of midrash commentary is sparse, to say the least. And, with the notable exception of the commentary on *Sifra* by Rabad of Posquières, the few commentaries which have come down to us prior to the late nineteenth century stem from rabbinic authors otherwise relatively unknown in the world of Jewish scholarship. Amongst them are Hillel ben Elyakim, who penned a

---

1 See Isadore Twersky, *Introduction to the Code of Maimonides* (New Haven: Yale University Press, 1980).

2 The marginal commentary of the 1567-68 Venice edition of Bereishit Rabbah attributed to Rashi was not written by Rashi. See R.N. Brown, "An Antedate to Rashi's Commentary to Genesis Rabba" (Hebrew), *Tarbiẓ* 53 (1983-84): 478.

commentary on *Sifra* and *Sifre* in twelfth-century Greece,[3] the Moroccan scholar Aaron ibn Ḥayyim, who authored a *Sifra* commentary known as *Korban Aharon* in the early seventeenth century, and a commentary on *Sifre* by an unknown author, apparently of the fourteenth century, which was mistakenly attributed to Rabad.[4] Likewise, we have an early medieval commentary on *Bereishit Rabbah* misattributed to Rashi and an anonymous twelfth-century commentary on both *Bereishit* and *Vayikra Rabbah*.[5] Yiẓḥak ben Yedayah also penned a commentary to the entire *Midrash Rabbah* in the thirteenth century,[6] and Isaachar Ber ben Naftali ha-Kohen wrote his *Matanot Kehunah* on *Midrash Rabbah* in 1584. It was followed a few years later by Shmuel Yaffe Ashkenazi's *Yefeh To'ar*.[7] And, in the seventeenth century, Avraham Abele Gombiner, author of the *Magen Avraham* commentary *on Shulḥan Arukh*, wrote his *Zayit Ra'anan* on the collection of midrash aggadah known as *Yalkut Shim'oni.*

This rather scant list includes all of the major works of midrash commentary which have come down to us from the time of the redaction of the classic works of midrash between the fifth and tenth centuries of the common era until the life of Eliyahu of Vilna (1720-1797), some thirteen centuries later. In the wake of the Vilna Ga'on, however, and due in part to his influence, the history of midrash commentary takes a rather sudden and rather dramatic turn.[8]

## *The "Vilna Circle"*

The first half of the nineteenth century, particularly in the Lithuanian Jewish community, witnessed a remarkable flowering of commentaries on compilations of midrash and similar extra-talmudic works thought to

3 We must, of course, allow for the possibility that other works were written, possibly even by authors of note, which never made it to print and whose manuscripts were lost or have yet to be discovered.

4 See H.W. Basser, *Pseudo-Rabad: Commentary to Sifre Deuteronomy Edited and Annotated According to Manuscripts and Citations* (Atlanta: Scholars Press, 1994).

5 See Yisrael Ta-Shema's "An Unpublished Early Franco-German Commentary on Bereishit and Vayikra Rabbah" (Hebrew), *Tarbiẓ* 55 (1985-86): 61-75.

6 See Marc Saperstein, "The Earliest Commentary on the Midrash Rabba," in Isadore Twersky, ed., *Studies in Medieval Jewish History and Literature* (Cambridge, MA: Harvard University Press, 1979), 283-306.

7 See Meir Benayahu, "R. Samuel Yaffe Ashkenazi and Other Commentators of Midrash Rabba" (Hebrew), *Tarbiẓ* 42 (1972-73): 419-460.

8 The role played by the Vilna Ga'on in bringing about this shift will be explored in Chapter Five.

be of tanaitic or amoraic origin.[9] Unlike the rabbinic intellectual society of the past, many of the Lithuanian community's premier intellectuals devoted significant time to editing and explicating a myriad of midrashic texts thought to contain halakhic and aggadic teachings of the talmudic sages. While no institutions existed in which midrash study was given a prominent or even a minor place in the official curriculum, a circle of intellectuals emerged, bound by a familial or student-teacher relationship, as well as by geographic location, to which much of the literary production in the realm of midrash study can be traced.

At the very center of this circle stands Avraham ben Eliyahu, son of the Vilna Ga'on (1750-1808) and Avraham's son Ya'akov of Slonim (d. 1849). Like his father, Avraham ben Eliyahu, also called Avraham ben ha-Gra, did not hold an official position as a communal rabbi, but his lineage and his own erudition secured him an honored place amongst the elite of the Vilna Jewish community. His scholarly endeavors had two clearly delineated foci: one was editing, annotating, and publishing the work of his father, and the other was his own study of midrash aggadah. In 1802, Avraham ben ha-Gra published *Midrash Aggadat Bereishit* along with his own critical comments and a lengthy introduction notable for its historical content. That introduction became part of a larger work in which Avraham ben ha-Gra set out to identify all of the midrashic works to which the earlier rabbinic authorities and commentators seem to have had access, much of which had been lost with the passage of time. This work was first published posthumously under the title *Rav Pe'alim* in Warsaw in 1894.[10]

Avraham ben ha-Gra also penned a commentary on the midrashic compilation known as *Pesikta' Rabbati*. The manuscript to this commentary was inherited by his son, Ya'akov of Slonim. Ya'akov of Slonim, in turn, gave the first half of the work to a midrash scholar living in Vilna named Ze'ev Wolf ben Yisrael Isser Einhorn.[11]

The decision to give Avraham ben Ha-Gra's commentary to *Pesikta'*

---

9 The latter category would include works such *Tosefta*, the so-called Minor Tractates, *Tanna de-Bei Eliyahu, Pesikta de-Rav Kahana*, the Passover Haggadah, as well as the Zohar and related kabbalistic texts such as *Sifre de-Ẓeniuta*, which were considered by the traditional community to have been of ancient origin.

10 On Avraham ben ha-GRA, see Shmuel Yosef Fuenn, *Kiriah Ne'emanah* (Vilna, 1905), 210-21.

11 *Midrash Pesikta Rabbati de-Rav Kehana* (Breslau, 1831), end of introduction. See also Solomon Buber's reference to this text in his preface to *Sefer Aggadat Bereishit* (New York: Menorah Institute, 1958), III.

*Rabbati* to Ze'ev Wolf Einhorn was probably motivated by the fact that Einhorn himself was engaged in studying and commenting on *Pesikta' Rabbati*. His commentary, which incorporates some of the comments of Avraham ben Ha-Gra, was published in Breslau in 1831. Einhorn also dedicated considerable energy to explicating the thirty-two hermeneutical principles of rabbinic aggadic exegesis. His comments on this subject were printed first in *Midrash Tana'im* (Vilna, 1838).[12] Einhorn's magnum opus, however, is a massive commentary on *Midrash Rabbah*, incorporated into the Vilna edition of that work under the name *Peirush MaHarZU* (Commentary of Moreinu ha-Rav Ze'ev Wolf) and published in 1855.

Avraham ben ha-Gra passed on not only his own unpublished manuscripts to his son Ya'akov, but also those of his father, the Vilna Ga'on. As a result, when a young midrash scholar from Vilna named Yiẓḥak Eliyahu Landau (1801-1876)[13] sought to obtain the Ga'on's notes on the compilation of midrash halakhah known as *Mekhilta'*,[14] he asked Avraham ben ha-Gra's son, Ya'akov of Slonim, to provide him with a copy. Ya'akov responded by telling Landau that the copy that had originally been in his possession had been sent off to be printed, but that its exact whereabouts were unknown. Yiẓḥak Eliyahu Landau, however, did succeed in locating a different copy of the manuscript.[15]

Landau's importance to the world of Lithuanian midrash commentary extends well beyond his connection to Ya'akov of Slonim. Born and raised in Vilna, Yiẓḥak Eliyahu Landau left for the home of his father-in-law in Dubno at the age of eighteen. While living in Dubno, Landau succeeded in business while earning a reputation as a scholar and an eloquent speaker. His success earned him a place amongst the elite of the Volhynian Jewish community, as reflected by the fact that he was chosen as a member of the rabbinical commission to the Russian Tsar in 1861. In 1868, Yiẓḥak Eliyahu Landau was appointed as a judge in Vilna's prestigious rabbinical court and as the official *maggid*, or preacher, to the Vilna Jewish community, and he remained in Vilna until his death in 1876.[16]

In addition to his success as a businessman, a preacher, and a scholar,

12 Cited in *EH* Re'eh 29 (III: 120).

13 Steinschneider, vol. I, 170.

14 Landau had been briefly shown a copy of the manuscript once before by another unnamed grandson of the Ga'on.

15 *Mekhilta im Be'ur Berure ha-Middot* (Vilna, 1844), 2 of introduction.

16 Ibid., 92-97; see also Feunn, *Keneset Yisrael*, 632; introduction to *Lishmo'a be-Limudim* (Vilna: 1876).

Landau was also one of nineteenth-century Jewish Lithuania's most prolific authors. And the majority of his literary production revolved around the study of extra-talmudic compilations of purportedly tanaitic and amoraic teachings. Of the fifteen books he published, most of which were written during his earlier years in Dubno, six focus exclusively on such texts,[17] five are Bible commentaries[18] which heavily employ midrashic texts, one is a commentary on the Passover Haggadah,[19] two are commentaries on various sets of prayers,[20] and one is a compilation of sermons which also makes extensive use of midrash.[21] Landau also wrote commentaries to the book of Samuel and the minor tractate known as *Masekhet Kallah*,[22] and is said to have also written a commentary on the compilation of talmudic *aggadot* known as *En Ya'akov*.[23] None of these last three were published.

Yiẓḥak Eliyahu Landau was not the only member of his family engaged in serious midrash study. Ẓvi Hirsch ha-Kohen Rappaport was married to Landau's wife's sister, another daughter of the wealthy Ẓadok Marshalkovitz of Dubno, and, like Landau, Rappaport resided in Dubno as a result.[24] While there, he composed a double commentary[25] on the halakhic midrash to the book of Leviticus known as *Torat Kohanim*,

17 *Ma'aneh Eliyahu* (Vilna: 1840) on *Tanna de-Bei Eliyahu; Berurei ha-Middot* (Vilna: 1844) on *Mekhilta'; Mikra' Soferim* (Suwalk: 1862) on *Masekhet Soferim; Aḥarit ha-shalom* (Vilna: 1871) on various *aggadot; Derekh Ḥayyim* (Vilna: 1872) on *Derekh 'Ereẓ Zuta'; Lishmo'a be-Limudim* (Vilna, 1876) on Talmudic *aggadot*.

18 *Patshegen* (Vilna, 1858) on Proverbs; *Kiflayim le-Toshiyyah* on Joel (Zhitomir, 1865) and on Psalms (Warsaw, 1866); *Patshegen ha-Dat*, on the Five Scrolls (Vilna, 1870) and on the Pentateuch (Vilna, 1872-75).

19 *Aḥarit le-Shalom* (Vilna, 1871). As the name Haggadah suggests, the Passover Haggadah is, in essence, a collection of midrashic material relating to the story and laws of Passover. As such, it is not surprising that this same period in Lithuania witnesses a flurry of activity in the realm of Haggadah commentary as well. Amongst the commentators are Landau, Avraham Danzig (1747-1820), and Bezalel ha-Kohen (1820-1878). See *Haggadah shel Pesaḥ 'im Peirushim Yikarim ve-Neḥmadim me-Rabanei Kehilat Kodesh Vilna* (Vilna, 1877).

20 *Simlah Ḥadashah*, on the Maḥzor (published in the Vilna editions of the Maḥzor); *Dover Shalom* (Warsaw, 1863) on the daily prayers.

21 *Derushim le-Kol Ḥefẓehem* (Vilna, 1871-77); he also published two of his funeral orations: *Kol Sha'on* (Vilna, 1872) and *'Evel Kaved* (Eydtkuhnen, 1873) on the death of Shmuel Strashun.

22 See introduction to his *Derekh Ḥayyim* (Vilna, 1872), 7-8.

23 Steinschneider, ibid.

24 Steinschneider, vol. I, 93, n. 8.

25 A double commentary generally consists of one section which provides a focused explanation of the text and a second, which adds notes to the commentary that are often only tangentially related to the text at hand. While this style of commentary long predates nineteenth-century Lithuania, it becomes a staple of Lithuanian commentary for reasons suggested in Chapter Three below.

published under the names *Ezrat Kohanim* and *Tosefet ha-'Azarah*. The first volume was printed in Vilna in 1845 and is cited by Neẓiv in his commentary on *Sifre*.[26]

Landau's interest in both the art of public preaching and the study of midrash may well have been fostered in his youth by exposure to the man whose position he would later fill, Yeḥezkel Feivel, the *maggid* of Vilna. Feivel assumed the position of *maggid*, or official city preacher, in 1811, when Landau was 10 years old, and held it until his death in 1833.[27] For seven years prior to his departure for Dubno, then, Landau must have heard the preaching of Yeḥezkel Feivel and might well have known that he was actively writing a commentary on *Midrash Rabbah*. That commentary was first published in the Vilna edition of *Midrash Rabbah* under the name *Peirush ha-Maharif* between 1885 and 1887.

In addition to Landau, there were a number of other young boys who grew up in Vilna during Yeḥezkel Feivel's tenure as *maggid* who went on to become noted scholars of midrash. Most prominent amongst them were Ḥanokh Zundel ben Yeshaya Luria (d. 1847), Shmuel Strashun (1794-1872), David Luria (1798-1856), and Ẓvi Hirsch Katzenellenbogen (1796-1868). Like Yeḥezkel Feivel, Ḥanokh Zundel ben Yeshayahu Luria became a *maggid* himself, first in New Zhagory and then in Novogroduk. He wrote a commentary entitled *Kenaf Renanim* on the aggadic mystical text known as *Perek ha-Shirah* (Krataschin, 1842).[28] Shmuel Strashun arrived with his family in Vilna in 1812, the year after Yeḥezkel Feivel was appointed as *maggid*. While best known for his notes to Talmud Bavli, which are published at the end of the standard Vilna editions of the books of Talmud (*Hagahot ve-Ḥidushei ha-Rashash*), Strashun authored extensive notes to *Midrash Rabbah* as well.

David Luria, later known by the acronym Radal, was born in 1798 in the town of Old Bihov and died there in 1856.[29] His father was Yehu-

26 E.g., *EH* Naso 1 (I: 2); *EH* Naso 2 (I: 14,17,18); *EH* Naso 2 (I: 18); *EH* Shelaḥ 3 (II: 23); *EH* Koraḥ 1 (II: 82).

27 See Edward Breuer, "The Haskalah in Vilna: R. Yeḥezkel Feivel's *'Toldot Adam'*," *Torah u-Madda Journal* 7 (1997): 15-40. Yeḥezkel Feivel was succeeded by his son Shelomoh Zev (who assumed the last name) Maggid. After Shelomoh Zev's death in 1868, Landau was appointed to the position.

28 Fuenn, *Keneset Yisrael*, 312.

29 The year of Radal's death is often listed as 1855. However, the date on the approbation which Luria wrote to Neẓiv in support of his commentary on *She'iltot* is dated the 28 of Tevet, 5616, which was January 6, 1856. In the letter which accompanied the approbation, Luria mentions that he is not well, and he probably passed away later that year. The letter

dah Yidel Luria, a seventh-generation descendant of Maharshal, and his mother was a daughter of Yisrael Rappaport, *av bet din* of Old Bihov.[30] In 1811, at age 13, he arrived in Vilna and soon became a student of Sha'ul Katzenellenbogen (1770-1825),[31] a member of the rabbinical court on which Avraham ben ha-Gra sat. Luria studied in Vilna with Katzenellenbogen for the next four years, which also coincide with the first four years of Yeḥezkel Feivel's tenure as *maggid* in Vilna. At age eighteen, Luria returned to Old Bihov, where he would assume the position of communal rabbi following the death of his father-in-law.[32] Luria's impressive erudition and broad knowledge in areas of traditional rabbinic learning and well beyond soon gained him a reputation as one of the elite scholars of his generation.[33]

David Luria's literary production was also impressive and, like many other scholars of his day, he chose to focus his energy on compilations of midrash and similar collections of rabbinic teachings. His works include notes on Talmud Bavli, which appear in the Vilna edition published by the Romm press, a commentary on Talmud Yerushalmi *Seder Mo'ed* (Koenigsberg, 1858), notes on GRA's commentary to Yerushalmi *Seder Zera'im* (Koenigsberg, 1858), a commentary on Tosefta of *Masekhet 'Ukẓin* (Vilna, Romm), a commentary on *Pirkei de-Rabbi Eliezer* (Warsaw, 1852), a commentary on *Midrash Shmuel* (Warsaw, 1852), *Kadmut Sefer ha-Zohar* on the antiquity of the Zohar (Koenigsburg, 1856), notes and a commentary to *Midrash Rabbah* (Vilna, 1843), a commentary and notes on *Pesikta' de-Rav Kahana* (Warsaw, 1893), *Nefesh David* on Zohar (Vilna 1882), notes on *Zohar Ḥadash Shir ha-Shirim* and *Ruth* (Warsaw, 1885), notes on *She'iltot* printed with Neẓiv's *Ha'amek She'elah* (Vilna, 1861), notes on *Shut ha-Ge'onim Sha'are Teshuvah* (Leipzig, 1858), notes and additions to *Sefer ha-Yuḥsin* and *Seder ha-Dorot* (Vilna, 1877), responsa known as *Shut Radal*

---

and approbation are found in *Ha'amek She'elah*, vol. I, "*Petaḥ ha-Emek*," 4.

30 *Sefer Kitve ha-Ga'on R. David Luria* (Jerusalem, 1990), 3.

31 On Katzenellenbogen, see *Kiriah Ne'emanah*, 237-238.

32 Ibid., 5.

33 Ḥayyim Davidsohn, rabbi of Warsaw at the time, describes Luria in the following manner in his approbation to Luria's commentary on *Pirkei de-Rabbi Eliezer*: "Because he is of the great Ge'onim of our time in sharpness and in breadth and because he has a broad heart [which encompasses] all knowledge, and he has ten hand breadths in the sciences." See *Toldot ha-Radal*, published as an introduction to *Kitvei ha-Radal: Sefer Pirkei de-Rabbi Eliezer* (Jerusalem, 1990), for further contemporary and posthumous accounts of the perception of Luria in Lithuanian rabbinic circles. See also Barukh ha-Levi Epstein's account of Luria in *Mekor Barukh*, vol. IV (Vilna, 1928), 1684.

(Jerusalem, 1898) and notes to *Sefer ha-Parnes* (Vilna, 1891).

While Radal's teacher, Sha'ul Katzenellenbogen, published no literary works of his own[34] his interest in midrash is evident from the work of another of his students, Ẓvi Hirsch Katzenellenbogen.[35] Ẓvi Hirsch's primary work is a commentary known as *Netivot 'Olam* (Vilna, 1822), on the Berayta ascribed to Eliezer ben Yose ha-Gelili which enumerates thirty-two hermeneutical rules for rabbinic aggadic exegesis.[36] Although Sha'ul Katzenellenbogen writes in a letter published at the beginning of the work that he will not make an exception to his policy against writing official approbations, his imprint is clearly left on the work through Ẓvi Hirsch's repeated citation of his teacher's insights into the world of midrash aggadah.[37] Ẓvi Hirsch also appends an entire section to *Netivot 'Olam*, which he describes as the "insights and additions to my book by my beloved friend the Ga'on, the Light of the World, the Splendor of the Generation, Our teacher, Shmuel Strashun, of Vilna."[38]

Thus, in the years following the death of the Vilna Ga'on, we begin to see the emergence of two generations of Vilna scholars for whom the study of non-talmudic collections of purportedly tanaitic and amoraic material is central to their scholarly endeavors. The first generation consists of influential rabbinic personalities such as Avraham ben ha-Gra, Sha'ul Katzenellenbogen, and Yeḥezkel Feivel. They, in turn, impart a passion for midrash study to a group of younger scholars, which included Avraham ben ha-Gra's son, Ya'akov of Slonim, Yiẓḥak Eliyahu Landau, Ḥanokh Zundel Luria, David Luria, Shmuel Strashun, and Ẓvi Hirsch Katzenellenbogen.

This circle of early nineteenth century midrash scholars, though, can be expanded beyond its center in Vilna by returning again to Ya'akov of Slonim, grandson of the Vilna Ga'on and resident of the Lithuanian town

34 Sparse notes from Katzenellenbogen to portions of the Talmud Bavli, however, are included at the end of each volume of the Romm Press edition of the Talmud.

35 According to Steinschneider, vol. I, 228, the young Naftali was originally known by the last name Simḥes, after his father Simḥah Bardes. It was due to his close kinship with Sha'ul Katzenellenbogen that the latter bestowed upon his student his own prestigious last name of Katzenellenbogen.

36 Zev Wolf Einhorn, who lived at the same time and in the same place, also composed a commentary which treats this alleged berayta. Einhorn's commentary was printed together with that of Katzenellenbogen in *Baraita de-Sheloshim u-Shetayim Middot de-Rabbi Eliezer beno Shel Rabbi Yosi ha-Galili* (Tel Aviv: Zion, 1969).

37 E.g., *Netivot 'Olam* 9a, 14b, 15a, 25a, 31a, 34b, 40a, 51b.

38 *Netivot 'Olam* (Vilna, 1858), 197-206.

of Slonim. Ya'akov of Slonim's engagement with midrash study was not limited to his role as a clearinghouse for the manuscripts of his ancestors, as evidenced by the fact that he composed his own set of exegetical notes to *Midrash Rabbah*. They were published at the end of his life, together with a commentary on *Midrash Rabbah* written by a contemporary of Ya'akov's who also happened to live in the town of Slonim. The commentary is entitled *'Eshed Neḥalim* (Vilna, 1843-45), and its author was Avraham Schick, another prolific early-nineteenth-century midrash commentator.[39]

*'Eshed Neḥalim,* however, is just a small piece of Schick's commentarial oeuvre. He also wrote a commentary on *Midrash Mishle* entitled *Zera' Avraham* (Vilna-Grodno, 1833), edited *Tanna de-Bei Eliyahu* and added a commentary entitled *Me'ore ha-'Esh* (Grodno, 1834), penned a commentary on *Shir ha-Shirim* entitled *Maḥazeh ha-Shir* (Warsaw, 1840), wrote a commentary on the compilation of talmudic aggadah found in Ibn Habib's *En Ya'akov* entitled *En Avraham* (Konigsberg, 1848), and edited the Genesis and Exodus volumes of Ya'akov of Dubno's *Ohel Ya'akov* (Johannesberg, 1859) as well.

It is very possible that the interest in midrashic texts of Ya'akov of Slonim and Avraham Schick was encouraged and possibly inspired by the famed *maggid* of their town, Yehudah Leib Edel (1757-1827). Edel, whom Yoseph Sha'ul Nathanson (1808-1875)[40] counted amongst the close associates of the Vilna Ga'on,[41] published a book on basic Hebrew

39 Steinschneider, vol. I, 170. I have not been able to determine Schick's years of birth or death. The title page to Schick's *Me'ore 'Esh* notes that his father was Aryeh Leib Schick, *av bet din* of Vashilishok (Vasilishki, on the outskirts of Vilna), who was the son of Yom-Tov Lipman who, in turn, was the son of Ḥanokh Henokh Schick, who served as *av bet din* of Shklov. It stands to reason that Avraham Schick was related to Eliyahu Schick, who was also born in the town of Vashilishok. Eliyahu Schick (1809-1876) also belongs to the intellectual circle we are here describing, as his great literary work, *'En 'Eliyahu,* is a commentary on Yosef ibn Habib's compilation of Talmudic *aggadot* known as *'En Ya'akov*. Eliyahu Schick served both as a maggid and as the rabbi of several notable Lithuanian communities, and is considered to have been one of the teachers of Yiẓḥak Elhanan Spektor.

40 Nathanson was the rabbi of Lvov (Lemburg), and widely considered one the foremost rabbinic scholars of nineteenth-century Poland. While best known for his voluminous collection of responsa, entitled *Shut Sho'el u-Meshiv* (Lemberg, 1865-79), he also authored commentaries on *Shulḥan Arukh* and Talmud Yerushalmi.

41 See his approbation to *Afike Yehudah* (Lemburg, 1863). The Vilna Ga'on did not have students in the traditional sense of the word. To be the student of a given person generally implies that there was formal instruction by the mentor to the disciple over a sustained period of time. The Vilna Ga'on, however, did not formally teach in any educational institution, and those who did study with him generally did not do so for more than a

grammar,[42] a collection of sermons,[43] a commentary on the Rambam's introduction to the mishnaic order of *Taharot*,[44] and a commentary on the *Mishnayot Taharot* and its earlier commentaries.[45] Most importantly for the present study, he also wrote a work edited by his son on the passages of midrash aggadah which appear in the Talmud Bavli, entitled *Iyye ha-Yam* (Ostrog, 1835).

Ya'akov of Slonim also seems to have left his mark, either through personal contact or through his writings, on Ḥanokh Zundel ben Yosef (d. 1867).[46] Twice in the early pages of Ḥanokh Zundel's commentary on *Midrash Rabbah*, which is entitled *'Anaf Yosef*, his comments are followed by parenthesis in which is written "from the Rav, our teacher, the Rabbi Ya'akov grandson of the GRA, of Slonim."[47] Radal left a clearly discernable imprint upon the work of Ḥanokh Zundel as well, as demonstrated by the numerous times Radal is referenced and cited throughout Ḥanokh Zundel's work.[48]

While both Avraham Schick and Yiẓḥak Eliyahu Landau were prolific midrash commentators, neither of them matched the literary output of Ḥanokh Zundel in the sphere of midrash commentary. His first publication was a double commentary on the *Midrash Rabbah* of the Five Megillot (Vilna and Grodno, 1829-1834).[49] His second was a double commentary on the aggadic *Midrash Tanḥuma* (Vilna, 1833).[50] In 1843, he published a commentary on the Passover Haggadah entitled *Meshiv Nefesh* (Warsaw,

---

few weeks or possibly a few months at a time. See Immanuel Etkes, *The Ga'on of Vilna: The Man and his Image*, trans. Jeffrey M. Green (Berkeley: University of California Press, 2002). For biographical information on Edel, see the introduction to his *Afike Yehudah* (Jerusalem: 1999).

42 *Kuntrus ha-Pe'alim be-Shem Safah le-Ne'emanim* (Lemberg: 1793).

43 *'Afike Yehudah* (Lemburg: 1802).

44 *Mei Niftoaḥ* (Bialystok: 1816).

45 *Mayyim Tehorim* (Bialystok: 1817).

46 To be differentiated from Ḥanokh Zundel ben Yeshayah Luria mentioned above.

47 *Midrash Rabbot*, Vol. I (Warsaw: 1867), 2b and 5a.

48 E.g., ibid., 38a, 39b, 40b, 41a, 42a, 43a, etc.

49 Traditional rabbinic scholarship views the collections of aggadic *midrash* on the Pentateuch and the Five Megillot known as *Midrash Rabbah* as a single entity. Radal, in his introduction to his commentary on *Aggadat* Shmuel (Warsaw, 1851), argues that *Aggadat Shmuel* also belongs to "the early Midrashim arranged by the Sages of Erez Yisrael which they called by the name Midrash Rabbot, of which much has been preserved on the books of Bereishit, Vayikra, and the Five Megillot."

50 His *Tanḥuma* commentary was reprinted immediately after his death as well (Stettin, 1863), and numerous times afterward.

1843). Two years later he published a triple commentary[51] on the rabbinic work of chronology, *Seder Olam* (Vilna, 1845).[52] The last major work Ḥanokh Zundel published during his lifetime was a double commentary on *Midrash Shmuel* (Stettin, 1860). Following his death, however, his massive triple commentary on *Midrash Rabbah* of the Pentateuch was published (Warsaw, 1867), as was his triple commentary on *Midrash Aggadat Bereishit* (Warsaw, 1876), and his commentary on the aggadic portions of the Talmud (Vilna, 1883). His introduction to his commentary on *Midrash Rabbah* of the Pentateuch states that he also penned commentaries on *En Ya'akov, Midrash Shoḥer Tov, Pesikta' Rabbati,* and *Yalkut Shim'oni.*[53] The *En Ya'akov* commentary was included in the Vilna edition of that work (1883), and the commentary ascribed to Ḥanokh Zundel and published in the Vilna *Tehillim* (1886) might be the work he referred to as a commentary on *Midrash Shoḥer Tov*. His commentaries on *Pesikta' Rabbati* and *Yalkut Shim'oni,* however, seem to have been lost.

We can thus begin to piece together a larger web of interconnected midrash scholars, many of whom spent their active or formative years in Vilna during the first two decades of the nineteenth century and seem to have had personal relationships with one another. Our point of departure is Ya'akov of Slonim. By virtue of the fact that he passed on the manuscript of his father's commentary to *Pesikta Rabati* to Ze'ev Wolf Einhorn, and the fact that he passed along his grandfather's notes to the *Mekhilta'* to Yiẓḥak Eliyahu Landau, we can assume he was well acquainted with these scholars and their personal intellectual pursuits, and that he trusted them with the care of his valuable family heirlooms.[54]

Ze'ev Wolf Einhorn maintained a close relationship with Ẓvi Hirsch Katzenellenbogen, as evidenced by the term "*yedidi,*" "my friend," which he employs to describe Katzenellenbogen in the introduction to his *Mi-*

51 Whereas the double commentary format is generally used to distinguish between simple explanatory notes and more tangential or complex commentary, Ḥanokh Zundel employs a triple commentary format, which adds a brief third commentary to reference parallel and source texts.

52 While not a work of Midrash in the strictest sense, *Seder Olam* does employ biblical exegesis for the purposes of establishing the chronology of events, and its authorship was traditionally ascribed to the second century tanna Yose ben Halafta.

53 *Midrash Rabbah,* vol. 1 (Israel: Wagshal, 2001), 35.

54 A similar suggestion can be made with regard to Ya'akov of Slonim's relationship with Shmuel Avigdor, *av bet din* of Karlin, to whom Ya'akov gives the Ga'on's commentary on *Tosefta*. Shmuel Avigdor later became known as Shmuel Avigdor Tosfa'ah due to the massive commentary he authored on the *Tosefta,* called *Tana Tosfa'ah*.

*drash Tana'im* on the thirty *middot* of aggadic exegesis. That work of Einhorn itself is a response to Katzellenbogen's *Netivot 'Olam.*[55] Ẓvi Hirsch Katzenellenbogen, in turn, was a favorite pupil of Sha'ul Katzenellenbogen, and it therefore stands to reason that he had a personal relationship with David Luria, who was also a student of Sha'ul Katzenellenbogen at the same time. As demonstrated above, the younger Katzenellenbogen considered Shmuel Strashun to be a close friend as well. Yeḥezkel Feivel, the *maggid* of Vilna who might well have influenced the young lives of Yiẓḥak Eliyahu Landau, Ḥanokh Zundel Luria, David Luria, Shmuel Strashun, and Katzenellenbogen, also maintained a close relationship with Ze'ev Wolf Einhorn, as evidenced by his very personal remarks in the approbation he gave to Einhorn's commentary on *Pesikta' Rabbati.*[56]

The residence in Slonim of both Ya'akov, son of Avraham ben ha-Gra, and Yehudah Leib Edel,[57] both of whom were prior residents of Vilna, provides the impetus for extending the Vilna Circle to include the midrash scholars of Slonim such as Avraham Schick. Schick, at the end of his lengthy introduction to *'Eshed Neḥalim,* thanks his "friend" David Luria of Bihov for having honored him by sending him his own notes to *Midrash Rabbah,* which Schick published alongside his commentary and the commentary of Ya'akov of Slonim. Schick also acknowledges Shmuel Strashun and Ze'ev Wolf Einhorn, who also assisted him in this publication.[58]

As noted above, Ḥanokh Zundel ben Yosef, a resident of Bialystok[59] for most of his active period, referred to Ya'akov of Slonim as "the Rav, our teacher the Rabbi Ya'akov grandson of the GRA, of Slonim."[60] In a similar fashion, we argued for the extension of this scholarly circle into Dubno,[61] where the young Yiẓḥak Eliyahu Landau settled after studying in Vilna and where both he and his brother-in-law, Ẓvi Hirsch ha-Kohen Rappaport, penned their commentaries on works of midrash.

---

55 *Midrash Tana'im* (Vilna, 1838), 3. More precisely, Einhorn refers to Katzenellenbogen as "My friend, the rabbi who is wise and complete, the famous master of many disciplines, our teacher, the rabbi Ẓvi Hirsch Katzenellenbogen of Vilna."

56 *Pesikta Rabati* (Breslau, 1831), 2.

57 Slonim is a Belarusian town, 108 miles south west of Minsk.

58 Avraham Schick, "*Tahalukhot ha-Midrash,*" *Midrash Rabbah* (Vilna, 1843), 72.

59 Bialystok is a northern Polish town 109 miles north west of Warsaw, near the Belarusian border. From the perspective of nineteenth-century Eastern European Jewry, both Bialystok and Slonim would have been considered towns in southern Lithuania.

60 *Midrash Rabbot,* Vol. I (Warsaw, 1867), 2b and 5a.

61 Dubno is a northern Ukrainian town 105 miles northwest of Kiev.

From this tapestry of interconnected scholars, all of whom were active in the first half of the nineteenth century in and around Vilna, emerge over forty different commentaries on midrashic literature.

### *The "Volozhin Circle"*

Once Landau, Radal, and Einhorn take their place amongst the leaders of the Lithuanian Jewish community in the 1830s and 1840s, a third generation of young Torah scholars emerges, which follows in the footsteps of the Vilna Circle in continuing to make midrash study a primary focus of their intellectual endeavors. At this point, however, the rural hamlet of Volozhin had established itself as a preeminent center for Torah study alongside the far larger city of Vilna, and hence it is not surprising that it is in and around Volozhin that this second circle of scholars takes root.

One of the most interesting members of this group is an author by the name of Yoel Dober ha-Kohen Perski (1825-1881). Born and raised in Volozhin, Yoel was the son of Meir ha-Kohen, who served as an emissary and fund raiser for the Eẓ Ḥayyim Yeshivah during its early years. Perski spent his formative years studying at the yeshivah in Volozhin, and is said to have enjoyed a particularly close relationship with Yosef Baer Soloveitchik (1820-1892).[62] After moving to Vilna, Perski's roots in Volozhin became part and parcel of his identity, and hence he was known as Yoel Dober me-Volozhin.[63]

The centerpiece of Perski's exegetical work is a double super-commentary published in 1857 in Koenigsburg on Avraham Abele Gombiner's seventeenth-century *Zayit Ra'anan*, which, in turn, is a commentary on the compilation of midrash *aggadah* known as *Yalkut Shim'oni*.[64] Prior to Perski's publication of his midrash commentary, though, he had translated into Hebrew and published François Fénelon's *Les Aventures de Télémaque* under the title *Kevod Elohim*.[65] And, after the Koenigsburg edition

62 Eliezer Laoni, *Volozhin: Sifrah Shel ha-Ir ve-shel Yeshivat Eẓ Ḥayyim* (Tel Aviv: Irgunim le-Bnei Volozhin, 1970), 52.

63 Zeitlin (*Kiryat Sefer*, 177).

64 Gombiner (c1637-1683) is best known for his commentary on the Oraḥ Ḥayyim section of Shulḥan Arukh entitled *Magen Avraham*. The commentary was first published in Dyhernfurth, 1692, and has been included in most standard printings of *Shulḥan Arukh* since then.

65 *Kevod Elohim* (books I, II, Königsberg, 1851; books III-XXI, Vilna, 1853). François de Salignac de La Mothe Fénelon was a seventeenth-century French archbishop and theologian whose

of his *Yalkut Shim'oni*, he published a biography of Æsop and translated some of his fables into Hebrew under the title *Ḥayye Asaf.*[66]

Despite his broad intellectual endeavors, Perski seems to have enjoyed the respect and support of several rabbinic figures central to Lithuanian rabbinic society. Evidence to that effect can be deduced from the approbations of Bezalel ha-Kohen, a well-respected halakhic decisor in Vilna, and the famed Ya'akov Ẓvi Meklenburg (1785-1865), author of the widely read Torah commentary *ha-Ketav ve-ha-Kabbalah,* which accompanied the first edition of Perski's commentary.[67] In 1864, he republished the commentary after it had been plagiarized by a former partner of his from the earlier printing. He included in this printing a vicious attack on the plagiarist and additional letters of support from Bezalel ha-Kohen and Dov Baer Miezeles, the rabbi of Warsaw.[68]

The core of the Volozhin Circle, however, was a group of young Torah scholars who studied in Volozhin's Eẓ Ḥayyim Yeshivah during the 1830s and 40s. Of this group, Matityahu Strashun (1817-1885), Yehoshua Heschel Levin (1818-1883), and Simḥah Edelman (1821-1893) all authored notes on *Midrash Rabbah.* Mordecai Gimpel Jaffe (1820-1891) wrote a commentary on the *Midrash Shoḥer Tov* on Psalms. And, Neẓiv, subject of the present study, authored notes on *Torat Kohanim,* as well as commentaries on *Mekhilta'* and *Sifre.*

This younger circle of Volozhin midrash scholars, whose active literary careers spanned the middle decades of the nineteenth century, were closely connected to the older Vilna Circle that preceded them. Matityahu Strashun was the son of Shmuel Strashun and like his father enjoyed a close relationship with Ẓvi Hirsch Katzenellenbogen.[69] In addition to acknowledging the assistance of Strashun, Luria, and Einhorn, Avraham Schick, in his *'Eshed Neḥalim,* notes:

---

*Les Aventures de Télémaque* was a satirical critique of Louis XIV's tyrannical reign. Its promotion of constitutional monarchy, and its advocation for the rights of the peasantry as well as a confederacy of nations to promote world peace, made it a popular work amongst Western European enlightened intellectuals.

66 *Ḥayye Assaf* (Warsaw, 1858).

67 On Ya'akov Ẓvi Mecklenburg, see Edward Breuer, "Between Haskalah and Orthodoxy: The Writings of R. Ya'akov Ẓvi Meklenburg," *Hebrew Union College Annual* 66 (1995): 259-287.

68 *Yalkut Shim'oni* (Vilna, 1864).

69 See *Netivot 'Olam* (Vilna, 1858), 225-227.

> And I also found a man of my own heart, the enlightened,[183] sharp, knowledgeable young man, Yehoshua Heschel the son of the extraordinary, famous, sharp and knowledgeable, enlightened in the pure fear of God, Eliyahu Zev Levin, who took upon himself to note the places in Talmud Bavli and Tosefta' which cite the words of the *Midrashot* from time to time and explain them, which is a guiding light in understanding them according to their straightforward sense.

Thus, like Strashun, Levin also maintained a scholarly relationship with the older generation of midrash scholars.

**Table 1: The "Vilna Circle" of Midrash Scholars**

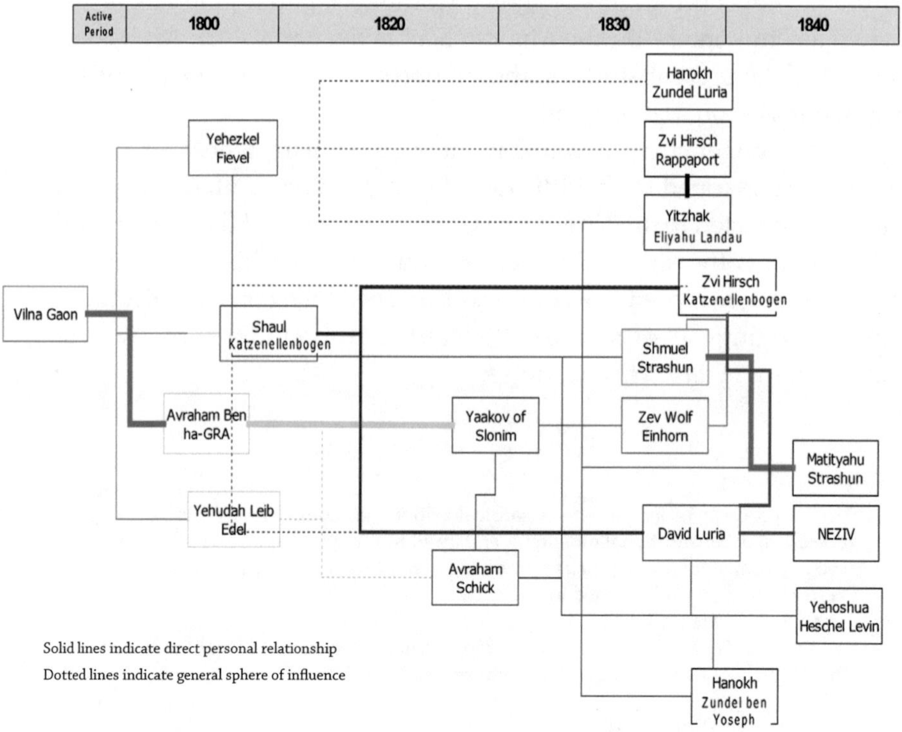

### *The Influence of Radal on the Young Neẓiv*

While the young Neẓiv cites from the midrash commentaries of Ẓvi Hirsch Katzenellenbogen,[70] Ze'ev Wolf Einhorn,[71] Shmuel Strashun,[72] Ẓvi Hirsch ha-Kohen Rappaport,[73] and Radal,[74] the clearest indication of direct contact between Neẓiv and the Vilna Circle of midrash scholars is manifest in his relationship with Radal, Rabbi David Luria (1798-1856).

Meir Bar-Ilan, Neẓiv's son and biographer, in describing the admiration that his father felt for Luria, the rabbi of Old Bihov, notes their common intellectual interests, the fact that Neẓiv corresponded with Radal, and the fact that Radal wrote an approbation for Neẓiv's work on the *She'iltot*.[75] Barukh ha-Levi Epstein ascribes greater intimacy to the relationship when he writes that Radal "gave Neẓiv motivation to press on in his studies" and that later in life Neẓiv said that "he owes everything to Radal."[76] The nature of this relationship, and hence Neẓiv's personal connection to the earlier generation of nineteenth-century midrash scholars, can be further illuminated by an examination of writings from both Neẓiv and Radal.

To begin, we must note that Radal is the only person other than Neẓiv's son, Ḥayyim Berlin, and his son-in-law, Raphael Shapira,[77] who is mentioned by Neẓiv as having played an integral role in editing and revising his magnum opus, the commentary on *She'iltot*. Furthermore, the text of Radal's approbation to that work clearly indicates that Neẓiv,

---

70 It is rather common to find the word "*maskil*" used in reference to rabbinic figures in the traditional Torah scholarship of the first half of the nineteenth century without connoting an association with the movement for modern Western Enlightenment. A careful study of the term's usage and its shifting connotations over the course of the nineteenth century may yield significant insight into the socio-intellectual history of this period. 184 *EH* 'Ekev 4 (III: 52). On the possible censorship of this reference, see Chapter 1 above.

71 185 *EH* Re'eh 29 (III: 120) "32 *middot 'im peirush Midrash tanaim.*"

72 186 *EH* Naso 39 (I: 152), Be-ha'alotekha 20 (I: 248). Also in his notes to *Torat Kohanim, Kedoshim* 2: 9 (32).

73 187 *EH* Naso 1 (I: 2); *EH* Naso 2 (I: 14); *EH* Naso 2 (I: 17); *EH* Naso 2 (I: 18); *EH* Shelaḥ 3 (II: 23); *EH* Koraḥ (II: 82).

74 188 *EH* Naso 42 (I: 168); *EH* Naso 46 (I: 179); *EH* Be-ha'alotekha 18 (I: 237); *EH* Be-ha'alotekha 20 (I: 248); *EH* Be-ha'alotekha 35 (I: 293). Neẓiv also cites Radal's work on *Midrash Rabbah* in a letter he wrote to the Hebrew newspaper *ha-Maggid*, published in 1862, issue #45. The letter is reprinted in *Iggerot ha-Neẓiv*, 56.

75 *Rabban*, 29. Neẓiv reproduces the approbation in *Ha'amek She'elah*, vol. I, "*Petaḥ ha-'Emek*," 4.

76 Epstein, (IV: 1684).

77 See *HS*, "*Kidmat ha-'Emek*," 12.

and his work, had a special place in Radal's heart:

> It is from Heaven that the great and elevated portion was granted to my kin[78] the rabbi -- ----- [sic] the Crown of Torah, our teacher Naftali Ẓvi Yehudah Berlin, head of the great academy of the holy community of Volozhin (his Maker and Redeemer should guard him) to compose an explanatory commentary on the *She'iltot* of Rav Aḥai Ga'on, may his memory be blessed, in which wellsprings of wisdom were opened before him with the help of Heaven, from which he drew in order to explicate the positions of our great halakhic decisors, Alfasi and Rambam, may their memories be blessed, [with] new insight[79] not previously conjured by any of the authors, may their names be blessed. And even though I have never given my approbation to any printed book, nonetheless, due to my great admiration for [this work], I have abandoned my usual constraints and lent my support so that the Torah may be strengthened by bringing this book to print, and the merit of the Ga'on, may his memory be blessed, will stand up for all those who participate in this *miẓvah*. Such are the words of the undersigned, Wednesday evening, 28th of Tevet, 5616 (1856), here in Old Bihov (its Maker and Redeemer should guard it). David Luria.[80]

Luria's influence on Neẓiv was not limited, though, to the study of *She'iltot*. Citations of Radal's work in Neẓiv's commentary on *Sifre* demonstrate Neẓiv's familiarity with Radal's notes to *Midrash Rabbah* as well. More significant, perhaps, in uncovering the relationship between Radal and the young Neẓiv is a curious passage at the end of the 1851 edition of Radal's commentary on *Aggadat Shmuel*. It is there that Shmuel Luria, a relative of Radal as well as the editor and publisher of his commentary, writes as follows:

---

78 The text contains the abbreviation "*shin-bet*" which stands for "*she'er bisari*" meaning "my relative." Neẓiv's brother, Avraham Meir, was married to Radal's niece, the daughter of his brother Ẓvi Hirsch Luria of Bihov.

79 Literally "new things."

80 *Ha'amek She'elah*, vol. I, "*Petaḥ ha-'Emek*," 4.

> And I want to acknowledge my relative, who brims with Torah, fears and trembles before the word of God, the sharp young man, Naftali Ẓvi Yehudah Berlin from the town of Shklov, who labored in the copying and arranging of the notes of Radal and arranged for them to be sent here for publication. May God repay him in full for his endeavors. And this is what I saw fit to collect from that which he added from his own broad knowledge when copying [this work]...[81]

The curiosity of this passage lies in its reference to Shklov as the town of origin for Naftali Ẓvi Yehudah Berlin, when Neẓiv was born and raised in the town of Mir. While I know of no plausible explanation for this oddity other than to ascribe it either to a printing error or to the author's misinformation, it is very difficult to seriously entertain the possibility that the reference is to someone other than Neẓiv.[82] Given the close relationship between Radal and Neẓiv described above, and given the documented fact that this was a relationship based on mutual intellectual interests, in which Neẓiv had sent the older Radal some of his work for review, it is most plausible to assume that this passage refers to the young Neẓiv, thus identifying him as the person who arranged, edited, and prepared Radal's work for publication.

In fact, it is possible that Radal shared with the young Neẓiv more than just his own work. On at least two occasions in *'Emek ha-Neẓiv,* Neẓiv writes in regard to a *Sifre* passage that "in the name of the GRA they emend" the text in a certain manner. However, the printed text of the Ga'on's emendations to *Sifre* appeared only in 1866 and thus it seems likely that the young Neẓiv might have had access to the Vilna Ga'on's work on *Sifre,* or more likely to parts of the Ga'on's work on *Sifre,* via some alternate source.[83] It might well be that his source was none other than Radal. After all, the publisher of the printed edition of the Ga'on's

81 *Aggadat Shmuel* (Warsaw, 1851), 56b. Luria then prints three short comments from Berlin on select passages from Radal's work.

82 As the passage was printed in 1851 prior to Neẓiv's appointment as Rosh Yeshivah, it is not that surprising that Neẓiv was not yet identified with Volozhin. Nonetheless, the association with Shklov rather than Mir remains perplexing.

83 Of course, it is also possible that these references represent post-1866 additions to the core text of Neẓiv's *Sifre* commentary.

work on *Sifre* notes that one of the primary sources for his printed text was a manuscript copy of the Ga'on's work which Radal had copied from Simḥah Bunim of Shklov. Thus, when one considers the fact that Radal and the young Neẓiv corresponded regarding the latter's endeavor in composing a commentary on *Sifre,* and the fact that Radal had in his possession a copy of a manuscript bearing the Vilna Ga'on's comments on *Sifre,* it would stand to reason that Radal might have shared some of the Ga'on's comments with Neẓiv.

Radal, therefore, serves as the direct personal link between the young Neẓiv and the world of early-nineteenth-century midrash commentary. As we shall see in the coming chapters, it is that world and its intellectual milieu which will guide Neẓiv in his literary endeavors both as a young man and well into his career.

## CHAPTER THREE:
### *'Emek ha-Neẓiv*: An Early Nineteenth-Century Midrash Commentary

In addition to the personal and geographic connections between the midrash scholars of early nineteenth-century Lithuania, there are strong stylistic commonalities which they share as well. In particular, many of the works listed in the previous chapter share a self-proclaimed interest in explaining the straightforward sense, or "*peshat*," of the text at hand and a propensity for emendation of the printed text, as well as citation from and reference to a broad range of texts and disciplines. As we will demonstrate below, all three of these elements are salient features of Neẓiv's commentary on *Sifre* as well.

*Straightforward Interpretation*

Ḥanokh Zundel ben Yosef[1] makes clear in the introduction to his commentary on *Midrash Rabbah* on the Pentateuch that unlike the commentators who preceded him, who tended to offer elaborate discussions of issues far from the text of the *Midrash Rabbah*, he intends to confine himself to the basic and straightforward meaning of a particular passage.

> And even though the intelligent kohen—the rabbi, author of the *Matanot Kehunah*—set out, with his broad knowledge and sustained effort, to explain [*Midrash Rabbah*] as is evident in his book, the obligation to adequately explain it remains unfulfilled. And this is all the more true [with regard to] the authors of *Yede Moshe* and *Zera' Avraham* and the like, who paid no attention to the basic meaning of the text but rather sought their own homilies in an unnecessary display of their cunning and breadth. The pages of this Torah of *Midrash Rabbah* are hidden and

---

1 Ḥanokh Zundel ben Yosef, a member of the Slonim branch of the Vilna Circle, see p. 50 above.

> sealed with ten clasps—nothing gets out.[2] And, behold, God placed in the heart of a gnat like me[3] [the ability] to strengthen its foundations, to straighten its walls, to illuminate its utility.[4]

In his commentary on *Masekhet Soferim*, Yiẓḥak Eliyahu Landau[5] explains his motivation for adopting a double commentary format by stating that the main commentary is designed to give the reader a straightforward understanding of the text, while the secondary commentary is for those readers who are interested in more complex analysis.

> In order to make it easier on the reader, I have divided my commentary into two parts. One will explain the words of the *mesekhta'* in order to gain a simple understanding. And the second is where I justly raise a question and an answer from new insights granted to me by the One Who Grants Knowledge. The first I called by the name *Mikra' Soferim* and the name of the second is *'Ittur Soferim*.[6]

Landau makes a similar statement at the beginning of his commentary on talmudic *aggadot*, writing that his work will contain no *pilpul*, no *ḥarifut*, and only *peshat*.[7]

Likewise, Avraham Schick[8] writes in his introduction to *Tanna de-Bei Eliyahu* that he will only treat in brief "those areas which contain deep philosophical concepts."[9] He also outlines a strikingly critical and plain-sense approach to the enterprise of rabbinic exegesis as a whole:

> It is the way of our rabbis *z"l* to associate a verse (in order to understand it better) with an event which happened

---

2 This is a play on the word *"poresh,"* so that the phrase "nothing gets out" or "nothing escapes" can also suggest "nothing explains" or "no one explains."

3 *"Yetosh ka-moni,"* a standard rabbinic phrase used to indicate, or perhaps at times to feign, the author's sense of humility.

4 *Midrash Rabbah* (Israel: Wagschal, 2001) *"Hakdamat Meḥaber 'Eẓ Yosef, 'Anaf Yosef, Yad Yosef"* (Ḥanokh Zundel).

5 On Landau, a member of the Vilna Circle, see pp. 44-46 above.

6 *Masekhet Soferim* (Suwalk, 1862), *Petaḥ Davar.*

7 *Lishmo'a be-Limudim* (Vilna, 1876), *Petaḥ Davar.*

8 On Schick, see p. 49 above.

9 *Tanna de-Bei Eliyahu, Rabba Zuta 'im Me'ore 'Esh* (Sudilkov, 1834), 2.

> in later times, which was not necessarily the intention of Scripture, only in order that through it the verse will be [properly] understood...Also, at times when something in the verse is difficult [to understand] they refer to some event through which the verse can be explained by comparison, even though the verse did not intend to refer to such an event.[10]

Ḥanokh Zundel Luria[11] states at the beginning of his commentary on *Perek ha-Shirah* that he too seeks to offer a plain-sense interpretation.[12] Other commentators, such as David Luria, do not explicitly state their goals before beginning their commentary, but one need only take a brief glance at their work to realize that they too try to offer a close and straightforward reading of the text at hand.

### *Straightforward Interpretation in* 'Emek ha-Neẓiv

*'Emek ha-Neẓiv* shares with the other works of early-nineteenth-century midrash commentary its emphasis on straightforward interpretation, or "*peshat*." Unlike the Torah scholarship created during the second half of the century, largely under the influence of Ḥayyim Soloveitchik of Brisk (1853-1918),[13] which often uses the text of the Talmud or that of Rambam's Code as a stepping stone for lengthy essays on concepts in Jewish legal theory, Neẓiv's primary goal in his commentary on *Sifre* is to explain the meaning and the relevance of the passages at hand.

That Neẓiv understands the scope of his comments to lie within the parameters of *peshat* is best evidenced by the occasions on which he writes that an interpretation he is about to offer appears to him as less convincing and more forced than his other comments. These he includes as secondary possibilities introduced by the phrase "*yesh le-faresh derekh ḥidud...*," meaning "one can explain in a cunning fashion..."[14] or "*u-ve-derekh ḥidud yesh lomar...*" meaning "and in a cunning fashion one can

---

10 Ibid.

11 On Luria, see p. 46 above.

12 *Kenaf Renanim* (Kratashin, 1842), 1.

13 Ḥayyim Soloveitchik, also referred to as Ḥayyim Brisker, was the son of the famed Yosef Baer Soloveitchik referred to in the Preface, n. 24, above. The younger Soloveitchik married the daughter of Rabbi Raphael Shapira who was also the granddaughter of the Neẓiv.

14 *EH* Naso 1 (I: 8).

explain…"[15] After offering his "cunning" approach, Neẓiv reiterates that "the primary [interpretation] is as I wrote above,"[16] or that "all this was in a cunning fashion, but the straightforward [interpretation] (*peshat*) is..."[17] From the fact that Neẓiv feels the necessity to note the instances in which he veers from *peshat,* we can infer that although he does have an appreciation for the "sharper" side of Torah study and possibly a desire to show his readers that he too can offer cunning insight, he understands the primary objective of his commentary to be squarely in line with the straightforward approach of other early-nineteenth-century midrash commentators.

It is important to note that on a number of occasions in his commentary on *Sifre,* Neẓiv characterizes his comments as "*derekh pilpul.*"[18] The word *pilpul* is often translated as casuistry, to which *peshat*, or straightforward commentary, is often portrayed as the antithesis. The former is generally associated with a method of study which constructs a series of hypothetical test cases only tangentially related to the text at hand, while the latter is associated with an interpretation which is narrow in scope and aims at elucidation of a particular passage. As such, the instances labeled by Neẓiv as *derekh pilpul* in *'Emek ha-Neẓiv* might be mistakenly regarded as equivalent to the instances of *derekh ḥidud* mentioned above.

However, close examination of the passages which include this phrase reveals otherwise. Unlike *derekh ḥidud,* which indicates weakness in the interpretive method through which a reading was deduced, and thus stands in opposition to *peshat,* Neẓiv uses the phrase *derekh pilpul* to introduce a complex analysis through successive steps which is required to resolve the textual or halakhic conundrum at hand. In the end, though, the complexities of *derekh pilpul* do not lead one to a secondary reading or a weak proposition as does *derekh ḥidud,* but to what Neẓiv considers the singular and proper resolution of the issue. Hence, unlike the instances of *derekh ḥidud,* the passages which are labeled as *derekh pilpul* include no alternative readings or interpretations, nor do they conclude with a retreat from the position offered by reminding the reader that a "straightforward" approach or the "primary" interpretation is preferable.

A similar conclusion can be drawn from other contexts within which

---

15 *EH* Naso 21 (I: 83).

16 Ibid., 8.

17 Ibid., 84.

18 *EH* Be-ha'alotekha 7 (I: 206); *EH* Be-ha'alotekha 12 (I: 224); *EH* Pinḥas 18 (II: 266).

Neẓiv employs the root *p,l,p,l* in his *Sifre* commentary. Thus, for example, when *Sifre* writes that the phrase in Proverbs (3:18) which states that the "supporters" of Torah will be "fortunate" refers to one who is truly wise, Neẓiv explains such a sage as one who is "*medakdek le-tareẓ u-lefalpel 'ad she-yihyeh ha-kol 'al ha-nakhon,*" that is, one who is "precise in answering and in engaging in *pilpul* until everything comes out correctly."[19] On another occasion, Neẓiv tells the reader to look at "the *pilpul* of *Tosafot* and you will find the essence of the matter."[20] It is therefore clear that unlike the word *ḥidud*, the word *pilpul* in Neẓiv's commentary on *Sifre* is not intended to stand in contradistinction to *peshat*.

This distinction between Neẓiv's usages of *ḥidud* and *pilpul* has important ramifications well beyond his commentary on *Sifre.* In fact, one of the single most dominant themes in Neẓiv's later writings is the importance of *pilpulah shel Torah.*[21] It is *pilpul* which the Tabernacle's candelabra came to symbolize,[22] it is his ability to engage in *pilpul* which set Moses above his brother Aaron,[23] it is *pilpul* which King David utilized to arrive at his legal pronouncements,[24] it is *pilpul* which the Sages of Babylonia employed in the halakhic deliberations recorded in the Talmud (in contradistinction to *torat ereẓ yisrael,* as developed by Neẓiv in his "Kidmat ha-'Emek" to *Ha'amek She'elah*),[25] and it is the salvific power of *pilpul* that sustains the Jewish people in the Diaspora.[26] Indeed, whereas the rabbis of old in the land of Israel had an intuitive sense which aided their understanding of biblical nuances, in Neẓiv's view subsequent generations lost that sense and the only vehicle which remained for arriving at true interpretation of the biblical text was *pilpul.*[27]

Given Neẓiv's own propensity for straightforward commentary and his disdain for casuistic interpretations, it may appear to be rather baffling that he accords such a distinctive place in Jewish history and Jewish

19 *EH* 'Ekev 12 (III: 78).

20 *EH* Pinḥas 3 (II: 220).

21 While the phrase "*pilpulah shel torah*" has a slightly different connotation than the word "*pilpul*" on its own, Neẓiv uses the phrase interchangeably with "*pilpul*" (e.g., HD Ex. 25: 21, HD Ex. 27: 20) "*pilpul ha-talmud*" (e.g., HD Ex. 15: 26,), "*torat ha-pilpul*" (e.g., Hrd Deut. 1: 3), and "*limud ha-torah be-derekh pilpulah*" (e.g., HD Deut. 27: 10), amongst others.

22 *HD* Ex. 25: 31, Lev. 16: 17.

23 *HD* Ex. 27: 20, Num. 15: 33.

24 *HS*, "*Kidmat ha-'Emek,*" 1: 6.

25 Ibid., 1: 10.

26 *HD* Num. 14: 34.

27 *HS* "*Kidmat ha-'Emek*" 2: 12.

theology to *pilpul*.[28] However, when the word *pilpul* is understood as Neẓiv uses it in *'Emek ha-Neẓiv*, this apparent tension is easily resolved. *Pilpul*, in Neẓiv's usage, does not oppose *peshat*. Rather, it is a complex and intellectually demanding method of arriving at *peshat*. Hence, it was the intellectual elite, such as Moses, David, and the talmudic Sages, who had mastered this method. And, as a result of the time commitment and intellectual effort which it demands, it is *pilpulah shel Torah*, rather than less demanding methods of study, which bears unique salvific rewards.[29]

Thus, his occasional foray into *pilpulah shel Torah* is not at odds with Neẓiv's primary commentarial objective in *'Emek ha-Neẓiv*. He, like so many of the midrash scholars of the early nineteenth century, saw his primary goal as the elucidation of the straightforward meaning of the text.

### *Textual Emendation*

The second feature shared by many of the commentaries which emerged during this period is an emphasis on textual emendation. In their quest to explicate their respective texts in a simple and straightforward manner, these authors recognized the need to first establish a reliable text, free of the errors and inaccuracies which had crept into it over the generations of copying. Thus, on the basis of their knowledge of textual witnesses and parallel texts, coupled with their own analytic and creative abilities, they set out to revise, repair, and restore these repositories of traditional legal, theological, and interpretive teachings.

Textual emendation is, therefore, a central component of early-nineteenth-century midrash study from the earliest members of the Vilna Circle to the work of the latest members of the Volozhin Circle and beyond.[30] Amongst the former, a distinctive interest in emending the text

28 See Hana Kats's approach to solving this problem in her *Mishnat Ha-Neẓiv*, 47.

29 Samuel Bialoblocki notes that rather than reject "*pilpul*" completely, both the Vilna Ga'on and Ḥayyim of Volozhin distinguish between proper *pilpul*, which leads to clarity, and improper *pilpul*, which leads to confusion. See his "*Merkaze ha-Torah be-Lita*," *'Em la-Masoret* (Tel Aviv: Bar-Ilan University, 1971), 217.

30 It should be noted that rabbinic commentary has a long history of textual emendation stretching back to the period of the *ba'alei tosafot*, and perhaps before. In the early modern period, however, this element of rabbinic writing loses popularity until it begins to regain prominence in the Yerushalmi commentaries and the proto-maskilic work of the mid-eighteenth-century. It isn't until the turn of the nineteenth century in Lithuania, however, that textual emendation reemerges as a central focus of a "school" of traditional rabbinic

can already be found in Yeḥezkel Feivel's commentary on *Midrash Rabbah*.[31] As noted above, Feivel's commentary was only first printed in the 1880s, but when one considers the fact that he was born in 1755 and died in 1833, it becomes reasonable to assume that he was engaged in such activity at least by the turn of the century.

In the commentary of Radal, a member of the second generation of the Vilna Circle,[32] textual emendation is not only an interest, but a passion. His commentaries display an acute sensitivity to a variety of different textual corruptions and are filled with attempts to correct the printed text. Thus, Radal often notes scribal errors,[33] later additions to the text,[34] and passages in which words or entire phrases seem to have been deleted.[35] Most of the time, however, he simply precedes his comments with the abbreviation *kaf, ẓade, lamed*, shorthand for "*kakh ẓarikh lomar*," or "so it should say," and then rewrites the text as he believes it should have appeared.[36]

Radal's friend, Avraham Schick,[37] set out in a manner quite similar to Radal's to produce a reliable text of *Midrash Rabbah*. Thus he writes in the introduction to his *'Eshed Neḥalim* that he has "set [his] eye and [his] heart upon emending the words of the midrash from the *aggadot* of the Yerushalmi and from other places...and to remove the injurious stones which prevent the straight thinker from studying it on its proper foundations."[38]

Producing a reliable text is one of the primary objectives of Ze'ev Wolf Einhorn's[39] commentary on *Pesikta' Rabbati* as well. In his approbation to the work, Solomon Tiktin, *av bet din* of Breslau, states that Einhorn "was also able to remove the innumerable thorns from the precious vineyard,

---

commentators. For more on rabbinic textual emendation, see Ya'akov Shmuel Spiegel, *'Amudim be-Toldot ha-Sefer ha-'Ivri*, 2nd ed. (Ramat Gan: Bar-Ilan University Press, 2005).

31 E.g., *Biur Maharif* in *Midrash Rabbah*, vol. 1 (Israel: Wagshal, 2001), 9: 9, 10 (100); 10: 9 (111); 13: 8 (142). On Yeḥezkel Feivel, the maggid of Vilna, see p. 46 above.

32 On Radal, see pp. 46-47 above.

33 E.g., *Pirkei de-Rabbi Eliezer* (Warsaw, 1852), 11a (of *Bet Ẓaddik* introduction), 7b (Hagahah), 20b; *Peirush Radal in Midrash Rabbah, vol. 1* (Israel: Wagshal, 2001), 2: 2 (111).

34 E.g., ibid., 17: 27 (484).

35 E.g., ibid., 1: 1 (12); *Pirkei de-Rabbi Eliezer*, 13a-b.

36 E.g., *Peirush Radal in Midrash Rabbah* (Israel: Wagshal, 2001) 2: 23 (185); 2: 24 (187); 2: 24 (188); 3: 1 (192); 3: 23 (225); 5: 29 (265); *Pirkei de-Rabbi Eliezer* 14a, 16a, 16b, 18b, 34b, 57b.

37 On Schick, see pp. 49 above.

38 *Midrash Rabbah*, "Author's Introduction," (Vilna, 1843).

39 On Einhorn, see pp. 43-44 above.

which arose in the earliest printings."[40] Einhorn himself states explicitly in his introduction that such was his primary motivation for composing the work.

> The *Hagahot*: these are the primary reason I was inspired, with the help of God, to begin the holy work on this holy Midrash; for the hands of mistaken copyists and faulty printers have prevailed upon it and introduced mistakes and perversions in four [different] manners: 1) missing [material]—for sometimes a few words or half a passage is missing, 2) additions in a similar fashion,[41] 3) switching words, lines, or passages from line to line and from page to page, 4) nonsensical passages and mixed up words. And, with the help of God, I labored and succeeded in establishing the proper text.[42]

As such, it is not surprising that the phrase "*kakh ẓarikh lomar*" or the shorter "*ẓarikh lomar*" appears on almost every page of his commentary on *Pesikta' Rabbati*.

Yiẓḥak Eliyahu Landau was similarly inclined, as evidenced by his description of the state of midrashic texts in his day in the introduction to his commentary on *Mekhilta'*. Instead of relying solely on his own analysis of the text, however, Landau sought out the emendations of the Vilna Ga'on, which he then incorporated into his commentaries on both *Masekhet Soferim* and *Mekhilta'*, with explanations and modifications where he deemed necessary.[43] In his introduction to the latter, he writes:

> Since men who understand its secrets have not ploughed through these *midrashim* in order to remove its rough spots, its stone fences have crumbled and its face has been covered with the thorns of printing errors…
>
> Like one blinded by an overpowering light, I felt my way through *Mekhilta'*, looking for a trodden path to remove

40 *Pesikta Rabati* (Breslau, 1831), 1.

41 This seems to refer to words or passages which were mistakenly added to the text.

42 Ibid., introduction, paragraph 4.

43 *Masekhet Soferim* (Suvalk, 1862), *Petaḥ Davar.*

> the stumbling block [placed by] the widespread errors. And, with a pure heart I asked my friend, the great rabbi Ya'akov of Slonim, grandson of the Ga'on, z"l, for the proper *Mekhilta'* which had once been before my eyes, in order to establish it with the notes of the Ga'on.[44]

Ḥanokh Zundel ben Yosef also suggests emendations of the text with regular frequency in his midrash commentaries.[45] In the introduction to his 1833 commentary on *Midrash Tanḥuma,'* he writes that in his day no one uses the work "because many places require extensive explanation, and its face has been covered with the thorns of printing errors, and [there are] changes in the wording, and misplaced passages, and some words and lines are missing and some have been added, and [since] these things commonly appear they blind even the eyes of the wise, who can not delve into the work and see its beauty."[46] It is Ḥanokh Zundel who likewise offers what might be the most eloquent description of this feature of nineteenth-century midrash commentary in the introduction to his commentary on *Midrash Rabbah,* part of which was cited above.

> And all who are wise know that the wisdom of the Sages is beyond the sight of man (*ge'eh me-'eyn 'enosh*). And even the form of the *peshat* is concealed in a cloak before all who learn her. And, [this is] specifically due to [the fact that] the mistaken hand of copyists prevailed upon it and covered it with meaningless lines (*natu 'alav kav tohu*), after which it fell into the hands of injurious printing presses (*defusim mafsidim*) which riddled it with empty stones (*u-regamu bo avnei vohu*). They left out, they added, they switched, they combined, they wasted their ink (*heshḥitu deyam*). They perverted its foundations, bent its walls, diminished its utility, darkened its light…
>
> … And I have prepared my heart to understand every text in its context (*kol ma'amar be-mikomo*), and how it

44 *Mekhilta'* (Vilna, 1844), 2 of introduction.

45 E.g., *Midrash Rabbah of the Pentateuch* (Warsaw, 1870), Genesis 86a.

46 *Midrash Tanḥuma, "Hakdamat Meḥaber Peirushei 'Eẓ Yosef ve-'Anaf Yosef"* (Vilna, 1833).

> is hinted at in the verse which is cited, and to establish the proper version of the text. And every verse will be cited properly as it appears in the Bible. And I labored extensively to find the books which cite the words of the midrash and what is said in it. And, thank God, I labored and I succeeded in gathering from them all interpretations that are sweet and pleasant to the ear which hears them. And they are founded in reason and knowledge; they are all the work of an artisan—never before heard and never before seen.[47]

For Shmuel Strashun and his son Matityahu as well,[48] the establishment of reliable texts was of the utmost importance. For the elder Strashun, this facet of his work is immediately evident from the constant appearance of "*kakh ẓarikh lomar*" and "*ẓarikh lomar*" throughout his notes to *Midrash Rabbah*. The younger Strashun, who was less prolific than his father, manifested his avid interest in the recovery of authentic texts through his passion for book collecting. His collection of rare printed texts and manuscripts later served as a valuable resource for scholars on their own searches for reliable texts. Today his collection is an important part of the YIVO library housed in the Center for Jewish History in New York City.

Amongst Matityahu Strashun's peers in the Volozhin Circle of midrash scholars, Yoel Dober ha-Kohen Perski[49] is another who counts textual emendation among the primary goals of his midrash commentary. Perski, however, was not content with introducing emendations of *Yalkut Shim'oni* in his commentary prefaced by the phrase "*kakh ẓarikh lomar*" as did Radal, Einhorn, and Shmuel Strashun.[50] Rather, Perski states that he wanted to insinuate his changes into the body text of *Yalkut Shim'oni* itself. The rabbinic authorities with whom he consulted, however, instructed him not to do so, and Perski conceded.[51]

Emendation of the text, then, played a leading role in the intellectual

---

47 *Midrash Rabbah, "Hakdamat Meḥaber 'Eẓ Yosef, 'Anaf Yosef, Yad Yosef"* (Ḥanokh Zundel), vol. 1 (Israel: Wagshal, 2001), 35.

48 On Shmuel, see p. 46 above. On Matityahu, see p. 54.

49 On Perski, see pp. 53-54 above.

50 Shmuel Strashun employs *kakh ẓarikh lomar* throughout his notes on *Midrash Rabbah* as well.

51 *Yalkut Shim'oni* (Koenigsburg, 1857), introduction.

endeavors of many of the early nineteenth century's Lithuanian midrash scholars. In light of the aforementioned proclivity of these same scholars for providing a straight forward and basic interpretation of the text, the tactic of emendation needs to be seen as an important means of doing so. And, as we will see below, the willingness to emend the text where necessary in order to provide a straightforward reading is a prominent feature of the young Neẓiv's work as well.

### *Textual Emendation in* 'Emek ha-Neẓiv

Neẓiv was not merely interested in establishing an authentic reading of the *Sifre* text, as Ḥanokh Zundel ben Yosef had been interested in rectifying the "perverted... foundations" and "bent...walls" of the printed *Midrash Rabbah*. Rather, the young Neẓiv had developed an instinctively critical eye to the point where he approached every text he read with a distinct sensitivity for its reliability or lack thereof. Thus, his *'Emek ha-Neẓiv* is filled with textually critical comments regarding the entire canon of traditional Jewish learning, with the important, though largely predictable, exception of the biblical text itself.

Neẓiv's emendations of the *Sifre* text can be found on almost every page of all three volumes of his *'Emek ha-Neẓiv*.[52] In the *parashah* of *'Ekev* alone, Neẓiv employs the abbreviation *"kof-ẓade-lamed,"* indicating an emendation of the printed text, on no less than seventy-three different occasions. The impetus and justification for these modifications to the printed text vary widely and are at times explicitly stated by Neẓiv. Of-

52 All indications are that the primary *Sifre* text from which Neẓiv was working was the Sulzbach 1802 edition. The publishers of *'Emek ha-Neẓiv* write in their preface that "it was made clear" to them "that the *Sifre* which was before the esteemed author was from this printing." While I have found no evidence to the contrary, Neẓiv's frequent citation of the *Sifre* commentary *Zera' Avraham* (Dyhernfurth, 1811 and 1819), published together with an annotated version of the original Venice *Sifre* (1545), indicates that, at the very least, he had access to the Venice edition as well. Neẓiv did not, however, have access to a manuscript of *Sifre*. It is important to note that on several occasions in his *Sifre* commentary Neẓiv does make reference to a *"ketav yad,"* and often such references are in regard to textual emendations [e.g., *EH* Pinḥas 3 (II: 220); *EH* Pinḥas 3 (II: 221); *EH* Pinḥas 12 (II: 247); *EH* Pinḥas 13 (II: 254); *EH* Pinḥas 15 (II: 261,262); *EH* Matot 1 (II: 274); *EH* Masa'ei 1 (II: 312)]. However, the source to which Neẓiv is referring in these instances is not a manuscript of *Sifre* but a medieval commentary, popularly attributed to Ra'avad, known as *"Ketav Yad Ga'on Sefaradi"* portions of which were published together with the *Zera' Avraham* edition of *Sifre* (Dyhernfurth 1811-1819). His emendations in *'Emek ha-Neẓiv*, then, must be distinguished from his emendations of the *She'iltot* text found in the second and third volumes of his *Ha'amek She'elah*, which do, in fact, stem from a manuscript of that text dating from 1460 which he was able to obtain. See *"Petaḥ ha-'Emek"* in *HS* 2: 1.

ten, however, *"kof-ẓade-lamed"* stands alone as Neẓiv's only comment following a header in which he cited the text of *Sifre* as he believed it should read without any explanation for the motivation or method behind his emendation.[53] In such moments of silence, he leaves it completely to the reader to decipher the reason and rationale behind his emendation of the text.

Amongst the instances in which Neẓiv does justify his emendations are those he describes as *"ta'ut sofer,"* thus ascribing the error to a faulty copying of the text by a medieval scribe.[54] Far more often, however, Neẓiv believes the corruption to have resulted from a mistake which can be attributed to the process of printing.[55] Thus, for example, Neẓiv suggests that the similarity between a passage in Sifre Shelaḥ and that of a *Mishnah* in the fourth chapter of *Shavu'ot* led the printer of *Sifre* to mistakenly print the *Sifre* passage with wording identical to that of the *Mishnah,* whereas according to Neẓiv, the words at the end of the passage belong only in the *Mishnah* and not in *Sifre.*[56]

Even without specific references to scribes or printers, Neẓiv's emendations display an acute awareness of the types of errors to which books that were copied and then printed for centuries are prone. Hence, we find that he divides a single word into two,[57] implying that the two original words must have been copied without the requisite space between them causing a later scribe to mistake them as a single entity. At times Neẓiv replaces a letter, or letters, of a word, with ones that look similar, in order to form what he believes to be the word originally intended by the author of *Sifre.* An example is the case of "Rabbi Ẓadok," in which Neẓiv suggests that an apostrophe of the abbreviated form of "Rabbi" had been mistaken for a *yud* and the letters *daled* and *vav* had been mis-

53 See *EH* 'Ekev 1 (III: 44 [two occurrences], *EH* 'Ekev 3 (III: 51); *EH* 'Ekev 4 (III: 53,54), 5 (III: 56), 15 (III: 81). Examples of this type of comment are found on innumerable occasions throughout the commentary. We will therefore limit ourselves here and below, where possible, to examples taken from the representative sample found in parashat *'Ekev,* which has a particularly high occurrence of emendations. A complete list of Neẓiv's emendations to parashat *'Ekev* , categorized and contrasted to those offered by the Ga'on and Louis Finkelstein in their editions of *Sifre,* can be found below in Appendix B.

54 E.g., *EH* 'Ekev 4 (III: 55).

55 E.g., *EH* 'Ekev 12 (III: 77). See also *EH* Naso 1 (I: 8); *EH* Naso 6 (I: 33); *EH* Naso 7 (I: 38); *EH* Naso 12 (I: 58); *EH* Naso 44 (I: 173); *EH* Be-ha'alotekha 2 (I: 196); *EH* Shelaḥ 9 (II: 63); *EH* Koraḥ 4 (II: 117); *EH* Pinḥas 1 (II: 212); *EH* Pinḥas 7 (II: 235); *EH* Matot 1 (II: 278); *EH* Matot 3 (II: 297); *EH* Masa'ei 2 (II: 317).

56 *EH* Shelaḥ 9 (II: 62).

57 E.g., *EH* 'Ekev 12 (III: 74).

taken for the letter *ḥet* thus rendering "Rabbi Yiẓḥak" rather than the intended "Rabbi Ẓadok."[58] Such emendations suggest that at one point in the transmission of the work there were letters in a hand-copied text which were slightly misshapen and thus mistaken by a later scribe or printer as different letters.

On other occasions, Neẓiv rearranges the letters of a word found in the printed text, which implies that the employee of the printing house charged with the task of setting the letters had taken the wrong letters and then set them in a fashion which made sense given the letters he had in hand. For example, he might have taken the letter *reish* when, in Neẓiv's view, he should have taken a *bet*, and thus he erroneously formed the word *"le-shivre"* rather than the word*"be-shvil."*[59] Or, on another occasion, the printer might have forgotten to set the letter *aleph* into the mold, while mistakenly taking the regular *mem* rather than the final *mem*, and, as a result of his carelessness, the printer created the word *"she-lamad"* in place of what Neẓiv believes should have been *"shel 'adam."*[60]

Neẓiv is also aware of the propensity for the human eye of a copyist or a printer to accidentally skip a word or letter and, thus, Neẓiv's emendations often consist of adding an element to the passage which he believes was erroneously deleted.[61] Likewise, Neẓiv recognizes that the similarity of a *Sifre* passage to another passage elsewhere in rabbinic literature with which the copyist or printer was well acquainted might have resulted in the mistaken insertion of words from the other passage into that of *Sifre.* Furthermore, he understands that prior editors might have erroneously inserted additional words in a misguided attempted to correct what they thought was a deletion of words. As such, Neẓiv often removes what he believes to be extraneous words in the printed *Sifre* text.[62]

Quite often, however, Neẓiv's emendations seem to be motivated less

58 *EH* 'Ekev 2 (III: 47). See also *EH* 'Ekev 7 (III: 68); *EH* 'Ekev 7 (III: 69); *EH* 'Ekev 12 (III: 75).

59 *EH* 'Ekev 2 (III: 48). *"Lamed-shin-vet-REISH-yud,"* rather than *"BET-shin-vet-yud-lamed."*

60 *EH* 'Ekev 12 (III: 75). *"Shin-lamed-regular mem-daled,"* rather than *"Shin-lamed ALEPH-daled-final mem."*

61 E.g., *EH* 'Ekev 2 (III: 47); *EH* 'Ekev 3 (III: 50); *EH* 'Ekev 4 (III: 53); *EH* 'Ekev 4 (III: 54) [x2]; *EH* 'Ekev 4 (III: 55); *EH* 'Ekev 5 (III: 57); *EH* 'Ekev 7 (III: 68); *EH* 'Ekev 11 (III: 71); *EH* 'Ekev 11 (III: 72); *EH* 'Ekev 12 (III: 74); *EH* 'Ekev 12 (III: 75); *EH* 'Ekev 12 (III: 76).

62 E.g., *EH* 'Ekev 2 (III: 47); *EH* 'Ekev 2 (III: 49); *EH* 'Ekev 3 (III: 50); *EH* 'Ekev 5 (III: 58); *EH* 'Ekev 7 (III: 66); *EH* 'Ekev 7 (III: 67); *EH* 'Ekev 7 (III: 67); *EH* 'Ekev 7 (III: 67); *EH* 'Ekev 7 (III: 69); *EH* 'Ekev 12 (III: 73); *EH* 'Ekev 12 (III: 77). For an explicit reference by Neẓiv to the work of earlier editors of the *Sifre* text, see Shelaḥ 1 (II: 15).

by his recognition of standard textual corruptions and more by his own sense of the passage's inner logic. This guiding sense is always informed by Neẓiv's sensitivity both to Hebrew grammar[63] and to the syntax employed by rabbinic literature.[64] On select occasions, though, it seems that Neẓiv's impetus for emending the printed text lies in the semantics of the passage rather than in its syntax, grammar, or his suspicion of scribal or printing error. And thus, with a slight emendation he might radically change the meaning of a seemingly intelligible printed text so as to conform to his conception of the passage's intended meaning.

Thus, for example, when the author of *Sifre* states that Jacob blessed Pharaoh with the mitigation of the seven years of famine (*EH 'Ekev* 1, III:48), it then proceeds to cite two verses, both of which speak of Joseph providing sustenance to his brothers in Egypt, as support for this position. Both verses employ the root *kh,l,kh,l,* but the verse cited second (Gen. 45:11) makes explicit mention of the sustenance coming as a means of relief for years of famine, whereas the verse cited first (Gen. 50:21) does not refer to a famine at all. The printed text of *Sifre* which follows these citations seems to be free of any discernable scribal errors and seems to make perfect grammatical and syntactical sense. Through the hermeneutical principle of *gezerah shavah,* which equates two disparate clauses in which two identical words are found, the rabbinic author derives that "just as the verse over there refers to the years of famine, so too the verse over here refers to the years of famine." That is to say that just as the second verse (Gen. 45:11), in which Joseph promised his brothers that he would mitigate the hardships of the famine should they come live with him in Egypt, refers to the years of famine, so too the first verse (Gen. 50:21), in which Joseph is on the verge of actually sustaining the brothers, refers to the years of famine. And, thus, the proposition of *Sifre,* that Pharaoh was blessed by Jacob with the mitigation of the years of famine is, according to midrashic standards, sufficiently proven.[65]

---

63 E.g., *EH* 'Ekev 3 (III: 50); *EH* 'Ekev 3 (III: 51); *EH* 'Ekev 6 (III: 61); *EH* 'Ekev 7 (III: 65); *EH* 'Ekev 12 (III: 74); *EH* 'Ekev 12 (III: 75). Nissim Eliakim deals extensively with Neẓiv's mastery of Hebrew grammar as evidenced in *Ha'amek Davar*. See, in particular, 89-192. Eliakim, though, seems unaware of the significant reading which the young Neẓiv did in this area, as we shall document below.

64 E.g., *EH* 'Ekev 1 (III: 44); *EH* 'Ekev 2 (III: 48); *EH* 'Ekev 3 (III: 50); *EH* 'Ekev 5 (III: 56); *EH* 'Ekev 5 (III: 57); *EH* 'Ekev 5 (III: 58); *EH* 'Ekev 7 (III: 63); *EH* 'Ekev 12 (III: 74); *EH* 'Ekev 12 (III: 75); *EH* 'Ekev 12 (III: 75); *EH* 'Ekev 12 (III: 75); *EH* 'Ekev 12 (III: 78); *EH* 'Ekev 15 (III: 82).

65 The fact that the blessing was supposedly to Pharaoh and yet the verses point to the family

Neẓiv, however, seems to be bothered by this reading, in which the first verse (Gen. 50:11) which takes place after the death of Jacob, is made to have taken place during the seven years of famine, when the biblical text is quite clear in stating that Jacob lived in Egypt for seventeen years (Gen. 47:28) and his death, therefore, was long after the seven years of famine would have passed. Neẓiv, as a result, takes the initial statement of *Sifre,* that the blessing of Jacob consisted of the mitigation of the years of famine, *"she-nimna' me-meno shenei ra'av,"* in the literal sense of the word *nimna'*, meaning withheld completely, rather than mitigated or lessened. If, then, the seven years of famine never took place, the statement following the citation of the verses, which states that just as one refers to the years of famine so too the other refers to the years of famine, becomes virtually unintelligible—how could they both refer to the years of famine, if the years of famine ended completely with the arrival of Jacob in Egypt? And how could stating that they both refer to years of famine possibly support the author's claim that Jacob's blessing to Pharaoh prevented Egypt from experiencing any further famine?

Neẓiv's response is to emend the text. In his version, the text reads "just as *kilkul* written over there does NOT refer to the years of famine, so *kilkul* written over here does NOT refer to the years of famine." That is to say that just as the first verse cited (Gen. 50:21), in which Joseph is on the verge of actually sustaining the brothers, does not refer to the years of famine—a reading far more in line with the straightforward sense of the text—so too, the second verse mentioned (Gen. 45:11), in which Joseph seems to be promising his brothers that he would mitigate the hardships of the famine should they come live with him in Egypt, does not actually refer to years of famine. Rather, Joseph is telling his brothers that if they come to Egypt there would be no more famine for, in the words of Neẓiv, "Joseph knew that in the merit of Jacob the famine would stop." Thus once again, but this time with a slight but semantically significant modification to the text, the original proposition, that Jacob blessed Pharaoh with the complete elimination of the years of famine, is midrashically proven.

While in this example Neẓiv offers his own reading of the text without invoking the support of any other rabbinic text, in many of the cases listed above he bolsters his decision to emend the text by referring the

---

of Jacob as having been the recipients is interesting but unrelated to our current discussion.

reader to a textual witness in which a reading similar to the one which he offered of the *Sifre* passage can be found. The text cited most often in this regard is *Yalkut Shim'oni*,[66] but references to variant readings found in Talmud Bavli,[67] Talmud Yerushalmi,[68] Tosefta,[69] one of the so-called minor tractates,[70] *Mekhilta'*,[71] *Midrash Rabbah*,[72] or medieval commentaries such as Rashi[73] or Tosafot[74] also abound.

The mere existence of a differing parallel text, however, is not sufficient cause for Neẓiv to emend the printed text. At times, therefore, Neẓiv mentions a variant parallel but determines that it does not justify emending the text of *Sifre*,[75] and elsewhere he expresses uncertainty in regard to emending the text in accordance with such a reading.[76] Often this reluctance stems from Neẓiv's belief that *Sifre* has its own distinctive voice, a voice which need not be in harmony with other rabbinic sources.[77]

An instructive illustration of such can be found in his comments on *Sifre, Naso* 39 (I: 155). *Sifre* there discusses the blessings which Aaron and his sons are commanded to give the Children of Israel in chapter six of Numbers (v. 22-27). In the context of his discussion, the author of this passage in *Sifre* notes that the verse uses the term "*Benei Yisrael*," which, as Neẓiv points out, could be translated as the Sons of Israel rather than the Children of Israel, which might suggest that proselytes, slaves, and women were not entitled to a blessing from Aaron and his sons. Thus,

---

66 E.g., *EH* 'Ekev 1 (III: 45); *EH* 'Ekev 1 (III: 46); *EH* 'Ekev 2 (III: 49); *EH* 'Ekev 3 (III: 50); *EH* 'Ekev 3 (III: 51); *EH* 'Ekev 4 (III: 54); *EH* 'Ekev 5 (III: 55); *EH* 'Ekev 5 (III: 56); *EH* 'Ekev 5 (III: 57); *EH* 'Ekev 5 (III: 58); *EH* 'Ekev 5 (III: 60); *EH* 'Ekev 5 (III: 61); *EH* 'Ekev 7 (III: 65); *EH* 'Ekev 7 (III: 66); *EH* 'Ekev 7 (III: 67); *EH* 'Ekev 7 (III: 68); *EH* 'Ekev 7 (III: 69); *EH* 'Ekev 10 (III: 71); *EH* 'Ekev 11 (III: 72); *EH* 'Ekev 12 (III: 74); *EH* 'Ekev 12 (III: 75); *EH* 'Ekev 12 (III: 76); *EH* 'Ekev 12 (III: 77); *EH* 'Ekev 12 (III: 78); *EH* 'Ekev 14 (III: 80); *EH* 'Ekev 15 (III: 82). It is interesting to note that Neẓiv rarely questions of the reliability of the *Yalkut* text—a text known to be rather corrupt.

67 E.g., *EH* 'Ekev 1 (III: 45); *EH* 'Ekev 2 (III: 47); *EH* 'Ekev 3 (III: 50); *EH* 'Ekev 5 (III: 59); *EH* 'Ekev 7 (III: 66); *EH* 'Ekev 11 (III: 73); *EH* 'Ekev 12 (III: 78).

68 E.g., *EH* Naso 12 (I: 58).

69 E.g., *EH* 'Ekev 7 (III: 63); *EH* Naso 38 (I: 150).

70 E.g., *Avot de-Rabbi Natan* in *EH* 'Ekev 11 (III: 73).

71 E.g., *EH* 'Ekev 7 (III: 64, 65, 66).

72 E.g., *EH* 'Ekev 3 (III: 50); *EH* 'Ekev 5 (III: 57); *EH* 'Ekev 11 (III: 73).

73 E.g., *EH* 'Ekev 3: (III: 50).

74 E.g., *EH* Naso 5 (I: 30); *EH* Naso 39 (I: 151).

75 E.g., *EH* 'Ekev 3 (III: 50); *EH* 'Ekev 12 (III: 74); *EH* 'Ekev 12 (III: 76); *EH* 'Ekev 12 (III: 77).

76 E.g., *EH* 'Ekev 7 (III: 68).

77 For more on Neẓiv's recognition of *Sifre's* distinctive voice, see the section on rabbinic methodology in Chapter Four below.

*Sifre* sets out to find an additional source which includes all members of the nation in the priestly blessing, and determines that the seemingly redundant phrase in verse twenty-seven in which God states "And I will bless them" proves the point. In his commentary Neẓiv notes that the same question is raised in a *berayta* cited in the Talmud (TB *Sotah* 38a), but the source offered in that text was the phrase "Say to them" from verse twenty-three, not the words "And I will bless them" from verse twenty-seven.[78] Despite his awareness of this parallel text, Neẓiv writes that the mere existence of a differing parallel is not sufficient justification for emending the text. In this case in particular, a later passage in *Sifre* suggests to Neẓiv that the verse cited in the printed text does indeed reflect the authentic voice of *Sifre,* a voice which need not be identical to that of the Talmud.

> And in the *berayta* [which appears] in the Gemara it states "hence it says 'Say to them.'" However, later on in *piska'* 43[79] it is evident that the primary [reading] is in accordance with our reading which extends [the recipients of blessings] from "And I will bless them." And I have already written in a number of places that there is not enough evidence to [merit] distorting *Sifre* due to the version of the Gemara in a place where there is no indication [of corruption] from [*Sifre* ] itself.[80]

For other rabbinic *Sifre* commentators, such as the Vilna Ga'on and Meir Leibush Malbim (1809-1879), the cacophony created by the printed text and its talmudic variant, along with the fact that *Sifre* in the very next line uses the phrase "and I will bless them" to derive a completely different ruling, leads them to emend this text, as well as its corollary in *piska'* forty-three.[81] For Neẓiv, however, these reasons alone, in the face of the seemingly unified voice of *Sifre,* do not justify an emendation of the printed text.

Despite examples such as this one, in which Neẓiv is reluctant to emend the text, the instances in *'Emek ha-Neẓiv* in which he does make

78 TB *Sotah* (38a).
79 *EH* Naso 43 (I: 170).
80 See also *EH* Naso 44 (I: 171).
81 See GRA in *'Emek ha-Neẓiv,* ad loc. For Malbim, see his *ha-Torah ve-ha-Miẓvah,* par. 142.

significant changes are far more prevalent. In fact, Neẓiv not only changes the wording of his printed edition of *Sifre* but takes the liberty of veering from the printed text's division of the text into *piska'ot* as well. Thus in 'Ekev, for example, Neẓiv believes *piska'* 8 should encompass all of what the printed edition calls *piska'ot* 9 and 10 as well.[82] *Piska'* 9, according to Neẓiv, corresponds to the printed *piska'* 11.[83] Neẓiv's version of *piska'* 10, however, contains that which is listed as both *piska'* 12 and 13 in the printed edition.[84] The remaining *piska'ot* in the *parashah* as conceived by Neẓiv correspond to those of the printed text. *Parashat 'Ekev*, for Neẓiv, therefore contains only thirteen *piska'ot*, while the printed edition contains sixteen.[85]

In general, the Neẓiv's division of *piska'ot* seems to reflect his understanding of the thematic segments which comprise the biblical text and his firm belief that the rabbinic exposition of verses which constitute a single thematic segment in the Bible should constitute a single *piska'* in *Sifre*. As such, *Piska'ot* 8, 9, and 10 in the printed text of 'Ekev correspond to Deuteronomy 11:18-19, which along with verse 20 seem to comprise a single unit in which a three-part directive is given by Moses to the people, instructing them to place the word of God on their hearts (11:18), to teach the word of God to their children (11:19), and to write the word of God on their doorposts (11:20). Thus, according to Neẓiv, the corresponding exposition on these verses in *Sifre* should constitute a single *piska'* (*piska'* 8). *Piska'* 11 in the printed text corresponds to Deuteronomy 11:21, which is an independent statement detailing the reward which will come as a result of keeping the above mentioned three part directive. Thus, here Neẓiv agrees with the printed text and assigns the corresponding text of *Sifre* its own *piska'* (*piska'* 9, according to his count). *Piska'ot* 12 and 13 of the printed text, however, correspond to the very same verse, Deuteronomy 11:22, in which a single introductory statement is made regarding the reward which comes from the observance of all of God's commandments. Thus, for Neẓiv these two *piska'ot* should, in fact, comprise one single *piska'*, *piska* 10 according to his division.

Similar patterns can be found throughout Neẓiv's *Sifre* commentary. For example, Devarim *piska'ot* 9-13 correspond to Deut. 1:9-13, which

82 *EH* 'Ekev 10 (III: 71).
83 *EH* 'Ekev 11 (III: 73).
84 *EH* 'Ekev 13 (III: 80).
85 *EH* 'Ekev 16 (III: 84).

represents a single proposal made by Moses to the people of Israel, and hence to Neẓiv they comprise a single *piska'*. Likewise, *piska'ot* 14-17 of the printed text in Devarim correspond to the people's response to the proposal of Moses and the ensuing action which was taken (Deut. 1: 14-17), and hence they too form only one *piska'*, according to Neẓiv.

Neẓiv's comments throughout *'Emek ha-Neẓiv* also demonstrate that his critical eye extended well beyond the text of *Sifre*. In the course of his commentary Neẓiv, following the lead of medieval commentators before him,[86] notes discrepancies in the text of the Mishnah as cited in Talmud Bavli and the same Mishnah as recorded in Talmud Yerushalmi.[87] Such discrepancies lead Neẓiv to suggest that the authors of *Sifre* might have been working from a version of a mishnaic text different than that found in the standard printed editions of the Talmud Bavli.[88] The Gemara texts of both Talmud Bavli[89] and Talmud Yerushalmi[90] are subject to emendations by Neẓiv as well. In addition, Neẓiv occasionally points out corrupt passages in Tosefta[91] and offers alternate readings of midrashic works such as *Midrash Rabbah*[92] and *Torat Kohanim*.[93] He constantly emends the printed renditions of medieval rabbinic literature such as Rif,[94] Rashi,[95] Rambam,[96] Ra'avad,[97] Ramban,[98] and Rosh.[99] In fact, he even accuses the early nineteenth-century editor of Avraham Lichtenstein's *Zera' Avraham* as having distorted the original eighteenth-century text.[100]

In addition to his penchant for identifying textual corruptions,

---

86 In his introduction to *Ha'amek She'elah*, Neẓiv explicitly refers to the example set in this regard by Tosafot in *Yevamot* 105b and *Bekhorot* 22b. See *Petaḥ Ha-'Emek*, #5.

87 E.g., *EH* Pinḥas 12 (II: 251); *EH* Teẓeh 15 (III: 253). For a contemporary look at the differing versions of Mishnah found in the Bavli and Yerushalmi, see Christine Elizabeth Hayes, *Between the Babylonian and Palestinian Talmuds* (New York: Oxford University Press, 1997).

88 See *EH* Teẓeh 35 (III: 287).

89 E.g., *EH* Naso 3 (I: 21); *EH* Naso 9 (I: 51); *EH* Naso 38 (I: 150); *EH* Shelaḥ 6 (II: 50); *EH* Matot 3 (II: 297); *EH* Masa'ei 2 (II: 317).

90 E.g., *EH* Naso 9 (I: 51); *EH* Naso 28 (I: 118,120); *EH* Naso 44 (I: 171).

91 *EH* Pinḥas 1 (II: 212): "*Mushgah be-defus harbeh.*"

92 E.g., *EH* Naso 6 (I: 35); *EH* Naso 12 (I: 58); *EH* Be-ha'alotekha 44 (I: 312); *EH* Pinḥas 7 (II: 235).

93 E.g., *EH* Be-ha'alotekha 45 (I: 315).

94 E.g., *EH* Be-ha'alotekha 12 (I: 223).

95 E.g., *EH* Be-ha'alotekha 44 (I: 211); *EH* Shelaḥ 1(II: 5); *EH* ve-'Etḥanan (III: 39).

96 E.g., *EH* Naso 7 (I: 38).

97 E.g., *EH* Naso 1 (I: 8); *EH* Naso 21 (II: 82).

98 E.g., *EH* Naso 44 (I: 174).

99 E.g., *EH* Shelaḥ 9 (II: 63).

100 E.g., *EH* Pinḥas 14 (II: 257).

Neẓiv was also keenly aware of questions regarding the authorship of earlier texts. In regard to *Sifre,* he identifies passages which he believes to be later additions to the original work, despite the lack of any such indication in the printed text itself.[101] Like many other rabbinic authors, when Neẓiv refers to medieval texts whose authorship is known to be questionable, he is careful to use the term *"meyuḥas le,"* "ascribed to," rather than assuming that the person to whom the work is ascribed is, in fact, the work's author.[102] At times, however, he distinguishes himself from the traditional rabbinic commentator by going so far as to suggest who the author of an "ascribed" work really was,[103] and by suggesting that works whose authorship had not previously been considered questionable by the rabbinic establishment were also misattributed. For example, the Talmud commentary which surrounds that of Alfasi in the printed editions of Nedarim appears under the name *Nemukei Yosef,* a reference to the commentary of Yosef Habiba (fourteenth century, Spain), but Neẓiv believes the work is actually that of Rabbeinu Yehonatan, authored almost two centuries earlier by Yehonotan ben David ha-Kohen of Lunel (c. 1135-c.1210).[104] Likewise, Neẓiv states that the commentary on Chronicles attributed to Rashi was really authored by Sa'adya Ga'on.[105]

---

101 E.g., *EH* Pinḥas 21 (II: 273) and *EH* Re'eh 59 (III: 148).

102 E.g., *EH* Naso 4 (I: 24) *"be-teshuvah ha-meyuḥeset le-ha-ramban"*; *EH* Matot 1 (II: 286) *"ha-peirush ha-meyuḥas le-Ritva."* For more on the printing of Ramban and Ritva, see Israel Ta-Shema, *"Seder Hadpasatam Shel Ḥiddushei ha-Rishonim le-Talmud," Kiryat Sefer* 50 (1975): 325-336. On the responsa of *Rashba* attributed to *Ramban,* see Ḥayyim Dov Chavel, *"Shut ha-Rashba ha-Meyuḥasot le-ha-Ramban," Hadorom* 46 (1978): 228-231.

103 *EH* Matot 1 (II: 277). From the fact that too many of the positions articulated in the Nedarim commentary attributed to *Ritva* are at odds with what Yosef Habiba cites in *Ritva's* name in his *Nemukei Yosef,* Neẓiv concludes that *Ritva* could not have been the author. Instead, he identifies a student of *Ra'ah* as the author of this commentary ascribed to *Ritva.* It is important to note, however, that this analysis bears a striking resemblance to the comments made by Aharon Fuld on the entry for *Nemukei Yosef* found in Yosef David Azulai's *Shem ha-Gedolim* (Vilna, 1852), 83. As this note was first published in the Krotozyn edition of *Shem ha-Gedolim* (1843), it is certainly possible that Neẓiv based his comment on that of Fuld. More recent scholarship has sided against Fuld and Neẓiv and views *Ḥiddushei ha-Ritva* on Nedarim as an authentic work of *Ritva.* See the introduction to *Ḥiddushei ha-Ritva Masekhet Nedarim* (Jerusalem: Mosad Harav Kook, 1977).

104 *EH* Naso 22 (I: 87). Ya'akov Spiegel, in an article on *Nemukei Yosef,* writes that there is, indeed, sufficient reason to doubt whether *Nemukei Yosef* on *Nedarim* is, in fact, the product of Yosef Habiba. Spiegel concludes, however, that there is insufficient evidence to decide the matter. He does not suggest, as does Neẓiv, that the true author of the work was Rabbeinu Yehonatan. See his *"Sefer Nemukei Yosef le-R. Yosef Ḥabiba," Sidra* 4 (1988): 111-162.

105 *EH* Koraḥ 1 (II: 81). While modern scholarship has agreed that what was traditionally called *Rashi* on Chronicles was not penned by *Rashi,* they do not ascribe its authorship to Sa'adya Ga'on. It is interesting to note, however, that this question is discussed in the

Neẓiv's penchant for textual emendation as well as his sensitivity to questions of authorship is clearly carried over into his work on *She'iltot* as well. The work opens with a discussion of the current form of *She'iltot* and the problems created by references to *She'iltot* passages in the works of medieval commentators which do not appear in the printed text. This leads Neẓiv to surmise that the work was originally written in segments, some of which had been lost over time,[106] and that the author subjected the work to multiple recensions, which similarly accounts for differences in the text. Neẓiv then proceeds to examine *She'iltot*'s date of composition, stating that he had originally believed the text to have preceded Shimon Kayara's *Halakhot Gedolot* due to the numerous passages found therein which seem to be based upon *She'iltot*.[107] Nonetheless, Neẓiv seems to have shifted his opinion on the matter after seeing that both Meiri in his introduction to Avot, and Sa'adiah ibn Danaan (of fifteenth-century Spain) in his *Seder ha-Dorot*, claim that *She'iltot* was written after *Halakhot Gedolot*. Thus, Neẓiv concludes, the references to *She'iltot* found in *Halakhot Gedolot* must represent later editorial insertions.[108] The body of his *She'iltot* commentary is similarly filled with attempts to establish an authentic reading of the *She'iltot* text, and he devotes consistent attention to the fact that *She'iltot* contains numerous citations of talmudic passages which deviate from the text found in standard printed editions.[109]

pages of the early Hebrew *wissenschaft* journals. Shlomo Yosef Rappaport first raises the issue in *Bikure ha-'Ittim* (Vienna, 1828): 35, and it surfaces again in a letter by Joseph Weiss published in *Kerem Ḥemed* 5 (Prague, 1841): 232-244. Both authors attribute authorship of *Rashi* on Chronicles to a student of Sa'adya Ga'on. Weiss explicitly states that the commentary penned by this "student" was intended to convey the insights of his teacher, Sa'adya Ga'on, on Chronicles. Thus, it is quite possible that Weiss's letter is the source upon which Neẓiv relies. While Neẓiv never cites directly from *Kerem Ḥemed*, the wide range of sources from which he does quote, including the maskilic newspaper *ha-Maggid*, makes it well within reason to suggest that he was a reader of *Kerem Ḥemed* as well. In fact, the constant attention given to topics such as biblical synonyms, textual emendation, and the lives and work of the Ge'onim in the pages of *Bikurei ha-'Ittim*, leads me to suspect that Neẓiv had access to some if not all of the volumes of that journal as well.

106 Robert Brody goes a step further and suggests that they might have been written by different people and that Aḥai of Shavha served as the editor rather than the author. See Brody, *The Ge'onim of Babylonia and the Shaping of Medieval Jewish Culture* (New Haven: Yale University Press, 1998), 208.

107 Such is the position adopted by Brody, ibid., 213. The position Neẓiv ascribes to Rashbam, namely, that *She'iltot* is a product of the Savoraic period, was argued in more elaborate fashion by J.N. Epstein in his *Meḥkarim be-Sifrut ha-Talmud u-ve-Leshonot Shemiyot*, vol. 2 (Jerusalem: Magnes Press, 1983), 382-391.

108 See *Ha'amek She'elah* vol 1, *Petaḥ ha-'Emek* 1: 1-5.

109 In an appendix to the *She'iltot* published by Moad ha-Rav Kook (Jerusalem, 1999), the

Another rather vivid portrayal of Neẓiv as a textual critic comes from the following story, which he relays in the second installment of his *Petaḥ ha-Emek.*

> And God further helped me to reveal the [proper] text of our Rabbi's book (i.e., *She'iltot*) [when], in the city of Minsk, a manuscript on the *She'iltot* was brought before me without any front matter (*ketivat ha-panim*), written with Spanish lettering, which had been a sealed book to its owner. And when I received it, I poured over it and analyzed the form of the writing, and I discovered the nature of this book. It was an abbreviated commentary, anthologized from the commentary of Rashi, like the commentary on Alfasi which is called 'Rashi on the Rif.'[110]

Thus, in the realm of rabbinics, Neẓiv's desire to establish reliable texts as well as his willingness to emend the printed text and to question the attribution of its authorship in order to do so are rather clear. This too, then, places him squarely in line with the intellectual interests and scholarly methods of the midrash scholars of early nineteenth-century Lithuania and suggests, perhaps, that he surpassed his mentors and col-

editor collects all of the passages in *She'iltot* in which the geonic author cites biblical verses in a manner which deviates from the masoretic text. He notes that despite Neẓiv's unquestionable knowledge of the masoretic text and his unique preoccupation with textual variants of rabbinic works, never in the course of his massive commentary does he so much as note the fact that the Bible which lay before the author of *She'iltot* differed rather significantly from that which lay before him. The editor seems to have missed Neẓiv's explicit reference in *Petaḥ ha-Emek* 1: 5 to the passage in *Mesekhet Soferim* (6: 4) which acknowledges the existence of different versions of the Torah text and states that in any particular instance one is to follow the text which appears in the majority of extant versions. Similarly, he notes that Targum Yonatan in Neviim and Ketuvim often seems to be working from a text different than the traditional masoretic text. Neẓiv has no doubt that the text of Targum Yonatan was also a legitimate text, but he writes that ultimately, "the voice of the multitudes is like the voice of God" and hence, today, one is to follow the text which has been accepted by the masses. Thus, it is clear that Neẓiv's critical eye was quick to notice discrepancies in the biblical text as well, but these instances were of little consequence to him as the masoretic text had long been accepted. Interestingly, in his Torah commentary (*HD* Num. 22: 4), when Neẓiv likewise acknowledges that *Rashi* seems to have had a biblical text which differed from the standard printed edition of the masoretic text, Neẓiv suggests that both versions of the text contain important messages for the reader, as if to suggest that God intentionally created both versions of the text, thus obviating any theological difficulties it might entail.

110 HS 1: *Petaḥ ha-'Emek*, 2: 3

leagues in the degree to which he pursued them.

*Intellectual Breadth*

The third distinguishing characteristic of early nineteenth-century Lithuanian midrash commentary is the breadth of source material and subjects which these authors incorporate into their commentary. Their citations and references, and the general subject matter of some of their comments, suggest that the authors were often conversant in the literature of Jewish philosophy, understood the basics of Aristotelian philosophy,[111] had at least a rudimentary knowledge of disciplines such as history and the natural sciences, and were familiar with the writings of the more critical German Jewish thinkers of the late eighteenth century. It is also evident that these authors felt no compunction about sharing their knowledge in these areas with their traditional Jewish readership.[112] Here too, the young Neẓiv follows the lead of his older Lithuanian contemporaries.

Ḥanokh Zundel Luria, the *maggid* of Novhardok, is a shining example of this type of intellectual breadth. In the approbations to the 1842 publication of his *Kenaf Renanim*, the *av bet din* of Novhardok refers to him as "*ha-Rav ha-Muflag ha-Ḥoker kalil ha-Mada'im*," "the extraordinary rabbi, scholar of all the sciences." Likewise Aharon Yosha Eliyahu Herzfeld in his approbation refers to Ḥanokh Zundel's "expertise in the natural sciences."[113] These descriptions are borne out by Ḥanokh Zundel's introduction to the work, where he writes of the time he spent engaging the works of Sa'adya Ga'on, Judah Ha-Levi, Baḥya Ibn Paquda, Rambam, Joseph Albo, and Isaac 'Aramah;[114] they can also be seen in the text of

111 The engagement with Aristotelian philosophy by most, if not all, of these authors seems to have been mediated through the work of medieval Jewish philosophers rather than through direct contact with the works of Aristotle. However, the pseudo-Aristotelian "*Sefer ha-Tapuaḥ*," which had been out of print since 1706, is printed again in Vilna (1799), in Frankfurt (1800), Luveville (1807), and Polonnoye (1813). Satanow's Hebrew edition of Aristotle's *Ethics* is printed in Berlin (1790) and could possibly have made its way to Lithuania as well.

112 By the later decades of the century this attitude will change drastically; see Chapter 7 below. It is important to note, as Yehuda Friedlander has, that the willingness to engage a broad array of sources in the pursuit of Torah learning is not synonymous with the ideological movement for Jewish enlightenment, known as *Haskalah*. See his "*Yaḥaso shel ha-GRA le-Haskalah*," in *ha-GRA u-Bet Midrasho*, eds. Moshe Halamish, et al. (Ramat Gan: Bar-Ilan University Press, 2003), 197-205.

113 *Kenaf Renanim* (Kratashin, 1842).

114 *Kenaf Renanim*, 5.

the commentary itself, in which he refers, amongst many other things, to the works of the "*ḥokerim ha-tevi'im*" or "those who study nature,"[115] to "*ha-rof'im be-Sifrehem*" or "the doctors in their books,"[116] to the theory of music,[117] and to the social and political nature of man.[118] He also offers translations of Hebrew into German[119] and Latin[120] and cites both the exegetical[121] and the philosophical writings of Moses Mendelssohn.[122]

It is important to note that the inclusion of such material in Ḥanokh Zundel Luria's work does not seem to have marginalized him in the eyes of the rabbinic establishment. In addition to those listed above, his work contains the approbations of the following leading Lithuanian Torah scholars: Aryeh Leib Katzenellenbogen, av bet din of Brisk (1836), Yitzhak, av bet din of Shavel (1838), Yosef David, av bet din of Mir (1837), and Ya'akov, av bet din of Karlin (1839). While it is quite possible that the above authors did not carefully examine the book, as noted above, the approbation from David of Novhardok (1769-1836), who was both a well known talmudist and the rabbi of the town in which Luria served as *maggid*, describes Luria as a "*ḥoker kalil ha-mada'im*" (scholar of all the sciences) while noting how well received his weekly sermons are amongst the community of Novhardok.

David Luria's breadth of knowledge is similar to that of Ḥanokh Zundel. In a note at the beginning of his commentary to *Pirkei de-Rabbi Eliezer*, Luria shares with his readers that which he has seen "in books of medicine."[123] In his commentary to *Midrash Rabbah* he writes of "a startling thing" he saw written by "the scholars of science" with regard to the area in which the "Mediterranean Sea meets the Atlantic Ocean by Gibraltar."[124] In the context of a discussion regarding Noah's Ark, Radal

---

115 ibid., 104.

116 Ibid., 52.

117 Ibid., 6.

118 "'*Inyan ha-'adam she-kol yesod kiyumo hu be-kibuẓ u-be-ḥevrah ha-medinati*," Ibid., 207, 297.

119 E.g., ibid., 206. Luria's translations into German are prefaced by the phrase "*nikra' be-lashon 'ashkenaz*," whereas his translations into Yiddish are prefaced by the phrase "*be-la'az nikra'*," as on 205.

120 E.g., ibid., 7. This translation is prefaced by the phrase "*u-be-lashon l'atyyn*."

121 Ibid., 224. The reference is to Mendelssohn's commentary on *Kohelet*.

122 Ibid., 135 "*Sefer igrot ha-filisofim le-ha-ḥakham ha-shalem moreinu ha-rav moshe ben Mendelssohn be-lashon ashkenaz be-mikhtav ha-rishon ve-ha-sheni*." In an editorial move reflective of the change in both time and place, this line was deleted from the 1859 Pressburg edition of *Kenaf Rennanim* (57b).

123 *Pirkei de-Rabbi Eliezer* (Warsaw, 1852), 1b.

124 *Peirush Radal* in *Midrash Rabbah, vol. 1* (Jerusalem: Wagshal, 2001), 4: 26 (255).

writes that he "saw amongst the books of the nations that someone in England successfully made the design of the ark and confirmed that it held far more than the amount held in other boats and that [nonetheless] it went easily on the water."[125] Elsewhere he suggests that the discovery of petrified fossils may explain the text on which he was commenting.

> And perhaps it is the hardening into stone of the bodies and bones of animals which the scholars of nature agree were from the days of the Flood because they are generally found in places which have climates in which such animals could not have lived at all, like in the northern lands.[126]

Ẓvi Hirsch Katzenellenbogen also displays a broad knowledge base in his commentary on the thirty-two *middot* of aggadic interpretation. His work, which is prefaced by the approbation of Avraham Abele Posvoler, Vilna's official rabbinic head, contains references to the philosophic work of Rambam[127] and Sa'adya Ga'on,[128] Mendelssohn's *Biur,*[129] basic works of geography,[130] geometry,[131] and the natural sciences.[132] In fact, this breadth has led to the classification of Katzenellenbogen as an early "maskil." Thus Hillel Noah Maggid Steinschneider writes, in his history of the Vilna Jewish community, "While he was still in his youth, the winds of the Haskalah began stirring the hearts of his older contemporaries…and the young Ẓvi Hirsch absorbed the spirit of these boys and became a youth enlightened in the true words of the Living God." Later, he "studied the works of German scholars and pored over the meanings of Hebrew words and proper Hebrew grammar."[133] From his own writing, and from the approbations which preface his work, it is clear that Katzenellenbogen did not view himself as being in a camp apart from the mainstream rabbinic world of Lithuania. It should also

125 Ibid., 6: 15 (310).
126 Ibid., 6: 16 (315).
127 E.g., *Netivot 'Olam* (Vilna, 1822), 9b.
128 E.g, ibid., 21b.
129 E.g, ibid., 33a.
130 E.g, ibid., 35a, 55a.
131 E.g, ibid., 52b.
132 E.g, ibid., 46b.
133 Steinschneider, vol. I, 228-232.

be clear from our present study that a broad knowledge base and citations therefrom were not unusual amongst Lithuanian Torah scholars of the early nineteenth century, thus making the line between traditional establishment and early Haskalah rather difficult to draw.

While Ḥanokh Zundel ben Yosef and Yiẓḥak Eliyahu Landau do not display a proficiency in scientific and philosophic literature equivalent to that of Radal or Ḥanokh Zundel Luria, nor the range of Katzenellenbogen, there is a discernable intellectual breadth apparent in their work as well. In his approbation to Ḥanokh Zundel ben Yosef's commentary to *Midrash Rabbah,* (1867), Binyamin David Rabinowitz, the *maggid* of Warsaw, notes that "people who are deep in wisdom and broad in science will also find in his commentary many things that are good and proper." In the commentary itself, there is evidence that Ḥanokh Zundel made use of the work of late eighteenth-century and early nineteenth-century Jewish thinkers such as Naftali Herz Wessely[134] and Menashe Illya, both of whom straddled the worlds of traditionalism and enlightenment.[135] The following passage from Landau's commentary on the Passover Haggadah also displays a genuine interest in and respect for the natural sciences.

> *Ve-afilu kulanu ḥakhamim, kulanu nevonim*...The relationship of *ḥakhamim, nevonim,* and *yod'ei ha-Torah* to the telling of the Exodus story is that God operates the world in three ways: a) through nature b) through the cosmic

---

134 *Ez̤ Yosef* in *Midrash Rabbah* (Warsaw, 1870), 90a.

135 *Masekhet Soferim* (Suvalk, 1862), 18b. While Wessely saw himself as a traditional Jew, and to some degree as a defender of rabbinic tradition, his manifesto on Jewish educational reform, *Divre Shalom Ve-Emet,* disenfranchised him to many in the traditional world. On the reaction of the Vilna community to this pamphlet, or their lack thereof, see Yehuda Friedlander's "The Ga'on's Relationship to Early Haskalah: The Ga'on and N.H. Wessely" (Hebrew) in *Ha-GRA u-Bet Midrasho,* eds. Moshe Halamish, et al. (Ramat Gan: Bar-Ilan University Press, 2003), 97-206. On his simultaneous alienation from the world of the Eastern European rabbinic establishment and the Western European Jewish Enlightenment, see Edward Breuer's "Naphtali Herz Wessely and the Cultural Dislocations of an Eighteenth-century Maskil" in Shmuel Feiner and David Sorkin, eds., *New Perspectives on the Haskalah* (Oxford: Littman 2001), 27-47. On the readership and reception of Mendelssohn's Bible commentary and translation, for which Wessely wrote the Leviticus volume, see Steven Lowenstein's "The Readership of Mendelssohn's Bible Translation" in *Hebrew Union College Annual,* 53 (1983) 179-213 and Moshe Samet's "M. Mendelssohn, N.H. Wessely and the Rabbis of their Generation" in *Studies in the History of the Jewish People and the Land of Israel,* A. Gilboa, et al., eds. (Haifa: The University of Haifa, 1970), 233-257. On Menashe of Ilya see Isaac Barzily's *Manasseh of Ilya: Precursor of Modernity among the Jews of Eastern Europe* (Jerusalem: Magnes Press, 1999).

> order[136] c) through miracles which are above both of them. And the lowest of the nations who are lacking enlightenment recognize the wonders of God only from the perspective of miracles that are above both nature and the [cosmic] order. But the enlightened ones understand that the analysis of nature reveals wonders as wondrous as those of miracles. So too in the systems of orbits of the spheres and the stars and the meteors in which there can be found the most astonishing secrets of wisdom. That is [the meaning of] "even if we were all wise," with the wisdom to comprehend the wonders of the analysis of nature, "even if we were men of understanding," who understood the wonders of the [cosmic] order… "even if we all were well versed in Torah" for it is the vehicle of the Blessed One in bringing about miracles…nonetheless, it is a commandment for us to tell the Exodus story.[137]

In a manner similar to that of Landau, Avraham Schick also felt the need to distinguish between the realms of physics and metaphysics. As such, his introduction to his commentary on *Tanna de-Bei Eliyahu* is dedicated to differentiating between the wisdom of nature and logic (*ha-tiv'it ve-ha-tevunah*) on the one hand, and "*ḥokhmat elohut*" on the other. In fact, he writes that one of his goals in composing the commentary was to distinguish between the nature of the intellectual endeavors of the Sages, who were assisted in their pursuit of wisdom by the Divine, and those individuals who rely solely on their intellectual faculties, the "*mitḥakmim be-sekhel levad*."[138] This distinction is, in itself, a testament to a certain degree of intellectual sophistication and belies an implicit respect for the independent discipline of scientific study. Both in the introduction and in the body of the commentary, Schick also displays a solid grasp of the medieval philosophic literature such as Sa'adya Ga'on's *'Emunot ve-De'ot* and the *Moreh Nevukhim* of Rambam.[139]

---

136 That is, the workings of the celestial spheres as opposed to "nature," which seems to refer to the workings of natural forces and phenomena on Earth.

137 *Haggadah shel Pesaḥ 'im Peirushim Yikarim ve-Neḥmadim me-rabanei Ge'onei k"k Vilna* (Vilna: 1877), 14.

138 *Tanna de-Bei Eliyahu, Rabba Zuta 'im Me'ore 'Esh* (Sudilkov, 1834), Introduction, 2.

139 E.g., ibid., 25a.

The medieval philosophic literature also figures prominently into the work of Yehudah Leib Edel, the *maggid* of Slonim.[140] In addition, Edel is clearly familiar with some historical literature, as evidenced by his lengthy attempt to identify the person known as "*Talmi*" in rabbinic literature with a known historical figure.[141] His explanation of thunder as the result of friction between "air" and "heat" suggests a certain familiarity with basic ideas of natural science as well.[142]

There were scholars known for their intellectual breadth amongst the Volozhin Circle as well. As mentioned above, Yoel Dober ha-Kohen Perski's intellectual pursuits beyond his midrash commentary consisted of Hebrew translations of *Telemaque* and *Aesop's Fables*. Simḥah Edelman published works on grammar, history, and poetry in addition to his work on *Midrash Rabbah*.[143] Mordecai Gimpel Jaffe is said to have educated himself in subjects beyond the traditional Jewish curriculum,[144] and below we will note that the same can be said of Neẓiv as well.

### *Intellectual Breadth in* 'Emek ha-Neẓiv

The diversity of disciplines and the range of authors cited by Neẓiv suggest that he, like the older midrash scholars of early nineteenth-century Lithuania, embraced avenues of knowledge wherever he could find them. His was a world in which books were printed to be read by the learned community. If they were deemed helpful in the pursuit of Torah knowledge, their content might be cited and referenced irrespective of the perceived religious orthodoxy of their authors or the prior absence of such works from the traditional canon of Torah study.

Hence, one finds Neẓiv citing approvingly from the grammatical section of a twelfth-century work by the Karaite author Yehudah Hadasi.[145] The work, entitled *Sefer Eshkol ha-Kofer*, was printed for the first time in the Ukrainian Black Sea port city of Eupatoria in 1832. Likewise Neẓiv cites the study of the masoretic tradition entitled *Masoret ha-Masoret*[146] and the Aramaic dictionary entitled *Tishbi*[147] both by the controversial

140 See *Afike Yehudah* (Jerusalem: 1999), 7.
141 Ibid., 28.
142 Ibid., 368.
143 See Steinschneider, vol. II, 173.
144 See Mordecai Gimpel Jaffe, *Zikhronot Mordecai* in *Mivḥar Ketavim* (Jerusalem: 1978).
145 *EH* Shoftim 17 (III: 189).
146 *EH* Matot 1 (II: 275).
147 *EH* Be-ha'alotekha 34 (I: 290).

Renaissance scholar, Eliyahu (ha-Baḥur) Levita (1468-1549). It was Levita who, in *Masoret ha-Masoret*, first argued that the cantilation and vocalization marks of the Bible were added at the close of the talmudic period and were not received from Sinai. The debate which ensued carried on right through the nineteenth century, in the works Yosef David Azulai, Yaakov Emden, Shadal, and many others.[148] As we shall examine in depth in the coming chapter, Neẓiv also makes extensive use of *Sefer Me'or 'Einayim*, by Levita's younger and more controversial Italian contemporary, Azariah de' Rossi.

As we move from the Renaissance to the Enlightenment, we should note that Neẓiv makes use of the work of a number of the great German Jewish authors of the late eighteenth century as well. For example, he refers his reader to the introduction of the *Biur*,[149] a Bible translation and commentary spearheaded and edited by Moses Mendelssohn, and to the Leviticus volume of that work authored by Naftali Herz Wessely.[150] He also cites Wessely's *Gan Naul* on Hebrew synonyms[151] and his commentary to the apocryphal Wisdom of Solomon entitled *Ruaḥ Ḥen*.[152] Works treating halakhic methodology and Jewish history are referred to as well, among them the medieval pseudo-Josephus known as *Yossipun* and Samson ben Isaac of Chinon's classic work on halakhic methodology, entitled *Sefer ha-Keritut*.[153] Classic works of Jewish theology and philosophy are likewise referenced throughout. Thus one finds mention of Yehuda ha-Levi's *Kuzari*,[154] Rambam's *Moreh Nevukhim*,[155] Joseph Albo's *Sefer 'Ikkarim*,[156] and Isaac 'Aramah's *'Akeidat Yiẓḥak*, amongst others.[157]

It is important to note that in all of these cases, Neẓiv is not the only member of Eastern European traditional society who was reading these works. The very fact that printers chose to print them reflects either their

148 For an overview of the issues surrounding this debate, see Dan Rabinowitz, ""Nekkudot": The Dots that Connect Us" in *Ḥakirah* 2 (2005): 49-69.

149 *EH* Shoftim 16 (III: 189). On this citation, see Chapter 1 above.

150 *EH* Re'eh 25 (III: 114).

151 *EH* Re'eh 49 (III: 135).

152 *EH* Be-ha'alotekha 41 (I: 306); 'Ekev 13 (III: 79).

153 For *Sefer ha-Keritut*, see *EH* Naso 1 (I: 2); *EH* Naso 24 (I: 102) and *EH* Balak 1 (II: 199); for *Yosippun*, see *EH* Masa'ei 3 (II: 331) and *EH* Balak 1 (II: 202).

154 For Neẓiv's use of *Kuzari*, see *EH* Shoftim 17 (III: 189). His citation of *Oẓar Neḥmad*, the commentary on *Kuzari* by Israel of Zamosc, indicates that Neẓiv was either using the 1796 Vienna edition of *Kuzari*, or one of the nineteenth-century Eastern European editions.

155 Cited in *EH* Be-ha'alotekha 45 (I: 314) [2x], *EH* Be-ha'alotekha 48 (I: 323); *EH* Re'eh 14 (III: 100).

156 Under the title *'Eẓ Shatul*.

157 For citations, see *EH* Naso 42 (I: 167); *EH* 'Ekev 5 (III: 56).

certainty or at the very least their assumption that a sizable market existed for their consumption. Such a market could not possibly have been limited to the tiny circle of individuals active in Eastern Europe during the first half of the nineteenth century who clearly identified themselves as proponents of Haskalah; their numbers were simply too small to constitute a feasible consumer market. Rather, it was the scholars at the very center of traditional Torah learning, like the circle of midrash scholars in and around Vilna, and like the young Neẓiv and his colleagues in Volozhin, for whom lines between traditional learning and maskilic learning had yet to be drawn, who bought, read, and assimilated the work of Hadasi and Levita, Mendelssohn and Wessely, ha-Levi and 'Aramah.

### *The Selection of* Sifre

The very choice of *Sifre* as the object of Neẓiv's commentary needs to be seen against the background of this scholarly coterie as well. By the time Neẓiv reached his early twenties in the late 1830s and was ready to begin his foray into the world of rabbinic composition, many of the great works of midrash had already been taken up by contemporary scholars. In the realm of midrash aggadah, *Midrash Rabbah* had been treated by the likes of Yeḥezkel Feivel, Ze'ev Wolf Einhorn, Ya'akov of Slonim, Avraham Schick, David Luria, Ḥanokh Zundel, and Shmuel Strashun. *Yalkut Shim'oni* had been treated at length by Ḥanokh Zundel, and a commentary was underway by Neẓiv's contemporary, Yoel Dober ha-Kohen Perski. *Midrash Aggadat Bereishit* was commented on by Avraham ben ha-Gra and Ḥanokh Zundel. *Midrash Tanḥuma'* was also taken up by Ḥanokh Zundel. *Pesikta' Rabbati* was treated by Avraham ben ha-Gra and Ze'ev Wolf Einhorn. The *Berayta of the 32 Middot* had been commented on at length by Einhorn and before him by Ẓvi Hirsch Kaztenellenbogen. *Pesikta' de-Rav Kahana* had been treated by Ḥanokh Zundel and David Luria. *Pesikta' de-Rabbi Eliezer, Tanna de-Bei Eliyahu*, and *Midrash Shoḥer Tov* had all been commented upon as well.

In the world of halakhic midrash (and Neẓiv's passion clearly lay in the world of *halakhah*), two of the three major works had been the subject of recent commentary as well. Yiẓḥak Eliyahu Landau published his commentary on *Mekhilta'* in 1844 after having worked on it for decades. His brother-in-law Ẓvi Hirsch ha-Kohen Rappaport published the first volume of his commentary on *Sifra* the following year.[158] Thus, by the late 1830s *Sifre* represented one of the last great works of midrash untouched by recent or contemporary midrash scholars.

### *Dual Commentary*

By the nineteenth century, it was commonplace to see a printed text of traditional Jewish literature in which the main text was supplemented by glosses or notes often referred to as "*hagahot*" or "*hasagot*." The most famous examples are undoubtedly the *hasagot* of Avraham ben David of Posquieres (1125-1198) on the halakhic code of Rambam and the *hagahot* of Moshe Isserles (1520-1572) on the halakhic code of Yosef Caro.

The work of Radal on *Pirkei de-Rabbi Eliezer* and the work of Neẓiv on *Sifre* continue the tradition of presenting a main commentarial text together with *hagahot*. The notable difference, though, is that whereas prior *hagahot* and *hasagot* generally reflected the questions, comments, and critiques of a secondary author who believed that the main commentary was at times incomplete or incorrect, the *hagahot* found interspersed amongst the commentaries of Radal and Neẓiv represent their own tangential comments and notes, which they felt did not belong in the body of their main commentarial text. As noted above,[159] the manuscript of *'Emek ha-Neẓiv* clearly indicates that while writing his main commentary on *Sifre*, Neẓiv opted to reserve certain points for his *hagahot* section, and they therefore can not be considered mere afterthoughts which, due to constraints of time or space, could not be included in the main text. Thus, for example, Neẓiv notes that in order to understand how *Sifre* could derive a law concerning a person who intentionally set someone else's property ablaze on Yom Kippur from a verse concerning a guilt offering, one must understand "that we find this often, that the verse teaches something tangential, unrelated to the topic of that *parashah*."[160]

158 Landau's status as a public figure in Dubno (the reputation he gained there as a successful preacher eventually won him the prestigious position of Maggid of Vilna in 1868), his close ties to Yaakov of Slonim, and his search for manuscripts of the Ga'on, might well have made him and his work known to the young Neẓiv (perhaps through Radal), prior to its publication in 1844. If Neẓiv did not, in fact, know about Landau's commentary or that of Rappaport, *Sifre* represents one of three major works of midrash halakhah that were in need of commentary, rather than the only remaining work.

159 See p. 34 above.

160 Ibid.

To Neẓiv, this rule helps explain a troubling talmudic passage which also involves the guilt offering. Lest he steer the reader away from *Sifre,* however, Neẓiv relegates the discussion of this passage to his *hagahot*. Radal and Neẓiv, therefore, employ a visual presentation quite familiar to the rabbinic reader—that of a main commentary dotted with notes referred to as *hagahot*. The content, though, differs from most prior presentations in that the *hagahot* reflect their own tangential thoughts rather than the later comments of a secondary author.

What Radal and Neẓiv call *hagahot* might well be seen as part of a much larger trend toward double and triple commentaries quite prevalent in early nineteenth-century Lithuanian Torah scholarship.[161] In general, the motivation behind writing multiple commentaries on a single text seems to stem from a sensitivity to multiple readerships, some of whom desire or are only capable of comprehending a straightforward explanation of the text, while others wish for an in-depth look at the legal, moral, or philosophical ramifications of the text as well as its parallels in other rabbinic works. Ḥanokh Zundel ben Yosef, whose voluminous writings are almost exclusively composed in this format, states his motivation clearly in the introduction to his 1833 commentary on *Midrash Tanḥuma*.

---

161 Two prime examples of this genre, Moshe Margolioth's Yerushalmi commentary *Pene Moshe* with its complementary *Mareh Penim* and David Frankel's Yerushalmi commentary *Korban ha-'Edah* with its complementary *Shire Korban*, date from the mid-eighteenth century. In Chapter Five below, we will argue that the flowering of this genre amongst early nineteenth-century Lithuanian Torah scholars was due to the concurrent flowering of the Hebrew print industry. It is important to note, then, that the Hebrew print industry in Western Europe was far more developed in the mid-eighteenth-century than was that of Eastern Europe. It is, therefore, not surprising to see that Western European Torah scholars such as Margolioth and Frankel developed this sensitivity to multiple readerships, as manifest in the creation of a simpler and more complex commentary on the same material. (Since Margolioth was originally from Lithuania, and began his work in Vilna, it is conceivable that he had already envisioned a dual commentary before coming to Western Europe, which would weaken the current hypothesis). It should also be noted that medieval examples of dual commentary, such as Solomon ibn Aderet's *Torat ha-Bayit,* belong to a different genre completely as the shorter commentary, in the case of ibn Aderet his *Torat ha-Bayit ha-Kaẓer*, is intended as an abridged version of the main commentary and generally does not contain material not found in the larger commentary. Due to the scarcity and relatively minimal circulation of intricate rabbinic texts in the pre-print period, it seems to me that the purpose of this genre was not to appeal to both advanced and less advanced audiences, as in the case of the nineteenth-century dual commentaries, but to serve as a quick reference guide to the small and elite readership of halakhic texts. On the other hand, Joshua ben Alexander HaCohen Falk's (1555-1614) *Derishah* and *Perishah* on the Tur may represent an early precedent for this type of dual commentary.

> The midrash in most places is like a sealed book, a concealed essay with no commentary, which needs explanation and commentary to which [task] most desist and [thus] steer their hands away from learning this midrash and [as a result,] it sits in a corner with no expounders and no seekers. For this [purpose] I gathered together for each of the sayings a nice—even a beautiful—commentary in concise language which I called *'Eẓ Yosef*. And it is a sufficient and overflowing[162] explanation [which seeks] to succinctly explain the words of the midrash, to enlighten and bring joy **to the hearts of the old and young**. Their eyes will gaze in it and together they will be happy for never before has there been an herb like this to [help] understand the nature and simple meaning of each phrase.
>
> The supplement called *'Anaf Yosef* is a crown which adorns it. Many novel insights are found there which will blossom into flowers and roses full of wisdom and perfect beauty to he who comes at length in order to demonstrate the base on which the splendor of the midrash's esteemed greatness is founded before the **sages of my nation and its wise men**, and in order to open its treasure chests and bolts and to expose its secrets before the [light of the] sun.[163]

Likewise, Yiẓḥak Eliyahu Landau writes in his introduction that in addition to the central text of his *Mekhilta'* commentary, entitled *Berurei ha-Middot,* he was including a secondary commentary entitled *Miẓuy ha-Middot* which contains a "synopsis of his explanation" intended "for all who look at them."[164] He similarly divides his commentary on *Masekhet Soferim* between *Mikra' Soferim* and *'Ittur Soferim*[165] and his commentary on *Derekh 'Ereẓ Zuta'* between *Derekh Ḥayyim* and *Orḥot Ḥayyim.*[166] This

---

162 From Josh. 3: 15.

163 Emphasis added. *Midrash Tanḥuma, "Hakdamat Meḥaber Peirusho 'Eẓ Yosef, 'Anaf Yosef"* (Vilna, 1833).

164 *Mekhilta'*, Author's Introduction, (Vilna, 1844), 2.

165 Suwalk, 1862.

166 Vilna, 1872.

type of double commentary is likewise employed by Ẓvi Hirsch ha-Kohen Rappaport in his *Ezrat Kohanim,* which is a simplified anthology of prior commentaries on *Sifra,* and his *Tosefet ha-'Azarah* in which he gives his own in-depth analysis of the *Sifra* text.[167] Yoel Dober ha-Kohen Perski similarly divides his commentary on Avraham Abele Gombiner's *Zayit Ra'anan* into two commentaries. *Heikhal Ra'anan* represents an anthology of prior commentaries selected due to the fact that they "appeared close to the primary intent of that passage's author according to its straightforward meaning."[168] In Perski's supplementary *Shemen Ra'anan* he "made holy emendations" and composed "wondrous things about which all whose palates taste them will praise him for the fruit of his labor."[169]

As noted above, in his *Sifre* commentary Neẓiv does not compose a full-fledged secondary commentary, but clearly intends to keep long tangential excurses out of the main text of his commentary and assigns them to the *hagahot* instead. While Avraham Yekutiel Lichtenstein's eighteenth-century *Sifre* commentary entitled *Zera' Avraham*[170] also contains an occasional authorial note under the name *hagahah,* these seem to represent thoughts which occurred to the author following the composition of the work's main text. Furthermore, there is no thematic distinction between the material found in his notes and that found in the main text. In *'Emek ha-Neẓiv,* however, the notes are clearly intended to address topics which Neẓiv felt were too far adrift from his central task, namely the explanation of the *Sifre* passage at hand.

### *Poetic Adornments*

Another facet of *'Emek ha-Neẓiv's* format which might be considered part of a larger trend of early nineteenth-century midrash commentary is its use of poetic adornments. Neẓiv begins the work with two couplets. One refers to the commencement of his commentary on *Sifre* and the other refers to the commencement of the section of his commentary treating *Parashat Naso.*[171] At the end of this *parashah,* there are again two couplets. One refers to the completion of *Naso,* and the other refers to the com-

167 Vilna, 1845.
168 *Yalkut Shim'oni, "Zevaḥ Todah,"* (Koenigsburg: 1857).
169 Ibid.
170 Dierenfurth, 1811. Neẓiv cites this text often in his own *Sifre* commentary.
171 *EH* Naso 1 (I: 1).

mencement of the section treating *Parashat Be-ha'alotekha*.[172] A similar pattern is maintained for every *parashah* in the first two volumes of the work.[173] At the end of the second volume there is a long poem consisting of two sections of nine rhyming lines. The first set of rhyming lines bears the acrostic NeẒIBeNYa'akov (Naftali Ẓvi Yehudah Berlin, son of Ya'akov). The second set bears the name of each of the *parashiyot* upon which he commented in the first two volumes.

While the use of basic poetry to introduce rabbinic commentaries dates well back into the Middle Ages, the consistent use of poetry to open and close sections of a commentary seems to have reemerged in the first half of the nineteenth century.[174] This format was particularly popular amongst the members of the circle of Lithuanian midrash and aggadah scholars that flourished in the second, third, and fourth decades of the nineteenth century. For example, Avraham Schick, in his 1834 commentary on *Tanna de-Bei Eliyahu*, begins the commentary with five couplets. A triplet appears at the end of the first section, *Eliyahu Rabba*, and a couplet marks the end of the second section, *Eliyahu Zuta*.[175] Yehudah Leib Edel, in his 1835 commentary on the aggadic portions of the Talmud Bavli, ends his comments on each tractate of the Talmud with a couplet, one line of which refers to the tractate just completed, and the other line of which refers to the tractate which will now begin.[176] Yiẓḥak Eliyahu Landau's 1844 commentary on *Mekhilta'* bears exactly the same format as Neẓiv's commentary on *Sifre*. That is, a double couplet is used to end every *parashah*, and the first set of lines marks the closing of the previous *parashah* and the second set of lines marks the opening of the new *parashah*.[177] In his work on the *aggadot* of the Talmud, Landau uses a double couplet to introduce the work as a whole[178] and a single couplet to introduce each tractate.[179] It is worth noting that such poetic flourishes were often the first parts of a work eliminated by a printer who, generally due to the cost of print, needed to shorten a commentary. As such,

172 *EH* Naso 58 (I: 190).

173 On the absence of such couplets in the third volume, see Chapter 1, p. 38.

174 E.g., Yosef Bekhor Shor's twelfth-century Pentateuch commentary is a notable example of rabbinic commentary bearing precisely this format long before the nineteenth century.

175 *Me'ore ha-Esh* (Grodno, 1834).

176 *Iyye ha-Yam* (Ostrog, 1835). E.g., 33b.

177 *Berurei ha-Middot* (Vilna, 1844). E.g., 18, 81.

178 *Lishmo'a be-Limudim* (Vilna, 1876), 5.

179 E.g., ibid., 51, 69.

poetic adornments may have been used more frequently than the printed texts which have come down to us would suggest. Nonetheless, such flourishes are nowhere to be found in the more traditional Talmud and *halakhah* scholarship of the very same time and place.[180] Thus, Neẓiv's usage of couplets throughout *'Emek ha-Neẓiv* ought to be seen as an additional, stylistic, indicator of the influence of early nineteenth-century midrash scholarship on Neẓiv's *Sifre* commentary.

In summary, then, the world from which Neẓiv's *'Emek ha-Neẓiv* emerges was one in which midrash commentary, notable for its plain-sense approach, its emphasis on textual emendation, and the intellectual breadth of its authors, enjoyed a prominent place in the endeavors of the scholarly elite. Less obvious, but equally important for the purposes of the present study, is the fact that many of these works also share a distinct interest in identifying and explicating the methods and methodologies of the rabbinic Sages. It is this trend, and its particular manifestation in Neẓiv's *Sifre* commentary, to which we turn our attention in the coming chapter.

---

180 For example, see the following traditional commentaries which represent the intellectual product of some of early nineteenth-century Lithuania's most respected Talmudic and halakhic authorities: David ben Moshe of Novogroduk, *Galya Masekhet* (Vilna, 1844) on Talmud and *halakhah*; Avraham Maskilieson, *Be'er Avraham* (Vilna, 1844) on Talmud (contains a single line of introductory verse, 5) and his *Naḥal Eitan* (Vilna, 1855) on Rambam's *Mishnah Torah*; Isaac of Karlin, *Keren Orah* (Vilna, 1851); Ya'akov Meir Padua, *Mekor Mayyim Ḥayyim* (Sudlikov, 1836) on *Shulḥan Arukh*, and his *Ketonet Pasim* (Koenigsburg, 1840) on the medieval Talmud commentary *Nemukei Yosef*; Ya'akov of Karlin, *Mishkenot Ya'akov* (Vilna, 1837) on Shulḥan Arukh and his *Kehilat Ya'akov* (Vilna, 1847) on Talmud; David Tevil, *Bet David* (Warsaw, 1854) on *halakhah* and his *Naḥalat David* (Vilna, 1864) on Talmud.

# CHAPTER FOUR:
## The Young Neẓiv and the Ancient Rabbis

Beyond the penchant for *peshat*, the tendency for textual emendation, and the broad range of source material described in the previous chapter, the text of *'Emek ha-Neẓiv* is dominated by the young Neẓiv's quest to define the inner-workings of rabbinic literature: its methods, its manner, and its relationship to the written Torah. As we shall see below, this element of Neẓiv's commentary on *Sifre* also bears the mark of the intellectual milieu of early nineteenth-century Lithuanian Torah scholarship. Here, however, the young Neẓiv seems to extend his work beyond that of his contemporaries.

### *Rabbinic Methodology*

Since any given work of midrash is considered by rabbinic commentators to be but one of numerous collections of tanaitic and amoraic teachings, much of rabbinic midrash study is devoted to the project of comparing and contrasting seemingly related statements in different works. Indeed, the act of comparing and contrasting disparate texts is germane to traditional Talmud commentary as well, in that the Talmud itself contain repetitions, reformulations, and reconstructions of similar statements which many a commentator has tried to sift through and sort out. From the period of the Tosafists onward, however, the approach most often adopted by rabbinic commentators was to try to harmonize the seemingly discordant texts. They might expand, restrict, or redefine one or all of the problematic texts so as to mitigate the tensions between them. This approach, for the most part, focuses on the content of each passage with little or no attention paid to its literary and historical context. That is, it begins with an assumption that all Torah texts, if properly understood, should fit neatly with one another regardless of when, where, and by whom the text was committed to writing. The job of the commentator, then, is to use his knowledge and his accumen to arrive at that proper understanding. When he fails to do so, and the tensions between texts remain unresolved, he ends his futile attempt with the statement of resignation *"ẓarikh iyyun,"* suggesting that an answer exists, but that more knowledge, more creativity, or more imagination are needed to arrive at it. Such was the general approach adopted by Jacob Meir Tam (1100-1171) and his school of Tosafists, as well as by Nahmanides (1194-1270) and his school of Spanish exegetes.[1] Later Talmud commentators such as Solomon Luria (1510-1573), Joshua Falk (1555-1614), Samuel Edels (1555-1661), and even the Vilna Ga'on (1720-1797) adopted a similar hermeneutic toward rabbinic texts, and so the trend continued right up to the nineteenth century.[2] In fact, this very same hermeneutic was central to the work of Ḥayyim Soloveitchik of Brisk and his students when, late in the nineteenth century, they began to offer brilliant conceptual analyses which explain away discrepancies in Maimonidean or talmudic texts.[3]

Neẓiv's approach to rabbinic texts, however, is different. Throughout his commentary, Neẓiv takes every opportunity to point out to his reader that a halakhic position, a literary format, an idiomatic phrase, or an exegetical device employed by a rabbinic text is typical of the given text or of the given text's author. Thus, Neẓiv often attributes the differences between seemingly similar tana'itic statements in different collections of tana'itic material to the methodology employed by the different editors.[4] For example, when faced with a statement of *Sifre* which seems to contradict a talmudic statement, instead of offering a clever reconciliation Neẓiv rather states simply, "I have already written many times that we find

1 While the Tosafists often note different *"girsa'ot,"* they generally do so in the hopes of establishing the reading which will best harmonize the seeming difficulties presented by the passage at hand, not as a means of validating multiple voices and multiple historical contexts within the rabbinic tradition. We should note, however, that they, along with a number of Spanish commentators, do acknowledge a select group of *sugeyot ḥalukot* for which no harmonization is possible. On Tosafot see Ephraim Elimelekh Urbach, *Ba'ale ha-Tosafot* (Jerusalem: Mosad Bialik, 1986) and Avraham Lifshitz, *Shiṭat ha-Limud (ha-Di'alekṭiḳah) shel Ba'ale ha-Tosafot* (PhD; Hebrew University, 2008). See also Israel Ta-Shema, *Creativity and Tradition: Studies in Medieval Rabbinic Scholarship, Literature and Thought* (Cambridge, MA: Harvard University Press, 2006).

2 The Vilna Ga'on was also a harmonizer in this sense. Instead of redefining one of the two seemingly contradictory passages, however, he would often emend one of the texts so as to eliminate the tension between them. See Jay M. Harris, *How Do We Know This?* (Albany: SUNY Press, 1995), Chapter 8, n. 74.

3 On the Brisker method see Norman Solomon, *The Analytic Movement: Ḥayyim Soloveitchik and His Circle* (Atlanta: Scholars Press, 1993); Yosef Blau, ed., *Lomdus: The Conceptual Approach to Jewish Learning* (Jersey City: Ktav Publishing House, 2006); Saiman, "Legal Theology: The Turn to Conceptualism in Nineteenth-Century Jewish Law," in *The Journal of Law and Religion,* 21 (2005-2006): 39-100; Norman Solomon, *The Analytic Movement: Hayyim Soloveitchik and His Circle* (Atlanta; Scholars Press, 1993).

4 E.g., *EH* Naso 3 (I: 20), *EH* Naso 4 (I: 24).

talmudic *sugyot* which oppose *Sifre*."[5] Similarly, he notes that the editors of *Sifre* opted for a more terse style of composition than did the editors of Mishnah which explains the occasional absence of particular words in a *Sifre* text that parallels a text in Mishnah.[6] Likewise, when Neẓiv notes that *Sifre* derives a ruling via a midrashic exegetical device when seemingly it could have been learned from an explicit verse, Neẓiv's instinct is not to offer an explanation for why the explicit verse cannot serve such a purpose, as one would expect from traditional rabbinic commentary. Instead, he writes that it was the exegetical preference of the Tanaim to derive laws from *derashot* rather than from explicit verses.[7] When *Sifre* contains a *derashah* which is also found in the Talmud, but the talmudic text follows the *derashah* with a question not found in *Sifre,* Neẓiv offers no apologetics for the difference. Rather he reminds the reader that "I have already written that according to the method of *Sifre* such [i.e., the difficulty raised in the Talmud] is not a [valid] question."[8]

Neẓiv also explains that the repetition of a particular passage multiple times within a single midrashic collection results from the editorial style of that work. Therefore, the fact that a *derashah* which was mentioned tangentially as part of a larger discussion in one place in *Sifre,* can then be stated again when *Sifre,* according to the chronology of the Torah text, reaches the verse in Numbers or Deuteronomy which the particular *derashah* expounds, reflects nothing more than the method adopted by *Sifre*'s editors.[9] Similarly, when a midrashic passage ends with an ethical statement[10] or includes a statement of *halakhah* unrelated to the verse being expounded,[11] Neẓiv notes that this too is the style of midrashic

5 *EH* Teẓeh 17 (III: 256).

6 *EH* Naso 31 (I: 134).

7 *EH* Naso 1 (I: 9).

8 *EH* Re'eh 20 (III: 109).

9 E.g., *EH* Naso 2 (I: 13); *EH* Naso 37 (I: 147). Neẓiv offers no indication that he understood *Sifre* on Numbers and *Sifre* on Deuteronomy as two distinct works, as modern scholarship has since ascertained. For an overview of the current understanding see D.Z. Hoffmann's *Zur Enleitung in die halachischen Midraschim* (Berlin: M. Driesner,. 1886–87), translated as "Le-ḥeker Midrashei ha-Tana'im" in A.Z. Rabinowitz, ed., *Mesilot le-Torat ha-Tanaim* (Tel Aviv, 1928); Saul Horovitz's introduction to his *Siphre D'be Rab* (Leipzig, 1917; repr. Jerusalem, 1966) as well as J.N. Epstein, *Introduction to Tannaitic Literature: Mishna, Tosephta and Halakhic Midrashim* (Hebrew), E.Z. Melamed ed. (Jerusalem: Magnes Press, 1957), 588-624

10 E.g., *EH* Naso 42 (I: 170).

11 E.g., *EH* Naso 17 (I: 71); *EH* Teẓeh 22 (III: 267).

literature. When the language of a midrash seems verbose[12] while the language of Rambam seems taciturn,[13] or when Rashi paraphrases *Sifre* rather than citing it directly,[14] Neẓiv notes that such reflects nothing more than their respective methods in commentarial composition.

Neẓiv adopts a similar approach toward resolving apparent contradictions in the work of Rambam as well. For example, when faced with an apparent contradiction between a statement of Rambam in his *Commentary on the Mishnah* and a statement by that same author in his *Mishneh Torah*, rather than suggest that the two statements are referring to different cases, or that each one is manifesting a different aspect of a single harmonious concept, Neẓiv states with the utmost simplicity that when Rambam authored his *Mishneh Torah* during his mature adult years, he thought better of some of what he had written in his Mishnah commentary, which he had composed in his youth.[15] Elsewhere he notes that when Rambam refers to a law considered by most to be of scriptural origin as "*de-rabbanan*," he does not mean to suggest that it is actually of rabbinic origin but that "it is the method of our Rabbi"[16] to refer to laws which are not explicit in the Torah as "*de-rabbanan*," though they are expounded by the rabbis from the words of the Torah and therefore have the status of "*de-'orayyta*."[17]

The elucidation of rabbinic methodology was not as widespread a phenomenon amongst early nineteenth-century midrash commentators as was the penchant for straightforward commentary, text emendation, and intellectual breadth.[18] Nonetheless, Neẓiv was not alone in

12 E.g., *EH* Shelaḥ 1 (II: 9); *EH* Shelaḥ 9 (II: 76); *EH* Ḥukat 4 (II: 171); *EH* Pinḥas 13 (II: 253); *EH* Pinḥas 14 (II: 257).

13 *EH* Shelaḥ 8 (II: 60).

14 *EH* Be-ha'alotekha 31(I: 282).

15 *EH* Naso 31 (I: 132); *EH* Naso 35 (I: 142); *EH* Naso 46 (I: 179); *EH* Ḥukat 2 (II: 158). For a critical look at this phenomenon, see Isadore Twersky, *Introduction to the Code of Maimonides* (New Haven: Yale University Press, 1980), 313-317, as well as Binyamin Ze'ev Benediḳṭ, *ha-Rambam le-lo Seṭiyah min ha-Talmud* (Jerusalem: Mosad Ha-Rav Kook, 1985), 20-24; 37.

16 "Rabbi" here refers to Rambam.

17 *EH* Naso 5 (I: 29). See Neẓiv's application of this principle in *HD* Lev. 33: 39. For Maimonides' distinction between laws which are considered of biblical origin and laws which are considered of rabbinic origin, see Harris, Chapter 4.

18 Although Avraham Schick notes in his introduction to his commentary on *Tanna de-Bei Eliyahu* (Sudlikov, 1834) that he has already begun composing a work called *Tahalukhot ha-Midrash*, "which is a general introduction to all of Midrash (2)," to the best of my knowledge, this work was never published. It is worth noting, however, that Barukh Goitein's (1770-1842) *Kesef Nivḥar* (Jerusalem, 1997), while a product of Hungary, was quite popular in Lithuania. Nonetheless, it does not seem to have been used by the young Neẓiv,

this endeavor. Avraham Schick, a friend of Radal who was assisted by Shmuel Strashun and Ze'ev Wolf Einhorn in composing his midrash commentaries,[19] prefaces his work on *Midrash Rabbah*, entitled *'Eshed Neḥalim*, with an introduction called "Tahalukhot ha-Midrash" whose purpose is to "explain the ways of the *midrashot* and *aggadot* [and] the techniques they employ, so as to assist all who delve into them in finding a simple and succinct path built on foundations of truth based on the ways of Torah and wisdom together."[20]

The interests of Neẓiv in this regard are also quite similar to the interest in the thirty-two hermeneutical rules of aggadic interpretation manifest in the work of Ẓvi Hirsch Katzenellenbogen and Ze'ev Wolf Einhorn. They, like Neẓiv, took a macrocosmic view of rabbinic literature and sought to understand individual midrashic passages through reference to underlying hermeneutic methods rather than through localized, microcosmic interpretation. Likewise, we might suggest that the propensity for comments of a methodological nature found throughout the Talmud commentary of David Tevele (1792 - 1861), a renowned Lithuanian rabbinic authority and a man closely tied to the world of the young Neẓiv, also reflects the same scholarly trend.[21]

### *Identification of* 'Asmakhta'

The single element of rabbinic methodology most often noted by Neẓiv in his commentary on *Sifre* is that, despite the seeming cohesiveness of *Sifre* 's project of rabbinic Scriptural exegesis, the nature of the rabbinic endeavor in *Sifre*—and in all other collections of midrashic texts, for that matter—differs from passage to passage. That is, most passages in *Sifre*, according to Neẓiv, reflect a creative process of rabbinic exposition whereby laws are derived through the act of interpreting biblical verses. There are select passages, however, which appear identical in both form and content to those in which laws are derived via creative interpretation, yet according to Neẓiv are quite different. In these passages the law which seems to have been derived from the verse actually pre-existed

---

as I found no references to it in his *Sifre* commentary.

19 Avraham Schick, "Tahalukhot ha-Midrash," *Midrash Rabbah* (Vilna, 1843), 72.

20 Ibid., 6.

21 See his *Naḥalat David*, first printed in Vilna, 1864. Neẓiv recounts having learned from David Tevele in person in *HS* 167: 17.

the exegesis, and the exposition found in *Sifre*, or elsewhere, is merely a means for the Sages to show that the Bible contains a non-normative hint to this law as well. Thus, time and again throughout his commentary, Neẓiv notes that a particular *derashah* is mere *'asmakhta'* or scriptural support for a pre-existing law.[22]

The precise nature of the term *'asmakhta'* in its original talmudic context and the variations thereof offered by later Talmud commentators has been treated at length by Jay Harris.[23] Specifically, he notes that in the Talmud *'asmakhta'* is generally used to denote a law of *de-rabbanan* status for which the Sages wished either to note a Scriptural hint or to create a mnemonic device by linking it, via rabbinic exegesis, to a particular verse.[24] Harris then tracks a startling shift in the term's usage through the work of Sa'adya Gaon, Ibn Ezra, and Rambam, wherein the term *'asmakhta'* also comes to denote laws of *de-'orayyta* status whose origin lies in tradition rather than in Scriptural exegesis.[25] Ramban, Harris notes, opposes this trend and limits the term *'asmakhta'* to a connotation of *de-rabbanan* status.[26] Harris' work then proceeds to describe the way in which these competing conceptions of the creative or non-creative nature of rabbinic exegesis become a centerpiece in the polemics and apologetics of the burgeoning denominations of modern Judaism in the nineteenth century.

Two points regarding Neẓiv's use of *'asmakhta'* in *'Emek ha-Neẓiv* are instructive in this regard. First of all, Neẓiv does not exclusively side with Rambam or Ramban on the status of laws whose exegesis is described as *'asmakhta'*. For Neẓiv, *'asmakhta'* merely indicates that the exegetical process in such a case is not the normative source of the law to which it is attached. In fact, the origin of the law may lie in the Sinaitic

22 E.g., *EH* Naso 2 (I: 16); *EH* Naso 39 (I: 153); *EH* Naso 16 (I: 69); *EH* Naso 23 (I: 92); *EH* Naso 49 (I: 182), *EH* Be-ha'alotekha 5 (I: 201); *EH* Be-ha'alotekha 19 (I: 241); *EH* Shelaḥ 9 (II: 71); *EH* Koraḥ 1 (II: 86); *EH* Koraḥ 6 (II: 129); *EH* Ḥukat 1 (II: 148); *EH* Ḥukat 2 (II: 153); *EH* Ḥukat 4 (III: 172); *EH* Ḥukat 5 (III: 190); *EH* Ma'asei 2 (II: 325); *EH* ve-'Etḥanan 9 (III: 28); *EH* ve-'Etḥanan 10 (III: 29); *EH* 'Ekev 7(III: 69); *EH* Re'eh 9 (III: 92); *EH* Re'eh 19 (III: 105); *EH* Re'eh 52 (III: 138,139); *EH* Re'eh 60 (III: 149); *EH* Re'eh 65 (III: 154); *EH* Re'eh 73 (III: 160); *EH* Re'eh 87 (III: 170); *EH* Shoftim 2 (III: 175); *EH* Shoftim 45 (III: 209); *EH* Teẓeh 22 (III: 265); *EH* Teẓeh 24 (III: 271).

23 See Harris, *How Do We Know This?*. See also David Weiss Halivni's *Peshat and Derash: Plain and Applied Meaning in Rabbinic Exegesis* (New York: Oxford University Press, 1991).

24 Ibid., 48.

25 Ibid., 78-90.

26 Ibid., 91.

tradition, thereby giving it the status of *de-'orayyta*, in an enactment of the Sages, or in accepted common law, which would grant it the status of *de-rabbanan*.

Thus, on one occasion Neẓiv rules that a particular law is "like *Rambam* who writes that it is *'asmakhta'* and *halakhah le-Moshe me-sinai*."[27] Similarly, in the midst of another discussion, he writes that according to Rashi, who maintains that the particular *halakhah* under discussion is *halakhah le-moshe me-sinai*, the passage in *Sifre* must be *'asmakhta'*.[28] That is, *'asmakhta'* in these cases is used by Neẓiv to indicate a non-generative *derashah* which restates a law known through the Sinaitic tradition, and hence deserving the status of *de-'orayyta*.

On the other hand, in an interesting passage discussing the service of the Levites in the Tabernacle, Neẓiv employs the term *'asmakhta'* in a very different manner. He writes that according to Ramban a practice developed amongst the Levites to begin learning the Tabernacle service at age twenty-five, five years prior to the age at which the Torah instructs them to begin actual service. As such, the *derashah* in *Sifre* which suggests that this training period can be derived from a verse is merely "*divrei 'asmakhta'*."[29] Here, then, *'asmakhta'* refers to a practice whose origin is in common law and whose status would therefore be *de-rabbanan*.[30] Elsewhere, a passage in *Sifre* derives from a verse the idea that a single witness's testimony that a married man has died is sufficient to allow the widow of the deceased to remarry. Neẓiv notes, however, that the Talmud (*Yevamot* 87b) contains a lengthy discussion of this matter, and concludes that this allowance derives from a rabbinic relaxation of the laws of testimony out of compassion for women who might otherwise become *'agunot*,[31] and not from exegesis of any verse. Neẓiv concludes, therefore, that either the Sages contributing to

---

27 *EH* Re'eh 19 (III: 105).

28 *EH* Ḥukat 4 (III: 172).

29 *EH* Be-ha'alotekha 5 (I: 201).

30 Members of the *wissenschaft* school of nineteenth-century Germany, such as Zechariah Frankel, will in fact argue that *halakhah le-moshe mi-sinai* refers to practices begun in antiquity which had since become common law. While Neẓiv makes a comment in the beginning of his introduction to *Ha'amek She'elah* which contains interesting, although far less radical, similarities to this approach, he certainly did believe that ideas explicitly referred to as *halakhah le-moshe mi-sinai* had their origin at Sinai. Hence, in the two examples above, he is using the term *'asmakhta'* to refer to two different types of laws.

31 "Bound women," or women who can never remarry due to the absence of a proper writ of divorce or sufficient testimony as to the death of their prior husband.

the talmudic debate were unaware of the *derashah* in *Sifre,* or that the *derashah* is *'asmakhta'.*[32] In other words, the second possibility which Neẓiv entertains is that the Sages of the Talmud did, in fact, know of *Sifre*'s *derashah,* but understood it as a playful hint at a rabbinic enactment, not as generative exegesis and not as a mnemonic device for a law given orally to Moses. On other occasions Neẓiv states outright *"de-kol derashot 'eilu 'asmakhtot ninhu ve-'einan 'ela' de-rabanan"* meaning "all these *derashot* are *'asmakhtot* and are nothing more than *de-rabbanan."*[33]

The second point which needs to be made in the context of Harris' discussion is that nowhere in *'Emek ha-Neẓiv* is there any indication that Neẓiv's project of identifying *derashot* as *'asmakhta',* or his insistence that a *derashah* labeled by others as *'asmakhta'* is not to be considered so,[34] is an attempt to advance a polemical agenda. Harris writes in his treatment of Neẓiv's Torah commentary, *Ha'amek Davar,* that

> Like his colleagues in the German lands, he knew full well that the foundations of the traditional world he inhabited were being shaken. He knew that there were those—whom he dismissed as heretics—who insisted that the Bible be appropriated without the mediation of rabbinic tradition. Like the Germans, he too responded

32 *EH* Shoftim 45 (III: 209). The two possibilities offered by Neẓiv in this passage to resolve the tension between *Sifre* and Talmud Bavli, namely that the *amoraim* of the Talmud were not acquainted with this berayta or that they knew of it but understood it as mere *'asmakhta',* seems to portray Neẓiv as belonging to the school of rabbinic harmonizers mentioned above, rather than as one who allows multiple voices to arise from multiple texts. After all, the simplest solution to his seeming conundrum is to suggest that *Sifre* understood the source of the law—and hence the law's legal status—differently than Talmud Bavli. The truth, however, is that the next line of his commentary testifies to the fact that Neẓiv did indeed believe in the legitimacy of such an approach. There he notes that the passage in *Sifre* actually works well if one adopts the position of Ritba, who argues that the legality of testimony from a single witness, in certain cases, has the status of *de-orayyta.* This passage in *Sifre,* then, becomes the source from which such a ruling is derived. In other words, the position of Ritba, which Neẓiv sees as rooted in *Sifre* and in opposition to the ruling of Talmud Bavli, is viewed by Neẓiv as completely legitimate. In fact, in the bracketed comment which follows Neẓiv writes that maintaining a scriptural basis for the legality of a single witness helps to explain a difficult passage in Yerushalmi *Shavuot,* which may suggest that Neẓiv believes the position which he has ascribed to Ritba is preferable to either of his earlier two solutions.

33 *EH* Be-ha'alotekha 19 (I: 241). See similarly in *EH* Naso 49 (I: 182); *EH* Shelaḥ 9 (II: 71); *EH* Teẓeh 24 (III: 271).

34 E.g., *EH* Naso 23 (I: 92) and *EH* Shelaḥ 4 (II: 31).

> by seeking to expand the range of traditionally transmitted law.[35]

Harris is quite accurate in ascribing an apologetic and reactive posture to Neẓiv's treatment of rabbinic exegesis in his Torah commentary.[36] However, there is no hint of such a stance in his commentary on *Sifre.* As we shall explore in the coming chapters, the contrast between the two works on this very point provides an invaluable window into the societal shift which the Lithuanian Jewish community undergoes in the second half of the nineteenth century and the impact it has on the work of Neẓiv.

### *De' Rossian Hermeneutics*

We cannot know whether the young Neẓiv's interest in rabbinic methodology led him to Azariah de' Rossi's *Sefer Me'or 'Einayim* or whether his exposure to de' Rossi helped foster his sensitivity to the methods and modes of the rabbis described above. What is clear, however, is that few books encountered and engaged by the young Neẓiv made as indelible an impact on his work as that of Azariah de' Rossi. From a cultural vantage point, Neẓiv's unabashed use of *Sefer Me'or 'Einayim,* which had been accorded contraband status by some of the leading rabbinic figures in generations prior to Neẓiv and by many traditionalist leaders in the generations that followed, attests to the intellectual openness of traditional Jewish scholarship in the first half of the nineteenth century. From an intellectual standpoint, Neẓiv's engagement with de' Rossi offers great insight into his development as a student of rabbinic literature.

Azariah de' Rossi, a sixteenth-century Italian Jewish scholar, first

35 Harris, 243.

36 Based on the presence of a few citations from *Ha'amek Davar* in Neẓiv's 1861 *She'iltot* commentary, Harris writes that Neẓiv's Torah commentary was completed prior to the 1860s, thus placing its composition at a time when the vocal advocates of Eastern European *Haskalah* "were just beginning to express some of the radical challenges to rabbinic tradition that had become common in the West (243)." In Chapter Six, however, I will argue that those select citations are actually later additions to the *She'iltot* commentary and, in contrast to *'Emek ha-Neẓiv,* much of *Ha'amek Davar* was in fact composed after his commentary on *She'iltot* during the 1860s, and precisely as the voice of the *Haskalah* reached full strength. This, in turn, explains the marked presence of apologetics in Neẓiv's Torah commentary, and its absence from his earlier *Sifre* commentary.

published his *Sefer Me'or 'Einayim* in Mantua in 1573.[37] The book is an amalgam of three separate works written by de' Rossi, entitled *Haderat Zekeinim, Kol Elohim,* and *'Imrei Binah.* The first consists of a Hebrew translation of the pseudepigraphic Letter of Aristeas, which recounts the rabbinic tale of the Septuagint's creation. The second section contains de' Rossi's exposition of the theological implications of the major earthquake which struck Ferrara in 1571. The final section, comprising the vast majority of the book, treats a variety of subjects pertaining to the chronology and intellectual history of Judaism during the Second Temple and early rabbinic periods.

Time and again throughout the fourth part of this third section of his *Sefer Me'or 'Einayim* de' Rossi advocates a hermeneutical stance toward rabbinic literature that circumscribes the canonical status of their teachings to the limited sphere of legal rulings. As a result, he allows for the possibility that the aggadic statements of the rabbis, most of which de' Rossi believes to contain pearls of valuable wisdom, might at times be reduced to hyperbolic statements invented for their pedagogic value, or sincere claims regarding the natural world which contemporary science has subsequently proven false.

De' Rossi's stance toward rabbinic aggadah is not without precedent. From the time of the Karaites of the Geonic period to the era of the Muslim and Christian polemicists of medieval Europe, aggadic literature surfaced time and again as the object of scorn and ridicule from the critics of rabbinic Judaism.[38] While a number of geonic authors such as Hai Ga'on, Sherira Ga'on, and Shmuel ben Ḥofni, not to mention Rambam and Ramban, seem to have expressed positions rather similar to that of de' Rossi in that they were at times willing to simply disregard those aggadic statements which seemed to contradict reason and common knowledge, and while such a position is echoed on occasion in the Jewish-Christian disputations of the thirteenth century, it is certainly not the method of

37 For biographical information on Azariah de' Rossi, see Salo Baron, "Azariah de' Rossi: A Biographical Sketch," *History and Jewish Historians*, eds. Arthur Hertzberg and Leon Feldman (Philadelphia: JPS, 1964), 167-173; Lester Siegel, *Historical Consciousness and Religious Tradition in Azariah de' Rossi's Me'or 'Einayim* (Philadelphia: JPS, 1989), introduction; *Kitvei Azariah min ha'Adomim*, ed. Robert Bonfil (Jerusalem: The Bialik Institute, 1991), Introduction; Azariah de' Rossi, *The Light of the Eyes*, ed. and trans. Joanna Weinberg (New Haven: Yale University Press, 2001), Introduction.

38 For an overview, see Marc Saperstein, *Decoding the Rabbis: A Thirteenth-Century Commentary on the Aggadah* (London: Harvard University Press, 1980), Chapter 1.

choice for medieval commentators in dealing with the difficulties presented by the literature of aggadah. Rather than rejecting statements of the Sages, the medieval Jewish exegete was far more inclined to reinterpret them through recourse to allegory or mysticism.

De' Rossi's return to a geonic hermeneutic toward rabbinic aggadah, then, raised the brow of many amongst the rabbinic establishment of the sixteenth century. The fact that he sought to prove the necessity of his approach by demonstrating that certain rabbinic aggadic statements, including the rabbinic account of the chronology of the Second Temple period, are clearly contradicted by third party sources, further aroused suspicion regarding his work. In the eyes of his rabbinic detractors, the fact that prominent amongst the third party sources in which de' Rossi looks for contradictions of aggadic statements are Justin Martyr, Origen, Jerome, Augustine, and Thomas Aquinas, engendered further distrust of *Sefer Me'or 'Einayim*.

In the introduction to her English translation of de' Rossi's work, Joanna Weinberg notes that Ḥayyim David Azulai (1724-1807) in his *Maḥazik Berakhah* on Yosef Caro's *Shulḥan Arukh* (OH 307:16), cites a 1574 letter from Moshe Alshekh and Elishah Gallico, students of Caro, stating that *Me'or 'Einayim* deserved to be burned.[39] In his *Be'er ha-Golah* Yehudah Loew ben Beẓalel, a contemporary of de' Rossi better known as the Maharal of Prague, spends pages upon pages delineating and decrying the heresies of *Me'or 'Einayim*.[40] The basic theme underlying his opposition is that statements of the rabbis which de' Rossi dismisses as rhetorical flourishes, hyperbole, or ignorance Maharal treats as allegory, in which secrets and mysteries of the world are to be found. Thus, for Maharal, the irreverence for such texts displayed by de' Rossi is tantamount to heresy of the highest order.[41]

39 Weinberg, xxi. See Ḥayyim David Azulai, *Maḥazik Berakhah* (Livorno, 1785), 133. A copy of this letter can be found in the rare book collection of the Yeshiva University Library, MS 1148.

40 Yehudah Loew ben Bezalel, *Sefer Be'er ha-Golah* (New York: Judaica Press, 1969), 126-141. See also M. Benayahu "The Polemic Regarding the *Me'or 'Einayim* of Azariah de' Rossi," *Asufot* 5 (Jerusalem: 1991), 213-265.

41 See Weinberg, 395, for de' Rossi's own acknowledgement of rabbinic opposition to his work amongst his peers. It is interesting to note that contemporary ultra-Orthodox society continues to view de' Rossi's work through the lens of Maharal, and cites it as precedent for the banning of contemporary works that display a similarly irreverent attitude toward the non-halakhic portions of rabbinic literature. The following is an excerpt from an open letter written in the winter of 2004 by Rabbi Moshe Shapira, an

As a result of this seemingly hostile reception within the ranks of traditional rabbinic scholarship, Weinberg, following Baron's lead,[42] suggests that de' Rossi's imprint can only be found amongst eighteenth-century Western European maskilic figures such as Mendelssohn and Wessely, or nineteenth-century scholars such as Zunz and Geiger.[43]

In his important introduction to selections from de' Rossi's work, Robert Bonfil has argued that the traditional historiographic account, as later reflected in Weinberg's work, which refers to an uncompromising opposition to de' Rossi by a seemingly unified rabbinic establishment, might have been significantly overstated by the maskilic historians of the nineteenth century. Bonfil makes his argument by placing de' Rossi's work in its Italian context and demonstrating both that *Me'or Eynayim*, which Bonfil understands as an apologetic defense of traditional Judaism, was not a radical departure from the scholarship of his time and place, and that the immediate contemporary rabbinic opposition was rather weak. It wasn't until a generation later that the strong opposition grew, and even then it was particularly scholars such as Alshekh and Maharal, who advocated a mystical reading of aggadah, who were most adamant in denouncing de' Rossi's hermeneutical stance as heretical.[44]

---

ultra-Orthodox halakhic authority in Jerusalem:

> They read before me a few paragraphs in literal translation from [Nosson] Slifkin's book and the words agitate the entire heart of one who trembles [before] the word of God [with] words of utter apostasy to the truth of the Torah, and a denial of its preachers...And these books are the books of heretics, and it is like that which was written by our rabbi Maharal about the book *Me'or 'Einayim* which came out in his generation, look at his words in the sixth *be'er* in the book *Be'er ha-Golah*, [And the books of the aforementioned are similar in their apostasy to *Sefer Me'or 'Einayim*] "Cursed shall be the day that these words were revealed and appeared. How did a man who does not know how to understand the words of the Sages, even one of their most minor points, etc., not fear to speak about the Sages and to speak of them as if they were people of his own generation and his friends etc. And moreover, since he has put forth his words etc, they are worthy of being burned like the books of heretics. And these are worse than those for he put them in print as if they were [to be considered] amongst the holy books." And look there at the many words which emerge from a seething heart and are said with the fire of holiness until he concludes, "And He, the blessed, should save the descendents of the remnant of Israel, so that there should not be found amongst us another breach which gives honor and glory to that which is foreign."

42 See Baron, 172-173.

43 See Weinberg, xxii.

44 See Azariah de' Rossi, *Kitvei Azariah min ha'Adomim*, ed. Robert Bonfil (Jerusalem: The

While Bonfil's suggestion that one cannot speak of a unified rabbinic establishment that opposed de' Rossi's work is borne out through his examination of exactly who did and did not ban *Me'or 'Einayim*, a more compelling argument might be made through an examination of those well within the world of the traditional rabbinate who made unapologetic use of *Me'or 'Einayim* in their own studies.

In a telling off-handed comment in the introduction to his *Bet Yehudah*, Isaac Baer Levinsohn (1788-1860), one of the pioneers of the Russian Haskalah, offers insight into the place of de' Rossi in the standard Lithuanian Jewish library. Levinsohn's *Bet Yehudah* was completed in 1829, although it was only published in 1838, and he begins by apologizing to his readers for the limited citations found in his work. He explains that this results from his current residence in Kremenitz, whose selection of communally and privately owned Jewish texts is severely limited. In listing the books not found in Kremenitz, Levinsohn writes:

> *'Arukh* with the *Musaf,*[45] Rambam's *Book of Miẓvot*, Jerusalem Talmud, *Aggadot Yerushalmi* with the *Yefeih Mar'eh,*[46] *BeHaG,*[47] *Pesikta'*, *Torat Kohanim*, *Sifre*, R' Azariah's *Me'or 'Einayim*, *Sefer ha-Ḥinukh,*[48] and the *SeMaG,*[49] and many others like them (which are, at times, found even in the small villages)[50]

Not only does Levinsohn include de' Rossi's work in a list of traditional classics of the Jewish library, which includes Rambam, the Talmud Yerushalmi, and *Sefer ha-Ḥinukh*, but he suggests that even in the small villages of Lithuania in the 1820s one might expect to find a copy of this text.

It is not surprising then that we find de' Rossi's work cited by leading figures of the traditional community without the least hesitation. For example, Yehudah Leib Edel, the *maggid* of Slonim, mentions in his *Afike Yehudah* that there is debate as to whether the Ptolemy referred to in the

---

Bialik Institute, 1991), 96-129.

45 Nathan ben Yehiel of Rome's twelfth-century *Sefer 'Arukh* with Benjamin ben Immanuel Mussafina's seventeenth-century *Musaf ha-'Arukh.*

46 Samuel Isaac ben Yaffe's sixteenth-century *Yafeh Mar'eh* on the *aggadot* of the Yerushalmi.

47 Shimon Kayara's ninth-century *Halakhot Gedolot.*

48 The anonymous fourteenth-century exposition of the *miẓvot.*

49 Moshe ben Ya'akov of Coucy's thirteenth-century *Sefer Miẓvot Gadol.*

50 Isaac Baer Levinsohn, *Bet Yehudah* (Vilna, 1839), xxiii.

Talmud is Claudius Ptolemaeus, the Alexandrian mathematician and astronomer who lived during the second century of the common era, or a member of the Macedonian House of Ptolemy which ruled Egypt in the third, second, and first centuries prior to the common era. For an elaboration on the latter opinion, Edel bids his reader to "look in the introduction to *Sefer Me'or 'Einayim*."[51] Similarly, Edward Breuer has pointed out that de' Rossi is often cited by Yeḥezekel Feivel, the *maggid* of Vilna, as well.[52] Likewise, Ya'akov of Slonim, in compiling a timeline of the Israelite kings at the end of the Ga'on's work on Chronicles, notes that he has used the work of de' Rossi, who gathered his information from an extensive range of authors both "circumcised and uncircumcised."[53]

By 1869, however, there is reason to believe that Lithuanian rabbinic society had grown far colder in its reception of de' Rossi. A telling sign can be found in a letter written in the fall of that year by Matityahu Strashun (1817-1886), a contemporary and associate of Neẓiv's, a fellow midrash scholar and a famed collector of books who, like other members of the Vilna and Volozhin circles mentioned above, walked the virtually invisible line between traditionalist and maskilic scholarship during the early- and mid-nineteenth century. The letter is addressed to Shmuel Yosef Feunn (1819-1891), a man closely associated with the Vilna Circle as well, but whose decision in 1848 to accept a position in the government-sponsored rabbinical school in Vilna identified him to some as leaning more heavily toward the world of Haskalah. In the letter, Strashun praises Fuenn for the important service he rendered in writing his history of Vilna, entitled *Kiriyah Ne'emanah* (Vilna, 1860). Strashun then writes that in reviewing the book he realized that there was additional information he could add to that which Feunn had already recorded, which might be of interest and of use to readers. He then proceeds to include his lengthy set of notes, which were later included in the second edition of Fuenn's book, printed in 1915.

Of importance here is the fact that Strashun includes an enormous footnote to his own notes on *Kiriyah Ne'emanah* regarding the use of Azariah de' Rossi's *Me'or 'Einayim*. In it, he refers to a list published by

---

51 See *Afike Yehudah* (Jerusalem: 1999), 7.

52 See Edward Breuer, "The Haskalah in Vilna: R. Yeḥezkel Feivel's '*Toldot Adam*'," *Torah u-Madda Journal* 7 (1997), 23.

53 Eliyahu of Vilna, *Aderet Eliyahu: Peirush al Neviim u-Ketuvim* (Jerusalem: 2001), 245. Neẓiv cites from the Ga'on's commentary on Chronicles in: *EH* Naso 46 (I: 179); *EH* Devarim 6 (III: 10).

Leopold Zunz which notes the major Jewish authors who made use of it. Strashun then feels compelled to let his readers, or, more precisely, the readers of Fuenn's *Kiriyah Ne'emanah*, know that many more revered rabbis also refer to de' Rossi. He then lists twenty-five different authors and the places in which they mention de' Rossi—from Yiẓḥak Lampornati to Avraham Gombiner to Yehudah Edels—after which he notes that "I have also seen *Me'or 'Einayim* mentioned in other books, which I no longer remember and I will [therefore] suffice with this small collection from twenty-five authors which still remain in my memory." Strashun's footnote then continues for another entire page, with a description of places in which de' Rossi is used by traditional rabbinic authors, although not mentioned by name.[54]

The strongly apologetic nature of Strashun's lengthy note suggests that by the 1860s Lithuanian rabbinic society no longer embraced de' Rossi as it had during the years of Strashun's youth. In the early decades of nineteenth-century Lithuania, *Me'or 'Einayim* was read, referenced, and cited by respected Torah scholars as it had been, in Strashun's estimation, for generations beforehand. It was in this world that Strashun was raised, and in this world that he acquired his intellectual breadth.

It was in this world, as well, that the young Neẓiv composed his *Sifre* commentary. And in *'Emek ha-Neẓiv* the influence of de' Rossi is unmistakable. Not only does the young Neẓiv repeatedly cite from de' Rossi's work and suggest that his readers look there for further clarification, but the elements of *Sefer Me'or 'Einayim* which Neẓiv borrows, both explicitly and implicitly, are precisely those elements which so enraged prior rabbinic authorities. Indeed, the young Neẓiv's basic hermeneutical approach to rabbinic literature throughout his *Sifre* commentary bears a striking similarity to that of de' Rossi. Thus, Neẓiv's explicit references to de' Rossi's work and his unreferenced applications of de' Rossian hermeneutics merit careful examination.

### *Explicit Use of* Me'or 'Einayim *in* 'Emek ha-Neẓiv

There are six occasions in his *Sifre* commentary in which Neẓiv explicitly cites the work of Azariah de' Rossi. However, when one reads through each of the chapters of *Me'or 'Einayim* which Neẓiv cites, and then re-

54 Matityahu Strashun, *Mivḥar Ketavim* (Jerusalem: Mosad ha-Rav Kook, 1969), 169-172, n. 11.

turns to the text of *'Emek ha-Neẓiv,* it becomes readily apparent that de' Rossi's imprint can be found in Neẓiv's early work even in places which contain no explicit reference to the text of *Me'or 'Einayim.*

Neẓiv first mentions de' Rossi's work in the second *piska'* of *Parashat Naso.* There Neẓiv is attempting to argue the rather novel position that there is no Torah prohibition against the entrance of a non-priest or Levite into the Tabernacle or even into the Temple's Holy of Holies. Amongst other supports for his argument, Neẓiv cites a passage in *Pirkei de-Rabbi Eliezer* (ch. 52) which states that King Hezekiah opened the Ark which was housed in the Holy of Holies. While the author of *Pirkei de-Rabbi Eliezer* wonders how such a righteous individual could transgress a commandment punishable by death, Neẓiv is quite confident that the only applicable prohibition is of rabbinic origin and had not yet been pronounced in the days of Hezekiah. Before offering this explanation of the passage, however, Neẓiv notes that "the author of *Me'or 'Einayim* already forced [an answer] for this in his notes [found] in the [later] editions, look there."[55]

Neẓiv's reference is to the third section of *Me'or 'Einayim,* known as *'Imrei Binah,* chapter fifteen. In that passage, de' Rossi writes that the story found in *Pirkei de-Rabbi Eliezer* is the invention of a rabbinic mind and need not be taken literally. In that passage, de' Rossi writes as follows:

> On the basis of this comment, it would appear that even more problematic is the sages' statement with regard to the verse, *There was no thing in his palace or realm that Hezekiah did not show them* [i.e., the Babylonians] (2K. 20:13). For in Pirqe d'Rabbi Eliezer it states that Hezekiah opened up the Ark and showed them the tablets of the Law. And in his commentary on Kings, Rashi uses the rabbinic Midrashim when he states that he [i.e., Hezekiah] showed them the Ark, the tablets, and the scroll of the Torah. You might say that this was done by instiga-

55 *EH* Naso 2 (I: 15). Neẓiv's reference to the "notes" of the later editions suggests that he was not using Feunn and Ben Ya'akov's 1865 edition of *Me'or 'Einayim,* which incorporated those notes into the main text without any notation. While Cassel's 1864 edition does demarcate the notes, our earlier conclusions regarding the early date of Neẓiv's composition of his *Sifre* commentary make it more plausible that he was using the Satanov edition of 1794, which was reprinted in Vienna in 1829.

> tion of the high priest that he should open up the Ark of the Covenant for the Queen of Sheba. Nevertheless, there is a problem with both passages. How was such an act possible given that it was prohibited according to the command, "Thus only Aaron shall enter the Shrine (Lev. 16:3)?" Moreover, according to Torat Kohanim, he was not even then allowed to enter at all times. However you could interpret the statement in line with the proposition "I am expounding Scripture." In other words, it would be actually tenable in the light of our other examinations to describe it as conjectural according to Sherira's definition. Then one might say that the expression "There was no thing that he did not show them" even includes the tablets and the scroll of the Torah which are called "things." In this way, our question is resolved.[56]

The mention of Sherira in this passage refers to de' Rossi's earlier citation of Isaac Aboab's fifteenth-century *Menorat ha-Ma'or*, in which Rav Sherira Ga'on is quoted as saying, "'Those statements which are derived from verses and are called midrash and aggadah are conjectural.'"[57] In other words, de' Rossi's explanation of the passage in *Pirkei de-Rabbi Eliezer* is that the story is a rabbinic rhetorical flourish and need not be taken literally. This reference by Neẓiv, then, is to a prime example of the allegedly heretical hermeneutic which Maharal and others so forcefully decried.

Of course, in the above citation from *'Emek ha-Neẓiv*, Neẓiv refers to the answer offered by de' Rossi as "forced" and rejects it in favor of his own interpretation. That Neẓiv is rejecting this specific application of de' Rossi's hermeneutic and not its underlying principle, however, is quite clear from elsewhere in his commentary on *Sifre*.

In Devarim, *piska'* 23, an anonymous passage in *Sifre* states that from the incident in Deuteronomy (1:25) recounting the Israelites' statement to Moses that upon completion of their mission in the Land of Israel the spies "will come down to us" in the wilderness, "Scripture is teaching that the Land of Israel is higher than all other lands." Rather than of-

56 Weinberg, 294. All translations of de' Rossi's text are from Weinberg.
57 Ibid., 288.

fer any original explanation of this statement, Neẓiv writes "See *Me'or 'Einayim le-ha-Adomi, 'Imrei Binah* chapter 11, which proves that it (i.e., the passage in *Sifre*) is talking about most [other lands] (i.e., not all other lands as a literal interpretation would suggest), or about lands which are noteworthy and deserving of praise, look there."[58] Here it is clear from Neẓiv's words alone that he is citing and affirming de' Rossi's non-literal approach to rabbinic statements of aggadah.[59] The fact that the passage in *Me'or 'Einayim* which Neẓiv here cites explicitly refers to this case as but one example of the general nature of rabbinic statements further suggests that Neẓiv is not adopting a single interpretation from de' Rossi but rather a hermeneutical approach.

> Sometimes, the idea of ascent is applied to a person of lowly stature who approaches a person of high station as in the case of Dathan and Abiram who said concerning our master Moses, *We shall not go up*. And although the standard division of Reuben was on the south, the Israelites were, in fact, at that time all in the same valley, and Moses would take the tent and place it in different directions. Likewise, one might speak of ascending to an important place. Among other usages, the term is also used in relation to those going out of exile and those making an assault on a city. From this perspective, then, given that some cities and countries are on high ground and some in the valleys, we might resume our discussion regarding the Land of Israel being on a higher level than all other lands. It would then be plausible to speak of going [down] both north and south from the Land of Israel. This is all the more feasible when you take into account that in such matters as these, one cannot draw conclusions from general rules in a dogmatic way and that the method of our Sages was to speak about the majority of cases as when they said in tractate Niddah and Bereishit Rabbah: "The fetus emerges from the womb in the position that it assumes during intercourse: the male with his

58 *EH* Devarim 23 (III: 21).

59 In contrast, see Maharal's treatment of this statement on *Be'er ha-Golah*, 131.

> face downwards, the female with her face upwards." But Jewish midwives say that this is only true of the majority of cases. Similarly, if one were to suggest that there are cities and countries on mountains with high peaks, it will not affect the statement about the Land of Israel.[60]

The affinity felt by Neẓiv for the work of de' Rossi is further highlighted by the fact that in delineating his understanding of what was and was not given to Moses at Sinai, a question which ranks amongst the weightiest in traditional Jewish theology, Neẓiv cites the work of no Jewish thinker other than Azariah de' Rossi.

*Sifre* in 'Ekev, *piska'* 12, states that one must study midrash, *halakhot*, and *aggadot*. From *Sifre* 's grouping of midrash, *halakhot*, and *aggadot* together Neẓiv understands the rabbinic author of the passage as alluding to three distinct categories of rabbinic teachings. The first, which *Sifre* refers to as "midrash," represents "expositions (*derashot*) of the verses like those in *Mekhilta'*, *Sifra'*, and *Sifre,* which connect the essence of the written Torah to the oral Torah, and without which a number of the *halakhot* would be forgotten like in the days of Joshua…"[61] Neẓiv writes further that the words of the verse cited by *Sifre* in support of the obligation to study *halakhot* and *aggadot* are intended to reinforce the idea that these teachings "were all said at Sinai…and included in this is the connecting of the *halakhot* which are derived via the *Midrashot*."[62] Thus, Neẓiv is reading into the words of *Sifre* the theory that much of Jewish law and lore originated at Sinai and was passed down orally, together with methods of linking these teachings to Scripture.

Following this description of midrash as mnemonic technique intended to prevent Sinaitic traditions from being forgotten, Neẓiv adds parenthetically "and look in *Me'or 'Einayim,* part four, chapter nine, which elaborates on this."[63] As Jay Harris has extensively documented,

---

60 Weinberg, 230-231.

61 *EH* 'Ekev 12 (III: 77).

62 Ibid.

63 Ibid., 77. The particular reference in this case, however, is a bit problematic. "Part four" of *Me'or 'Einayim* could only be a reference to part four of the *'Imrei Binah* section, since the book itself consists of three, not four parts. *'Imrei Binah,* on the other hand, which comprises the vast majority of the book, is in fact, divided into four separate sections. Part four of *'Imrei Binah,* though, begins at chapter forty, thus suggesting that the printed text of *'Emek ha-Neẓiv*'s citation of "part four, chapter nine" is flawed. De' Rossi does indeed

the theory of *midrash halakhah* as mnemonic has a long history in rabbinic writings and can be found in the classic works of Sa'adya Ga'on, Yehudah ha-Levi, Ibn Ezra, and Rambam, among many others.[64] It is noteworthy, then, that Neẓiv, who certainly was no stranger to those works, refers his readers only to the treatment of this critical subject found in the work of Azariah de' Rossi.

In this regard, de' Rossi cites Solomon ibn Aderet (Rashba) and Menachem Recanati as precedent for the notion that *aggadot* sometimes originate as oral traditions later appended to Scripture as a mnemonic device. He then extends the principle to the sphere of *halakhah* as well.

> Similarly, in his explanation of the *Aggadot* on Berakhot and Bava Batra cited by Aboab, Rashba [Solomon ben Aderet] of blessed memory…writes: "In Midrashim such as these, the point of our sages is to provide support from Scripture by using expressions which render them memorable; but they had no intention whatsoever of interpreting the verses as such." Moreover…the wise Recanati writes: "You should realize that our rabbis sometimes make a true pronouncement based on tradition or clear-cut evidence and then cite a verse as a mnemonical allusion to it or simply as a support." This method is even applied to the precepts. For example, ibn Ezra discusses the precept of procreation linked to the verse, *Be fruitful and multiply* (Gen. 1:28) and writes: "This precept was transmitted by our ancestors and they used the verse as an aide-memoire and as a support." Likewise, there is the statement of the rabbis of blessed memory in tractate Eruvin: "the laws relating to minimum quanti-

---

discuss *midrashei halakhah* as mnemonics, though, in section two of *'Imrei Binah*, chapter fifteen. Neẓiv's familiarity with this chapter is evident from his reference to it in Naso, discussed above. In all probability, then, the editor of *'Emek ha-Neẓiv* probably misread Neẓiv's letter *bet* for a *daled*, rendering what should be chapter two as chapter four, and mistook Neẓiv's letter *vav* following the *tet* as an apostrophe, rendering what should be fifteen as nine (Neẓiv's handwriting does have a tendency, at times, to extend the end of a cursive *bet* bellow the rest of the letter, thus creating a striking similarity to the cursive *daled*).

64 Jay M. Harris, *How Do We Know This? Midrash and the Fragmentation of Modern Judaism* (Albany: SUNY Press, 1995).

> ties, interpositions, and partitions fall into the category of laws transmitted from Sinai. They objected: 'But are they not scriptural for it is written *A land of wheat and barley* (Deut. 8:8)?' Rabbi Isaac [Hanan] said "The entire verse refers to measures and sizes.' They responded, 'Yes, it does fall into the category of *halakhah* transmitted [orally] from Sinai, and the scriptural verse is used simply as a support.'" In a similar vein is Rav Ashi's statement: "A divorce given by a levir is a rabbinic enactment for which Scripture is used as a mere support." In other words, since we are fully conversant with the verses of Scripture, we should similarly commit to memory the words of wisdom which they [i.e., the Sages] linked to them…[65]

In fact, Neẓiv relies on de' Rossi not only for his treatment of the nature of the oral Torah, but for clarification on the nature of the written Torah as well. In *Sifre Be-ha'alotekha, piska'* 26, there is a long list of verses which according to *Sifre* contain euphemistic language. Since a straightforward statement of the verse's intended meaning would have been disrespectful to God, the midrash states *"kinah ha-katuv,"* a phrase which can be translated as either "[he] modified the verse,"[66] or "Scripture modified [the verse]."[67] The former interpretation, which allows for the possibility of a human editor who modified Scripture in deference to the honor of God, poses serious challenges to traditional Jewish theology. While the language in *Sifre* lends itself more to the interpretation that Scripture itself did the modification, Neẓiv nonetheless notes that in other places these verses are referred to by the term *"tikkun soferim,"* or scribal emendation. In response to the possibility of human emendation of the biblical text implied by the appellation *tikkun soferim*—a problem which he himself raised—Neẓiv writes

> And the meaning is that Scripture itself fixed and built [it] in the manner of a scribal emendation, and [it is] not to say that the Men of the Great Assembly emended and

65 Weinberg, 281-282.

66 Although if *"ha-katuv"* is the object of the verb rather than the subject it would be more properly rendered if prefaced with an *"et."*

67 "Scripture" here being understood as a reference to God, the author of Scripture.

> changed the language of Scripture, heaven forbid. And look in *Me'or 'Einayim* of de' Rossi, part four,[68] chapter 19, who spoke correctly about this.[69]

In this instance, it is de' Rossi's conservative stance which Neẓiv admires. De' Rossi cites, in this regard, a passage in *Midrash Yelamedeinu* which states rather explicitly that the euphemistic emendations to which the midrash refers were introduced by the Men of the Great Assembly. Yet, de' Rossi quickly relegates that passage to a misinformed note written by some later author in the margin of his copy of *Midrash Yelamedeinu* which was mistakenly later incorporated into the main text.[70] In other words, for the sake of denying any emendation of the biblical text, de' Rossi freely emends a midrashic text.[71]

In his comments on *Be-ha'alotekha*, Neẓiv mentions another rabbinic passage which similarly suggests the possibility of human additions to the Pentateuchal text. Once again, Neẓiv responds by referring his readers to the work of de' Rossi. In this instance, the issue at hand is a passage in *Avot de-Rabbi Natan* which suggests that Ezra the Scribe had the authority to choose whether or not to include certain passages in the Torah text, and to demarcate potentially troubling passages with dots over its letters.[72] In discussing these dots, which appear in the masoretic text of the Torah, Neẓiv cites this passage and states at its conclusion that "it is a puzzling passage." His next words, and his final comment on the issue, instruct the reader to look at what de' Rossi wrote about this passage in *Me'or 'Einayim*, part four, chapter 19. There is possibly no more lucid and succinct example of de' Rossi's hermeneutic toward rabbinic texts than his comments concerning this passage from *Avot de-Rabbi Natan*.

> And was Ezra great enough to have the capacity to add or to detract from the divine script in any way? God forbid

---

68 Once again, there is no chapter 19 in part of four of *'Imrei Binah*. The correct reference is to part two, chapter 19.

69 *EH* Be-ha'alotekha 26 (I: 268).

70 Weinberg, 326-327.

71 While not necessarily a sign of de' Rossian influence, Neẓiv employs this very technique in *EH* Pinḥas 21 (II: 273), when he identifies the final line of the *piska'* in the printed edition of *Sifre* as the gloss of a later "Ga'on" or "talmid," which was then anonymously incorporated into the text.

72 *Avot de-Rabbi Natan*, chapter 34.

> that he or we should do such a thing. The responsibility may perhaps be laid on some pupil who wrote the passage without permission of his teacher, as was said in the Kuzari quoted above. Alternatively, one must necessarily account for it in terms of the statement of Rabbeinu Hai Ga'on of blessed memory that we may disregard those Midrashim and *Aggadot* which were not fixed in the Gemara. Alternatively, it may be understood in the manner of the author of the *Guide* that we mentioned previously, namely, that it is a statement of an individual according to a certain manner of thinking. This implies that it is not to be taken literally but has some artificial reason.[73]

This liberal attitude toward rabbinic texts coupled with a fierce conservatism regarding the biblical text is a fundamental tenet of Neẓiv's work as well.[74]

The final explicit reference to *Me'or 'Einayim* in Neẓiv's *Sifre* commentary is found in his comments on the first *piska'* of Balak. The passage in *Sifre* mentions a kingdom it calls "*Cartigni*," which Neẓiv identifies as "The famous Carthage in Jossipon which was conquered by the Roman warrior Scipio." He then adds,

> And look in *Sefer Me'or 'Einayim* of de' Rossi, *'Imrei Binah* chapter 11, and you will find its place in Africa. And it is Tarshish [about which] it is written in Kings and Chronicles in regard to the ships of Solomon and Jehoshaphat which were destroyed. And it is [about which] it is written in Ezekiel "Tarshish, Pul, and Lud, and distant islands" and look there for more.[75]

While it is interesting to note that de' Rossi states explicitly that his source for identifying the place called Tarshish in Ezekiel with Carthage is "the Christian translator," or Saint Jerome,[76] it is perhaps of greater significance that this passage in *Me'or 'Einayim* also stems from a discus-

73 Weinberg, 328.
74 See Chapter 3 above on textual criticism.
75 *EH* Balak 1 (II: 202).
76 Weinberg, 212.

sion that de' Rossi's detractors label as heretical hermeneutics. Here de' Rossi is not treating examples of rabbinic hyperbole or moral fiction, but statements of the Rabbis which were based on the science of their day, and which have since been proven wrong. Only a few paragraphs after having identified and located Carthage, de' Rossi comments,

> On the basis of all these observations, a general conclusion may be drawn. You might take our sages' statements on the subject of the heavens, their constellations, their shapes and movements in a literal way and likewise, their treatment of the earth's shape and all related matters. You then might notice that their view is contradicted by the philosophers whose views were promulgated at a later date. However, even if one were to regard the opinions of the Gentile sages as having a firmer foundation, and that proof could possibly be adduced to verify the truth of their contentions, this should not be accounted as an inherent defect in the teachings of the rabbis of blessed memory or in the other traditions they transmitted to us. For they were not speaking on matters such as these through prophetic tradition, but rather as ordinary human beings who evaluate the evidence as they see it or argue on the basis of what they come to hear.[77]

These six citations, then, clearly demonstrate that Neẓiv made significant unapologetic use of de' Rossi—and that he uses precisely those elements considered by Maharal and others to be the most offensive. There is good reason to believe, however, that the influence of de' Rossi on Neẓiv's *Sifre* commentary extends well beyond the instances in which *Me'or 'Einayim* is explicitly cited, and into the fundamental hermeneutics which the young Neẓiv adopted in approaching rabbinic texts.

### *The Unattributed Influence of de' Rossi*

Our investigation of Azariah de' Rossi's impact on the work of Neẓiv in places where there is no explicit reference to *Me'or 'Einayim* will

77 Ibid., 218.

proceed in two stages. First we will look at instances in which concepts and phrases found in de' Rossi's work also appear in the work of Neẓiv. Afterward, we will explore more generally the similarity between de' Rossi's hermeneutical stance and that of Neẓiv

Toward the beginning of chapter fifteen, de' Rossi cites a passage from Isaiah of Trani (thirteenth century), in which he classifies midrashic literature into three categories, the first of which is "*guzma'*,'" or hyperbole. While the characterization of a particular rabbinic statement as *guzma'* can be found on seven different occasions in Talmud Bavli, in five of those places the term is used to signify a legal ruling in which the numbers or measurements rendered extend beyond the minimum legal requirement, with the intent of emphasizing the strength of that particular position.[78] In such cases *guzma'* signifies imprecision, but there is no element of falsehood. On only two occasions, then, is the term used to indicate that a literal reading of a rabbinic statement would render it untrue, and thus one must consider it mere hyperbole intended as a pedagogic tool, not as a factual account.[79] While Rashi in *Arakhin* (11a) does suggest that it is "the way of Mishnayot to teach [via] *guzma'*," the use of this term in its second sense as a category of rabbinic literature, under whose heading large numbers of rabbinic statements deserve to be classified, is unique to Isaiah of Trani, and to de' Rossi who follows his lead.

Neẓiv, possibly on cue from de' Rossi, also recognizes a category of midrashim which are to be treated as *guzma'* in the sense of non-factual hyperbole. A passage in *Sifre Korah, piska'* 1, states "that the [Divine] judicial decree on the people of Jerusalem [during the era of the first Temple] was sealed only because of [the fact] that they were disdainful of the sacred [sacrifices]." Neẓiv, commenting on the words "only because of," writes

> Not exactly, for their main transgressions were idolatry, sexual promiscuity, and murder, as is written in the Tosefta at the end of *Menahot* and in *Yoma'*... Rather, the Tana wrote *guzma'*, and its intent [is that] this was also

78 TB *Eiruvin* 2b, *Beẓah* 4a, *Bava Meẓia'* 38a and 104b, *Ḥullin* 98a. See de' Rossi's discussion of these examples in Chapter 20, 333-341.

79 *Ḥullin* 98a (cited in 29a), *Arakhin* 11a.

> a transgression which brought about the judicial decree on Jerusalem. **And there are many such cases in the Talmud**, [e.g.,] "Jerusalem was only destroyed because the trustworthy people left her,"[80] and there are many like it, and they are all similar in intent.[81]

In other words, Neẓiv bids his reader not to take the statement "only because of" in its literal sense. Nor should any other statement of its kind in rabbinic literature be taken as such. The tanaitic authors employed such language as a colloquial means of emphasizing the point at hand, according to Neẓiv, with the knowledge that they are overstating their case and with the intent that others would understand them as such.

Neẓiv broadens this category in his comments on the first *piska'* of Balak. There, the passage in *Sifre* referring to the process of penalizing a promiscuous daughter of a priest states that "the High Priest goes out before her and says to her 'if you had acted in the ways of your mothers, you would have merited that a High Priest like this would have emerged from you.'" Neẓiv, though, writes that "the law is not so, but rather the method of *derush* is the method of *guzma'*."[82] In the previous examples, *guzma'* was employed by Neẓiv as a means of altering the degree to which a statement was made so as to conform with the accepted reality. Thus, the Temple was not destroyed "only because" the people were disdainful of the sacrifices—that was only one, and perhaps a minor, reason why it was destroyed. The rabbinic author upped the ante—through the use of *guzma'*—to emphasize that disdain of sacrifices was also an egregious sin. In this example, however, *guzma'* is used by Neẓiv to justify a statement which is completely non-factual. The rabbis in the case of the promiscuous daughter of a priest did not overstate the matter, they restated the matter. According to Neẓiv, the authors of this *Sifre* passage invented what seem to be normative instructions for the high priest to chastise the promiscuous girl, but it is, in truth, simply a midrashic means of relaying the severity of such impropriety. This type of reading bears distinct similarities to the hermeneutics which de' Rossi employs toward rabbinic texts throughout his *Me'or 'Einayim*.

---

80 *Ḥagigah* 14a

81 *EH* Koraḥ 1 (II: 80). Emphasis added.

82 *EH* Balak 1 (II: 200).

It is also instructive that while Neẓiv writes in the first passage that there are many such cases of *guzma'* found in talmudic literature, he does not refer to any of the passages actually labeled as *guzma'* in the Talmud itself. Rather, he draws the reader's attention to a class of otherwise unidentified hyperbolic midrashim, much the same way Isaiah of Trani and Azariah de' Rossi do.

Another parallel between the work of de' Rossi and that of Neẓiv is to be found with regard to the theory known amongst modern scholars of midrash as the conservation of personalities. That is, there is an exegetical trend in rabbinic literature of identifying multiple biblical characters as the same person under different aliases or identifying an anonymous biblical character with one who is named. In his discussion of the rabbinic statement which identifies the Persian kings Cyrus, Darius, and Artaxerxes as the same person, de' Rossi notes that on several occasions in rabbinic literature "the sages of blessed memory are intending to point out the similarity and compatibility that may be detected between different persons whether in respect to their acts or words," and do not mean that the two biblical characters are actually a single historical individual.[83]

In a famous midrashic statement of this ilk, the Israelite midwives charged by Pharaoh with casting newborn Israelite males into the Nile are named Shifrah and Pu'ah by the biblical text (Ex. 1:15) and are identified by the rabbis as Miriam and Yokheved, the mother and sister of Moses. In response to this rabbinic exegetical maneuver, Neẓiv writes that the rabbis did not mean that the two sets of women were literally a single historical entity. Rather, he explains that this is a common rabbinic technique which results from the fact that we "know no other respected women of the generation."[84] The adoption, then, of the theory of conservation of personalities is but another example of Neẓiv's non-literal hermeneutical stance toward rabbinic literature and of the possible unspoken influence of de' Rossi.

In regard to Neẓiv's more general hermeneutic posture, we also find what we might call de' Rossian elements. For example, *Sifre* on *Parashat*

---

83 Weinberg, 318-319.

84 *EH* Be-ha'alotekha 20 (I: 250). It is interesting to note that in a discussion which centers on the servant Abraham sends to find a wife for Isaac [*EH* Be-ha'alotekha 21 (I: 254)], who is identified by rabbinic literature and many later commentaries as Eliezer, Neẓiv is careful to refer to him only as "the servant" and not by the name Eliezer.

*Shelaḥ* cites two biblical verses which lend themselves to what *Sifre* considers to be heretical exegesis. In a move which runs directly counter to the tendencies of those who impart mystical or allegorical significance to rabbinic texts, and which is directly in line with de' Rossi's critical historical approach, Neẓiv writes that these two examples have no inherent significance and were selected by the midrash simply because they were the most popular heresies in the times of the authors.[85] Later in the same *parashah* he dismisses the details of a story which appears in *Sifre* because "it is the way of midrash to say things through stories."[86] Similarly, in his comments on Korah he cautions his readers that one "cannot ask questions" based on the literal meaning of "a *derush*."[87]

In addition to his critical historical approach to rabbinic statements, Neẓiv's emphasis on the methodology of *Sifre* and other rabbinic texts echoes de' Rossi's explicit call for all Jewish exegetes to do precisely that.

> The statement of our Master Moses (which we mentioned previously), *Show me your ways that I may know you* (Ex. 33:13) serves as an illuminating example for every intelligent person. It enables one to realize that in order to understand anything which is difficult or obscure in the meaning or statements of the other, one must become acquainted with his methods and characteristics. Surely, even the physician, politician, or person who wants to read a foreign script must in each case immediately apply himself to understanding the humors, human character, and the practice of one who forms the shapes of the letters? Then he will attain the expertise needed to reach the truth. We should act in the same way with our sages to ensure that we gain deep insight into their thought, and then we and they will be untouched by folly or sin. We should attain knowledge and understanding of their methods. In commenting on Scripture they were not using the methods of the literalists who were intent on understanding the actual words in the

85 *EH* Shelaḥ 6 (II: 48). See also *EH* Koraḥ 4 (II: 113), in which Neẓiv comments that *Sifre* 's selection of a particular parable was due to its common usage in that generation.

86 *EH* Shelaḥ 9 (II: 76).

87 *EH* Koraḥ 4 (II: 112).

> light of their context and would take into account the entire scope of what is being communicated in the narrative. Rather, external considerations determine their statements and teaching.[88]

This passage, like so many of the passages whose echoes distinctly reverberate in *'Emek ha-Neẓiv*, also comes from chapter fifteen of de' Rossi's *'Imrei Binah*. In fact, it directly precedes the discussion of midrash halakhah as a mnemonic device to which Neẓiv refers his readers in *piska'* 12 of *parashat* 'Ekev.

Furthermore, we might note that this tendency toward elucidating midrashic method, found in both de' Rossi and Neẓiv, is closely related to their adoption of a critical historical exegetical hermeneutic. For at the very core of the methodological exegesis employed by de' Rossi and Neẓiv stand the frailties and peculiarities of the distinctively human authorship of rabbinic texts. An allegorical or mystical hermeneutic, however, which views the author as divinely inspired and as intentionally crafting his work so as to connote multiple meanings, is far more likely to overlook the human tendencies and vulnerabilities which bear upon the composition of any literary work. Once, though, one has divested such statements of their secondary meanings and the words of the rabbis are seen as the wise, although at times hyperbolic or misinformed, teachings of human authors, there is room to note that differences in biological composition and environmental influences account for differences in semantics, syntax, and idioms, as well as the variety in authorial motivations, goals, and techniques.[89] Only then can one state, as does Neẓiv, that a ruling which appears one way in *Sifre* and in a different form in the Mishnah reflects differences in halakhic writing, not differences in halakhic reasoning.[90] It is then that one can state, as does Neẓiv, that Rambam's method is to refer to laws expounded from Scripture as "*de-rabbanan*" even though their legal status is "*de-'orayyta*."[91] And it is then that one can explain, as Neẓiv often does, divergent *derashot* for the same

88 Weinberg, 280.

89 Throughout his work, Neẓiv displays acute sensitivity to the inherent dissimilitude amongst human beings. See my "No Two Minds are Alike: Pluralism and Tolerance in the Work of Neẓiv," *Torah u-Madda Journal* 12 (2004): 74-98.

90 *EH* Naso 31 (I: 134).

91 *EH* Naso 5 (I: 29).

legal ruling by stating that "it is the way of [the authors of] the Talmud to cite the *derashot* which were on the tips of their tongues."[92]

The similarity in exegetical hermeneutics between Neẓiv's commentary on *Sifre* and de' Rossi's *Me'or 'Einayim*, then, is clear. At the very least we can say that the young Neẓiv found in de' Rossi a kindred spirit whose work he read, approved of, and cited at critical junctures in his *Sifre* commentary. Given the fact, though, that no single person or single text in the sphere of influence of Neẓiv—neither the work of the Vilna Ga'on nor that of Ḥayyim of Volozhin, nor what we know of the teachings of Radal or Reb 'Iẓele—bears so strong a resemblance in hermeneutics to Neẓiv's early work, we might suggest that de' Rossi's work served not simply as support for Neẓiv's preconceived hermeneutic, but played a formative role in shaping the development of Neẓiv's approach to rabbinic texts and in spurring his quest to define the parameters of the oral Torah.

Our exploration of Neẓiv's use of de' Rossi leads us back to Bonfil's argument regarding the reception of *Me'or 'Einayim.* And we can now assert quite definitively that if there ever was a rabbinic establishment which opposed *Sefer Me'or 'Einayim,* Neẓiv certainly did not belong to it. In fact, Neẓiv's use of de' Rossi suggests that he, and perhaps the larger rabbinic culture of early-nineteenth-century Lithuania to which he belonged, may well have understood *Me'or 'Einayim* as a defense of traditionally held beliefs—as Bonfil suggests was de' Rossi's intent—and did not consider his hermeneutics to be heretical. It is, therefore, an exploration of this broader rabbinic culture and the factors which gave it rise to which we move in the coming chapter.

92 *EH* Shelaḥ 1 (II: 16).

# CHAPTER FIVE:
## *'Emek ha-Neẓiv* in its Cultural Context

Though not completely absent from the portfolio of eighteenth-century rabbinic exegesis, midrash commentaries produced prior to the nineteenth century are few in number and scattered amongst various decades and geographic locations. In the second half of the nineteenth century, following the lead of Eliezer Gordon (1841-1910) of Telz, Ḥayyim Soloveitchik of Brisk (1853-1918), as well as Meir Simḥah (1843-1926) and Yosef Rosen (1858-1936) of Dvinsk[1] amongst others, incisive commentaries on Talmud and Rambam came to dominate the literary endeavors of the Lithuanian rabbinic elite. And while the conceptual method of study employed by the Briskers was rather novel,[2] the renewed emphasis on Talmud and Rambam signifies a return to the subject matter which had preoccupied rabbinic authors for centuries, and an end to the remarkable flourishing of Lithuanian midrash commentary described in the previous chapters.[3] This brief intellectual effervescence thus elicits the question of what cultural factors unique to Lithuanian Jewish society at the turn of the nineteenth century gave rise to it. And, if we can better understand the culture which led the minds of early-nineteenth-century Jewish Lithuania to explore the world of midrash, we can better understand the culture from which *'Emek ha-Neẓiv* was born.

### *The Influence of the Vilna Ga'on*

A brief glance at the members of the Vilna Circle whose contours we

---

1 The latter is often referred to as the Rogatchover.

2 See Chapter 4, n. 3 above.

3 Yisrael Meir ha-Kohen (1838 -1933) is a notable exception. While best known for his work on the laws of proper speech, *Ḥafeẓ Ḥayyim*, and his halakhic compendium, *Mishnah Berurah*, he also wrote a lengthy commentary on *Sifra* first published in Piotrków Trybunalski, 1918. Of course, there were some Lithuanian Torah scholars who continued to focus in less traditional areas of study, such as Yaakov Dovid Wilovsky (1845–1913), Ridbaz, who focused his energies on Yerushalmi and later Yeḥezkel Abramsky (1886–1976), who wrote a major commentary on Tosefta, but they are the rare exception in a world that was largely preoccupied with Talmud Bavli and Rambam's Mishneh Torah.

outlined earlier and from whom much of early-nineteenth-century Lithuanian midrash commentary emerges, suggests that its animating force might have been the influence of the Vilna Ga'on himself.[4] From the direct influence of the Ga'on on his son Avraham and through his personal relationships with Sha'ul Katzenellenbogen, Yehudah Leib Edel, and Yeḥezkel Feivel, to the role played by Ya'akov of Slonim in passing on the manuscripts of his father Avraham and his grandfather the Ga'on, the influence of the Ga'on seems to lie at the very heart of this intellectual coterie.

Nonetheless, the Ga'on's influence on Lithuanian rabbinic scholarship has been called into question in recent years both by Immanuel Etkes in his important work on the image and reality of the Vilna Ga'on[5] and by Shaul Stampfer in his insightful response essay, entitled "The Image of the Ga'on."[6] Neither scholar, however, incorporates the world of Lithuanian midrash study into their assessment of the Ga'on's influence. The intellectual developments described in the previous chapter suggest that a look at the scholars who comprised this world, the work they produced, and their connection to the Vilna Ga'on may offer a valuable new perspective on the issue.

In the first chapter of Etkes' work, he states that unlike the Ga'on's role in the fight against Hasidism, his impact on the world of Torah study was indirect and unclear. According to Etkes the major contribution of the Ga'on to the world of Lithuanian learning is to be found in the inspiration provided by the popular reconstruction of the Ga'on's image, rather than in the reality of the method and content of the Ga'on's own studies.[7] However, the Ga'on's well documented penchant for plain-sense, text-critical midrash study, combined with the flourishing of such study in his latest years and immediately following his death in 1797, raises considerable doubt as to Etkes' conclusions.

Shaul Stampfer nonetheless adopts the perspective of Etkes and restates it in a more categorical fashion. Like Etkes, he writes that, "The role often popularly attributed to the Ga'on in the formation of a 'mit-

4 See Chapter 2, Table 1.

5 Immanuel Etkes, *The Ga'on of Vilna: The Man and His Image*, trans. Jeffery M. Green (Berkeley: University of California Press, 2002), 9.

6 Shaul Stampfer, "The Image of the Ga'on," *Ha-GRA u-Bet Midrasho*, eds. Moshe Halamish, et al. (Ramat Gan: Bar-Ilan University Press, 2003).

7 Etkes, 9.

nagdic' ideology also has to be questioned."[8] He goes further, though, by definitively stating that, "After his death, the Ga'on's memory was not perpetuated by the study of his writings."[9] Likewise he writes that the Vilna Ga'on was one of those scholars who "were talked about by name—but not read."[10] Thus, as his essay draws to a close he reiterates that, "The Ga'on's works did not play a central role in Lithuanian Torah scholarship in the first half of the 19th century."[11]

Stampfer's assessment is based on two bodies of evidence. The first consists of the intellectual products of Lithuanian society immediately following the death of the Ga'on, which he argues are bereft of citations of the Vilna Ga'on's work. As a case in point he cites the example of Ḥayyim of Volozhin's *Nefesh ha-Ḥayyim*:

> An indication of the limited visibility of the Ga'on's impact can be seen in *Nefesh HaHaim* [sic], written by the Ga'on's illustrious student, Rabbi Hayim of Volozhin. While there is absolutely no doubt as to the formidable influence of the Ga'on's person on Rabbi Hayim, and while the book's ideology, which emphasizes the centrality of Torah study over all other activities, fits the Ga'on's view, there are few explicit references to the Ga'on in it. A reader studying the book would come out with few impressions of the Ga'on. Without citation, thinkers lose their impact.[12]

In a footnote, Stampfer also notes that Professor Haym Soloveitchik points out the glaring paucity of references to the Vilna Ga'on in Yeḥiel Mikhel Epstein's (1829-1888) *Arukh ha-Shulḥan*, a well-respected halakhic code and commentary which emerges from the center of Lithuanian rabbinic society later in the nineteenth century.[13]

The second body of evidence cited by Stampfer to support the notion

8 See Alan Nadler, *The Faith of the Mitnagdim: Rabbinic Responses to Hasidic Rapture* (Baltimore: 1997).

9 Stampfer, 41.

10 Ibid., 59.

11 Ibid.

12 Ibid.

13 Ibid., 48, n. 31 referring to Haym Soloveitchik, "Rupture and Reconstruction: The Transformation of Contemporary Orthodoxy," *Tradition* 28, 4 (1994): 110-112.

that the Vilna Ga'on had little impact on the intellectual endeavors of Torah scholars in the first half of the nineteenth century is the publishing history of the Ga'on's work. Here Stampfer notes that the majority of the Vilna Ga'on's writings remained unpublished until the 1830s and 40s, by which point the generation of Lithuanian Torah scholars following the Ga'on had already matured well into adulthood, and some had already completed their life's work. Thus, the Torah scholars of early-nineteenth-century Lithuania could not have counted such publications as primary influences on their intellectual development.

Both lines of reasoning employed by Stampfer, however, have notable weaknesses. While *Nefesh ha-Ḥayyim* and *Arukh ha-Shulḥan* rank amongst the important works of Torah scholarship produced by the scholars of nineteenth-century Lithuania, they alone do not form a representative sample of the voluminous material which that society produced.[14] And, as we shall demonstrate below, if one turns to the sphere of midrash commentaries, citations of the Ga'on abound.[15] Stampfer's second line of reasoning, namely that the dramatic rise in publication of the Ga'on's work only begins in the 1830s and hence the Ga'on's work could not have had a major impact on earlier scholarship, merits reconsideration as well.

Let us first look, however, at the question of citation of the Ga'on amongst early-nineteenth-century rabbinic scholars. We have noted already that Yiẓḥak Eliyahu Landau's commentary on *Masekhet Soferim* includes the emendations of the Ga'on.[16] Likewise, in the introduction to his commentary on *Derekh 'Ereẓ Zuta'*, he writes, "I have arranged the tractate according to the emendations of *ha-rav ha-GRA* of Vilna."[17]

Landau's commentary on *Mekhilta'* is composed of three different sections. One section, entitled *Eifat Ẓedek*, consists solely of the notes on *Mekhilta'* by the Vilna Ga'on, given to him by Ya'akov of Slonim. This section of Landau's work is not explicitly referred to as the work of the

14 The selection of Yeḥiel Mikhel Epstein's *Arukh ha-Shulḥan* as an example of the Ga'on's lack of influence on Torah scholars in the first half of the nineteenth century is a curious one given that Epstein was active only in the second half of the nineteenth century and given that his older brother-in-law, Neẓiv, who was in fact active in the 1840s refers to the Ga'on on at least 200 occasions in his collection of halakhic responsa entitled *Meshiv Davar*.

15 There are halakhic works from the first half of the nineteenth century which draw heavily from the Ga'on as well. One example would be Shmuel ben Yosef ha-Levi of Bialostok's *Shut Bigdey Yesha'* (Vilna, 1844).

16 *Mikra' Soferim* (Suvalk: 1862).

17 *Derekh Ḥayyim* (Vilna: 1872), 6.

Ga'on due to the prohibition proclaimed by the Vilna *bet din* against officially ascribing any work to the Ga'on which they, the *bet din*, did not sanction.[18] Furthermore, a second section of Landau's *Mekhilta'* commentary, entitled *Berurei ha-Middot*, is devoted in large measure to an explanation of the Ga'on's emendations.

Radal and Ẓvi Hirsch Katzenellenbogen make frequent use of the Vilna Ga'on's writing as well. In Katzenellenbogen's work on the thirty-two hermeneutic rules, the Ga'on's Torah commentary, *Aderet Eliyahu*, is often cited.[19] Radal's commentary on *Midrash Rabbah* also includes a number of citations of the Ga'on's commentaries and notes.[20] Likewise, Radal's commentary on *Pirkei de-Rabbi Eliezer* draws heavily on the work of the Ga'on throughout.[21]

Most importantly for the purposes of this study, Neẓiv's commentary on *Sifre*, which we have already shown belongs in large part to the 1830s and 1840s, cites the Vilna Ga'on more than it does any other post-talmudic source. His work contains in excess of sixty different citations of the Ga'on's work.[22]

With regard to the publication history of the Ga'on's work, Stampfer's implicit suggestion, that the publication frequency of the Ga'on's

18 *Mekhilta' im Beiur Berurei ha-Midot* (Vilna: 1844), 2 of introduction.

19 Katzenellenbogen, *Netivot 'Olam* (Vilna: 1822) 14a, 47b, 50a, 59a, etc.

20 E.g., *Midrash Rabbah, vol. 1* (Israel: Wagshal, 2001), 8: 9 (90) "*hagahot* to *Yerushalmi*;" 17: 3 (168) "*Aderet Eliyahu*;" 39: 16 (404) "*Peirush ha-GRA* (on *Torat Kohanim*)"; vol. 2, 51: 3 (530) "*hagahot ha-GRA*;" etc.

21 E.g., *Pirkei de-Rabbi Eliezer* (Warsaw, 1852), introduction, 5; Main text, 3a, 3b, 12a "*Hagahot ha-Meyuḥasot le-ha-GRA* (on *Pirkei de-Rabbi Eliezer*);" 5b, 9b "*Peirush le-Sefer Yeẓirah*;" 6a, 7a "*Tikkunim*;" 8a "*Aderet Eliyahu*;" 9b "*Be'ur Sefer Yeẓirah le-ha-GRA*;" 10b, 11a, "*Peirush ha-Heikhalot*", etc.

22 *EH* Naso 1 (I: 6); *EH* Naso 1 (I: 8); *EH* Naso 3 (I: 21); *EH* Naso 15 (I: 65); *EH* Naso 16 (I: 69); *EH* Naso 2 (I: 15); *EH* Naso 22 (I: 88); *EH* Naso 23 (I: 97); *EH* Naso 31(I: 132); *EH* Naso 39 (I: 150); *EH* Naso 4 (I: 23); *EH* Naso 40 (I: 156); *EH* Naso 42 (I: 167); *EH* Naso 44 (I: 172); *EH* Naso 46 (I: 179); *EH* Naso 5 (I: 29); *EH* Naso 9 (I: 51); *EH* Be-ha'alotekha 1 (I: 191); *EH* Be-ha'alotekha 11(I: 217); *EH* Be-ha'alotekha 16 (I: 233); *EH* Be-ha'alotekha 2 (I: 196); *EH* Be-ha'alotekha 20 (I: 252); *EH* Be-ha'alotekha 45 (I: 317); *EH* Shelaḥ 1 (II: 10); *EH* Shelaḥ 3 (II: 24); *EH* Shelaḥ 4 (II: 28); *EH* Shelaḥ 4 (II: 26); *EH* Shelaḥ 6 (II: 51); *EH* Shelaḥ 6 (II: 43); *EH* Shelaḥ 9 (II: 63); *EH* Koraḥ 3 (II: 101); *EH* Koraḥ 6 (II: 126); *EH* Koraḥ 6 (II: 126,127); *EH* Ḥukat 1 (II: 139); *EH* Ḥukat 2 (II: 157); *EH* Ḥukat 2 (II: 160); *EH* Ḥukat 4 (II: 170); *EH* Ḥukat 4 (II: 174,179); *EH* Ḥukat 5 (II: 183); *EH* Ḥukat 7 (II: 194); *EH* Ḥukat 7 (II: 196); *EH* Pinḥas 11 (II: 243); *EH* Pinḥas 15 (II: 10); *EH* Pinḥas 3 (II: 225); *EH* Matot 1 (II: 10); *EH* Matot 1 (II: 279); *EH* Matot 2 (II: 10); *EH* Matot 3 (II: 10); *EH* Matot 6 (II: 10); *EH* Masa'ei 2 (II: 10); *EH* Devarim 6 (III: 10); *EH* ve-'Etḥanan 10 (III: 40); *EH* ve-'Etḥanan 11 (III: 41); *EH* ve-'Etḥanan 7 (III: 33); *EH* 'Ekev 9 (III: 70); *EH* Re'eh 10 (III: 94); *EH* Re'eh 10 (III: 94); *EH* Re'eh 58 (III: 147); *EH* Re'eh 63 (III: 151); *EH* Shoftim 21 (III: 192); *EH* Teẓeh 17 (III: 296); *EH* Teẓeh 21 (III: 264); *EH* Teẓeh 22 (III: 265); *EH* Teẓeh 24 (III: 264).

books is directly proportional to his intellectual influence, is highly problematic. Specifically, there are three additional factors which need be taken into account. The first relates to the nature of those works of the Ga'on which were in fact printed during the first decades of the nineteenth century. The second factor is the place of the Vilna Ga'on's publications within the larger context of the Eastern European Hebrew print industry, and the third is the degree to which the Ga'on's work circulated in manuscript form.

While the publication history of the Ga'on's work seems to suggest that many of the earliest works printed fell out of favor amongst Lithuanian Torah scholars of the later nineteenth century, it is critical to point out that these works were squarely in line with the dominant intellectual milieu of the earliest decades of the century—a milieu perhaps molded and bolstered by the availability and accessibility of these texts. They consist of commentaries on midrashic literature and similar collections of extra-talmudic rabbinic teachings, such as the 1799 and 1804 printings of the Ga'on's commentary on *Tosefta,* the 1800 printing of his commentary on selected *aggadot,* the 1801 printing of his commentary on *Seder Olam,* the 1803 printing of his commentary on the *baraita* of the thirty-two hermeneutical rules of aggadic interpretation, the 1804 printing of his commentary on Torah, and the 1805 printing of his Passover Haggadah.

One cannot help but take note of the fact that many of the scholars teaching and studying in Vilna during the first few decades of the nineteenth century made these texts central to their intellectual endeavors. Shmuel Avigdor Tosfa'ah produced a massive commentary on the *Tosefta,* published in the Vilna edition of the Talmud in 1854. In 1822, Ẓvi Hirsch Katzenellenbogen published his commentary on the *baraita* of the thirty-two hermeneutical rules, and in 1838 Ze'ev Wolf Einhorn wrote one of his own. Yehudah Leib Edel devoted much of his intellectual energy to the study of talmudic *aggadot,* and the products of his labor were published posthumously in 1835 under the title *Iyye ha-Yam.* In addition to Ḥanokh Zundel ben Yosef's work on *Midrash Rabbah, Midrash Tanḥuma,* and *Midrash Shmuel,* he also penned a commentary on the Passover Haggadah in 1843 and a triple commentary on *Seder Olam* published in Vilna in 1845. Yiẓḥak Eliyahu Landau published two works on selected *aggadot,* commentaries on five different areas of the Bible, and a commentary on the Passover Haggadah. And, of course, Neẓiv also authored a commentary on the Torah and another on the Passover Haggadah. Thus, despite the paucity of published books by the Vilna Ga'on printed in the early decades of the nineteenth century relative to the number printed from the 1840s and on, the subject matter of these books was central to the endeavors of the intellectual elite, and thus may well have been more influential than the printing record suggests.

The second factor unaccounted for in Stampfer's examination of the impact of the Ga'on on early-nineteenth-century Torah scholarship is the historical context of the Hebrew print industry in Eastern Europe as a whole. As we will outline in greater detail below, the industry was still in its infant stages at the turn of the nineteenth century. Therefore, the fact that fewer works of the Ga'on were published in the first decade of the nineteenth century than in the fifth decade of the nineteenth century may reflect the technical inability of the community to publish more, or the economic difficulties associated with setting commentaries for print (which often required the setting of the commentary's source text as well), rather than a relative disinterest in the Ga'on's work, as suggested by Stampfer. In other words, the fact that fifty works attributed to the Ga'on were published between 1798 and 1808 may be just as significant as the fact that one hundred works of the Ga'on were published between 1855 and 1865.[23] In fact, if we take into account the population explosion of Eastern European Jewry over the course of the nineteenth century, it becomes highly possible that whereas the number of works of the Ga'on published by mid-century increased greatly, their per capita influence might well have remained the same as it had been at the turn of the century. And, as demonstrated in the table below, if we take the rate at which new printing houses opened in Eastern Europe as an indicator of the growth of the Hebrew printing industry, we find that the number of the Ga'on's works published during the turn of the century outpaced the growth of the industry as a whole. This trend would suggest that once the mechanism for Hebrew printing in Eastern Europe was put in place, the market demand for the Ga'on's books was quite high.

---

23 The computations of printed works of the Ga'on are based on Yeshayahu Vinograd, *Oẓar Sifre ha-GRA* (Jerusalem: 2003).

**Table 1: The Publication History of the Vilna Ga'on in Historical Context**[24]

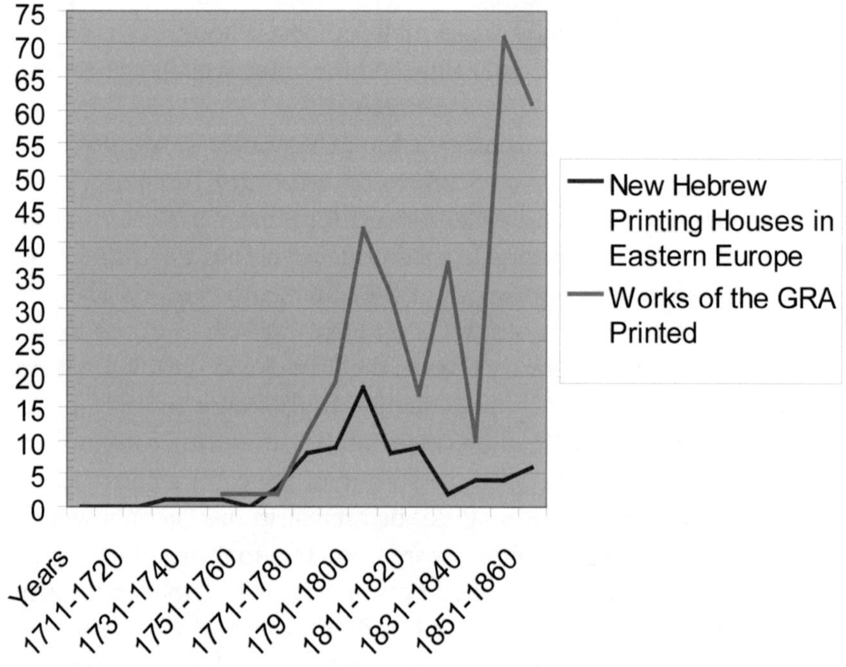


Printing houses based on Joshua Bloch, *Hebrew Printing and Bibliography*, ed. Charles Berlin (New York, 1976).

Works of the GRA based on Yeshayahu Vinograd, *Oẓar Sifre ha-GRA* (Jerusalem, 2003).

The third factor which needs to be considered when assessing the impact of the Vilna Ga'on on the scholars of early-nineteenth-century Lithuania is the circulation of the Ga'on's unpublished manuscripts. Given the fact that many of the scholars in and around Vilna shared personal relationships with one another and with the family of the Ga'on, it stands to reason that they might well have had access to works that had not yet been printed. Indeed, we have already seen evidence of such in the anecdote related above concerning Yiẓḥak Eliyahu Landau and

24 This graphic representation demonstrates that Stampfer was clearly right in noting the spike in interest during the 1850s and 1860s, but it also shows that there were previous spikes, possibly just as meaningful, given the smaller population and the lesser capacity to print.

Ya'akov of Slonim. Landau first encountered the Ga'on's work on the *Mekhilta'* via an unnamed grandson of the Ga'on who, upon visiting Dubno, showed him a copy of the manuscript. Landau then approached Ya'akov of Slonim in an effort to obtain a copy for himself. Ya'akov of Slonim responded by informing Landau that he had submitted his copy of the work to a printer for publication, but it had since mysteriously disappeared. However, Landau writes that he later learned of the existence of yet another copy of this same work, which was held by a different member of the Ga'on's progeny. He secured access to that copy and published it under the name *Eifat Ẓedek* together with his own *Mekhilta'* commentary. Thus, from Landau's story we have evidence of three different manuscripts of the Ga'on's work—one in the possession of the anonymous visitor, one which was lost on its way to the printer, and one to which Landau succeeds in gaining access—all of which were passed amongst the scholars of his day.

The notes of Shmuel Luria, the printer who first published the Ga'on's work on *Sifre* in 1866, suggest that numerous copies of his *Sifre* commentary similarly circulated amongst members of the Lithuanian rabbinic elite during the first half of the nineteenth century. Luria writes on the book's title page that the text he has printed is based on the

> Copies made by the Ga'on R' David Luria, *Za"L,* who copied it from amongst the writings of our teacher R' Simḥah Bunim of Shklov, a student of the GRA, *Za"L;* and on a copy that I found amongst the copies of the GRA's manuscripts (upon which his son…our teacher R' Avraham signed)…of [*Sifre* to] the book of Deuteronomy. I also had a copy made by one of his students who copied the entire book according to the version of his Rabbi.[25]

From this description alone we have evidence of three copies of the Ga'on's work on *Sifre* in its entirety—one held by Simha Bunim of Shklov, one copied therefrom by David Luria, and one from an unnamed student—as well as an additional copy of his comments on *Sifre* to Deuteronomy found amongst the manuscripts certified by Avraham ben ha-Gra.

---

25 *Sifre* (Shklov: 1866), title page.

Radal himself alludes to the fact that he had a copy of an unprinted work of the Ga'on when he remarks in his comments on *Pirkei de-Rabbi Eliezer* that the hand-copied version of the Ga'on's notes to *Pirkei de-Rabbi Eliezer* in which he is looking are illegible in a particular passage.[26] Likewise, Louis Finkelstein notes that Ẓvi Hirsch ha-Kohen Rappaport, author of *Tosefet ha-'Azarah* on *Sifra*, had a manuscript of the Ga'on's work before him, which he cites on occasion in his own work.[27]

Possibly the most dramatic evidence of the widespread circulation of manuscripts purportedly containing teachings of the Ga'on is the 1799 *pesak din* of the Vilna *bet din*. It famously stated that only seven works of the Vilna Ga'on were certified as authentic and that all of the other works in circulation which purport to represent the teachings of the Ga'on must be considered forgeries.[28] While the statement is clearly intended to protect the economic interests of the Ga'on's descendents by validating only the works they had published as authentic, by inference we can deduce that there was a considerable amount of intellectual material claiming to reflect the work of the Ga'on, as early as 1799. Indeed, the ruling explicitly states that one "must not listen to nor believe anyone who says he heard something in the name of ha-Ga'on ha-Hasid, nor one who comes with a manuscript [said to be] copied from the manuscripts of the Ga'on, until it is certified with utter certainty that they came from the writings of the Ga'on himself."[29]

In fact, a story recorded by Barukh ha-Levi Epstein in his *Mekor Barukh* suggests that the unpublished manuscripts of the Vilna Ga'on continued to influence the world of Lithuanian scholarship well into the middle of the nineteenth century. While describing time he spent as a young man studying in what was known as the *bet midrash* of the Vilna Ga'on, Epstein recounts the entry of a distinguished rabbi, later identified as Yisrael Salanter, into the study hall. As the boys studying there looked on, the study hall's caretaker brought a copy of one of the Ga'on's manuscripts to Salanter for him to study. In a sense, the picture Epstein draws is rather similar to that of a rare book room in a modern research library. Those with qualified credentials were free to sit with the texts

26 *Pirkei de-Rabbi Eliezer* (Warsaw: 1852), 15a.

27 Louis Finkelstein, *Sifra on Leviticus*, vol. 1 (New York: Jewish Theological Seminary, 1989), 14.

28 Printed in the introduction to the Ga'on's commentary on Mishle (Shklov: 1799).

29 Ibid.

and examine them to their heart's content, provided that the work did not leave the confines of the *bet midrash*.[30]

We might add, with regard to the copies of the Ga'on's work on *Mekhilta'* mentioned above, that Landau first had to verify that the manuscript which he had obtained was in fact a genuine rendition of the Ga'on's work. While he states that he was able to do so, Landau still did not officially ascribe the work to the Vilna Ga'on. Rather he printed it under the name *Eifat Ẓedek* and mentioned the Ga'on's authorship of it in his introduction.[31] Thus, in addition to the hand copied works of the Vilna Ga'on which circulated during the first half of the nineteenth century, there was at least one printed work—and perhaps there were more—which contained the intellectual products of the Ga'on but did not bear his name as author. This too, then, suggests further caution is required in gauging the impact of the Ga'on's writings on the rabbinic circles of early-nineteenth-century Lithuania solely from the publication history of works attributed to the Ga'on.

Thus, contrary to the suggestions made by Etkes and Stampfer, it seems that the Ga'on might well have exerted substantial influence in the world of early-nineteenth-century rabbinic scholarship. A close examination of Neẓiv's earliest work, classified earlier as a product of this world, further supports this conclusion.

## *The Vilna Ga'on in* 'Emek ha-Neẓiv

Much as the image and the work of the Vilna Ga'on loomed large in the world of Ya'akov of Slonim, Ẓvi Hirsch Katzenellenbogen, Radal, and Yiẓḥak Eliyahu Landau,[32] his presence is unmistakably felt throughout Neẓiv's commentary on *Sifre*. Neẓiv constantly cites, questions, and refutes interpretations, rulings, and emendations which he found in *Aderet*

---

30 Epstein (IV: 1801). We might also note in a similar vein that Neẓiv's first contact with the work of Radal on *She'iltot* was not through a printed text, but through a hand-written copy of Radal's notes which was in the possession of Neẓiv's father-in-law, Reb 'Iẓele (*Ha'amek She'elah, "Petaḥ Ha-Emek,"* I: 4). It therefore stands to reason that a significant amount of scholarly material was still being circulated in hand-copied form, and thus printing records are not an entirely accurate gauge of intellectual influence during this period.

31 See *Eifat Ẓedek* in *Mekhilta' im Be'ur Berurei ha-Midot* (Vilna: 1844).

32 See Chapter 3.

*Eliyahu;*[33] the Ga'on's commentary to *Avot de-Rabbi Natan;*[34] his notes on the Mishnah;[35] his explanations of *Shulḥan Arukh Oraḥ Ḥayyim,*[36] *Yoreh De'ah,*[37] and *'Even ha-'Ezer;*[38] his commentary on Chronicles;[39] *Eliyahu Rabba;*[40] *Shenot Eliyahu;*[41] and *Taharat ha-Kodesh.*[42] Conspicuously absent from this list of the Ga'on's writings cited by Neẓiv are the commentaries and notes on works of *midrash halakhah* generally ascribed to the Vilna Ga'on. When one considers our earlier assertion, however, that the core of Neẓiv's commentary on *Sifre* was composed in the late 1830s and early 1840s, the absence of the Ga'on's work on midrash is easily explained. After all, the first of the Ga'on's work on midrash was not published until 1844,[43] while all of the above works of the Ga'on, from which the young Neẓiv does cite in his commentary on *Sifre,* were published well before Neẓiv began his commentarial career.[44]

Despite the absence of citations of any of the Ga'on's published work

---

33 *EH* Naso 9 (I: 51); *EH* Naso 39 (I: 150); *EH* Naso 40 (I: 156); *EH* Naso 42 (I: 167); *EH* Be-ha'alotekha 2 (I: 196); *EH* Be-ha'alotekha 16 (I: 233); *EH* Shelaḥ 1 (II: 10); *EH* Pinḥas 3 (II: 225); *EH* Re'eh 58 (III: 147); *EH* Shoftim 21 (III: 192).

34 *EH* Be-ha'alotekha 45 (I: 317); *EH* Re'eh 10 (III: 94).

35 *EH* Shelaḥ 6 (II: 51).

36 *EH* Naso 16 (I: 69); *EH* Be-ha'alotekha 1 (I: 191); *EH* Be-ha'alotekha 11 (I: 217); *EH* Shelaḥ 9 (II: 63); *EH* Pinḥas 15 (II: 10); *EH* ve-'Etḥanan 10 (III: 40); *EH* ve-'Etḥanan 11 (III: 41).

37 *EH* Naso 5 (I: 29); *EH* Naso 22 (I: 88); *EH* Naso 23 (I: 97); *EH* Shelaḥ 4 (II: 28); *EH* Koraḥ 3 (II: 101); *EH* Koraḥ 6 (II: 126,127); *EH* 'Ekev 9 (III: 70); *EH* Re'eh 63 (III: 151); *EH* Teẓeh 17 (III: 296).

38 *EH* Naso 15 (I: 65).

39 *EH* Naso 46 (I: 179); *EH* Be-ha'alotekha 20 (I: 252); *EH* Devarim 6 (III: 10); *EH* Re'eh 10 (III: 94),

40 *EH* Naso 1 (I: 6); *EH* Shelaḥ 4 (II: 26); *EH* Shelaḥ 6 (II: 43); *EH* Ḥukat 1 (II: 139); *EH* Ḥukat 2 (II: 157); *EH* Ḥukat 4 (II: 174); *EH* Ḥukat 4 (II: 179); *EH* Ḥukat 5 (II: 183); *EH* Ḥukat 7 (II: 196).

41 *EH* Naso 4 (I: 23); *EH* Koraḥ 6 (II: 126); *EH* ve-'Etḥanan 7 (III: 33); *EH* Teẓeh 21 (III: 264); *EH* Teẓeh 22 (III: 265); *EH* Teẓeh 24 (III: 264).

42 *EH* Ḥukat 2 (II: 160).

43 *Mekhilta'* (Vilna: 1844). Unlike the older members of the Vilna Circle, the young Neẓiv does not seem to have been privy to manuscript copies of the Ga'on's work on midrash.

44 *Shenot Eliyahu* (Lemburg: 1799); *Eliyahu Rabba* (Brno: 1802); *Be'urei ha-GRA* on *Shulḥan Arukh, OH,* (Shklov: 1803); *Taharat ha-Kodesh* (Zholkva: 1804); *Be'urei ha-GRA* on *Shulḥan Arukh, YD* (Grodno: 1806); *Aderet Eliyahu* (Dubrovno: 1804); *Hagahot* on *Mishanyot* (Grodno: 1818); *Be'urei ha-GRA* on *Shulḥan Arukh, EH* (Vilna: 1819); *Divre ha-Yamim* (Grodno: 1820); Avot de-Rabbi Natan (Vilna: 1833). Such is also the case for Neẓiv's notes to *Torat Kohanim.* In this short and terse volume which also dates from Neẓiv's youth, Neẓiv cites from the work of the Ga'on on thirteen different occasions, all of which refer to the above list of books. For citations of *Aderet Eliyahu,* see *Vayikra Dibura' de-Ḥovah* 21: 13: 3 (13); *Ẓav* 2: 9 (13); *Shemini Mekhilta' de-milu'im* 2: 10 (20), 4: 1 (20), 4: 12 (21), 10: 2 (23), 17 (18); *Nega'im* 9: 6 (27), 13: 2 (27); *Emor* 4: 5 (35). For citations of *Shenot Eliyahu,* see *Kedoshim* 1: 7 (32), 3: 2 (33). A citation of *Eliyahu Rabba* is found in *Nega'im* 1: 5 (26).

on midrash, it is clear that Neẓiv was well acquainted with the Ga'on's approach to midrashic literature. The references Neẓiv makes to *Aderet Eliyahu* all refer to the way in which the Ga'on treats a midrashic text cited in his commentary. On one occasion Neẓiv writes in reference to a passage in *Mekhilta'* that he "saw that they emend in the name of the Ga'on" in a particular fashion.[45] On at least three occasions Neẓiv writes in regard to a *Sifre* passage that "in the name of the Ga'on they emend" the text in a certain manner.[46] The late date of publication of the Ga'on's notes to *Sifre*,[47] and Neẓiv's implication that these emendations may not have stemmed from the Ga'on himself, suggest that Neẓiv had access to some source, written or oral, in which at least some of the emendations of the Ga'on to *Sifre* were recorded or reported.[48] A comparison of the entire *Sifre* according to the Ga'on's emended text and *Sifre* as emended by Neẓiv, however, suggests that either Neẓiv did not have access to the complete work of the Ga'on on *Sifre*, or that he chose to ignore the overwhelming number of occasions in which the Ga'on's emendations differed from his own.[49] Irrespective of which means Neẓiv employed to acquaint himself with the material, it is clear that he was well aware of the extensive emendational endeavors of the Vilna Ga'on. And, as such, despite the dissimilarity between the content of their emendations to *Sifre*, the very propensity of Neẓiv for unapologetic emendation of rabbinic texts can be traced, at least in some measure, to the influence of the Vilna Ga'on.[50]

Neẓiv's repeated citation of the Ga'on's commentary on *Shulḥan Arukh* provides additional insight into the potential influence of the Ga'on on the developing Neẓiv. Many of the earlier biographers of Neẓiv have noted that his method in talmudic and halakhic study centers around the search for literary antecedents for the passage under consideration that offer insight into how a particular legal position developed,

45 *EH* Naso 2 (I: 15). This particular emendation also appears in Isaac Eliyahu Landau's rendition of the Ga'on's notes to *Mekhilta'* printed under the name *Eifat Ẓedek* in *Mekhilta' 'im be'ur Berurei ha-Midot* (Vilna: 1844).

46 *EH* Naso 44 (I: 172); *EH* Be-ha'alotekha 45 (I: 316); *EH* Matot 1 (II: 279). In *EH* Be-ha'alotekha 16 (I: 233) Neẓiv does not ascribe the emendation to a third party in the name of the Ga'on, but to the Ga'on himself.

47 *Sifre* (Vilna: 1866).

48 See below on the influence of Radal.

49 See Appendix B for a comparison of their emendations to *Sifre* 'Ekev.

50 For a description of the Ga'on's method of emendation and speculation on what motivated him to do so, see Israel of Shklov's introduction to his *Pe'at ha-Shulḥan* (Safed: 1836), 8

or what a particular statement was intended to mean.[51] Such is precisely the method of the Vilna Ga'on in his commentary on *Shulḥan Arukh*. His point of departure is most often the identification of earlier sources of material pertinent to the position advocated by Yosef Caro in his halakhic code. Such material, often found in unsuspected areas of Talmud Bavli, Talmud Yerushalmi, Tosefta, the halakhic *midrashim*, or in a comment by one of the Ge'onim or Rishonim, is used by the Ga'on either to elucidate the statement at hand or as a means of arguing that the ruling issued by Caro or by commentaries on *Shulḥan Arukh* is flawed due to incorrect interpretation of the earlier sources or a failure to account for such sources at all.

The Ga'on's commentary on *Shulḥan Arukh* is also one of the earliest sources of biographical and hagiographical information about the life and methods of the Ga'on. In their introduction to the volume on *Oraḥ Ḥayyim* (Shklov, 1803), the sons of the Ga'on note both the breadth of the Ga'on's Torah study and his emphasis on establishing the correct text:

> For six years he carefully examined and weighed Talmud Bavli and Yerushalmi, Toseftot, *Mekhilta'*, *Sifra*, and *Sifre*, and enlightened the obscurity [caused by] the darkness of the texts [*ha-nusḥa'ot*] and [blazed]the path of wisdom that had been vanquished by excessive *pilpul* which no one could enter and from which no one could leave. And he opened it wide and everyone said "praised is the nation to whom such belongs."

Toward the end of their introduction, in recounting the curriculum the Ga'on was said to have advocated for budding Torah scholars, his sons write that one must first master the twenty-four books of the Bible "and atop their battalions [shall fly] the banner of the wisdom of grammar." And once one has mastered the Bible one should engage in studying the Mishnah "and atop its battalion [shall fly] the banner of its proper readings."

Likewise Ya'akov of Slonim, the grandson of the Ga'on, asks in his introduction to the work, *Commentary on* Shulḥan Arukh:

51 E.g., Epstein (IV: 1694); Zevin, 20.

> Is anything like it to be found? A man in whom the spirit of God spoke and whom God granted [the] wisdom and knowledge [*madda'*] to know how to make the set table [*shulḥan ha-'arukh*] along with its cloth and all of its vessels—those are warriors, the setters of the table whose sources he (i.e., the Ga'on) revealed. And he opened the crate from its side and onto our doorsteps [came] all of the sweets—Mishnah, Gemara, *Tosefta*, and *berayta*; minor tractates, *midrashim*, *Sifra*, and *Sifre*, etc. And also new readings which he raised and brought from tractate to tractate and from Yerushalmi to Bavli, and from Bavli to *Tosefta* and *berayta*, wonderful and pleasant things which all who preceded him never considered.

Thus, time and again in the introduction to a work which was clearly read carefully by the young Neẓiv, the breadth of the Vilna Ga'on's Torah study and the emphasis he placed on emending texts in order to establish an authentic reading is noted, reiterated, and extolled. A mere glance at Neẓiv's *Sifre* commentary reveals that both the consistent use of "Mishnah, Gemara, *Tosefta*, and Berayta; minor tractates, midrashim, *Sifra*, and *Sifre*" as well as the constant attempt to emend and improve the printed text of *Sifre*, are central to the young Neẓiv's endeavor as well.

We might, then, summarize the impact of the Vilna Ga'on on early-nineteenth-century Lithuanian rabbinic scholarship in general, and on Neẓiv's early work in particular, as follows. Certainly his impact is not unknown, as suggested by Etkes, nor is it absent, as suggested by Stampfer. The Ga'on's work was clearly of great importance to scholars such as Einhorn, Radal, Landau, Neẓiv, and others. The Ga'on's work is referred to, cited, discussed, and, at times, copied completely, and the subject matter and methods of study popular amongst these scholars clearly reflect the methods and interests of the Ga'on before them. Of course, the personal ties to the Ga'on through Ya'akov of Slonim, Yehudah Leib Edel, and Sha'ul Katzenellenbogen only strengthen this conclusion.

At the same time, even within the sphere of midrash commentary the Ga'on's influence certainly does not dominate in the way hagiographical accounts might suggest. Furthermore, it seems that for many of the authors discussed above, the Ga'on's work is an important support to their own endeavors but not necessarily the force which drove them to midrash study, plain-sense interpretation, textual emendation, or intellectual breadth in the first place. Rather, it seems that the Ga'on's work was one important factor amongst others in the flourishing of midrash study in the early decades of the nineteenth century. It is to some of the additional factors that we now turn our attention.

### *The "Halakhic" Progression of Torah Commentary*

If we broaden our scope for a moment, and look more generally at the progression of Torah scholarship up until the early nineteenth century, an interesting pattern emerges. Namely, the chronological progression of new foci for rabbinic commentary through the centuries largely follows the order of importance ascribed to such subject matter in the halakhic decision-making process. Thus, rabbinic commentary begins in earnest with the groundbreaking work of Rashi in the eleventh-century[52] on the Talmud Bavli, which had emerged as the unequivocal primary source for all halakhic decision-making. Rashi's work opens the floodgate of Talmud commentaries, first in the lands of Western Europe and then in Christian Spain, which dominate rabbinic exegetical activity for the next few centuries.

The Middle Ages also gives rise to works which seek to simplify and codify the halakhic material found in the talmudic sources. Beginning with the code of Alfasi, and continuing with those of Rambam, Moshe of Coucy, Asheri, and Rabbeinu Asher, and finally concluding with his son's *Arba'ah Turim* and Yosef Caro's *Bet Yosef* and *Shulḥan Arukh*, the works of halakhic codification begin to compete with the books of the Talmud itself as the primary foci of rabbinic study. Hence we find that the new vistas of rabbinic exegetical material in the sixteenth and seventeenth centuries are commentaries on the Codes, such as *Bayit Ḥadash*, *Sefer Me'irat 'Einayim*, *Sifte Kohen*, and *Ture Zahav*.[53]

Throughout this sizable literature of medieval and early modern Talmud and code commentary, the Talmud Yerushalmi is generally treated as

52 The Ge'onim engaged in very little commentarial work. See Robert Brody, *The Ge'onim of Babylonia and the Shaping of Medieval Jewish Culture* (New Haven: Yale University Press, 1998). Rashi was, though, preceded by the commentarial work of Rabbeinu Gershom, only some of which has come down to us.

53 The most comprehensive overview of halakhic literature is Menachem Alon, *Jewish Law: History, Sources, Principles*, trans. Bernard Auerbach and Melvin J. Sykes (Philadelphia: JPS, 1993).

being on the second tier of halakhic material. Its decisions are given normative force only in cases where the Bavli is silent, or where it is unclear as to what the *halakhah* should be.[54] Due in part to its secondary halakhic status, the Talmud Yerushalmi receives almost no serious consideration as an object of rabbinic commentary in and of itself. It seems, though, that by the eighteenth century a critical mass of code commentaries had been reached, and thus rabbinic scholars began to push downward on the halakhic hierarchy and apply themselves, for the very first time, to wide-scale Yerushalmi commentary.[55]

Yehoshua Benveniste seems to have paved the way for this literary shift with his seventeenth-century publication of *Sedeh Yehoshua*, a commentary on the Yerushalmi order of *Zera'im*.[56] This was followed by Eliyahu ben Yehudah Leib Fulda's commentary on *Zera'im*, the tractate *Shekalim*, and some of the order of *Nezikin* in the first half of the eighteenth century.[57] Eliyahu ha-Kohen (d. 1729) added his commentary on *Zera'im*, which was published in 1755.[58] The most significant contributions to Yerushalmi study to emerge from the eighteenth century, however, belong to David Frankel (1704-1762) and Moshe Margolioth. The former's *Korban ha-'Edah*[59] along with its complementary *Shiyare Korban*, and the latter's *Pene Moshe*[60] with its *Mar'eh Penim*, effectively open the world of Talmud Yerushalmi to students of the Bavli who might previously have shied away due to the Yerushalmi's uniquely challenging vocabulary,

54 See Shlomo Luria's "Introduction to Bava Kama" in his *Yam Shel Shlomo* for an explicit statement to this effect. See also Malakhi ha-Kohen's *Yad Malakhi*, Kelalei Shenei ha-Talmudim, #2. While it is true that when weighing the normative force of a text found in Talmud Bavli versus a text found in Talmud Yerushalmi, preference is given to that of Bavli, halakhic decisors also grant considerable weight to common law or *minhag*, which is based on communal practice rather than codified instructions. Historians of Jewish Law have in recent years, noted that much of *Ashkenazic* and Italian *minhag*—and thus, in many cases, *halakhah*—has roots in the case law and rulings found in the Talmud Yerushalmi.

55 A trend most certainly aided by the newfound availability of printed copies of Yerushalmi in the 18th century. While only there was only one printing of Yerushalmi in the seventeenth century (Cracow: 1609), it went through five editions during the first half of the eighteenth century alone (Amsterdam: 1710; Offenbach: 1725; Frankfurt de Main: 1741; Dessau: 1743; Kushta: 1745). Of course, the multiple printings also attest to the significant interest taken in Yerushalmi by mid-eighteenth-century Jewish scholars.

56 Joshua Benveniste, *Sedeh Yehoshua* (*Zera'im*, Constantinople: 1662; *Mo'ed, Nashim Nezikin, ib.* 1754).

57 Eliyahu b. Yehudah, *Peirush on Yerushalmi* (*Zera'im* and *Shekalim*, Amsterdam: 1710; *Bava Kama, Bava Meẓtia, Bava Batra.*, Frankfurt: 1742).

58 Eliyahu ha-Kohen, *Iggeret Eliyahu* (Smyrna: 1755).

59 David Fränkel, *Korban ha-'Edah* (*Seder Mo'ed*, Dessau: 1743; *Seder Nashim, ib.* 1757).

60 Moshe Margolioth, *Pene Moshe* (*Nashim*, Amsterdam: 1750; *Nezikin*, Leghorn: 1770).

syntax, structure, and textual lacunae.

By all accounts, the tannaitic teachings which make up Yehudah ha-Nassi's Mishnah form the foundation of normative halakhah. The gemaras, therefore, both Bavli and Yerushalmi, which are conceived primarily as elucidation and interpretation of the Mishnah, rank one and two in the halakhic pyramid, with primary value accorded to Bavli over Yerushalmi.[61] If we were to speak of a third tier, therefore, it would contain the works thought of as repositories for tanaitic teachings recorded after the Mishnah, which include *Tosefta, Sifra, Sifre*, and other collections of midrash.[62] It is therefore not surprising that in the wake of Frankel and Margolioth's elucidation of the Yerushalmi came interest in composing commentaries on *Tosefta* and the *midrashei halakhah* in the late eighteenth and early nineteenth century. When combined with the influence of the Vilna Ga'on, who gave such works a prominent place in his method of Torah study, this intellectual progression begins to shed light on the flurry of interest in midrash commentary during the first decades of the nineteenth century.

In fact, this pattern can be taken one step further. If we had to define a fourth tier in the hierarchy of primary halakhic source material, it might well consist of the literature of the Ge'onim. The Ge'onim were privy to longstanding halakhic traditions often undocumented in the work of the *tana'aim* and *amora'im*. As a result, their work is at times referred to as a source of law, rather than as applications or explanations of the law. Once again, it is striking to note that following the upsurge in midrash commentary in the late eighteenth and early nineteenth century comes the beginning of commentary on works of the Ge'onim.

Zev Wolf Lipkin (1780-1858)[63] begins this trend with his commentary on the *Sefer Halakhot Gedolot* entitled *Ben Aryeh.*[64] In addition to his work

---

61 See Luria, *Yam Shel Shlomoh*, ad loc.

62 In the final paragraph of his *Kelalei Shenei ha-Talmudim*, Malakhi ha-Kohen writes that "any time Midrash Rabbah contradicts Yerushalmi, the halakhah follows the Yerushalmi." He does not mention any of the halakhic midrashim, but it stands to reason that they fall under the same category. (In fact, we might suggest that the rather strange inclusion of Midrash Rabbah, without reference to *Sifra, Sifre*, or *Mekhilta'*, reflects the fact that Midrash Rabbah was the only collection of midrash even somewhat available to rabbinic scholars during the active period of Malakhi ha-Kohen [1700-1790].)

63 Ze'ev Wolf Lipkin was the father of Yisrael Salanter.

64 The manuscript of this commentary consists of notes Lipkin wrote on his copy of Zolkiev (1811) of *Halakhot Gedolot*. It was first printed in *Sefer Halakhot Gedolot* (Jerusalem: Makhon Yerushalayim, 1992).

on midrash, Radal devotes considerable time to the study and exegesis of *Sefer Halakhot Gedolot*[65] as well as the *She'iltot of Rav Aḥai Ga'on.*[66] He also publishes a compilation of Geonic responsa entitled *Teshuvot Geonim.*[67] Avraham Shimon Traub (1811-1874) also composes a commentary on *Sefer Halakhot Gedolot,*[68] as does Yosef Zekhariah Stern (1831-1903) later in the century.[69] Neẓiv, of course, publishes his massive commentary on the geonic *She'iltot* in 1861. Avraham Harkavy, a student and friend of Neẓiv, dedicates much of his scholarly work as a librarian in the Imperial Library in St. Petersburg to the study of the Ge'onim, as evidenced by his *Zikkaron la-Rishonim ve-Gam la-Aḥaronim,*[70] which contains biographies and works of Shmuel ha-Naggid, Shmuel ben Ḥofni, Sa'adya Ga'on, and Hai Ga'on, amongst others. Yeruḥam Perlow (1846-1934) brings the genre of traditionalist Geonica study into the twentieth century with the printing of his elaborate commentary on Sa'adya Ga'on's *Sefer ha-Miẓvot* in 1914.[71]

**Primary subjects of rabbinic commentary over time**

| Halakhic "Rank" | *11th Century* | *16th Century* | *18th Century* | *19th Century* |
|---|---|---|---|---|
| 1 | Talmud Bavli ⇨ | | | |
| | | Halakhic Codes ⇨ | | |
| 2 | | | Talmud Yerushalmi ⇨ | |
| 3 | | | | Midrash / Tosefta ⇨ |
| 4 | | | | Geonim ⇨ |

65 Luria's comments on *Halakhot Gedolot* were also composed as notes to his copy of the 1811 Zolkiev edition.

66 In a clear display of the profound influence of Radal on the young Neẓiv, Neẓiv also dedicates much of his intellectual energy toward the composition of a massive commentary on the *She'iltot*. Neẓiv will go so far as to publish Radal's comments along with his own in *Ha'amek She'elah* (Vilna: 1861).

67 David Luria, *Teshuvot ha-Ge'onim* (Leipzig: 1868).

68 *Sefer Halakhot Gedolot* (Warsaw: 1874), reprinted in *Sefer Halakhot Gedolot* (Jerusalem: Makhon Yerushalayim, 1992).

69 Stern mentions this work amongst several others that remain unpublished in his *Teshuvot Zekher Yehosef*, vol. III (Jerusalem: 1967), 82.

70 Avraham Harkavy, *Zikkaron la-Rishonim we-gam la-Aḥaronim. Studien und Mittheilungen aus der St. Petersburg Kaiserlichen Bibliothek*, 5 vols. (St. Petersburg: 1879-82).

71 Yeruḥam Perlow, *Peirush Sefer Ha-Miẓvot le-Rabbi Sa'adia Ga'on* (Warsaw: 1914-1917). It should be noted that Sa'adya Ga'on's original work took the form of an *'azharah*, and it was Perlow who formatted it as a *Sefer ha-Miẓvot*.

As noted above, the chronological progression of commentaries in order of halakhic authority may help to explain the interest of the Vilna Ga'on, Ẓvi Hirsch ha-Kohen Rappaport, Yiẓḥak Eliyahu Landau, Ḥanokh Zundel ben Yosef, and Neẓiv in *midrash halakhah*. For Neẓiv and Radal it might help to explain their interest in *She'iltot* as well. It does little, however, to increase our understanding of the distinct interest in the aggadic portions of midrash which clearly grows during this period as well.

### *The Lithuanian* Maggid

Insight into the rise of midrash aggadah commentary in the early nineteenth century might be gained by noting the large number of scholars engaged in such activity who also served their community in the capacity of official *maggid*, or preacher. Yeḥezkel Feivel served as the *maggid* of Vilna in the beginning of the 19th century, as did Yiẓḥak Eliyahu Landau several years later. Yehudah Leib Edel was the *maggid* in Slonim, and Ḥanokh Zundel Luria served as *maggid* in both New Zhagory and Novogroduk. Yehoshua Heschel Levin, a member of the Volozhin Circle who authored notes to *Midrash Rabbah,* served as the official *maggid* to the Jewish community of Paris. The correlation of *maggid* and aggadic midrash study is a natural one in that one of the primary responsibilities of a *maggid* was to deliver weekly sermons based on the Sabbath Torah reading. As midrash aggadah is often organized according to the weekly Torah portions and offers insights and teachings generally less technical than its halakhic counterpart, it stands to reason that it would be a resource often tapped by the *maggidim*. The mere fact that the aggadic midrash aided the *maggidim* in performing their official responsibilities, though, does not alone explain the rise in focused study of midrash aggadah and in the subsequent flourishing of commentary devoted to it. However, a closer look at the position of *maggid* in the Lithuanian Jewish community may serve to further explicate the matter.

While the *maggid* is often imagined as an itinerant preacher who enjoyed the status of a second-rate intellectual at best, this was certainly not the case in the major towns of Lithuania. Hillel Noah Maggid Steinschneider points out that the position of "*maggid mesharim*" in Vilna consisted of a judicial appointment to the city's official court of Jewish law, along with the additional responsibility of publicly preaching at the city's main synagogue on Sabbath afternoons.[72] While appointments to this official position ended with the controversy surrounding the deposed official rabbi of Vilna in 1777, it is clear from the scholars selected to fill Vilna's post-1777 independent *maggid* position that it was reserved for a man of exceptional eloquence and extraordinary intelligence.[73] Thus, of the first three *maggidim* to serve Vilna in the nineteenth century, both Yeḥezkel Feivel and Yiẓḥak Eliyahu Landau proved their intellectual prowess through their writings. Only Shelomoh Zev Maggid does not do so, in that his sole literary work is largely a reformulation of his father's insights rather than an intellectual product of his own.[74] It is important to note, however, that Shelomoh Zev effectively inherits his position from his father, Yeḥezkel Feivel, whereas Yeḥezkel Feivel and Landau are appointed solely on the basis of their own merits.[75]

Following Landau's death in 1876, the community of Vilna is said to have desired Meir Leibush Malbim (1809-1879) to assume the position of *maggid*. His candidacy is reported to have been rejected due to his prior expulsion from the Russian town of Mohilev, though his cantankerous personality might have contributed as well. Nonetheless, Malbim's candidacy makes perfect sense in that his proven intellectual prowess, as well as his interest in Bible commentary and midrashic literature, precisely fit the mold of what a Vilna *maggid* should be. In the end, the young Ya'akov Yosef (1848-1902) assumed the position of Vilna *maggid* in 1883. Although not a prolific author like Landau or Malbim, from his early days as a student of Neẓiv in Volozhin to his final days as one of New York's prominent rabbinic authorities Ya'akov Yosef was similarly known for his sharp intellect.[76] The eigteenth-century endeavors

---

72 Steinschneider, vol. I, 102.

73 For a history of the controversy see Israel Klausner, *Vilna: Yerushalayim de-Lita* (Israel: Ghetto Fighter's House, 1988), 88-102.

74 Shelomoh Zev Maggid, *Mussar ve-Da'at* (Vilna: 1868).

75 Nonetheless, Shelomoh Zev Maggid, also known as Zalman Zev, was appointed to the committee of rabbinic elite who were to decide whether Neẓiv or Yosef Baer Soloveitchik was to take over the leadership of the Volozhin yeshivah following the death of Eliezer Yiẓḥak Fried, which testifies to his standing as one of the Lithuanian community's most revered rabbinic authorities.

76 On Ya'akov Yosef in New York, See Abraham J. Karp, "New York Chooses a Chief Rabbi," *Publications of the American Jewish Historical Society* 44, 3 (March 1955): 129–198; Arthur Goren, New York Jews and the Quest for Community: the Kehillah Experiment, 1908-1922 (New York: Columbia University Press, 1970); Jeffrey S. Gurock, "How 'Frum' Was Rabbi Jacob Joseph's Court? Americanization Within the Lower East Side's Orthodox Elite, 1886-1902," *Jewish History* 8, 1-2 (Winter 1994): 1-14; Kimmy Caplan, "Rabbi Jacob Joseph,

of Ya'akov ben Wolf Kranz, the famed *maggid* of Dubno and Ḥayyim Avraham ben Aryeh Leib, *maggid* of Mohilev,[77] as well as the nineteenth-century work of Yehudah Leib Edel, *maggid* of Slonim, and Ḥanokh Zundel Luria, *maggid* of Novogroduk, suggest that the intellectual *maggid* was a widespread phenomenon and not unique to Vilna alone.

As the position of *maggid* in large Lithuanian towns was more akin to that of a public intellectual than a soapbox preacher, many of them proved capable not only of reading works of *midrash* aggadah and incorporating them into a sermon but also of analyzing them, emending them, and composing commentaries on them. In fact, the intellectual breadth reflected in these commentaries might also at least partially result from the *maggid*'s quest for material that would pique the interest of his audience. Hence the *maggid* would cite a wide range of relevant material, whether it came from *Arabian Nights*, as in the case of the Dubno Maggid, or from ha-Levi, 'Aramah, de' Rossi, or Mendelssohn, as in the case of the nineteenth-century *maggidim.*

Furthermore, it stands to reason that if the position of *maggid* was well respected in major Lithuanian communities, we might expect to find young men who at an early age decide that being a communal *maggid* might be their calling. These students, therefore, might concentrate their studies on the midrashic and philosophic material which would aid them in their pursuit of a *maggid* position. Such an account is explicitly related by Ḥanokh Zundel Luria in the introduction to his *Kenaf Renanim*. He writes that at an early age he "realized his strengths reside in his ability to understand and his desire to learn." However, since it was apparent that his interests were a bit broader than those of the typical Talmud student, he decided to channel his energy into preparing for the position of *maggid*. He did so by studying "the books of early sages, people of repute, pillars of Torah, mightiest of leaders, *sefer ha-Kuzari, sifre ha-Ga'on Rabbeinu Sa'adiah, ve-Rabeinu Baḥya, ha-rav hagadol Rambam…mahari 'Albo,*

---

New York's Chief Rabbi - New Perspectives," *Hebrew Union College Annual* 67 (1996): 1-43 (Hebrew Section); Edward T. O'Donnell, "Hibernians Versus Hebrews?: A New Look at the 1902 Jacob Joseph Funeral Riot," *Journal of the Gilded Age and Progressive Era* (forthcoming).

77 His *Pat Leḥem* commentary on Baḥya ibn Paquda's, *Ḥovot ha-Levavot* (Shklov, 1803) [reprinted in *Ḥovot ha-Levavot* (Jerusalem: Masoret Yisrael, 2003)] makes extensive use of classical philosophy and science (see 14, 72, 133, 137, 149, 162) and also displays his proficiency in German (see 27, 204). Also see David E. Fishman, *Russia's First Modern Jews: The Jews of Shklov* (New York: New York University Press, 1995), 73.

*Ba'al ha-'Akeidah*" as well as "*agadot, midrashim,*" and "*mikra'ei kodesh.*"[78]

While a basic sketch of the position of the Lithuanian *maggid* helps to explain the general interest in aggadic midrash, the scholarly nature of such study, and the intellectual breadth which often accompanied it, the question remains as to why a flourishing of such activity should take place specifically during the first few decades of the nineteenth century. After all, as stated above, the position of *maggid* and the scholarly nature of the position, well preceded the nineteenth century. In the simplest of terms, the answer to that question lies in the fact that it was only during the first decades of the nineteenth century that the texts necessary for such study became readily available.

### *Hebrew Print and the Study of Midrash*

The startling fact that Hebrew printing did not blossom in Eastern Europe until the late eighteenth and early nineteenth century, three hundred and fifty years after Gutenberg invented his press, has already been well documented.[79] While Hebrew printing houses were established in Eastern European centers such as Cracow and Lublin by the first half of the sixteenth-century, by the middle of the seventeenth century the growth of Eastern European Hebrew print industry slowed dramatically. This trend is all the more significant when compared to the population explosion of the Eastern European Jewish community during the same period. From 1613 to 1734 only one new Hebrew printing house opened in the Polish-Lithuanian Commonwealth.[80] Gershon Hundert, in his work on the Jews of Poland and Lithuania, calls it "most puzzling…that the massive market for Jewish books in the Commonwealth was served by only one domestic center of production during the entire period between 1692 and about 1760."[81] Even if we expand the range to include the one hundred and sixty-three years between 1613 and 1776, we find that

78 *Kenaf Renanim* (Pressburg: 1859), *Hakdamat ha-Mefaresh*, 2.

79 E.g., Bernhard Friedberg, *Ha-Defus ha-'Ivri be-Polaniyah* (Tel Aviv: 1950); Israel Halperin, "*Va'ad Arba Arazot be-Polin ve-ha-Sefer ha-'Ivri,*" *Yehudim ve-Yahadut be-Mizraḥ Eiropa*h (Jerusalem: 1968); and, more recently, Moshe Rosenfeld, *ha-Defus ha-'Ivri me-Reishito Ad Shenat 1948* (Jerusalem: 1992).

80 The Zolkiev press was founded in 1691 by Uri (Phoebus) ben Aaron ha-Levi (1625-1715) of Amsterdam under orders of Johan Sabieski. See Friedberg, 52.

81 Gershon David Hundert, *Jews in Poland-Lithuania in the Eighteenth Century: A Genealogy of Modernity* (Berkeley: University of California Press, 2004), 54-55.

only six new Hebrew printing houses opened in all of Eastern Europe. In the ten years following 1776, however, six more printing houses open. Over the next decade eleven more follow suit. And according to Moshe Rosenfeld and Joshua Bloch, the fifty years between 1782 and 1832 witnessed the establishment of at least fifty new Eastern European Hebrew printing houses, thus completely reversing the trend set over the previous century and a half.[82]

**Table 2: The Rise of Hebrew Print in Eastern Europe**

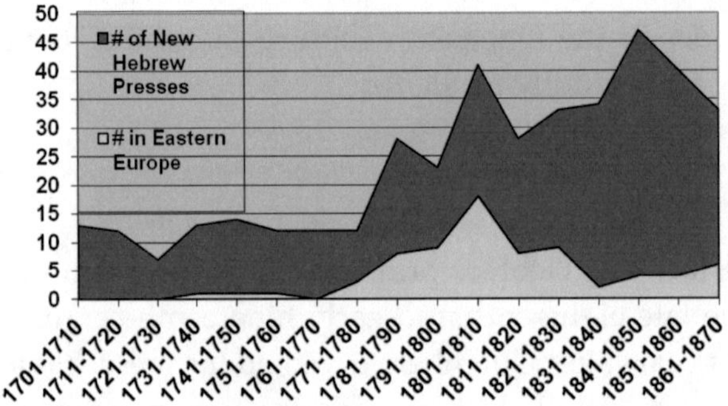


Based on Joshua Bloch, *Hebrew Printing and Bibliography*, ed. Charles Berlin (New York: New York Public Library and Ktav Publishing House, 1976).

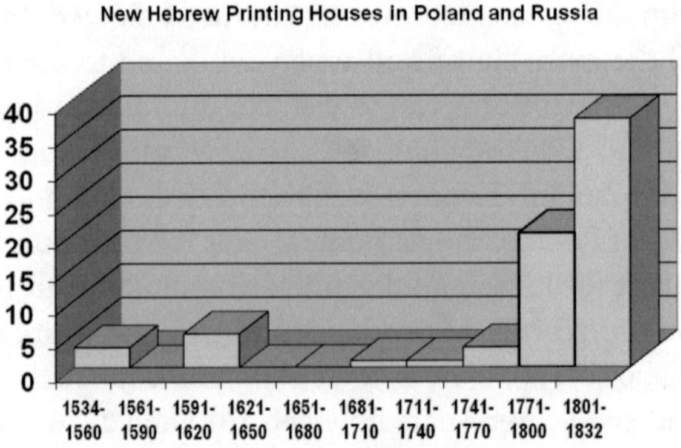


Based on Moshe Rosenfeld, *Ha-Defus Ha-Ivri Me-reishito ad shenat 1948*, (Jerusalem, 1992), 26-43.

82 It is important to note that many of these presses did not last more than a few years. Some of them were transferred to a different location, and thus what Rosenfeld and Bloch list as two new printing houses may be the same house but displaced. Others closed down completely without ever significantly contributing to the flow of Hebrew books in Eastern Europe. Nonetheless, the rapid growth of the Eastern European Hebrew print industry over the last decades of the eighteenth century and into the first few decades of the nineteenth century is undeniable.

A number of significant political factors affecting the Polish Lithuanian Jewish community during the seventeenth and eighteenth centuries undoubtedly played a significant role in stymieing the growth of the Eastern European Hebrew press. The first was the climate of instability, invasion, and rebellion which plagued the Commonwealth from the Cossak-Ruthenian revolt of 1648 and the subsequent Muscovite-Swedish invasion in 1654 until the partition of Poland by Russia, Prussia, and Austro-Hungary in the last decades of the eighteenth century. The 1648 uprising, led by Bogdan Chmielnicki, inflicted significant damage on the region's two major centers of printing, Cracow and Lublin.[83] Moreover, the harsh toll inflicted upon the Jewish communities of Poland and Lithuania by this century of unrest resulted not only in physical losses of life, property, and sources of income, but in psychological losses of security and stability which were often replaced by a paralyzing fear of impending crisis. Such circumstances did not encourage the establishment of new business enterprises that required imported technology and significant machinery which would be lost if and when Jews were again forced to flee. Furthermore, the lack of stability seems to have led to a general decline in the establishment of centers of learning and scholarship, which in turn diminished the market for Hebrew books.[84] However, following the return of political stability to the region in the late decades of the eighteenth century, Hebrew print immediately began to flourish.

The second factor of significance in this regard is the fact that Hebrew print was an industry highly controlled and regulated in the seventeenth and eighteenth centuries both by the internal political systems of the Jewish community and by the regulations set by the nobility and government of the Polish-Lithuanian Commonwealth. Thus, for example, the *Va'ad 'Arba' 'Araẓot* in 1594 proclaimed that "no printer shall print any book without the consent of the rabbis and leaders" and "if the printer violates [this prohibition], they (the rabbis and leaders of the *Va'ad*) will nullify the work of their press and excommunicate the printer and all

---

83 See Friedberg, 39, as well as Aryeh Tauber, *Meḥkarim Bibliographiim* (Jerusalem: Hebrew University, 1932), 17.

84 See M.J. Rosman, "The Image of Poland as a Center of Torah Learning after the Massacres of 1648," *Zion* 51 (1986): 435-48. Interestingly, the very same trend will help to bolster the success of *Ḥasidut*, which, in turn, leads to the creation of new genres and new markets for Hebrew books. See Ze'ev Gries, *Sifrut ha-Hanhagot* (Jerusalem: Mosad Bialik, 1989) and his *Sefer, Sofer ve-Sipur be-Reshit ha-Ḥasidut* (Jerusalem: Kibutz ha-Meuchad, 1992).

of his associates."[85] Furthermore, in order to protect the interests of the Polish printing houses, the *Va'ad* declared that the Hebrew publishing houses of Italy were prohibited from printing any works which were also being printed by the presses of Cracow and Lublin, and if they did so, these works were not to be sold in the Polish lands for a designated period of time.[86] Similar pronouncements from 1594 and 1595 banned books printed in Basel and in Moravia from being imported into Polish lands.[87]

When the third Eastern European Hebrew press opened its doors in Zolkiew in 1692, a similar process ensued. The *Va'ad* recognized the great need for an additional publishing house and applauded the high standards Uri Phoebus promised to bring to this new endeavor. The *Va'ad* demonstrated its support by issuing an explicit ban on the printing or importing of any book which might compete with a similar volume printed in Zolkiew. Furthermore, they restricted the three Polish presses to printing no more then 700 copies per annum of the "*kuntresim*," the basic study texts which formed the basis of their business, by sending "controllers" to each of the publishing houses and ordering them to sign each printed copy, while simultaneously issuing a ban on any copies which did not contain such a signature.[88]

In 1726 and again in 1754 the *Va'ad* reiterated its ban on the publication of books that were not explicitly granted its approval.[89] While the need for such repeated decrees suggests that its authority and control over the Hebrew print industry was beginning to erode, the fact that the members of the *Va'ad* made such proclamations demonstrates that Hebrew print remained a highly regularized industry right through the first half of the eighteenth century.

In addition to the restrictions levied by the rabbinic leadership, the overwhelming tendency of Jews in the Polish-Lithuanian Commonwealth to live in private cities subjected them to the demands of the

---

85 Israel Halperin, "The Council of Four Lands and the Hebrew Book," *Kiyat Sefer* 9 (Jerusalem: 1932): 370. The Council could prevent competition by invoking the Jewish stricture of *hasagat gevul*, which limits business establishments in a given region to the number thought sustainable by the local population.

86 Ibid.

87 Ibid., 372.

88 Ibid., 374. See also *Pinkas Va'ad Arba Araẓot*, ed. Israel Halperin (Jerusalem: Bialik Institute, 1945), 237-241.

89 Ibid., 378.

nobility as well. It was not uncommon for the nobleman to set limits on the number and type of industries which he allowed on his estate and to regulate the import of foreign goods through steep tariffs.[90] Hence, the charter of the Jewish community of Zamosc in 1684, for example, limits the ownership of Hebrew books to those used for liturgical purposes, and prohibits the import or export of any goods for which explicit permission had not been granted.[91] Furthermore, Gershon Hundert has shown that the one center of Hebrew print which did exist in eighteenth-century Eastern Europe, that of Zolkiew, was under the control of the Radziwill family, one of the most powerful noble families in the Commonwealth. Thus, Hundert writes, "The role of the powerful Radziwills in protecting their own interests was likely the critical ingredient in this story [of the stymied growth of the Eastern European Hebrew print industry]."[92]

Several events transpired, though, during the second half of the eighteenth century which substantially advanced the growth of the Eastern European Hebrew print industry. To begin, the disbanding of the *Va'ad Lita* in 1762 and the *Va'ad 'Arba' 'Araẓot* in 1764 diminished the power of Jewish communal leadership to control regional industries and to limit competition amongst Hebrew presses. The power of the Polish nobility was also compromised over the last decades of the century. 1772 marks the beginning of a three-stage process in which the Austrian and Russian Empires, along with Prussia, divided the lands of the Polish-Lithuanian Commonwealth for themselves. The Russian Tsarina Catherine the Great demanded an oath of allegiance from the Polish nobility before granting them continued control of their estates. When some refused, Catherine usurped their lands and gave them to loyal members of the Russian gentry.[93] These lands, then, and the Jewish communities located within them, were extricated from their Polish charters and came under the rule of the Tsar. Catherine, who fancied herself an enlightened absolutist,

90 See Raphael Posner and Israel Ta-Shema, eds., *The Hebrew* Book: *An Historical Survey* (New York: Leon Amiel, 1975), 112. For an overview of the regulations set by Polish nobility on Jewish commerce in the Commonwealth, see M.J. Rosman, *The Lord's Jews: Magnate-Jewish Relations in the Polish-Lithuanian Commonwealth During the 18th Century* (Cambridge, MA: Harvard University Press, 1990), 75-105.

91 Jacob Goldberg, *Jewish Privileges in the Polish Commonwealth*, vol. I (Jerusalem: The Israel Academy of Sciences and Humanities, 1985), 397.

92 Hundert, 56.

93 See David E. Fishman, *Russia's First Modern Jews: The Jews of Shklov* (New York: New York University Press, 1995), 46.

signed a ukase on January 27, 1783, permitting the creation of Hebrew language printing presses. The Jewish communities of the formerly Polish towns in the Vitebsk region took immediate advantage by opening a Hebrew press in Shklov the very same year. In 1802 another printing house opened in neighboring Kopyss and another in nearby Dubrowna. The following year, yet another printing house opened in the Vitebsk region, this time in the Hasidic stronghold of Lyady.

As Catherine the Great paved the way for the founding of printing houses in her newly conquered territory, a similar process took place within the remaining lands of Poland. King Stanisław August Poniatowski, the last ruler of the Polish-Lithuanian Commonwealth and a former lover of Catherine's, focused his reign on two major objectives. One was to solidify the power of the Polish monarchy, thus wresting from the Polish nobility their traditional status as virtual monarchs in their own lands. The other was to reform the Polish educational system, thereby fostering the enlightenment of the Polish people. Thus, it was Stanislaw who ordered the printer Peter Defour to establish a multi-lingual printing house in Warsaw. When Defour sought permission from Stanislaw to expand his printing capacity to include Hebrew, Stanislaw responded with instructions to create a state-of-the-art Hebrew printing house so as to keep monies previously spent by the Jewish community on imported books within the state. Defour eventually determined that such a project was beyond his means, and leased his rights to Jan Anton Krieger, who opened the Hebrew publishing house in Nowy Dwor, outside Warsaw, in 1781.[94] A similar process took place in Grodno where, under Stanislaw's orders, the capacity of the local printing house was expanded to include Hebrew in 1785.[95]

In the southern regions of Poland, the spread of Hassidut and its polemics against the community of mitnagdim spurred the opening of several additional printing houses in the region of Volhynia. The press in Korec opened in 1776, one in Polonoyye opened in 1783, another in nearby Slavuta opened in 1790, and the press of neighboring Ostrog opened in 1793. Zhitomir's press opened in 1804, and in 1812 the Sudylkov press was founded.[96]

---

94 Friedberg, 75.
95 Ibid., 96.
96 Ibid.

The Polish territories acquired by Austria, however, underwent a very different transition. In an effort to ensure that all books printed in the Austrian Empire passed through the government censor's office, the old Polish Hebrew press of Zolkiew, established in 1691, was moved to Lvov, the Austrian government center in the Galician region and the home of the government censor. As a result, though, Lvov quickly emerged as a major center for the Eastern European Hebrew print industry.[97]

While the number of extant publishing houses prior to 1780 and the number of different titles printed therein suggest a limited availability of Hebrew books in Eastern Europe prior to the nineteenth century, the fact that Jewish communities of the East imported books from printing centers such as Amsterdam, Frankfurt, Dyhernfurth and Sulzbach requires that we offer additional evidence to support the contention that there was a general paucity of printed Hebrew material available in late eighteenth- and early nineteenth-century Eastern Europe. In particular, our interest is in determining that works of midrash, and the wide range of texts used by early nineteenth-century midrash scholars, were not readily available in Eastern Europe prior to the turn of that century. To do so, we will first look at anecdotal evidence which supports such a claim. Then we will turn our attention to the publication history of such works to further demonstrate not only the unavailability of these texts during most of the eighteenth century, but their dramatic resurgence at the dawn of the nineteenth.

In the anecdotal realm, Gershon Hundert's examination of the library in Volozhin's *bet midrash* in the eighteenth century provides important insight.[98] Hundert frames his study of the minute book of Volozhin's Mishnah Society as a corrective to the work of Simḥah Assaf and Ze'ev Gries, who suggested that the *batei midrash* of the eighteenth century were overflowing with thousands of books.[99] In contrast, Hundert argues

97 See Friedberg, 62-65 and 82-86.

98 Gershon David Hundert, "The Library of the Study Hall in Volozhin, 1762: Some Notes on the Basis of a Newly Discovered Manuscript," *Jewish History* 14, 2 (2000): 225-244. See also the words of Moshe Yosef of Krinick, cited in Tanhum Frank, *Toldot Bet ha-Shem be-Volozhin* (Jerusalem: 2001), 7.

99 See Simḥah Assaf, "*Am ha-sefer ve-ha-sefer,*" *Be'ohalei Ya'akov* (Jerusalem: 1943), 1-26, and his "*Sifriyot Batei Midrash,*" *Yad la-Kore* 1, 7-9 (Nov./Dec. 1946-Jan. 1947), 170-172; Ze'ev Gries, *Sefer Sofer, ve-Sipur bi-Reishit ha-Ḥasidut* (Israel: Ha-Kibutz ha-me'uhad, 1992). Cited in Hundert.

that Volozhin's *bet midrash* contained only 87 different titles.[100] He also notes that those books which contain places of publication were largely imported from Western Europe, thus suggesting the inability of the local presses to serve even the modest needs of the local *bet midrash* in Volozhin.[101]

Most striking for our present purpose, however, is Hundert's list of the books that were present in Volozhin's *bet midrash*. Or, more precisely, which books were not present in Volozhin's *bet midrash*. Of the eighty-seven books available to the scholarly-minded residents of 1760s Volozhin,[102] none were works of midrash. While there was a copy of Ya'akov ibn Habib's anthology of talmudic aggadah, *En Ya'akov*, there was not a single copy of *Midrash Rabbah, Mekhilta', Tanḥuma, Sifre, Sifra, Pesikta' de-Rav Kahana*, or any of the other midrashic works which so captivated the Lithuanian scholars of the first decades of the nineteenth century. In the philosophic realm, ibn Pakuda's *Ḥovot ha-Levavot* was represented, but there were no copies of the philosophic writings of Sa'adya Ga'on, Rambam, ha-Levi, Albo, or 'Aramah. While there was a basic Hebrew grammar, there were no Hebrew works or translations of books on history, geography or the natural sciences, all of which become commonplace amongst Lithuanian rabbinic scholars by the end of the century.

Other writings of the period contain similar accounts of the unavailability of the aforementioned midrashic Torah texts. Avraham Yekutiel Lichtenstein, rabbi of Plonsk (near Warsaw) in the eighteenth century, remarks in the introduction to his commentary on *Sifre* that he has taken up the task of publishing *Sifre* along with his comments due to the fact that the work simply couldn't be found.[103] Despite his noble intentions, Lichtenstein did not succeed in publishing his commentary, and it is only his son, in 1811, who actually brought *Sifre* together with the commentary *Zera' Avraham* to press. Similarly, Ẓvi Hirsch ben Aryeh Margoliot, the Shklov printer of Yehudah Leib Margoliot's *Bet Middot* (1786) notes in

100 Hundert, 231.

101 Ibid. Similar texts printed locally would undoubtedly have been cheaper, and thus the presence of imported books implies that locally printed versions simply were not available.

102 Hundert also notes that Aryeh Leib Ginsburg, author of the responsa *Sha'agat Aryeh*, was rabbi of Volozhin during this period (230). We might also note that it is during this period in Volozhin that Ginsburg trained a promising young scholar named Ḥayyim of Volozhin, to whom he married his daughter.

103 *Sifre 'im peirush Zera' Avraham* (Dyhernfurth, 1811), Hakdamah Sheniah: Ma'aleh Harishonah.

the preface that in most cities one would be hard pressed to find a single copy of Sa'adya Ga'on's *'Emunot ve-De'ot,* Joseph Albo's *'Ikkarim,* or Isaac 'Arama's *Akeidat Yiẓhak.*

By the middle of the nineteenth century, however, anecdotal evidence suggests that Hebrew books such as these had become far more accessible. Indeed, the availability of basic Hebrew books grew so rapidly over the first decades of the nineteenth century that one hundred years after Volozhin's Mishnah Society reported having only the third volume of Rambam's *Mishneh Torah* in their library and not a single volume of the Talmud Yerushalmi, the interest of many Eastern European scholars turned toward the establishment of an Antiquarian Society for the publication and distribution of rare manuscripts. Eliezer Lipman Zilberman, editor of the Hebrew newspaper *ha-Maggid,* spearheads the effort to establish this society which he calls *Mekiẓe Nirdamim,* Awakers of the Slumbering.[104] In trying to raise support for his society in September of 1861, Zilberman anticipates that some will see no need for his endeavors, due to the fact that books are now readily available. "After all," they will say, "such printing houses are now numerous in [our] lands and people have already started to print old manuscripts and also books that are expensive, so for what do we need such a society?"[105]

Likewise, Neẓiv notes in his 1861 introduction to *Ha'amek She'elah* that the later Torah scholars have done great injustice to Rambam's *Mishneh Torah* in that they "have tried to fit everything into the Rambam and explain him with *pilpulin* (casuistry)" rather than explore the primary sources, often Geonic or midrashic, upon which Rambam's statements are based. However, Neẓiv refrains from passing judgment on these earlier commentators and states instead that "they are not to be blamed, as printing had not developed enough to facilitate it—thus they would only understand the Talmud according to Rashi and other known commentators" rather than the way it was understood by midrashic sources

104 Although *ha-Maggid* was not an Eastern European newspaper, much of its readership was in Eastern Europe. Likewise, although *Mekiẓe Nirdamim* was an international society with representatives all over the world, a large percentage of those who subscribed lived in Eastern Europe. The Lithuanian towns of Vilna, Lomza, Minsk, Brisk, Kovno, and Dvinsk alone accounted for 225 of the 1107 subscribers listed in *Reshimah shel Shemot Ha-ḥaverim le-ḥevrat mekiẓe nirdamim 1865*-66 (Lyck: 1866).

105 *Ha-Maggid,* Sept. 12, 1861 (no. 36). The November 28 edition of that same year announces the membership of "*Ha-Rav ha-Ga'on Moreinu ha-Rav Naftali Ẓvi Yehudah Berlin, Volozhin*" in the newly created society.

and the Ge'onim.[106] The implication, of course, is that by 1861 the state of printing had advanced to a point where a proper study could—and, in Neẓiv's case, would—now be done.

The publication histories of midrashic texts further support our contention.[107] Many of the works which become the foci of early nineteenth-century Lithuanian scholars were hardly printed at all over the course of the preceding century. The few which did enjoy steady publication were printed in Western Europe and thus were subject to the costly import process. However, once the printing houses of Eastern Europe began to flourish in the late eighteenth century, these books immediately returned to circulation.

Thus, for example, *Sifra* was first printed in Constantinople in 1530. It then went through three more editions over the next 80 years. From 1609 to 1818, however, *Sifra* was printed only once, in Dessau in 1742. In 1818, it was printed in Kopyss (in the Vitebsk region), and another edition was produced in Vilna in 1845.

*Sifre,* the text most germane to our present study, was first published in Venice in 1545. It was not printed again until 1789, when it was republished in Hamburg. Thereafter, however, it was printed in Sulzbach in 1802 and then in Eastern Europe on the Mencowice press in 1803. In the same year it was also printed in Salonica and the next year it was printed in Dyhernfurth as well.

*Mekhilta',* the last of the *midrashei halakhah,* has a similar history. It was first printed in Constantinople in 1515 and again in Venice in 1545. The next printing of *Mekhilta'* was close to two hundred years later in

---

106 *HS* Kh 1: 16.

107 The publication records presented here are based on the Institute for Hebrew Bibliography's software, entitled *The Bibliography of the Hebrew Book 1473-1960,* and on Chapter B. Friedberg, *Bet Eked Sefarim,* 2nd ed. (Tel Aviv: 1952). A methodological note is in order here. Above we argued that Stampfer's reliance on printing records to determine the influence on the Vilna Ga'on's writing was flawed in that it did not account for the circulation of hand-copied manuscripts. Here, we are about to offer our own arguments based on printing records, but with a significant difference. Stampfer was arguing his point from the silence of the printing histories—a silence which might have been disrupted had manuscripts been taken into account. While we too will note the absence of certain works from publication histories, we will not conclude that such works had no influence during that period. We will leave open the possibility that such works were imported, preserved in private libraries or communal *batei midrashim,* or circulated in manuscript form. We will argue, however, that the dramatic emergence of certain works in a short period of time definitively indicates the increased availability of such works, particularly in the immediate surroundings of the press from which they emanate.

Amsterdam in 1712. It was printed again, though, in Livorno in 1801, and Yiẓḥak Eliyahu Landau's edition was published in Vilna in 1844.

The publication histories of the aggadic *midrashim* are perhaps even more striking. *Midrash Tanḥuma* was first printed in Constantinople in 1520. It then went through five more editions over the next century. From the Prague printing of 1613 until its printing in Frankfurt der Oder in 1792, only two printings were made (Frankfurt der Oder, 1701 and Amsterdam 1733). Over the next twenty years, however, from 1792 until 1812, *Midrash Tanḥuma* was printed ten times, in such places as Cracow, Lvov, Mencowice, Zolkiew, and Shklov.

The histories of *Midrash Tehillim,* also referred to as *Shoḥer Tov*, and that of *Tanna de-Bei Eliyahu,* are virtually identical to that of *Tanḥuma*. *Shoḥer Tov* went through four printings between 1512 and 1613. It was then printed once in the course of the next one hundred and eighty years (Amsterdam, 1730). From 1794 to 1808, however, it went through four editions, all of them in the newly founded printing centers of Eastern Europe: Polonoyye (1794), Zolkiew (1800), Mohalov (1803), and Berdichev (1808). *Tanna de-Bei Eliyahu* went through two early editions in 1598 (Venice) and in 1676 (Prague). For the next one hundred and twenty years, as the European Jewish community grew by leaps and bounds, *Tanna de-Bei Eliyahu* was printed only once (Zolkiew, 1753). From 1796 to 1826, however, the work enjoyed nine different printings and, with the exception of the Prague edition of 1815, all of the printings took place in Eastern Europe.

Unlike *Shoḥer Tov, Tanḥuma,* and *Tanna de-Bei Eliyahu, Yalkut Shim'oni* enjoyed regular publication through the end of the seventeenth century. In Frankfurt am Main in 1709, however, it was printed for the first and last time in the eighteenth century. It next resurfaced in the Eastern European press of Polonoyye in 1805.

The publication histories of *Pirkei de-Rabbi Eliezer* and *Midrash Rabbah,* however, were slightly different. Both of these works remained in regular circulation throughout the sixteenth, seventeenth, and eighteenth centuries. It is significant, though, that the 1608 Cracow edition of *Midrash Rabbah* and the 1617 Cracow edition of *Pirkei de-Rabbi Eliezer* represent the last Eastern European printings of either work until the late eighteenth century. Beginning with its 1784 printing in Shklov, however, *Pirkei de-Rabbi Eliezer* goes through four more Eastern European printings before 1806, and from 1818 until 1850 it is printed eleven more times, all of them in Eastern Europe. The history of *Midrash Rabbah* is quite similar.

It is printed in Mencowice in 1798 and then reprinted ten times over the next twenty years, each time in one of the new centers of Hebrew print in Eastern Europe.

*Neẓiv's Use of Newly Available Books*

It is clear, then, that midrashic literature was newly available to the Jewish world as a whole, and to the Eastern European Jewish community in particular, in and around the turn of the nineteenth century. Thus, when we add to this our understanding of the influence of the Vilna Ga'on, the general progression of rabbinic commentary, and the position of the Lithuanian Maggid, we begin to better understand why midrash commentary flourished in Lithuania during this period. Furthermore, the rise in the availability of Hebrew texts not only presented rabbinic scholars with a greater array of primary sources upon which to comment, but in composing their commentaries, they now had a greater array of secondary sources from which to draw. A close look at the sources used by the young Neẓiv in composing his commentary on *Sifre* reveals that beyond the works of midrash discussed above, many of the works he regularly cites had also just recently been published in Eastern Europe—some for the first time and others for the first time in a very long while.

One of the most striking examples of this, and one that offers great insight into other areas of Neẓiv's illustrious literary career, is the *She'iltot of Rav Aḥai Ga'on*. This early halakhic work is referenced throughout his *Sifre* commentary[108] and is the primary focus of what will become Neẓiv's magnum opus, his *Ha'amek She'elah.*[109] Like many of the midrashic works, *She'iltot*, published in 1546, was first printed in Venice. Unlike others, however, *She'iltot* was not printed again until 1786, when it was

108 *EH* Naso 2 (I: 14); *EH* Naso 3 (I: 20,21); *EH* Naso 5 (I: 29); *EH* Naso 6 (I: 34,36); *EH* Naso 7 (I: 43); *EH* Naso 15 (I: 65); *EH* Naso 16 (I: 68,69); *EH* Naso 22 (I: 87); *EH* Naso 23 (I: 95,98); *EH* Be-ha'alotekha 14 (I: 229); *EH* Shelaḥ 4 (II: 32); *EH* Shelaḥ 6 (II: 54); *EH* Shelaḥ 9 (II: 70); *EH* Pinḥas 13 (hagah) (II: 254); *EH* Matot 1 (II: 276); *EH* Matot 6 (II: 310); *EH* Shoftim 1(III: 174); *EH* Teẓeh 36 (III: 288); *EH* Teẓeh 38 (III: 292).

109 E.g., *EH* Naso 2 (1: 18); *EH* Naso 3 (I: 21); *EH* Naso 7 (I: 43); *EH* Naso 15 (I: 65); *EH* Naso 16 (I: 69); *EH* Naso 23 (I: 93); *EH* Naso 23 (I: 94); *EH* Naso 39 (I: 154); *EH* Be-ha'alotekha 1 (I: 192); *EH* Be-ha'alotekha 34 (I: 291,292); *EH* Shelaḥ 9 (II: 70,72); *EH* Koraḥ 1 (hagah) (II: 79); *EH* Ḥukat 1 (II: 147); *EH* Balak 1 (II: 204,207); *EH* Pinḥas 3 (II: 223); *EH* Matot 1 (II: 285); *EH* Matot 6 (III: 309,310); *EH* Shoftim 1 (III: 174) [x2], *EH* Shoftim 21 (III: 193); *EH* Shoftim 45 (III: 207); *EH* Teẓeh 6 (III: 237); *EH* Teẓeh 36 (III: 288); *EH* Teẓeh 37 (III: 290); *EH* Teẓeh 38 (III: 292).

published by the Dyhernfurth press. In 1811 *She'iltot* was printed once more, this time in Salonika. While it was not published in Eastern Europe until it appeared with Neẓiv's commentary in 1861, the very fact that it had returned to circulation made it feasible for the young Neẓiv to study it, and its status as an ancient halakhic compendium virtually untouched by rabbinic commentary made it an alluring challenge similar in many respects to the works of midrash which had so fascinated Lithuanian scholars over the previous few decades.

Other early medieval halakhic works cited by Neẓiv had also only recently returned to circulation. For example, Moshe Ben Ya'akov of Coucy's thirteenth-century *Sefer Miẓvot Gadol* was first published in 1475 and then four more times before 1550.[110] It was not printed again, though, until 1807, in Kopyss. Isaac of Corbiel's thirteenth-century *Sefer Miẓvot ha-Katan,* also cited in *'Emek ha-Neẓiv,*[111] went through three editions in the sixteenth century and was then out of circulation for more then two hundred years before being printed in Lyady in 1805.

The same is true with regard to works of methodology cited by Neẓiv in his *Sifre* commentary. Samson of Chinon's fourteenth-century *Sefer ha-Keritut* on talmudic methodology was out of print for most of the eighteenth century.[112] It was printed twice in the sixteenth century, once in the seventeenth, and again in 1709. The next printing, and the one apparently used by the young Neẓiv when studying the methodology of Talmud and midrashic texts, was in Zolkiew in 1799. Azariah de' Rossi's *Me'or 'Einayim,* whose usage by Neẓiv was discussed at length in the previous chapter, was printed in 1573 and not again until Isaac Satanow's edition in 1794. It was published again in Vienna in 1829. Eliyahu Levita's dictionary, known as *Tishbi,* was published three times between 1541 and 1601.[113] Its next printing was two hundred and four years later, in the Lithuanian city of Grodno.

Another book which is referred to consistently throughout Neẓiv's *Sifre* commentary is the Pentateuch commentary of Baḥya ben Asher ben Ḥalāwah (d. 1340), commonly known as Rabbeinu Baḥya.[114] Its publica-

---

110 Cited by Neẓiv in *EH* Naso 5 (I: 27); *EH* Koraḥ 1 (II: 83); *EH* Pinḥas 11 (II: 245); *EH* Pinḥas 13 (II: 254); *EH* Pinḥas 21 (II: 271).

111 *EH* Shelaḥ 9 (II: 74).

112 See, for e.g., *EH* Naso 1 (I: 2); *EH* Naso 24 (I: 102); *EH* Balak 1 (II: 199).

113 See, for e.g., *EH* Be-ha'alotekha 34 (I: 290).

114 Or, mistakenly, as Rabbeinu Behayye. *EH* Naso 23 (I: 96); *EH* Naso 40 (I: 157); *EH* Naso 42 (I: 167); *EH* Naso 44 (I: 171); *EH* Naso 46 (I: 179); *EH* Be-ha'alotekha 12 (I: 223); *EH* Be-

tion history follows the very same pattern as *She'iltot* and the works of midrash. Following its 1544 printing in Venice, Rabbeinu Baḥya's commentary was published twice, once in Cracow in 1610 and again in Naples in 1724. In 1799 the commentary was made available again in Eastern Europe due to its printing in Korec, a Volhynian town whose printing house was first opened in 1776. In 1811, the Korec press reprinted the commentary of Rabbeinu Baḥya. From 1824 to 1827, another Volhynian printing house published the commentary, this time in Sudylkov, whose press had been in operation only since 1812. Thus, whereas the Pentateuch commentary of Rabbeinu Baḥya went through only three printings in the two and a half centuries from 1544 to 1798, it was published three times in Volhynia alone during the first quarter of the nineteenth century.

Amongst the various talmudic and halakhic works authored by Nahmanides (1195-1270) and his prolific student Solomon ibn Abraham Aderet (Rashba) (1235-1310), Neẓiv takes particular interest in a tract on Divine reward and punishment by Nahmanides, entitled *Sha'ar ha-Gemul*,[115] and on Rashba's work dedicated to the laws pertaining to Jewish holidays, entitled *Avodat ha-Kodesh*.[116] When one looks at their respective publication histories, the same pattern emerges. *Sha'ar ha-Gemul* was published as part of *Torat ha-'Adam* in Constantinople in 1518, and again in Venice in 1595. There is no record of it having been printed at all over the course of the seventeenth century. The next recorded printing of *Torat ha-'Adam* is in Berlin in 1750. *Sha'ar ha-Gemul* was published for the first time in Eastern Europe, and this time without the rest of *Torat ha-'Adam*, in the Ruthenian town of Zolkiew in 1793. It was then printed again in

---

ha'alotekha 14 (I: 228); *EH* Be-ha'alotekha 25 (I: 263); *EH* Be-ha'alotekha 26 (I: 264); *EH* Be-ha'alotekha 27 (I: 272); *EH* Be-ha'alotekha 34 (I: 288,289); *EH* Be-ha'alotekha 37 (I: 296); *EH* Be-ha'alotekha 45(I: 314,316); *EH* Be-ha'alotekha 47 (I: 320); *EH* Shelaḥ 5 (II: 38); *EH* Shelaḥ 7 (II: 55); *EH* Shelaḥ 8 (II: 59); *EH* Shelaḥ 9 (II: 72); *EH* Pinḥas 3 (II: 229); *EH* Pinḥas 9 (II: 239); *EH* Pinḥas 11 (II: 242); *EH* Pinḥas 11 (II: 244); *EH* Pinḥas 11 (II: 246); *EH* Pinḥas 12 (II: 250); *EH* Pinḥas 13 (hagah) (II: 254); *EH* Pinḥas 14 (II: 257); *EH* Pinḥas 19 (II: 268); *EH* Pinḥas 21 (II: 272); *EH* Matot 1 (II: 274); *EH* Matot 1 (II: 281); *EH* Matot 1 (II: 282); *EH* Matot 1 (II: 285); *EH* Matot 1 (II: 288); *EH* Matot 5 (II: 305); *EH* Devarim 8 (III: 12); *EH* Re'eh 10 (III: 95).

115 *Sha'ar ha-Gemul* is actually the last chapter of the work by Nahmanides entitled *Torat ha-'Adam*. Due to the theological import of its subject matter, it was at times printed independent of the larger work. For citation in *'Emek ha-Neẓiv* see *EH* Naso 2 (I: 18); *EH* Naso 40 (I: 158); *EH* Be-ha'alotekha 12 (I: 222); *EH* Be-ha'alotkha 45 (I: 314); *EH* Shelaḥ 6 (II: 53); *EH* Shelaḥ 6 (II: 54); *EH* Shelaḥ 6 (II: 55); *EH* ve-'Etḥanan 9 (III: 39).

116 *EH* Naso 39 (I: 154); *EH* Naso 40 (I: 158); *EH* Naso 42 (I: 164); *EH* Be-ha'alotekha 12 (I: 322); *EH* Be-ha'alotekha 34 (I: 288); *EH* Be-ha'alotekha 41 (I: 310); *EH* Be-ha'alotekha 45 (I: 314); *EH* Shelaḥ 1(II: 10); *EH* Shelaḥ 6 (II: 54).

the Lithuanian town of Grodno two years later, in a printing house which had only opened seven years earlier in 1788. Similarly, *Avodat ha-Kodesh* was printed for the first time in Venice in 1602 and not again for the next one hundred and fifty years. It then appeared as part of a larger compendium entitled *Aseifat Zekeinim* in Meẓ, 1764 but was only printed for the first time in Eastern Europe in Warsaw in 1803.

For the classical works of medieval Jewish philosophy from which Neẓiv draws in his *Sifre* commentary, the story is no different. Rambam's *Moreh Nevukhim* was printed only once between 1553 and 1791.[117] It was printed twice in 1828, however, and again in 1833. Yehuda ha-Levi's *Kuzari* went through three editions in the sixteenth century and was reprinted again in 1660.[118] The next printing of his work, however, was not until 1795 in Berlin. It was published twice over the next two years and again in 1826, 1833, and 1840. Likewise, Isaac 'Arama's *Akeidat Yiẓḥak* was published in 1522 and again in 1547.[119] Its next printing was in Frankfurt der Oder in 1785, after which it was printed in Lvov in 1808.

Generally speaking, the availability of new texts is a necessary prerequisite for a resurgence in their study, but it is not sufficient for explaining why such a resurgence occurred. Thus, we can return to the previous socio-cultural factors: the influence of the Vilna Ga'on and his breadth of study, the natural progression of Torah commentary from Yerushalmi study to midrash, and the influence of the Lithuanian *maggid* to understand why the newfound availability of texts led to a flourishing in their study. However, in an intellectual society such as nineteenth-century Lithuania, where a premium was placed on Torah study above all other endeavors, the very availability of texts might indeed be seen as sufficient cause for explaining their increased popularity. When books which have not been in circulation for decades or perhaps centuries suddenly become available, the intellectual, and especially the young intellectual, looking to make his mark amongst the scholarly elite is naturally drawn to them and to the challenge of uncovering their mysteries and secrets. Such certainly seems to be the case amongst the intellectual elite of early nineteenth-century Lithuania.

It is therefore apparent that the dramatic rise in the availability of

117 Yesnitch, 1742. For citations see *EH* Be-ha'alotekha 45 (I: 314) [2x], *EH* Be-ha'alotekha 48 (I: 323); *EH* Re'eh 14 (III: 100).

118 *EH* Shoftim 17 (III: 189).

119 *EH* Naso 42 (I: 167); *EH* 'Ekev 5 (III: 56).

Hebrew texts in the early nineteenth century had a formative effect in creating the *Weltanschauung* of the young Neẓiv. The newfound availability of midrashic texts undoubtedly played a significant role in leading him toward the study of *Sifre.* And, within the pantheon of books to which he looked for guidance in understanding and elaborating upon the ideas and instructions of *Sifre,* a prominent place was given to those books which had only recently become accessible to an Eastern European Jewish audience. Thus the classic commentaries of Rashi, Tosafot, and the novellae of Ramban and Rashba, all of which had been in print throughout the decades and had consumed the minds and pens of many rabbinic authors,[120] seem to fascinate the young Neẓiv far less than the relatively virgin territory of *She'iltot* and *Rabbeinu Baḥya, Torat ha-'Adam* and *'Avodat ha-Kodesh, Tishbi* and *Sefer ha-Keritut, Moreh Nevukhim* and *'Akeidat Yiẓḥak.*

The effects of Hebrew print's rapid growth in the late eighteenth and early nineteenth centuries, however, extend beyond the choice of texts studied by Neẓiv and his Lithuanian colleagues. The cultural impact of newfound accessibility to printed material has been studied extensively in other cultural contexts, and many of the conclusions drawn there are equally applicable to early-nineteenth-century Lithuania.[121] Thus, for example, Elizabeth Eisenstein notes that due to the fact that "by its nature a reading public was more atomistic and individualistic than a hearing one," since "reception of a printed message in any place requires at least temporary isolation,"[122] a print culture is far more susceptible to innovation than a society dominated by oral teaching. As is well known, nineteenth-century Lithuanian Torah scholars considered the notion of exegetical innovation, or *ḥiddush,* the ultimate goal of all Torah study.

---

120 The *Ḥiddushim* of Rashba' to various *mesekhtot* were printed on a few occasions in the sixteenth century and on many occasions throughout the eighteenth century. The *Ḥiddushim* of Ramban, however, were not published (except for the occasional volume mistakenly attributed to Rashba') until the 1850s, but his work on Alfasi enjoyed considerable circulation.

121 See, e.g., Elizabeth Eisenstein, *The Printing Press as an Agent of Change* (New York: Cambridge University Press, 1979), Miriam Usher Christman, *Lay Culture Learned Culture: Books and Social Change in Strasbourg* (New Haven: Yale University Press, 1982), Michael T. Clanchy, "Looking Back from the Invention of Printing," in *Literacy in Historical Perspective,* ed. Daniel P. Resnick (Washington, DC: Library of Congress, 1983), 7-22; Anthony T. Grafton, "The Importance of Being Printed," *Journal of Interdisciplinary History* 11 (1980): 265-86; idem., *Defenders of the Text: The Traditions of Scholarship in an Age of Science, 1450-1800* (Cambridge, MA: Harvard University Press, 1991).

122 Eisenstein, 132.

Even the cultural movements rooted in nineteenth-century Lithuanian society which abandon Torah study as the ideological center of Jewish existence bear the imprint of a society newly exposed to print. It has often been noted that the availability of texts reduces the need for ecclesiastical interpretation of religious texts, and thus spurs the growth of religious reformist programs.[123] The Eastern European program for Haskalah, which emerges from the first few decades of the nineteenth century certainly deserves mention as a case in point. Eisenstein also notes that in numerous societies the growth of print is linked to a growth of nationalist sentiment,[124] a trend clearly reflected in the birth of modern Zionist ideology in nineteenth-century Eastern Europe.

However, it is in the realm of midrash study that Eisenstein's work proves most relevant. On the most basic level, her study suggests that the decision to study midrash in the early decades of the nineteenth century results not only from the increased availability of midrashic texts but because, more generally, "the search for ancient wisdom was rapidly propelled by print."[125] That is, wide-scale availability of basic texts of ancient wisdom, be it the Gospels or the Talmud Bavli, sparks interest in further exploration of ancillary ancient texts, be they Augustine or *Mekhilta'*. The process does not end, though, with the mere publication of ancient wisdom for, as Eisenstein writes, "recovery spurs discovery,"[126] and hence scholars of ancient texts in a print culture are inspired to add their own comments and insights into the teachings of antiquity.

The content of these studies also bears the mark of a print culture. Eisenstein cites David Hume's statement that "the Power which Printing gives us of continually improving and correcting our works in Succes-

123 See, e.g., Miriam Usher Chrisman, *Lay Culture, Learned Culture,* Books *and Social Change in Strasbourg, 1480-1599* (New Haven: Yale University Press, 1982) and Elizabeth Eisenstein, *The Printing Revolution in Early Modern Europe* (Cambridge: Cambridge University Press, 1983) 148-146; Roger Chartier, *The Cultural Uses of Print in Early Modern France,* Lydia G. Cochrane trans. (Princeton: Princeton University Press, 1987). While Eisenstein and Adrian Johns continue to debate whether or not advances in print brought about a cultural "revolution," the fact that print played a major role in the Protestant Reformation and the ensuing Counter Reformation is undeniable. See their exchange in *The American Historical Review* 107 (February 2002).

124 Ibid., 118. See Lucien Febvre, *The Coming of the Book: The Impact of Printing 1450-1800*, trans. David Gerard (London: Verso, 1990), 262, in this regard as well.

125 Ibid., 124. For the sake of clarification, note that Eisenstein makes no mention of Lithuanian Jewish society and certainly not the study of Midrash. The above comments reflect inferences made from her more general study of the impact of print on culture.

126 Ibid., 193.

sive Editions appears to me the chief Advantage of that art" as reflective of the centrality of text emendation to the process of recovery and discovery of ancient texts common to cultures newly exposed to print.[127] Scholars of such texts in a world of readily accessible books come to the realization that "as long as ancient learning had to be transmitted by hand-copied texts, it was more likely to be blurred or blotted out than to be augmented and improved over the course of centuries."[128] Thus, it was their task in the dawn of the printing age to gather extant variants of an ancient text and restore it to its original format. Once again, then, we might return to Ḥanokh Zundel ben Yosef's poignant mission statement in the preface to his commentary on *Midrash Rabbah,* where he states that he has undertaken precisely this endeavor:

> because the mistaken hand of copyists prevailed upon it and created senseless schemes (*natu 'alav kav tohu*). And, afterward, it fell in the hands of the injurious printing presses (*defusim mafsidim*) which stoned it with empty stones. They left out, they added, they switched, they combined, they destroyed their ink (*heshḥitu deyam*). They perverted its foundations, bent its walls, darkened its utility, diminished its light…
>
> … And I have prepared my heart to understand every text in its context, and how it is hinted at in the verse which is brought, and to establish the proper version of the text. And every verse will be cited properly as it appears in the Bible. And I labored extensively to find the books which cite the words of the midrash and what is said in it. And, thank God, I labored and I succeeded in gathering from them all interpretations that are sweet and pleasant to the ear which hears them. And they are founded in reason and knowledge, they are all the work of an artisan—never before heard and never before seen.[129]

---

127 Ibid., 112.

128 Ibid., 289.

129 *Midrash Rabbah, "Hakdamat Meḥaber," 'Eẓ Yosef, 'Anaf Yosef, Yad Yosef"* (Ḥanokh Zundel), vol. 1 (Israel: Wagshal, 2001), 35.

While the elucidation of rabbinic methodology was not as widespread a phenomenon amongst early-nineteenth-century midrash commentators as was the penchant for straightforward commentary, text emendation, and intellectual breadth, it is most reasonable to assume that the dramatic rise in print over the first few decades of the nineteenth century played an important role in fostering and facilitating Neẓiv's interest in this area as well. After all, a rabbinic author studying in the *bet midrash* of Volozhin, seventy years prior to Neẓiv's arrival, would have had great difficulty describing a particular rabbinic technique as "*derekh midrashim*" when, in all likelihood, there was not a single copy of *Midrash Rabbah, Tanḥuma, Mekhilta', Sifre,* or *Sifra* on the shelf. It is only once texts became readily available that a rabbinic author could rise above a particular passage or a particular subject matter in order to view the totality of a body of literature and juxtapose it with other similar or dissimilar texts. Indeed, Neẓiv makes this point himself in the introduction to his commentary on *She'iltot,* first published in 1861, when he credits the development of the Hebrew print industry for having allowed him access to the source material upon which Rambam built his Code.[130]

In sum, we can conclude that numerous cultural factors gave rise to the flowering of midrash study in the early decades of the nineteenth century. Among these factors were the palpable influence of the Vilna Ga'on and his intellectual work, the natural progression of Torah study from the Talmud Yerushalmi to compilations of midrash, the nature and function of the Lithuanian *maggid,* the dramatic rise in availability of printed material, and the cultural shift which results therefrom. The effects of all of these phenomena are clearly reflected in *'Emek ha-Neẓiv,* and thus they constitute the cultural building blocks from which the young Neẓiv's approach to Torah study was built. As we shall explore in the coming chapters, the commentarial approach taken by the young Neẓiv reverberates well into his later work. And, where the mature Neẓiv diverges from the methods and style of his youth, there is reason to question what new factors might have arisen to bring about such a change.

130 HS KH 1: 16.

## CHAPTER SIX:
### From *'Emek ha-Neẓiv* to *Ha'amek Davar*

In the preceding chapters we have sought to place Neẓiv's commentary on *Sifre*, *'Emek ha-Neẓiv*, in the context of early nineteenth-century Lithuanian midrash study. Doing so affords us a glimpse into the larger intellectual world which informed the young Neẓiv's intellectual development. What remains to be explored, however, is the degree to which the intellectual trends of the early nineteenth century, so prominent in *'Emek ha-Neẓiv*, continue to guide and shape Neẓiv's later literary endeavors. As we shall see below, setting Neẓiv's later work against the background of his work on *Sifre* yields valuable insight into the mature Neẓiv's commentarial method and motivation.

#### *From* 'Emek ha-Neẓiv *to* Ha'amek She'elah

As we noted above, the numerous references to Neẓiv's *She'iltot* commentary scattered throughout his commentary on *Sifre* suggest that he began his work on *She'iltot* as a young man, while still actively engaged in penning his work on *Sifre*.[1] We have also mentioned, albeit in passing, several important areas in which his *She'iltot* commentary is closely related to his work on *Sifre*. *She'iltot*, like *Sifre*, was a recently published repository of primary halakhic sources, which had been long neglected by rabbinic scholarship. *She'iltot*, as a geonic work, represented a logical frontier for new commentarial endeavors, as study of works of midrash had by the 1840s been increasingly engaged in by Lithuanian scholars. Neẓiv's penchant for text criticism, which is so apparent in his work on *Sifre*, is clearly visible throughout his work on *She'iltot* as well.

Nonetheless, the nature of the project which Neẓiv undertakes in *Ha'amek She'elah* is rather different than that of *'Emek ha-Neẓiv*. Neẓiv's primary goal in his *Sifre* commentary, like that of so many of his contemporaries in midrash scholarship, is to open a "sealed book" to the scholarly public. In doing so, he often takes the opportunity to show his

---

1 See Chapter 1, n. 18, above.

readers how he believes a particular *Sifre* text fits into the larger world of halakhic discourse. In his commentary on *She'iltot*, however, Neẓiv's priorities seem reversed. Throughout his introductory chapters, he makes it clear that he set his sights upon *She'iltot* for the express purpose of gaining insight into the works of Shimon Kayara, Alfasi, and Maimonides. Thus, unlike in his commentary on *Sifre*, almost every comment in *Ha'amek She'elah* is a lengthy halakhic essay aimed at elucidating the halakhic relevance of the statement in *She'iltot*, and very rarely does Neẓiv restrain himself to merely explicating the words of the passage at hand. Furthermore, the project of *Ha'amek She'elah* differs significantly from that of *'Emek ha-Neẓiv* in that the latter revolves entirely around scriptural exegesis, whereas the former focuses almost exclusively on the world of *Torah she-Be'al Peh*, with little interest shown in its biblical foundations.

In both of these regards, then, Neẓiv's Bible commentary, *Ha'amek Davar*, represents a more natural continuation of his early work on *Sifre*. *Ha'amek Davar* aims to offer a close reading of the biblical text, not to provide lengthy halakhic excurses. And, of course, *Ha'amek Davar* is wholly dedicated to the realm of biblical exegesis. Indeed, the fact that, as we will demonstrate below, the core composition of *Ha'amek Davar* seems to date to the period directly following the core composition of *'Emek ha-Neẓiv* indicates that a comparison of these two works is, perhaps, a better indicator of Neẓiv's intellectual growth and development than a comparison of *'Emek ha-Neẓiv* and *Ha'amek She'elah*.

## *Dating* Ha'amek Davar

Before examining the continuum between Neẓiv's early work on *Sifre* and his later commentary on Torah, we must establish that the Torah commentary, the now-celebrated five-volume work known as *Ha'amek Davar,* does indeed date to a later period in Neẓiv's life than does the commentary on *Sifre.* It is well known and self-evident from a close study of Neẓiv's various works that he subjected his literary creations to constant revision and reworking. As a result, the 1879 publication date of *Ha'amek Davar* alone need not dictate a late date of composition for it. Indeed, his *Sifre* commentary, which we have dated to the 1830s and 1840s, was first published only in 1959. Nonetheless, there is ample evidence that suggests that the vast majority of *Ha'amek Davar* was indeed composed during the 1860s and 1870s.

To begin, when Neẓiv in 1861 lists his early literary endeavors in a passage which introduces his *Ha'amek She'elah,* he makes no mention of a commentary on Torah, thus suggesting that, unlike *'Emek ha-Neẓiv, Ha'amek Davar* is a product of his later years.[2] A similar conclusion can be deduced from the fact that his earlier work, such as the commentary on *Sifre* and the commentary on *She'iltot,* do not regularly reference his Torah commentary,[3] whereas the Torah commentary does consistently reference those earlier works.[4] The implication, therefore, is that *Ha'amek Davar* was composed after Neẓiv's commentary on *Sifre* and his commentary on *She'iltot* had been completed. The consistent references to his father-in-law, who died in 1849, with the appellation "of blessed memory,"[5] and to his son, who was born in 1832, with the appellation "*Ga'on*"[6] similarly suggests that such passages date, at the very earliest, to the 1850s.

---

2 HS KH 1: 17.

3 The printed edition of *'Emek ha-Neẓiv* does contain two references to a commentary on Torah, one in *EH* Naso 44 (I: 176) "[*u-be-perush al ha-Torah her'eiti la-da'at…*] and one in *EH* Koraḥ 1 (II: 78) "*ve-'ayyen mah shekatavti be-H'"D parashat* Naso *parashat nazir.*" There is good reason to believe, though, that neither reference was part of the original *Sifre* commentary. First of all, the sheer number of instances in which the comments made by Neẓiv in his *Sifre* commentary relate to comments he makes in his Torah commentary, yet the latter goes unmentioned, calls into question the authenticity of these two references. Second, I was able to look at the Naso reference in the manuscript of *'Emek ha-Neẓiv* and saw that it is a marginal addition to the core text. While I was not able to see the Koraḥ reference in the manuscript, the fact that it appears as a self-contained sentence at the end of a passage rather than mid-sentence in the course of a larger discussion makes it quite plausible that it was inserted by a later editor. In our discussion of the printed edition of Neẓiv's *Mekhilta'* commentary below, we will demonstrate clear indications of precisely this type of reference inserted without demarcation by the editors. Likewise, the references to Neẓiv's Torah commentary found in the recent printed editions of *Ha'amek She'elah* (*Kidmat ha-'Emek* 2: 2, 3: 9, 10 and in the main commentary 14: 1) are clearly later insertions of an editor as they do not appear in the original 1861-1867 edition.

4 For references to *'Emek ha-Neẓiv,* see *HrD* Ex. 4: 3; *HrD* Num. 6: 19; *HrD* Num. 7: 14; *HD* Num. 7: 15; *HrD* Num. 7: 48; *HD* Num. 15: 32, 41; *HD* Num. 18: 9; *HrD* Num. 18: 19; *HD* Num. 24: 8; *HD* Num. 31: 23. For references to *Ha'amek She'elah,* see *HrD* Gen. 19: 27; *HrD* Gen. 22: 3; *HrD* Gen. 49: 10, 15; *HD* Gen. 49: 22; *HD* Gen. 49: 33; *HD* Ex. 14: 29; *HD* Ex. 21: 30; *HD* Ex. 23: 15; *HD* Ex. 31: 14; *HD* Ex. 32: 9; *HD* Ex. 33: 11; *HrD* Ex. 34: 22; *HrD* Ex. 36: 8; *HD* Lev. 5: 1; *HD* Lev. 6: 21; *HrD* Lev 8: 35; *HrD* Lev 8: 36; *HD* Lev. 14: 2; *HD* Lev. 14: 21; *HD* Lev. 15: 16, 25; *HD* Lev.16: 8; *HD* Lev. 20: 20, 21, 25; *HD* Lev. 22: 21; *HD* Lev. 23: 3, 31, 32; *HD* Lev. 27: 29; *HrD* Num. 3: 48; *HrD* Num. 5: 10; *HD* Num. 15: 38, 39; *HD* Num. 18: 12; *HD* Num 24: 5; *HD* Num 24: 6; *HD* Num. 30: 6; *HD* Num. 31: 23; *HrD* Num. 35: 3; *HrD* Num. 35: 30; *HD* Deut. 5: 12; *HD* Deut. 6: 7; *HD* Deut. 6: 20; *HD* Deut. 7: 3; *HD* Deut. 7: 25; *HD* Deut. 14: 23; *HD* Deut. 19: 14; *HD* Deut. 22: 8; *HD* Deut. 22: 12; *HD* Deut. 23: 2; *HD* Deut. 32: 37.

5 E.g., *HD* Gen. 30: 29; *HD* Gen. 34: 21; *HD* Num. 1: 42; *HD* Num. 25: 12.

6 *HD* Ex. 25: 39; *HrD* Ex. 34: 22; *HD* Lev. 26: 43; *HD* Deut. 2: 6; *HD* Deut. 16: 11.

Other references made by Neẓiv in the context of his Torah commentary, however, unequivocally date to the 1860s or later. For example, in *HD* Num. 6:7 and in Num. 28:31, Neẓiv refers to Elazar Moshe Hurwitz as *av bet din* of Pinsk. Hurwitz only assumed that position in 1859. In a parenthetical remark found in *HD* Gen. 2:9, Neẓiv states that he read *Iggeret ha-Neḥamah,* written by Rambam's father, in the fortieth edition of the eighth year of the newspaper *ha-Levanon*. That edition was issued on June 11, 1872. Similarly, in the fourth volume of *Ha'amek Davar* Neẓiv includes a reference to an exegetical insight he "heard from [his] brother-in-law, *moreinu ha-rav B, n"y*."[7] The reference seems to be to Barukh ha-Levi Epstein who was only born in 1860 and therefore could not have been offering his own exegetical insights until the mid-1870s at the very earliest. Indeed, Epstein, who was Neẓiv's nephew by his first marriage, only became Neẓiv's brother-in-law in 1873, when Neẓiv was remarried to Epstein's sister.[8] Likewise, in *HD* Deut. 21:16 Neẓiv refers to Yom-Tov Lipman Baslavsky as *av bet din* of Mir; Baslavsky came to Mir in 1874. In what might be the latest passage in *Ha'amek Davar*, Neẓiv in *HrD* Ex. 31:17 follows a reference to Bezalel ha-Kohen of Vilna, who died in 1878, with the words "of blessed memory." In the same passage he cites "my [grand] son-in-law, the rabbi, the Ga'on, moreinu Ḥayyim ha-Levi," a reference to Ḥayyim Soloveitchik of Brisk, who was only born in 1853. While all of the above passages could represent later additions to a core text, when combined with the references to *'Emek ha-Neẓiv* and *Ha'amek She'elah* and a lack of similar passages suggesting an earlier composition, the evidence leans toward dating the *Ha'amek Davar* to the 1860s and 1870s.

### 'Emek ha-Neẓiv *as the Foundation for* Ha'amek Davar

Having established *Ha'amek Davar* as a product of Neẓiv's more mature years, we can return to our investigation of the degree to which the intellectual trends of early-nineteenth-century Lithuania impacted Neẓiv's later work. As we shall see below, it is quite clear that in both form and content *Ha'amek Davar* bears the unmistakable imprint of Neẓiv's earlier foray into the world of midrash.

The most apparent sign of his years spent engaged in midrash study

7 *HD* Num. 28: 11

8 See Epstein, *Rabban Shel Yisrael*, 127.

is simply the frequency with which he cites not only the *derashot* found in the Talmud, but those found in the collections of *midrashe aggadah*, and the books of *Midrash Rabbah* in particular,[9] as well as the *midrash halakhah* found in *Sifra*, *Sifre* and *Mekhilta'*.[10] In fact, his very first comment on the very first verse in Genesis contains a citation of *Sifre*.[11] On select occasions, while discussing a passage from *Sifre*, Neẓiv even lets the reader of his Torah commentary know that he has discussed the matter previously in the commentary he wrote (but had yet to publish) on *Sifre*. Thus, for example, Neẓiv closes his comments in *Harḥev Davar* to Numbers 6:19 by stating that "there is much more to explain about this [matter], and when God grants me the privilege of publishing the commentary on *Sifre* I will explain at length."[12] Furthermore, when citing rabbinic exegesis in

9 E.g., in the book of Genesis, see *HD* Gen. 1: 4, 7; *HD* Gen. 2: 9; *HD* Gen. 3: 9, 17; *HD* Gen. 4: 19; *HD* Gen. 14: 23; *HD* Gen. 15: 1; *HD* Gen. 17: 17, 22; *HD* Gen. 18: 2; *HD* Gen. 22: 1; *HD* Gen. 24: 7; *HD* Gen. 26: 5; *HD* Gen. 31: 46; *HD* Gen. 37: 27; *HD* Gen. 39: 8; *HD* Gen. 41: 1; *HrD* Gen. 1: 1; *HrD* Gen. 2: 14; *HrD* Gen. 2: 15; *HrD* Gen. 2: 18; *HrD* Gen. 16: 7; *HrD* Gen. 24: 1; *HrD* Gen. 27: 9; *HrD* Gen. 33: 4; *HrD* Gen. 34: 1; *HrD* Gen. 37: 12; *HrD* Gen. 40: 23; *HrD* Gen. 41: 8; *HrD* Gen. 41: 51; *HrD* Gen. 45: 16.

10 For *Mekhilta'*, see *HD* Ex. 6: 6; *HD* Ex. 11: 6; *HD* Ex. 12: 21; *HD* Ex. 12: 22; *HD* Ex. 12: 23; *HD* Ex. 12: 28; *HD* Ex. 12: 39; *HD* Ex. 13: 17; *HD* Ex. 13: 19; *HD* Ex. 14: 31; *HD* Ex. 15: 27; *HD* Ex. 16: 20; *HD* Ex. 16: 24; *HD* Ex. 18: 13; *HD* Ex. 19: 6; *HD* Ex. 20: 6; *HD* Ex. 21: 5; *HD* Ex. 21: 30; *HD* Ex. 22: 12; *HD* Ex. 22: 26; *HD* Ex. 23: 10; *HD* Ex. 23: 11; *HD* Ex. 23: 12; *HD* Ex. 24: 4; *HD* Ex. 25: 2; *HD* Ex. 27: 8; *HD* Ex. 31: 14; *HD* Ex. 34: 22 and *HrD* Ex. 3: 15; *HD* Ex. 12: 11; *HD* Ex. 15: 11; *HD* Ex. 15: 18; *HD* Ex. 22: 2; *HD* Ex. 24: 3. For *Sifre*, see *HD* Gen. 13: 7; *HD* Num. 3: 12; *HD* Num. 3: 39; *HD* Num. 5: 31; *HD* Num. 6: 20; *HD* Num. 6: 21; *HD* Num. 7: 1; *HD* Num. 7: 15; *HD* Num. 8: 1; *HD* Num. 9: 1; *HD* Num. 9: 6; *HD* Num. 9: 7; *HD* Num. 10: 6; *HD* Num. 10: 9; *HD* Num. 10: 10; *HD* Num. 11: 1; *HD* Num. 11: 6; *HD* Num. 11: 11; *HD* Num. 11: 12; *HD* Num. 11: 25; *HD* Num. 11: 26; *HD* Num. 11: 30; *HD* Num. 11: 35; *HD* Num. 12: 2; *HD* Num. 12: 3; *HD* Num. 12: 4; *HD* Num. 12: 11; *HD* Num. 15: 5; *HD* Num. 15: 26; *HD* Num. 15: 35; *HD* Num. 15: 41; *HD* Num. 18: 7; *HD* Num. 18: 9; *HD* Num. 19: 4; *HD* Num. 19: 19; *HD* Num. 21: 22; *HD* Num. 23: 28; *HD* Num. 24: 2; *HD* Num. 24: 4; *HD* Num. 24: 8; *HD* Num. 24: 15; *HD* Num. 26: 53; *HD* Num. 27: 17; *HD* Num. 28: 2; *HD* Num. 28: 4; *HD* Num. 28: 10; *HD* Num. 30: 6; *HD* Num. 31: 21; *HD* Num. 31: 23; *HD* Num. 31: 24; *HD* Num. 35: 34 and *HrD* Num. 6: 19; *HrD* Num. 7: 48; *HrD* Num. 8: 6; *HrD* Num. 8: 15; *HrD* Num. 10: 10; *HrD* Num. 10: 33; *HrD* Num. 12: 3; *HrD* Num. 12: 7; *HrD* Num. 18: 19; *HrD* Num. 28: 4 as well as *HD* Deut. 1: 3; *HD* Deut. 1: 5; *HD* Deut. 1: 7; *HD* Deut. 1: 14; *HD* Deut. 3: 26; *HD* Deut. 3: 28; *HD* Deut. 4: 1; *HD* Deut. 4: 3; *HD* Deut. 4: 46; *HD* Deut. 6: 7; *HD* Deut. 11: 24; *HD* Deut. 12: 1; *HD* Deut. 12: 21; *HD* Deut. 13: 9; *HD* Deut. 14: 3; *HD* Deut. 14: 23; *HD* Deut. 15: 5; *HD* Deut. 17: 8; *HD* Deut. 18: 1; *HD* Deut. 18: 5; *HD* Deut. 18: 8; *HD* Deut. 18: 13; *HD* Deut. 19: 9; *HD* Deut. 21: 14; *HD* Deut. 21: 16; *HD* Deut. 21: 18; *HD* Deut. 22: 8; *HD* Deut. 22: 19; *HD* Deut. 22: 22; *HD* Deut. 22: 24; *HD* Deut. 22: 26; *HD* Deut. 22: 24; *HD* Deut. 22: 15; *HD* Deut. 25: 2; *HD* Deut. 25: 11; *HD* Deut. 30: 19; *HD* Deut. 31: 14. References to *Sifra'*, which Neẓiv generally refers to as *Torat Kohanim*, can be found on just about any page in the Leviticus volume of *Ha'amek Davar*.

11 *HD* Gen. 1: 1.

12 See also *HD* Lev. 8: 4; *HD* Num. 4: 23; *HD* Num. 7: 15; *HD* Num. 31: 23; *HrD* Num. 7: 14; *HrD* Num. 7: 48; *HrD* Num. 18: 19.

*Ha'amek Davar*, whether from a work of midrash or from one of the Talmuds, Neẓiv's purpose is quite often to demonstrate the way in which the rabbinic exposition is grounded in the words of the verse.[13] This is one of the central goals of *'Emek ha-Neẓiv* as well.

Less noticeable, though, are the points in his Torah commentary in which Neẓiv makes no mention of *Sifre* or his commentary thereon, yet his comments in *Ha'amek Davar* echo those he had written earlier in *Sifre*. For example, in the context of his discussion regarding the Sotah waters in *HD* Numbers 5:18 and 23, Neẓiv repeats his reconciliation of the seemingly contradictory passages in *Sifre* and Talmud Sotah regarding the nature of the Sotah water precisely as he did in *EH Naso* 11 (I:57).[14]

Certain features of *Ha'amek Davar* bear close resemblance to Neẓiv's *Sifre* commentary as well. Thus, for example, Neẓiv's choice to divide his work into two different commentaries—*Ha'amek Davar*, which contains his comments directly related to the Torah verse at hand, and *Harḥev Davar*, which contains his tangential comments and excurses—harkens back to what was the dominant trend in midrash commentary during the first decades of the nineteenth century. Although they are not nearly as prominent in *Ha'amek Davar* as in *'Emek ha-Neẓiv*, echoes of the intellectual milieu of early-nineteenth-century Lithuanian midrash commentary reverberate in the freedom and frequency with which Neẓiv emends rabbinic texts in his *Ha'amek Davar*. Thus, one finds the mature Neẓiv noting possible printing errors in Onkelos,[15] Rif,[16] and Rashi[17] and variant readings of talmudic texts,[18] as well as corruptions in the text of Tosefta[19]

13 E.g., *HD* Gen. 5: 5; *HD* Gen. 14: 7; *HrD* Gen. 15: 1; *HD* Gen. 29: 10; *HD* Gen. 22: 1; *HD* Gen. 23: 2; *HD* Gen. 30: 27; *HD* Ex.12: 15; *HD* Ex. 13: 18; *HD* Ex. 14: 21; *HD* Ex. 15: 16; *HD* Ex. 16: 26; *HD* Ex. 17: 8; *HD* Ex. 21: 2; *HD* Ex. 22: 1; *HD* Ex. 22: 30; *HD* Ex. 23: 12; *HD* Ex. 27: 14; *HD* Ex. 28: 20; *HD* Ex. 36: 13; *HD* Ex. 36: 29; *HD* Ex. 38: 21; *HD* Ex. 39: 37; *HD* Ex. 40: 2 ; *HD* Lev. 2: 2; *HD* Lev. 13: 3; *HD* Lev. 21: 6; *HD* Num. 12: 11; *HD* Num. 15: 5; *HD* Num. 15: 29; *HD* Num. 16: 16; *HD* Num. 18: 28; *HD* Num. 32: 30; *HD* Num. 35: 30; *HD* Num. 35: 34; *HD* Deut. 1: 27; *HD* Deut. 2: 1; *HD* Deut. 5: 16; *HD* Deut. 10: 20; *HD* Deut. 11: 15; *HD* Deut. 16: 15.

14 Compare also *EH* Naso 2 (I: 15) with *HD* Num. 18: 1; *EH* Naso 5 (I: 29) with *HD* Lev. 19: 19; *HD* Lev. 19: 27 and *HD* Lev. 33: 39; *EH* Shelaḥ 9 (II: 74) with *HD* Num. 15: 41; *EH* Re'eh 76 (III: 162) with *HD* Deut. 16: 2, and many others.

15 *HD* Num. 17: 27; *HD* Num. 18: 26.

16 *HD* Lev. 11: 14.

17 *HD* Num 6: 21.

18 *HD* Lev. 23: 3; *HD* Lev. 25: 4; *HrD* Num. 15: 40.

19 *HD* Num. 6: 20; *HrD* Num. 10: 33.

and in the printed editions of the various collections of midrash.[20] In fact, his critical eye even leads him to note that the Torah text which Rashi and Ibn Ezra had before them seems to have contained a letter "*vav*" which does not appear in the standard Torah text used in his day.[21]

Neẓiv's early interest in the methodology of rabbinic texts also seems to have carried over into his Torah commentary. While there are far fewer explicit statements in *Ha'amek Davar* elucidating the methodology of rabbinic authors than there are in *'Emek ha-Neẓiv*,[22] the former's distinctly macrocosmic perspective of the Torah text can be seen as an extension of the same trend. Throughout his *Ha'amek Davar*, Neẓiv displays great sensitivity not only to the verse at hand, but also to the way in which the verse at hand and Neẓiv's interpretation thereof fits within the broader context of the *parashah*, of the Pentateuchal book in which that *parashah* is found, and in the context of the language and themes of the Torah in general. Thus, each of the five volumes opens with an introduction to the general themes of the given Pentateuchal book. And, time and again, Neẓiv repeats the same idea he presented elsewhere in *Ha'amek Davar*, or builds upon it, when applicable to another similar verse. Likewise, from time to time Neẓiv notes that a stylistic feature of the biblical text is "the way of the Torah" and not an isolated or random occurrence.[23] It is for this reason that Meir Bar-Ilan noted that in order to truly appreciate the Torah commentary of his father, one must read it in its entirety rather than selected verses devoid of their larger context.[24]

It is also quite clear that the mature Neẓiv of *Ha'amek Davar*, like the younger Neẓiv of *'Emek ha-Neẓiv*, has a broad range of intellectual interests which extends well beyond the realms of traditional Bible and Talmud study. The most apparent field of study in which Neẓiv in *Ha'amek Davar* displays not only interest, but mastery, is that of Hebrew grammar, syntax, and semantics. While Nissim Eliakim devotes much of his work on Neẓiv to elucidating precisely this point, when it comes to

---

20 E.g., *HD* Num. 10: 35; *HrD* Num. 20: 13.

21 *HD* Ex. 25: 22

22 On select occasions such statements can be found. E.g., in *HD* Gen. 26: 16 he refers to the method of *Ramban*, in his introduction to Leviticus he distinguishes between the style of *Sifre* and that of *Sifre Zuta*, and in *HD* Deut. 26: 13 he refers to the method of *Rambam* in his *Mishneh Torah*.

23 E.g., *HD* Gen. 5: 5; *HD* Ex. 24: 1; *HD* Ex. 29: 21; *HD* Num. 3: 47; *HD* Num. 25: 65, HD. Deut. 5: 5.

24 Bar-Ilan, *Rabban*, 54.

the question of where Neẓiv acquired this knowledge Eliakim has very little to offer.[25] Seen against the backdrop of his work on *Sifre,* however, one can begin to offer an answer. For it is there that one learns that the young Neẓiv devoted significant time to the study of the grammatical section of a twelfth-century work by the Kaarite author Yehudah Hadasi, *Sefer Eshkol ha-Kofer,*[26] as well as Eliyahu (ha-Baḥur) Levita's (1468-1549) *Masoret ha-Masoret*[27] and his Aramaic dictionary entitled *Tishbi.*[28] It is in *'Emek ha-Neẓiv,* as well, that one learns that the young Neẓiv studied Mendelssohn's *Biur*[29] and Wessely's *Gan Naul* on Hebrew synonyms,[30] as well as the work of the German Bible scholar and grammarian, Zev Wolf Heidenheim.[31] Thus, there is no question that the foray into the world of grammar and Hebrew language undertaken by the young Neẓiv in the context of his early study of midrash forms the basis of much of his later Torah commentary.

Beyond the realm of Hebrew language, *Ha'amek Davar* contains comments which relate to numerous other areas of study as well. In his introduction to the work he compares the process of interpreting Torah to that of interpreting poetry,[32] and the discovery of new meaning in a biblical verse to the discovery of new scientific data.[33] These allusions not only place Neẓiv within the broad intellectual world common amongst the midrash commentators of the early nineteenth century, but also make his introduction as a whole rather reminiscent of Ḥanokh Luria's intro-

---

25 While Eliakim (44) notes that a glance at the sources used by Neẓiv in his *Mekhilta'* and *Sifre* commentaries might "teach us about the sources he used to construct his spiritual, ethical, and exegetical world," he also admits (22) that he only considered other works of Neẓiv *"be-sha'at ha-ẓorekh."* Thus, without having seriously engaged Neẓiv's commentary on *Sifre,* Eliakim can do no more then speculate as to what works Neẓiv might have read.

26 *EH* Shoftim 17 (III: 189).

27 *EH* Matot 1 (II: 275).

28 *EH* Be-ha'alotekha 34 (I: 290).

29 *EH* Shoftim 16 (III: 189). On this citation, see Chapter 1 above. As a result of a few striking similarities between the work of Neẓiv and that of Moses Mendelssohn, Eliakim (45-48) perceptively states that "with great care I would guess that Mendelssohn's *Biur* did not escape the sight of Neẓiv." Again, Neẓiv's commentary on *Sifre* furnishes the evidence which Eliakim lacks.

30 *EH* Re'eh 49 (III: 135).

31 *EH* Pinḥas 11 (II: 246).

32 *HD Kidmat ha-'Emek* 3, 5. The significance of this metaphor has been discussed by Jay Harris in his *How Do We Know This? Midrash and the Fragmentation of Modern Judaism* (Albany: SUNY Press, 1995). It also serves as the basis for Nissim Eliakim's analysis of Neẓiv's approach to *parshanut*. While the metaphor is indeed interesting and significant, I believe Eliakim has overstated the case.

33 *HD Kidmat ha-'Emek* 4.

duction to his *Kenaf Renanim* (Pressburg, 1859) in which he compares the music of the mind to music of the ear,[34] as well as Avraham Schick's introduction to his commentary on *Tanna de-Bei Eliyahu* (Sudilkov, 1834), in which he compares "*ḥakhmot ha-tiv'it ve-ha-tevunah*" to "*ḥokhmat elohut.*"[35] Indeed, the references to poetry come as no surprise to one who has read Neẓiv's commentary on *Sifre,* for there one sees the young Neẓiv composing poems of his own.

The reference to scientific discovery in the introduction to *Ha'amek Davar* is not the only instance in which Neẓiv displays a marked interest in the natural world. On a number of occasions in the early chapters of *Ha'amek Davar* on Genesis, Neẓiv hints to his readers that his knowledge extends beyond the proverbial four cubits of *halakhah.* For example, he displays familiarity with the concept of a genus from which a variety of species emerge,[36] he makes a comment regarding the inadaptability of animals to foreign climates,[37] he notes that the period directly preceding the Flood was marked by a disruption in the world's food chain,[38] and he suggests that the modern discovery of prehistoric fossils is related to the manner in which God brought about the Flood's waters upon the Earth.[39] While such comments are rare within traditional Jewish scholarship of the second half of the nineteenth century, remarks regarding the natural world and the popular science of the day are found throughout the work of Luria, Schick, Radal, Yiẓḥak Eliyahu Landau, and Reb 'Iẓele of Volozhin, as well as that of their intellectual predecessor, the Vilna Ga'on.[40]

Throughout his Torah commentary, Neẓiv also displays a distinct historical consciousness and a particular interest in the context in which biblical events unfold. Thus he notes that amongst ancient Near Eastern peoples it was common for a master to force his slave to look more youthful by cutting off his sidelocks and beard "as is still the practice amongst the Children of Ishmael today."[41] He notes that such people

34 *Hakdamat ha-Mefaresh,* 2.
35 *Tanna' de-Bei 'Eliyahu 'im Me'ore 'Esh,* introduction, 2.
36 *HD* Gen. 1: 21.
37 *HD* Gen. 2: 7.
38 *HD* Gen. 6: 12.
39 *HD* Gen. 7: 23.
40 See Chapter 3 above on the intellectual breadth of early-nineteenth-century Lithuanian Torah scholars.
41 *HD* Lev. 19: 27.

would also cut themselves as a sign of mourning or engrave the names of the deceased into their skin. Those who preferred not to do so would hire a poor person to do so for them "as is still the practice [amongst Middle Eastern peoples] to hire criers and drummers."[42] Likewise, Neẓiv writes that in biblical times there were no inns along the road; instead, travelers would sleep at abandoned buildings known as "*einayim*."[43] Neẓiv in *Ha'amek Davar* also displays a keen sensitivity to the geo-political structure of the ancient Near East. He is therefore quick to note that when Bil'am's prophesy (Num. 24:22) refers to a people called "*Ashur*" raiding the descendants of Cain, the reference couldn't possibly be to the Assyrian kingdom of the first Temple period, as is the common translation of "*Ashur*," since "we don't find that Assyria [ever] harmed the descendents of Cain." Rather, Neẓiv suggests that the reference is to the Persian kingdom which had overtaken Assyria and were "*me'usharim*" or "pleased" with their success, hence Bil'am's reference to them as "*Ashur*."[44] He also writes of ancient Near Eastern punitive measures,[45] courtship practices,[46] and defense protocols.[47] Probably the most celebrated example of Neẓiv's interest in the ancient Near East, though, is his statement that the name Moses is derived not from the Hebrew verb "*mishitihu*" meaning "she drew him [from the water]," but from the Ancient Egyptian word for son.[48]

Of course, Neẓiv lacked the linguistic tools, research skills, and, perhaps, the motivation to engage in serious historical study, and thus many of his accounts have little, if any, credible evidence upon which to stand. His information was undoubtedly gleaned from his study of Ibn Ezra, Maimonides, Yossipun, de' Rossi, Levita, Mendelssohn, and other similar Hebrew works, as well as his regular reading of Hebrew newspapers and periodicals.[49] Nonetheless, his consistent interest in the

---

42 *HD* Lev. 19: 28.

43 *HD* Gen. 38: 14—It was in such a building that the adulterous incident between Yehudah and Tamar occurred.

44 *HD* Num. 24: 22.

45 *HD* Deut. 21: 22.

46 *HD* Deut. 21: 10; *HD* Gen. 14: 16.

47 *HD* Num. 13: 22.

48 *HD* Ex. 2: 10. In this instance, Neẓiv does provide a source for his knowledge. However, the name he provides, Shmuel from "*medinat Boheim*," is one that neither I nor anyone else I have consulted with in the field to date have been able to identify. It would seem, though, that Ibn Ezra ad loc., also aided Neẓiv in drawing such a conclusion.

49 As noted earlier, Neẓiv cites the newspaper *Ha-Maggid*, in *EH* Naso 45 (I: 177).

ancient world and his implicit recognition of the importance of historical information not found in the biblical text sets Neẓiv, along with many of his contemporary midrash scholars, apart from much of traditional Jewish Bible commentary.[50]

In a similar vein, Neẓiv on several occasions alludes to the competing religio-political factions which developed during the First and Second Temple periods.[51] While a general knowledge of such events can be gained from talmudic and midrashic literature, a close reading of *Harḥev Davar* on Exodus 13:16 indicates that Neẓiv's knowledge of the subject was considerably more extensive. In his discussion there of the three different "sects" which emerged during the Second Temple period, he refers to the sect on the religious "right" who were hermits, ascetics, and pietists, as "*'issiyim*" or Essenes.[52] The term Essenes is found nowhere in traditional rabbinic literature. Azariah de' Rossi, however, does refer to the Essenes in his *Sefer Me'or 'Einayim* and, as noted above, *Me'or 'Einayim* is a work with which the young Neẓiv was intimately familiar. De' Rossi even mentions that Eusebius and Philo refer to them as "*kedoshim*" or holy ones, thereby associating them with a religious right wing of sorts, similar to Neẓiv's portrayal of them.[53]

In fact, the identification of the Essenes with one of the Second Temple sects mentioned in rabbinic literature was given considerable attention amongst Lithuanian scholars of the first half of the nineteenth century. In the 1820s, Isaac Baer Levinsohn took issue with de' Rossi's equation of the Essenes with the heretical "*beitusim*" mentioned in rabbinic literature

---

50 On the debate over Jewish sensitivity or insensitivity to non-biblical historical events, see Robert Bonfil's "Jewish Attitudes Toward History and Historical Writing in Pre-Modern Times" in *Jewish History* 11, 1 (Spring 1997): 7-39.

51 E.g., "Petiḥah Le-Sefer Bereishit," *Ha'amek Davar; HD* Deut. 32: 6; *Harḥev Davar* Ex. 13: 16. See also *Meshiv Davar* (Jerusalem: 1993), I: 44; *Ma'amar 'al Yamin u-Semol*, III: 10.

52 The additional detail in this version leads me to believe that the famous passage in the undated *Ma'amar 'al Yamin u-Semol* (*Meshiv Davar* 1:44) is a later abridged version of this one. The fact that that letter was written to members of the nascent Hungarian ultra-Orthodox movement, whom Neẓiv was encouraging to take a more moderate stance vis a vis the Jews of their communities who had embraced elements of modernity, provides sufficient cause for Neẓiv to have deleted an obviously foreign term, such as *issiyim*, from his homily, whereas I see little motivation for adding such a term to a pre-existing homiletical piece before including it in his *Harḥev Davar*. Hence my suggestion that the piece in *Harḥev Davar* represents the original and that of *Ma'amar al Yamin u-Semol* is an abbreviated reformulation.

53 *Me'or 'Einayim, 'Imrei Bina*, 3. Cassel, 94; Weinberg, 107.

and identified them instead as "*nezirim*" or nazarites.[54] In his *Te'udah be-Yisrael,* Levinsohn describes the Essenes as "*ḥasidim ha-kedoshim,*" or "holy pietists," terms identical to those of de' Rossi and quite close to those of Neẓiv. Yisrael Böhmer (1820-1860), whose father Yosef Böhmer (1796-1864) was the rabbi of Slutsk and was widely regarded as one of the premier students of Ḥayyim of Volozhin,[55] dedicated an entire monograph to precisely this question. Once again, then, the intellectual world of Neẓiv's youth offers important insight into his later *Ha'amek Davar.*

Beyond the general breadth of knowledge displayed by Neẓiv in his *Ha'amek Davar,* which is reminiscent of the intellectual interests of the Vilna Ga'on, the direct impact of the Ga'on's thought, so strikingly apparent in Neẓiv's work on *Sifre,* is also evident in his later commentary on Torah. Neẓiv in *Ha'amek Davar* cites from a full range of the Ga'on's work, including *Aderet Eliyahu,*[56] his commentaries on *Eliyahu Rabba,*[57] *Seder Olam Rabba,*[58] and *Shulḥan Arukh.*[59] He also refers to teachings of the Ga'on which were unprinted but recounted in his name.[60] At times, however, he dismisses such teachings as spurious, such as when he writes that, "We heard the opposite in the name of the Gaon, z"l...and I don't believe in the rumors spread in the name of the Gaon...a lie has been uttered in his name."[61]

Furthermore, as Jay Harris has shown, the sharp distinction which the Ga'on draws between *peshat* and *derash* is unmistakable in the work of Neẓiv as well.[62] Although both readings legitimately emanate from the text, one is not to be mistaken for the other. Neẓiv, in *Ha'amek Davar,* is adamant and explicit in this regard. Thus, we find comment after comment in which Neẓiv carefully points out to his readers that one reading

54 Levinsohn, *Bet Yehudah,* 201.

55 On Yisrael and Yosef Böhmer, see Fuenn, *Keneset Yisrael,* 493. On Yosef Böhmer's role in adjudicating the dispute between Neẓiv and Yosef Baer Soloveitchik, see Ya'akov Ha-Levi Lifshitz, *Sefer Toldot Isaac* (Warsaw, 1896), 61. On his familial connection to Isaac Elḥanan Spektor, see Ephraim Shimoff, *Rabbi Isaac Elchanan Spektor: Life and Letters* (Jerusalem: Sura Institute for Research, 1959), 23.

56 E.g., *HD* Num. 5: 2.

57 E.g., *HD* Num. 27: 11.

58 E.g., *HD* Deut. 9: 18.

59 E.g., *HD* Num. 6: 3; *HrD* Num. 27: 11; *HrD* Deut. 22: 4.

60 E.g., *HD* Num. 11: 32. Neẓiv also refers to the Ga'on, without naming the source, in *HD* Gen. 1: 31; *HD* Gen. 2: 19; *HD* Ex. 32: 30; *HD* Lev. Intro; *HrD* Lev. 25: 15; *HD* Deut. 4: 28; *HD* Deut. 5: 23; *HD* Deut. 24: 15; *HD* Deut. 29: 8; *HD* Deut. 32: 6.

61 *HD* Deut 21: 15.

62 See Harris, 235-44.

of the verse is to be considered *derash*, while another is what he believes to be *peshat*.[63] Of course, the young Neẓiv's study of de' Rossi and of Hebrew grammar, as well as his thorough understanding of the nature of midrashic literature, significantly contributes to this element of his later commentarial approach as well.

### *Exegetical Positions Rooted in* Sifre

A number of the exegetical positions the mature Neẓiv advances in his *Ha'amek Davar* also seem to be rooted in his early work on *Sifre*. Thus, for example, the young Neẓiv, based on a position he ascribes to Rambam, suggests that *halakhot* stated explicitly in the Torah text have weightier legal status than *halakhot* exegetically derived from the text.[64] The older Neẓiv then uses this distinction to explain several difficulties raised in his Torah commentary.[65] More striking is a comment in *EH Pinḥas* 5 (II: 233), in which the verb "*ẓav*," literally meaning command, is interpreted by *Sifre* as a reference to "*divre talmud*." Neẓiv, ad loc, offers an explanation of the semantic connection between *ẓav* and *talmud*, stating that the "*talmud*" referred to by *Sifre* is a reference to the oral Torah. This con-

63 *HD* Gen. 3: 9; *HD* Gen. 9: 20; *HD* Gen. 10: 12; *HD* Gen. 11: 29; *HD* Gen. 17: 1; *HD* Gen. 18: 15; *HD* Gen. 20: 13; *HD* Gen. 22: 1; *HD* Gen. 23: 2; *HD* Gen. 24: 2, 9, 28; *HD* Gen. 27: 9, 27; *HD* Gen. 28: 19 ; *HD* Gen. 30: 23; *HD* Gen. 32: 26, 29; *HD* Gen. 33: 18; *HD* Gen. 36: 21; *HD* Gen. 41: 54; *HD* Gen. 43: 16; *HD* Gen. 44: 18; *HD* Gen. 46: 3; *HD* Gen. 48: 8, 22; *HD* Gen. 49: 24, 27; *HD* Ex. 7: 12, 27; 12: 21; *HD* Ex. 21: 2 ; *HD* Ex. 21: 3; *HD* Ex. 21: 7; *HD* Ex. 21: 11; *HD* Ex. 21: 30; *HD* Ex. 21: 36; *HD* Ex. 22: 2 ; *HD* Ex. 22: 4; *HD* Ex. 22: 14; *HD* Ex. 22: 17, 30; *HD* Ex. 23: 3, 7, 18; *HD* Ex. 24: 12; *HD* Ex. 25: 12; *HD* Ex. 26: 24; *HD* Ex. 31: 2, 14, 15; *HD* Ex. 33: 22; *HD* Ex. 34: 7; *HD* Ex. 34: 20, 27; *HD* Ex. 35: 3 ; *HD* Ex. 36: 29; *HD* Ex. 39: 37; *HD* Lev. 1: 8; *HD* Lev. 2: 8, 14; *HD* Lev. 3: 9; *HD* Lev. 4: 1, 5, 12; *HrD* Lev. 5: 4; *HD* Lev. 6: 4; *HD* Lev. 6: 11 ; *HD* Lev. 7: 9, 16, 18, 24; *HD* Lev. 9: 6; *HD* Lev. 9: 17; *HD* Lev. 10: 11; *HD* Lev. 11: 8, 23; *HD* Lev. 13: 3, 45; *HD* Lev. 14: 13, 17, 19; *HD* Lev. 15: 31; *HD* Lev. 16: 3, 16, 20, 23; *HD* Lev. 17: 2, 15, 16; *HD* Lev. 18: 5; *HD* Lev. 18: 28; *HD* Lev. 19: 3, 7, 17, 22; *HD* Lev. 19: 23; *HD* Lev. 20: 10; *HD* Lev. 21: 4, 6; *HD* Lev. 22: 3; *HD* Lev. 23: 1, 39; *HD* Lev. 25: 6, 13, 15; *HD* Lev. 25: 24 ; *HD* Lev. 27: 2, 21, 26, 29, 33; *HD* Num. 3: 12; *HD* Num. 5: 9, 13, 14, 24; *HD* Num. 6: 23; *HD* Num. 10: 9; *HD* Num. 11: 19; *HD* Num. 12: 3; *HD* Num. 14: 38; *HD* Num. 15: 5; *HD* Num. 15: 26 ; *HD* Num. 15: 28, 35; *HD* Num. 16: 15; *HD* Num. 17: 5; *HD* Num. 18: 7, 28; *HD* Num. 19: 7; *HD* Num. 19: 17; *HD* Num. 20: 23; *HD* Num. 21: 3, 8; *HD* Num. 24: 14; *HD* Num. 27: 2; *HD* Num. 28: 7; *HD* Num. 29: 35; *HD* Num. 32: 30; *HD* Deut. 1: 17; *HD* Deut. 2: 1; *HD* Deut. 6: 20; *HD* Deut. 8: 3; *HD* Deut. 11: 15, 26; *HD* Deut. 12: 4, 8; *HD* Deut. 13: 9; *HD* Deut. 14: 7; *HD* Deut. 15: 19; *HD* Deut. 16: 1, 3, 4; *HD* Deut. 17: 11; *HD* Deut. 18: 3; *HD* Deut. 20: 20; *HD* Deut. 21: 22; *HD* Deut. 22: 22; *HD* Deut. 23: 12, 24; *HD* Deut. 24: 1; *HD* Deut. 5: 1, 8; *HD* Deut. 26: 7; *HD* Deut. 31: 2; *HD* Deut. 32: 18.

64 *EH* Naso 5 (I: 29). While they are both considered *de-orayyta*, certain stringencies apply only to explicit *halakhot* and not to those which result from rabbinic exegesis.

65 E.g., *HD* Ex. 22: 27; *HD* Lev. 23: 39; *HD* Deut. 13: 15.

nection, between the word *ẓav* in its various forms and the oral Torah, becomes a centerpiece of Neẓiv's exegetical approach in *Ha'amek Davar*. That is, Neẓiv interprets the verb *ẓvh* as referring to oral instructions, which form the basis of the oral Torah and hence the Talmud. This exegetical tool, therefore, becomes Neẓiv's preferred method of explaining the discrepancy between the commonly accepted corpus of *halakhot* on a given topic and its treatment in the biblical text. If the latter is missing items or seems to contradict the accepted norms but contains the verb *ẓvh* (as legal portions of the Torah text most often do), Neẓiv understands the Torah to be stating that additional instructions or explanations were given orally, hence alleviating any seeming dissonance.[66] In fact, Neẓiv states quite clearly in *Ha'amek Davar*, Deuteronomy 3:28, that his position is based on *Sifre*.[67]

Another *Sifre* passage which becomes a hallmark of Neẓiv's Torah commentary is *Sifre*'s statement that the biblical word "*ḥukim*" refers to the "*midrashot*."[68] The young Neẓiv there explains that by "*midrashot*" *Sifre* means the *halakhot* which are not explicitly stated in the Torah text but derived instead through exegesis. The word *ḥukim*, however, literally means laws or rules. Neẓiv, therefore, ever mindful of exegetical method, understands the midrash as referring to the rules or principles of rab-

66 E.g., *HD* Gen. 2: 16; *HD* Gen. 6: 22; *HD* Gen. 9: 7; *HD* Ex. 7: 6; *HD* Ex. 12: 28; *HD* Ex. 16: 34; *HD* Ex. 18: 23; *HD* Ex. 34: 4; *HD* Ex. 34: 32; *HD* Ex. 36: 1; *HD* Ex. 39: 5; *HD* Ex. 39: 7; *HD* Ex. 39: 26; *HD* Ex. 39: 43; *HD* Ex.40: 33; *HD* Lev. 6: 1; *HD* Lev. 7: 38; *HD* Lev. 8: 5; *HD* Lev. 8: 21; *HD* Lev. 8: 35; *HD* Lev. 8: 36; *HD* Lev. 9: 7; *HD* Lev. 10: 13; *HD* Lev. 17: 2; *HD* Num. 2: 33; *HD* Num. 3: 42; *HD* Num. 5: 4; *HD* Num. 7: 12; *HD* Num. 8: 3; *HD* Num. 9: 5; *HD* Num. 15: 23; *HD* Num. 15: 36; *HD* Num. 17: 26; *HD* Num. 20: 27; *HD* Num. 27: 11; *HD* Num. 27: 22; *HD* Num. 31: 7; *HD* Num. 31: 41; *HD* Num. 31: 47; *HD* Num. 35: 34; *HD* Num. 36: 10; *HD* Deut. 1: 2; *HD* Deut. 3: 28; *HD* Deut. 26: 14.

67 It is important to note that the ubiquitous equation of *ẓvh* with oral instruction seems to be a position adopted by Neẓiv, based on the passage above, only later in life. Thus, whereas such is the standard explanation of the verb in *Ha'amek Davar*, Neẓiv never mentions this passage on any other occasion in *'Emek ha-Neẓiv*. And this is not for lack of opportunity. The first two pages of Neẓiv's commentary on *Sifre* alone contain six comments surrounding the meaning of the word *ẓav*, yet the only mention Neẓiv makes of the interpretation offered in Pinḥas is an aside when *Sifre* itself cites the verse used for the *derashah* in Pinḥas. For other similar remarks, see *EH* Naso 53 (I: 185); *EH* Naso 58 (I: 188); *EH* Be-ha'alotekha 2 (I: 195); *EH* Be-ha'alotekha 7 (I: 206), and many others. In fact, in *EH* Matot (II: 208), Neẓiv writes that the phrase "*ka'asher ẓivah*" is unnecessary in regard to the oral Torah, which everyone knows is from God, whereas the written Torah requires the phrase lest one think that it came from Moshe and not God himself. As we shall see below, the transformation of this single *Sifre* passage into a universal meaning accorded to the verb *ẓvh* is in line with the general transformation Neẓiv undergoes as he enters his later years.

68 *EH* Re'eh 5: 6 (III: 89).

binic exegesis such as the thirteen *middot* of Rabbi Ishmael and other similar rabbinic techniques. In his commentary on Torah, therefore, virtually every time the Torah text includes the word "*ḥukim*" Neẓiv writes that the word does not simply mean laws or statutes, as one might have imagined. Instead, based on this passage in *Sifre*, "*ḥukim*" throughout the Torah text, according to *Ha'amek Davar*, refer to the principles of rabbinic exegesis.[69]

### Ha'amek Davar *as Nineteenth-Century Midrash*

In addition to the individual elements of the intellectual milieu of Neẓiv's youth which surface in *Ha'amek Davar*, much of Neẓiv's general approach to the task of interpreting the Torah text hints at a past immersed in the world of midrash. In fact, one might well characterize significant parts of *Ha'amek Davar* as nineteenth-century midrash. That is, in *Ha'amek Davar* Neẓiv not only borrows, interprets, and explains passages of rabbinic midrash, but continues the process of rabbinic midrash by applying markedly similar, if not identical, exegetical techniques where the Sages of old failed to do so.

From a close reading of Neẓiv's introduction to *Ha'amek Davar* one can already begin to discern that his intent is to continue the process of interpretation found in the classic works of midrash. Building off his metaphor of the Torah as poetry, Neẓiv writes that in order to best understand the work of a poet one must acquaint oneself with the techniques used by the individual poet to convey meaning in his poems.[70] Sometimes the methods of a given poet are well known, and at other times they must be deduced from careful analysis of the totality of that poet's work. The same is true, says Neẓiv, regarding the interpretation of the Torah. Some of the techniques through which the Torah text expresses meaning are already known, like "the seven [hermeneutical] principles" of Hillel, the thirteen principles which "*Tana de-ve Rabbi Yishmael* added to them," and "the thirty-two rules of aggadah which

---

69 E.g., *HD* Gen. 26: 5; *HD* Ex. 15: 26; *HD* Lev. 18: 4; *HD* Lev. 10: 11; *HD* Lev. 18: 5; *HD* Lev. 19: 37; *HD* Lev. 20: 8; *HD* Lev. 26: 3; *HD* Lev. 26: 46; *HrD* Num. 7: 9; *HD* Num. 9: 3; *HD* Num. 15: 16; *HD* Deut. 4: 1; *HD* Deut. 4: 45; *HD* Deut. 5: 28; *HD* Deut. 6: 20, 24; *HD* Deut. 11: 1; *HD* Deut. 12: 1; *HD* Deut. 16: 12; *HD* Deut. 17: 19; *HD* Deut. 26: 17; *HD* Deut. 27: 10; *HD* Deut. 30: 16. *HD* Deut. 4: 1 and 12: 1 refer explicitly to *Sifre* as the source of this position.

70 Here too one senses Neẓiv's affinity for methodology.

Eliezer the son of Yosi ha-Gelili derived from scrutiny of the [biblical] text."[71] Unlike other traditional Torah commentators, however, Neẓiv believes that the authors of the classical midrashic literature did not exhaust the application of those principles or the process of illuminating new principles. Thus he concludes the above passage by stating, "So we should [continue] to add and to explain in every generation, even if it has not been explained beforehand."[72] This point is reinforced in the next section of his introduction when, in listing some of the exegetical principles which he applies in his own commentary, he notes that one of his basic exegetical techniques is identical to the eleventh rule of Rabbi Eliezer's thirty-two hermeneutical principles of aggadah. Furthermore, in the course of his commentary Neẓiv refers to the project of rabbinic biblical exegesis via the *middot* of Rabbi Eliezer, Rabbi Ishmael, and the like as *pilpulah shel Torah,* while simultaneously and repeatedly reminding his readers that the project of *pilpulah shel Torah* remains the lifeblood of the Jewish people down to his day.[73]

Neẓiv, however, not only states that the process of midrash is an ongoing endeavor, but sets a personal example as well. In the narrative sections of the Torah he often inserts a detail into the story which has no basis either in the text or in any rabbinic tradition, but which was necessitated by an inconsistency in the text, or by a gap in the narrative sequence. For example, the story in Numbers of the spies sent to the Land of Israel describes their ascent from the Negev and their approach to the city of Hebron (Num. 13:22). The masoretic text, though, describes the ascent through the Negev with a verb in the plural form and the approach to Hebron in the singular form. According to the Sages, this shift in number indicates that while all of the spies ascended through the Negev, only one actually entered the city of Hebron. From a combination of the verse in Deuteronomy (1:36) which states that Caleb was granted "the land which he traversed" and a verse in Judges (1:20), the Sages

---

71 *HD "Kidmat ha-'Emek"* 5.

72 Ibid.

73 E.g., *HD* Ex. 15: 25; *HD* Ex. 18: 23; *HD* Ex. 25: 21; *HD* Ex. 27: 6; *HD* Ex. 27: 20; *HD* Ex. 29: 39; *HD* Ex. 29: 41; *HD* Ex. 30: 7; *HD* Ex. 34: 1; *HD* Ex. 34: 27; *HD* Ex. 37: 19; *HD* Ex. 39: 37; *HrD* Ex. 13: 16; *HrD* Lev. Intro, 4: 17; *HrD* Lev. 8: 36; *HrD* Lev. 10: 11; *HrD* Lev. 16: 16; *HrD* Lev. 18: 5; *HrD* Lev. 24: 4; *HrD* Lev. 24: 5; *HrD* Lev. 25: 18; *HrD* Num. 4: 6; *HrD* Num. 4: 9; *HrD* Num. 8: 2; *HrD* Num. 9: 6; *HrD* Num. 14: 34; *HrD* Num. 15: 23; *HrD* Num. 15: 33; *HrD* Num. 21: 20; *HD* Deut. 1: 3; *HD* Deut. 3: 23; *HD* Deut. 4: 7; *HD* Deut. 4: 9; *HD* Deut. 4: 14; *HD* Deut. 4: 46; *HD* Deut. 7: 11; *HD* Deut. 10: 2; *HD* Deut. 10: 8; *HD* Deut. 26: 17.

deduce that the single spy who entered Hebron was Caleb. They further suggest that the Torah's (veiled) reference to Caleb's separation from the rest of the spies in the approach to Hebron teaches us that Caleb went into Hebron to perform an act of great spiritual merit which the other spies were not motivated to do. As Hebron is best known in the Bible as the burial place of the forefathers, the Sages conclude that such was the purpose of Caleb's visit.[74] That is, the seemingly nebulous verse means to say that Caleb separated from the other spies so as to pray at the Cave of Mahpelah, where his forefathers were buried.

The obvious shift from plural to singular in this verse clearly disturbs the well-honed grammatical sensibilities of Neẓiv as well. While he accepts the basic approach of the Sages in suggesting that the verse refers to Caleb approaching Hebron alone, he describes a completely different set of circumstances which surrounded the event. While it is not uncommon for traditional Torah commentaries to reject the aggadic narrative of rabbinic midrash, what is most striking about Neẓiv's comments is the fact that he, much like the rabbis of the talmudic period long before him, inserts "historical" events which are not recorded in the text, nor anywhere else for that matter, in order to allow for an easier reading of the verses as hand.

Neẓiv's interpretation of the verse in Numbers (13:22) focuses on the fact that the next verse reverts to the plural form, suggesting that Caleb was reunited with at least one of his fellow spies. He also takes into account the report which the other spies relay upon their return to the Wilderness (Num. 13:31-33), which emphasizes the strength and size of the land's inhabitants, and the fact that the entire mission was completed in the span of forty days. Therefore, Neẓiv begins his comments here by stating in a matter-of-fact fashion that the spies did not travel in a single group but spread out through the land in pairs. This explains their ability to cover so much terrain in only forty days, and also explains the return to the plural after Caleb's visit to Hebron, for his partner in espionage waited for him on the outskirts of the city. The partner's refusal to enter, according to Neẓiv, was motivated purely by cold feet. He was afraid of the city's inhabitants and anxious over the fact that "in a fortified city it is difficult to escape in an emergency."[75]

---

74 TB *Sotah* 34b.

75 *HD* Num. 13: 22. Neẓiv makes mention of his version of this narrative in *HD* Num. 32: 9 as well.

The rabbinic narrative, then, has twelve spies emerging from the Negev and Caleb slipping away to pray at the graves of his forefathers; Neẓiv's narrative, based on many of the same scriptural anomalies which motivated the talmudic sages, has six pairs of spies emerging from the Negev on individual routes, only one of which has Hebron on its itinerary. When the spies on that route reach the city, however, one of the pair is panicked by rumors of the city's frightening inhabitants and thus Caleb, undaunted by the rumors and faithful to his mission, scouts the city alone before returning to his partner so they can proceed on their way. While the story as Neẓiv tells it makes logistical sense and brilliantly harmonizes a variety of verses, it has no source other than Neẓiv's fertile imagination. But, then again, the talmudic contention that Caleb entered to visit the Cave of Mahpelah had no known prior source either, and as Neẓiv's *pilpulah shel Torah* is no different from that engaged in by the Sages, he feels that he too has the right to insert historical circumstances which fill in the gap of anomalous texts.

In *Ha'amek Davar*, Neẓiv also inserts "historical" events to account for what might otherwise appear to be repetition in the biblical text. For example, when the biblical narrative repeatedly relates that Abraham's servant left the house of Betu'el together with his daughter Rebecca, Neẓiv writes that there were, in fact, two distinct departures from the city. The first was a public sendoff which included a large procession through town, during which Rebecca was embarrassed to ride together with the servant on the same camel. The second was upon actually leaving the city limits, at which time Rebecca joined the servant on his camel, hence the otherwise repetitive phrase (Gen. 24:61) "and the servant took Rebecca and they went."

This transfer from her own camel to that of the servant then sets the stage for Neẓiv's well-known account of Rebecca's initial encounter with her groom, Isaac, in which she falls off the camel, frightened by the spiritual state exhibited by Isaac who, according to the midrash, had been immersed in prayer. Had she been riding behind the servant, though, Neẓiv suggests that she would have seen the normal interaction between the servant and Isaac, and thus would have realized that the man was not the frightening Divine agent that she imagined. Hence, by the time the servant would have introduced Isaac to Rebecca as her future husband, she would have overcome her initial state of panic. However, in Neẓiv's account of the narrative, since Rebecca was riding together with the servant, all she knew was that they were approaching some man who looked "like a terribly awesome angel" with "his arms prostrated in prayer." As a result she was overcome by a fear so traumatic that even in later years Rebecca, unlike her mother-in-law Sarah, cowered before her husband.[76]

In a fashion quite similar to his account of Caleb described above, Neẓiv in commenting on this story of Rebecca readily accepts certain elements of the rabbinic embellishment of the biblical narrative, such as the notion that Isaac was engaged in prayer prior to Rebecca's arrival. But, as in the aforementioned example, Neẓiv then alters the rabbinic account, which has Rebecca prostrating herself before her groom, by inserting a number of embellishments of his own—the public sendoff, the transfer between camels, and the sudden panic upon their encounter—so as to allow for a narrative which alleviates the problem of repetitions in the text and fits well with the later narratives found in the biblical text itself. Thus, once again Neẓiv has embraced the approach of rabbinic exegesis and advanced the project of *pilpulah shel Torah* with his own novel contribution.

As many of the classical works of midrash are wont to do, Neẓiv also employs the technique of *mashal*, or parable, in poignant fashion throughout his commentary. More often than not, the characters in Neẓiv's parables are those of the midrashic literature—the king and his officers,[77] the master and his slave,[78] the father and his son,[79] the bride and her groom.[80] Time and again, Neẓiv invokes the midrashic simile "*malkhuta' de-raki'a ke-'ein malkhuta de-'ar'a,*" "the kingdom of Heaven is like a kingdom on Earth," to explain the actions and methods of God.[81] While, on the one hand, Neẓiv's use of *mashal* has its roots in the world of the *maggidim* and *darshanim* of his day, his frequent employment of it as a means of explaining the ways of God and in terms identical to those

76 H.D. Gen. 24: 61-65. For similar insertions into the biblical narrative, see *HD* Gen. 11: 1-9; *HD* Gen. 33: 18; *HD* Ex. 1: 7; *HD* Ex. 2: 25; *HD* Ex. 3: 7; *HD* Ex. 9: 35; *HD* Num 14: 1; *HD* Num 20: 14; *HD* Num 21: 1; *HD* Num 21: 130; *HD* Num 22: 16; *HD* Num 22: 22; *HD* Num 31: 11, and many others.

77 E.g., *HD* Ex. 24: 10, *HD* Lev. 10: 2; *HD* Num. 1: 1; *HD* Deut. 29: 12.

78 E.g., *HD* Deut. 29: 13.

79 E.g., *HD* Lev. 26: 3.

80 E.g., *HD* Ex. 19: 4; *HD* Lev. 9: 1; *HrD* Deut. 32: 2.

81 In rabbinic literature, see TB *Berakhot* 58a, TB *Shavuot* 35b, and *Yalkut Shim'oni* I Kings, *remez* 319. See, also; *HD* Ex. 7: 28; *HD* Ex. 18: 19; *HD* Ex. 23: 20; *HD* Ex. 23: 21; *HD* Ex. 33: 1; *HrD* Lev. 23: 24; *HrD* Lev. 33: 43; *HD* Num. 1: 1; *HD* Deut. 7: 12; *HD* Deut. 11: 13, and others.

used in the midrashic literature seems to similarly suggest that Neẓiv understands the purpose of *Ha'amek Davar* as but a continuation of the rabbinic exegetical endeavor.

The characterization of *Ha'amek Davar* as nineteenth-century midrash is probably best exemplified by Neẓiv's comments pertaining to the realm of *midrash halakhah*. As clearly demonstrated in his commentary on *Sifre*, Neẓiv understands the role of the rabbis in *midrash halakhah* to be twofold. At times they are creatively deducing heretofore unknown halakhic rulings from the wording of the biblical text, and at times they are merely looking for scriptural support for a ruling which was received orally via tradition. In his commentary on Torah, Neẓiv engages in both activities. At times he offers a novel halakhic ruling based on his own analysis of the biblical text. For example, he writes that the wording of a verse pertaining to the appointment of the Levites as priests in place of the first-born Israelites indicates that the contemporary Jewish ceremony of redeeming the first born (*pidyon ha-ben*) requires the father to specify which child is being redeemed, lest his halakhic obligation to redeem his son go unfulfilled.[82] Likewise, his analysis of the biblical text leads him to the halakhic conclusion that a defiled Priest is forbidden from performing not only the duties of a priest, but also the duties of a Levite.[83]

Far more frequently, however, Neẓiv in *Ha'amek Davar* links *halakhot* recorded elsewhere to a scriptural source. In his introduction to the book of Leviticus, Neẓiv makes this element of commentarial endeavor quite clear when he states explicitly that he, like the Geonic author of the *She'iltot* before him, has come to pick up where *Sifra* left off.

> And there are many more verses in which the nuances of the language have not been explained in *Sifra* because they had no received traditions [about them] and they did not extract it from the verse. And we, with humility and with the help of God the blessed Giver [of knowledge], have explained the nuances of a number of verses, not in order to extract something new of our own accord,

82 *HD* Num. 3: 48. Neẓiv refers to a passage in Tosafot Ketubot 102a in this regard, but, to the best of my knowledge, neither that Tosafot nor any of the standard halakhic codes record the ruling as stated here by Neẓiv.

83 *HD* Num. 18: 2. See also *HD* Lev. 7: 29; *HD* Lev. 7: 30; *HD* Deut. 23: 12; *HD* Deut. 24: 3, and others.

> Heaven forbid, but because through nuanced [explanation] we can explain many received traditions and *halakhot* found in the Gemara.[84]

Indeed, there may be no exegetical technique employed more frequently by Neẓiv in *Ha'amek Davar* than the identification of a word, a phrase, and, at times, an entire verse which appears extraneous.[85] After noting such, Neẓiv continues with the phrase *"u-ba' le-lamdeinu…,"* meaning "it (the extra word or words) comes to teach us…" The next sentence generally contains a legal or narrative detail which was previously recorded elsewhere in rabbinic literature but never previously linked to the verse at hand. At times Neẓiv means to identify the source from which the rabbinic tradition was generated, and at times he seeks merely to show the way in which the verse alludes to a component of the Oral Torah.[86] Both exegetical moves, of course, are identical to the rabbinic techniques which Neẓiv identifies time and again throughout his commentary on *Sifre*.[87] In other words, as a young man Neẓiv ex-

84 *HD* Lev. intro.

85 E.g., *HD* Gen. 4: 25; *HD* Gen. 12: 17; *HD* Gen. 14: 12; *HD* Gen. 17: 22; *HD* Gen. 24: 10; *HD* Gen. 26: 26; *HrD* Gen. 27: 9; *HD* Gen. 28: 10; *HD* Gen. 32: 26; *HD* Gen. 33: 18; *HD* Gen. 34: 1; *HD* Gen. 34: 25; *HD* Gen. 36: 11; *HD* Gen. 36: 32; *HD* Gen. 38: 26; *HD* Gen. 40: 5; *HD* Gen. 47: 28; *HD* Ex. 6: 23; *HD* Ex. 12: 14; *HD* Ex. 13: 22; *HD* Ex. 14: 29; *HD* Ex. 16: 15; *HD* Ex. 16: 26; *HD* Ex. 17: 7; *HD* Ex. 22: 6; *HD* Ex. 25: 9; *HD* Ex. 25: 19; *HD* Ex. 27: 9; *HD* Ex. 27: 11; *HD* Ex. 27: 18; *HD* Ex. 30: 20; *HD* Ex. 33: 8; *HD* Ex. 36: 8; *HD* Ex. 38: 21; *HD* Ex. 39: 9; *HD* Lev. 1: 14; *HD* Lev. 4: 5; *HD* Lev. 4: 6; *HD* Lev. 4: 18; *HD* Lev. 5: 26; *HD* Lev. 6: 9; *HD* Lev. 7: 11; *HD* Lev. 7: 29; *HD* Lev. 8: 32; *HD* Lev. 11: 9; *HD* Lev. 12: 2; *HD* Lev. 13: 3; *HD* Lev. 13: 18; *HD* Lev. 14: 7; *HD* Lev. 16: 30; *HD* Lev. 18: 5; *HD* Lev. 19: 3; *HD* Lev. 23: 31; *HD* Lev. 23: 44; *HD* Lev. 25: 6; *HD* Lev. 27: 21; *HD* Lev. 27: 32; *HD* Num. 1: 19; *HD* Num. 3: 17; *HD* Num. 3: 42; *HD* Num. 4: 40; *HD* Num. 5: 4; *HD* Num. 6: 3; *HD* Num. 6: 5; *HD* Num 7: 72; *HD* Num. 9: 1; *HD* Num. 9: 12; *HD* Num. 10: 30; *HD* Num. 11: 29; *HD* Num. 15: 29; *HD* Num. 15: 35; *HD* Num. 7: 12; *HD* Num. 18: 2; *HD* Num. 19: 4; *HD* Num. 20: 26; *HD* Num. 20: 27; *HD* Num. 23: 12; *HD* Num. 26: 46; *HD* Num. 27: 4; *HD* Num. 27: 13; *HD* Num. 27: 22; *HD* Num. 27: 7; *HD* Num. 28: 14; *HD* Num. 1: 6; *HD* Num. 1: 29; *HD* Num. 33: 3; *HD* Num. 1: 39; *HD* Num. 35: 1; *HD* Num. 36: 10; *HD* Deut. 1: 2; *HD* Deut. 1: 14; *HD* Deut. 1: 15; *HD* Deut. 1: 27; *HD* Deut. 1: 41; *HD* Deut. 5: 19; *HD* Deut. 10: 5; *HD* Deut. 12: 21; *HD* Deut. 13: 9; *HD* Deut. 17: 11; *HD* Deut. 18: 19; *HD* Deut. 21: 23.

86 For other examples of Neẓiv's linking pre-existent *halakhot* to the words of the text, see *HD* Gen. 17: 11; *HD* Gen. 17: 13; *HD* Gen. 24: 7; *HD* Gen. 24: 8; *HD* Gen. 24: 53; *HD* Gen. 24: 6; *HD* Ex. 22: 21; *HD* Num. 6: 21; *HD* Num. 15: 19; *HD* Num. 19: 16; *HD* Num. 19: 18; *HD* Num. 19: 19; *HD* Lev. 9: 3; *HD* Lev. 12: 2; *HD* Lev. 12: 6, and many others.

87 It should be noted, however, that in classical midrashic texts the phrase *ba' lelamdeinu* generally indicates generative midrash and not *'asmakhta'*. In *Ha'amek Davar*, however, most—although not all—of the new midrashic readings offered by Neẓiv do not generate new legal rulings.

plored the methods and modes of rabbinic exegesis, as demonstrated in *'Emek ha-Neẓiv*, and in his later years he set out to practice those methods, thereby continuing the ever-evolving process of *pilpulah shel Torah*.

Thus, in many ways the foundations of *Ha'amek Davar* can be traced to Neẓiv's earlier work in *midrash halakhah*. His propensity in the Torah commentary to cite from the *derashot* of the Sages, his broad range of intellectual interests, the freedom with which he emends rabbinic texts, and his focus on the macrocosmic elements of the text all neatly align with the central features of *'Emek ha-Neẓiv*. In a sense, though, *Ha'amek Davar* represents a bold step beyond his earlier work, in that as a young man he was content to explain and interpret the exegesis of the rabbis, whereas in his later work, as head of the world's most prestigious institution of talmudic study, he carried on the exegetical endeavor of the midrashic authors by engaging the biblical text itself.

Despite the fact that these trends clearly place *Ha'amek Davar* on a continuum which flows directly from Neẓiv's early work in the realm of midrash commentary, there are a few salient features of *Ha'amek Davar* which seem to be at odds with the *Weltanschauung* adopted by the young Neẓiv. In the coming chapter we will examine these features and note the way in which they directly reflect the changes to Lithuanian Jewish society, as well as Neẓiv's place within that society, that took place over the years which separate *'Emek ha-Neẓiv* from *Ha'amek Davar*.

# CHAPTER SEVEN:
## The Polemics of *Ha'amek Davar*

The fact that much of Neẓiv's *Ha'amek Davar* can be understood as nineteenth-century midrash need not be at odds with the fact that Neẓiv considered his project, first and foremost, as a Torah commentary bent on giving the straightforward reading of the biblical text. After all, like Rashi and many other medieval commentators, Neẓiv believed that the exegesis of the sages did, at times, reflect the *peshat* of a given verse. Thus, when Neẓiv employs similar techniques it can be understood in a similar fashion. What is more striking, though, in a commentary aimed at *peshat*, is the very definite polemical streak which runs throughout *Ha'amek Davar* and which at times seems to blur the distinction between Torah commentary and social commentary. Placing *Ha'amek Davar* against the backdrop of the work of *'Emek ha-Neẓiv*, which as we've seen in the last chapter is quite similar to *Ha'amek Davar* in its commentarial approach yet also markedly non-polemical, allows the social issues which the older Neẓiv takes up in his Torah commentary to come to the fore.[1]

Thus, for example, we have already noted that two centerpieces of *Ha'amek Davar* have their source in *Sifre*. The verb "*ẓav,*" is interpreted by *Sifre* as a reference to "*divre talmud*" which Neẓiv, ad loc, understands as a reference to the Oral Torah.[2] In his *Sifre* commentary, this point is made and then dropped—never to be taken up again in three volumes of *'Emek ha-Neẓiv*. In his Torah commentary, however, the equation of the root *ẓvh* with Divine instructions received orally and hence unrecorded in the biblical text is repeated over and over again.[3] Neẓiv's purpose in

---

1 In noting the differences between the two works, clearly consideration need be given to the fact that *'Emek ha'Neẓiv* is a commentary on a work of rabbinic midrash while *Ha'amek Davar* is a commentary on Torah. I believe, however, that the particular areas of divergence which we will now explore are unrelated to the difference in subject matter of the two commentaries. In Appendix D, I have used Neẓiv's work on *Mekhilta'*, *Birkat ha-Neẓiv*, to demonstrate this point.

2 *EH* Pinḥas 5 (II: 233),

3 E.g., *HD* Gen. 2: 16; *HD* Gen. 6: 22; *HD* Gen. 9: 7; *HD* Ex. 7: 6; *HD* Ex. 12: 28; *HD* Ex. 16: 34; *HD* Ex. 18: 23; *HD* Ex. 34: 4; *HD* Ex. 34: 32; *HD* Ex. 36: 1; *HD* Ex. 39: 5; *HD* Ex. 39: 7; *HD* Ex. 39: 26; *HD* Ex. 39: 43; *HD* Ex.40: 33; *HD* Lev. 6: 1; *HD* Lev. 7: 38; *HD* Lev. 8: 5; *HD* Lev. 8: 21; *HD* Lev. 8: 35; *HD* Lev. 8: 36; *HD* Lev. 9: 7; *HD* Lev. 10: 13; *HD* Lev. 17: 2; *HD* Num. 2: 33; *HD*

repeating this is clearly to respond to those who had begun to doubt or to attack the integrity of the Oral Torah—a goal which simply was not part of Neẓiv's earlier commentary on *Sifre*.

A similar phenomenon can be seen in regard to *Sifre*'s statement that the biblical word *"ḥukim"* refers to the *"midrashot,"* which Neẓiv understands as a reference to the principles of rabbinic exegesis, such as the thirteen *middot* of Rabbi Ishmael and other similar rabbinic techniques.[4] In his *Sifre* commentary, this line remains an isolated comment, never again applied to similar biblical statements. In his commentary on Torah, however, virtually every time the Torah text includes the word *"ḥukim,"* Neẓiv writes that the word does not simply mean laws or statutes, as one might have imagined. Rather, God's call for the people of Israel to follow his *"ḥukim"* is actually, in Neẓiv's view, a call for the people of Israel and their descendents in future generations to engage in rabbinic exegesis and talmudic study.[5] Certainly, this too rings a polemical note, one which had no place in Neẓiv's earlier commentarial endeavor.

Indeed, the polemical strains in *Ha'amek Davar*, from its relentless call to Torah study to its defense of rabbinic exegesis and forceful derision of heretical sectarianism, as well as its near silence in referencing books beyond the pale of the traditional cannon, account for virtually all of *Ha'amek Davar*'s divergence from its intellectual roots in *'Emek ha-Neẓiv*. The shifts within Lithuanian Jewish society between the decades of the 1830s and 1840s, when Neẓiv was penning his *Sifre* commentary, and the decades of the 1860s and 1870s, when he was composing his Torah commentary, coupled with the marked change of Neẓiv's place within that society, help to explain why the later work is both Torah commentary and social commentary, while the earlier one was strictly confined to the realm of intellectual endeavor.

---

Num. 3: 42; *HD* Num. 5: 4; *HD* Num. 7: 12; *HD* Num. 8: 3; *HD* Num. 9: 5; *HD* Num. 15: 23; *HD* Num. 15: 36; *HD* Num. 17: 26; *HD* Num. 20: 27; *HD* Num. 27: 11; *HD* Num. 27: 22; *HD* Num. 31: 7; *HD* Num. 31: 41; *HD* Num. 31: 47; *HD* Num. 35: 34; *HD* Num. 36: 10; *HD* Deut. 1: 2; *HD* Deut. 3: 28; *HD* Deut. 26: 14.

4 *EH* Re'eh 5: 6 (III: 89).

5 E.g., *HD* Gen. 26: 5; *HD* Ex. 15: 26; *HD* Lev. 18: 4; *HD* Lev. 10: 11; *HD* Lev. 18: 5; *HD* Lev. 19: 37; *HD* Lev. 20: 8; *HD* Lev. 26: 3; *HD* Lev. 26: 46; *HrD* Num. 7: 9; *HD* Num. 9: 3; *HD* Num. 15: 16; *HD* Deut. 4: 1; *HD* Deut. 4: 45; *HD* Deut. 5: 28; *HD* Deut. 6: 20, 24; *HD* Deut. 11: 1; *HD* Deut. 12: 1; *HD* Deut. 16: 12; *HD* Deut. 17: 19; *HD* Deut. 26: 17; *HD* Deut. 27: 10; *HD* Deut. 30: 16. *HD* Deut. 4: 1 and 12: 1 refer explicitly to *Sifre* as the source of this position.

### *Literal Aggadah in* Ha'amek Davar

As noted in the previous chapter, Neẓiv's comments in *Ha'amek Davar* quite frequently distinguish *derash* from *peshat*.[6] Furthermore, in good de' Rossian fashion, he explicitly states that the purpose of "*aggadot*" is "to pull the heart of a person toward his father in heaven."[7] It is therefore rather jolting when, from time to time in his Torah commentary, Neẓiv seems to accept statements of midrash aggadah in their most literal sense. For example, he relates to the rabbinic story of Abraham's salvation from the fiery furnace as historical fact and not as a literary device intended to convey a religious message.[8] It goes unmentioned in the biblical text, according to Neẓiv, only because it predates Abraham's encounter with Torah study.[9] He also seems to accept at face value the aggadic statement, found in *Midrash Rabbah*, that during his stay in Egypt Joseph forgot all of the Torah he had studied with his father. Neẓiv goes on to state that had Joseph continuously reviewed his studies, thereby maintaining his engagement in Torah study, he never would have fallen prey to the wife of Potiphar.[10]

Similarly, Neẓiv embraces the aggadic statement that Jacob spent fourteen years studying in the yeshivah of *Shem va-`Ever*.[11] A comment he makes in this regard might well suggest that Neẓiv had abandoned the hermeneutics of his youth. When the Torah text records (Gen. 29:11) "And Jacob kissed Rachel and he raised his voice and he cried," Neẓiv ad loc in *Ha'amek Davar* first cites Rashi, who explains that Jacob's tears resulted from the fact that Elifaz, Esau's son, had robbed him along the way, thus leaving him with nothing to give to his beloved Rachel. Neẓiv rejects this aggadic answer and writes that "according to the *peshat*, when he was in the house of *Shem va-`Ever* for fourteen years he spent everything he had." That is, for Neẓiv, the aggadic story of Elifaz's heist runs against his literary sensibilities, but the notion that Jacob spent fourteen years studying in yeshivah he considers to be *peshat*.

Even when Neẓiv does question the literal meaning of an aggadic passage, the resolution he provides in *Ha'amek Davar* seems, at times,

---

6 See Chapter 6, note 60, above.
7 *HD* Ex. 15: 26
8 *HD* Gen. 11: 3.
9 *HrD* Gen. 12: 17.
10 *HrD* 39: 6.
11 *HD* 28: 10.

rather distant from what we would imagine the young Neẓiv to have suggested. A passage particularly insightful in this regard is found in Neẓiv's *Harḥev Davar* to Genesis 26:5. In the beginning of the passage the reader catches a brief glimpse of the young Neẓiv as he cites the comments of Rashi, which seem to take at face value a rabbinic exegetical statement in the Talmud (*Yevamot*, 21) that suggests that the forefathers adhered to the minutiae of rabbinic *halakhah* centuries before any rabbis existed. In response, Neẓiv wonders, "But I am dumbfounded for it is explicitly stated in *Yevamot* that this [rabbinic exegetical comment] is only an '*asmakhta*'!" But whereas the young Neẓiv might have left his reader on this troubling note, the older Neẓiv is quick to comment that "there is, in this, another meaning." From there he goes on to explain, with the help of a number of other aggadic sources, that what is meant by Rashi and the passage in *Yevamot* is not that the forefathers observed all of rabbinic law, but that they actively engaged in its study. This, according to the older Neẓiv, like his explanation of Jacob's tears, is an explanation according to "*peshat*." For one well schooled in the approach of de' Rossi, well-read in the commentaries of Mendelssohn and Wesseley, and who constantly distinguishes between *peshat* and *drash*, these passages seem strikingly out of place.

### *Hermeneutics of a* Rosh Yeshivah

It is no mere coincidence, however, that the passages just cited, in which Neẓiv seems to have broadly expanded his sense of *peshat*, all relate to the act of Torah study. After all, the young Neẓiv of the *Sifre* commentary had, by the time of his composition of *Ha'amek Davar*, transitioned from the realm of a *lamdan*—an up-and-coming scholar devoted wholeheartedly to the parochial world of books and study—to the realm of *Rosh Yeshivah*—a communal leader charged with the responsibility of engaging Lithuania's best and brightest Jewish youth with the world of Torah study. The young Neẓiv began the decade of the 1840s as one of many young talented Talmudists in Jewish Lithuania. By 1853 he had been catapulted into a position which made him a member of the tiny cadre of Lithuanian Jewry's most prominent rabbinic leaders. The shift was rapid and seems to have been relatively unexpected.

While Max Lilienthal does describe Neẓiv as a close confident of Reb 'Iẓele as early as 1841, and he mentions as well that Neẓiv had already begun to teach in the yeshivah,[12] it was his older brother-in-law, Eliezer Yiẓḥak Fried, who had been marked as the successor to Reb 'Iẓele when the latter would pass away. In 1849, following what Meir Bar-Ilan describes as the sudden death of Reb 'Iẓele, Eliezer Yiẓḥak assumed the mantle of *Rosh Yeshiva* and the Neẓiv began his ascent by assuming Eliezer Yiẓḥak's former position of second in command. Only four years later, at the age of forty-three, Eliezer Yiẓḥak also passed away. Once again the Neẓiv's career was moved forward—this time into the position of Volozhin's *Rosh Yeshiva*.[13] While his appointment in 1853 was initially challenged from numerous fronts, by 1855 a distinguished rabbinic panel cemented his position as head of the yeshiva with Yosef Baer Soloveitchik assuming the position of second in command. Thus, the period from the mid-1840s to the mid-1850s marks the period of Neẓiv's emergence as a communal leader. For the young Neẓiv, then, full time Torah study is the ideology which informed the way he lived his life. For the mature Neẓiv, Torah study is the ideology which he must instill in the lives of hundreds of young men, each and every day.

Furthermore, significant developments in the 1850s and 1860s made the call to Torah study even more charged and more forceful than it had been during the decades of Neẓiv's youth. First of all, the world of the yeshivah had grown dramatically. Aided in part by the publication of Ḥayyim of Volozhin's *Nefesh ha-Ḥayyim* in 1824, the ideology of full-time Torah study had begun to extend its reach beyond the inner circles of the intellectual elite; by the time Neẓiv was appointed *Rosh Yeshivah* in Volozhin, many other smaller yeshivot had sprung up, built largely in Volozhin's mold.

Just as important, however, is the fact that the ideology of full-time Torah learning also met its first serious challenge by the late 1850s. It was a challenge from within—the challenge of Yisrael Salanter's Mussar movement—which, while accepting and advocating the notion of full-time Torah study, argued that classic Torah study as practiced in yeshivot such as Volozhin was insufficient for the purposes of molding the character and behavior expected of Torah-abiding Jews. To the proponents of the Mussar movement, sustained introspection, passionate study of moral tracts, habituation techniques, and self deprecating measures were

12 See pp. 15-16 above.
13 Bar–Ilan, *Rabban*, 26.

often necessary complements to Talmud study.[14] To purists such as Neẓiv, these were distractions wholly unnecessary if one was to truly devote oneself to proper Torah study, and thus the call to Torah study took on new meaning as Neẓiv assumed his new role as *Rosh Yeshivah* and began to compose his *Ha'amek Davar*. In fact, there is at least one occasion in his Torah commentary where Neẓiv is unmistakably responding to the challenge of the Mussar movement:

> From here we learn that one whose actions have led him to anger or cruelty or to hatred for other human beings, must engage in Torah for its own sake. And in the merit of such he will find the strength to place himself on the good and proper path.[15]

Neẓiv of *Ha'amek Davar*, therefore, is so immersed in a world highly charged with the call to Torah study that the aggadic statements ascribing Torah study to the biblical forefathers seem to have jumped over the divide from the realm of *derash* into the realm of *peshat*. To Neẓiv, the notion that Abraham, Jacob, and Moses spent their days engaged in Torah study is *peshita*, simple, because that is what life for Neẓiv the *Rosh Yeshivah* is all about.

As such, these instances in which Neẓiv takes aggadic statements at face value may not be at odds with the approach of de' Rossi. De' Rossi, after all, never advanced an utter rejection of all aggadic material.[16] Rather, in more dramatic form than Maimonides before him, he argued that the modern reader is not obliged to accept the literal meaning of an aggadic statement which is at odds with accepted contemporary truths. For the Sages "were not speaking on matters such as these through prophetic tradition, but rather as ordinary human beings who evaluate the evidence as they see it or argue on the basis of what they come to hear."[17]

---

14 See Immanual Etkes, *Rabbi Salanter and the Mussar Movement: Seeking the Torah of Truth* (Philadelphia: Jerusalem Publication Society, 1993).

15 *HD* Deut. 13: 19.

16 Proponents of the Mussar Movement argued that "the study of Torah for its own sake" alone was an insufficient remedy for such character flaws. For a good comparison of the respective approaches of Maimonides and de' Rossi to *aggadah*, see Lester Segal's *Historical Consciousness and Religious Tradition in Azariah de' Rossi's* Me'or 'Einayim (Philadelphia: JPS, 1989), 115-132.

17 Weinberg, 218.

In fact, Samuel ibn Nagrela made the same point in more succinct fashion when he wrote in regard to *aggadah* that

> What [the Sages] explained in regard to [non-halakhic interpretations of] biblical verses is in accord with that which occurred to them and the way they understood things, and, of these interpretations, those which seem reasonable we learn from and the rest we do not rely upon.[18]

Thus, what has changed for Neẓiv is not his sensitivity to *peshat* and *derash*, nor his belief that *aggadot* need not be taken literally. What has changed is the barometer by which aggadic statements are deemed reasonable or unreasonable. That is, in the world of the yeshivah, aggadic statements regarding Abraham's *pilpul* and Jacob's years in yeshivah seem perfectly in confluence with the realities of the time and hence need not be relegated to the world of moral teachings intended solely to "to pull the heart of a person toward his father in heaven."[19]

This insight into the worldview of Neẓiv and its hermeneutic consequences explains more than just Neẓiv's literal acceptance of *aggadot* relating to Torah study. As described in the previous chapter, Neẓiv in *Ha'amek Davar* often sees himself as engaging in the very same project of exegesis as performed by the tanaitic and amoraic authors of midrash. And, just as those rabbinic authors took the liberty of inserting Torah study into the narratives of the biblical text, insertions which Neẓiv takes quite literally, so does Neẓiv. In fact, hardly a chapter goes by in *Ha'amek Davar* without Neẓiv finding a reference to Torah study within the biblical text. Through such allusions, metaphors, and creative interpretation, *Ha'amek Davar* becomes a poignant polemic arguing for both the antiquity and the salvific power of intense Torah study.

### *The Antiquity of* Pilpulah Shel Torah

As noted above in relation to Neẓiv's understanding of *ḥukim* as the principles of *pilpulah shel Torah*, Neẓiv did not view the Torah study in which he, his disciples, and a growing number of young Lithuanian men were

18 Nagrela, *Mevo'*, 91.
19 *HD* Ex. 15: 26

engaged as a product of early modern or medieval Europe, and not even as a product of the tanaitic and amoraic periods. To Neẓiv, the study of Torah was a discipline in which his earliest forefathers had engaged and which was later mastered by Moses; a discipline to which the written Torah itself repeatedly refers and one which has remained the prized possession of the Jewish people down to the present time. And, while the notion of the antiquity of Torah learning long predates Neẓiv, the lengths to which he goes to prove it and the detail which he provides in doing so are distinctive. If we may borrow a term from contemporary Western culture, we might say that Neẓiv's *Ha'amek Davar* functions almost as a prequel to Ḥayyim of Volozhin's *Nefesh ha-Ḥayyim*. While the latter articulates the unrivaled place of traditional Torah study within the Jewish religious experience, Neẓiv's work, published fifty years after *Nefesh ha-Ḥayyim*, ventures back into biblical history in an effort to explain how Torah study came to occupy the elevated position described by the earlier scholar, his wife's grandfather, in *Nefesh ha-Ḥayyim*.

At times, Neẓiv makes the argument for the antiquity of traditional Torah study explicitly, as he does, for example, when he contrasts the constancy of Torah study through the ages with the changed nature of Jewish prayer.

> Furthermore, the power of [learning] Torah is different from the power of [Divine] worship in that the Torah is exalted by [the Jewish people today] in the same manner that it was exalted in the Wilderness and in the Land of Israel. Even though there were changes in the nature of the analysis of Torah (*iyyun ba-Torah*) according to the times, nonetheless it is all of the same character, [that is,] to scrutinize the language of Scripture and to add interpretations (*le-hosif lekaḥ*). Such is not the case with [Divine] worship [where] even though prayer came in the place of sacrificial worship, nonetheless the form of these worships are different from each other.[20]

Often, though, this argument is made more subtly, such as when Neẓiv states that Abraham traveled to the south of Canaan because it

20 *HD* Ex. 27: 6.

was more suitable to the study of Torah[21] and that there he devised new *halakhot* using the thirteen hermeneutical principles.[22] Other examples appear when he makes an off-handed remark that the Land of Israel was a place already sanctified by Torah and religious worship in the days of Jacob,[23] that the plight of Joseph was linked to his failure to study in depth,[24] and when he notes that the *Tamid* sacrifice brought daily in the desert was intended as an aid to Torah study.[25]

A similar effect is created by the symbolic significance Neẓiv accords to the crossbeam upon which the Israelites were commanded to sprinkle the blood of their sacrificial lambs prior to the last of the ten plagues. Neẓiv writes that a door consists of three parts: two side posts and a crossbeam which lies on top of them. The three parts correlate to the three forefathers, each of whom embodied one of the three foundations of Jewish existence. Jacob correlates to one of the sideposts and represents peace, Isaac correlates to the other sidepost and represents kindness and acts of charity, and Abraham correlates to the crossbeam and represents Torah and the act of traditional Torah study.[26] While it is true that the crossbeam of Torah must have the pillars of kindness and peace in place before it can be laid securely upon them, it is equally true that ever since the times of the forefathers, it is, in Neẓiv's view, the act of Torah study which occupies the sole position atop the list of Jewish values.

Similar symbolic significance is accorded by Neẓiv to a verse which seems to suggest that the kindling of the Tabernacle's menorah was dependent on the act of burning the incense which precedes it in the daily priestly ritual. The burning of the incense, write Neziv, symbolizes the giving of charity, while the fire of the menorah represents *pilpulah shel Torah*. Much as Abraham's crossbeam of Torah relies on the support of Isaac's sidepost of charity, so too the menorah of *pilpulah shel Torah* must be preceded by acts of charity. After all, it is charity and communal support which allow a young Lithuanian Torah scholar to devote himself entirely to Torah study, thus enabling the fire of *pilpulah shel Torah* to burn bright. Here, in a nod toward those of his own generation, Neẓiv

21 *HD* Gen. 12: 9.
22 *HD* Gen. 26: 5.
23 *HD* Gen. 37: 1. See also *HrD* Gen. 26: 5.
24 *HD* Gen. 39: 6.
25 *HD* Ex. 29: 41.
26 *HD* Ex. 12: 22. See also *HD* and *HrD* Gen. 12: 17.

states quite explicitly that the symbolism of the biblical text is intended to "teach us the order of Torah and charity for all generations."[27]

Despite Abraham's predilection for Torah study, it is Moses, the greatest of prophets and the original teacher of God's Torah, who amongst all biblical figures most actively engaged in *pilpulah shel Torah*. Moses, according to Neẓiv, received the tools to engage in creative Torah study directly from God, although he did not share them with the people until they reached the plains of Moav.[28] These tools, which were later codified by Rabbi Ishmael into the thirteen principles of rabbinic exegesis,[29] were used with proficiency by Moses[30] to decide legal cases[31] and later to preside over the Sanhedrin.[32]

Neẓiv does recognize that the *pilpulah shel Torah* in which the forefathers and Moses engaged was not identical to the process of Torah learning with which later generations were occupied. However, he maintains that it was the core from which all later scholarship grew and from which traditional Torah scholarship continued to grow in nineteenth-century Lithuania. In the early verses of Deuteronomy, Neẓiv outlines his understanding of the history of traditional Torah learning by comparing it to a tree which took root at Sinai and which has grown in every generation thereafter.

> The growth of the Torah of Talmud is like the growth of a live tree. For the tree's growth and sustenance is dependent on its central roots [which lie] deep in the ground. And even though the strength of its roots are not apparent to the eye, nonetheless, everyone understands

---

27 *HD* Ex. 30: 7. Likewise, Neẓiv writes in *HD* Ex. 26: 35 that the *Shulḥan* was placed in the Tabernacle first, and the *menorah* afterward, to symbolize the necessity of sustenance in order to provide for those engaged in *pilpulah shel Torah*. On the *menorah* as symbolic of *pilpulah shel Torah*, see *HD* Ex. 25: 31; *HD* Ex. 27: 20; *HD* Ex. 27: 21; *HD* Ex. 30: 7; *HD* Ex. 37: 19; *HD* Ex. 39: 37; *HD* Lev. 4: 17; *HD* Lev. 16: 17; *HD* Lev. 24: 4; *HD* Lev. 24: 5; *HD* Num. 4: 6; *HD* Num. 4: 9; *HD* Num. 8: 2. On the communal obligation to support Torah scholars see *HD* Ex. 35: 24; *HD* Num. 31: 30; *HD* Deut. Intro; *HD* Deut. 27: 26; *HD* Deut. 33: 2; *HD* Deut. 26: 3; *HrD* Deut. 33: 4.

28 *HD* Ex. 15: 25; *HD* Ex. 25: 21; *HD* Lev. 8: 36; *HD* Num. 8: 6; *HD* Num. 14: 34; *HrD* Num. 21: 20.

29 *HD* Lev. 25: 18; *HD* Deut. 1: 3; *HD* Deut. 26: 17.

30 *HD* Ex. 27: 20; *HD* Ex. 32: 18; *HD* Num. 3: 1; *HD* Num. 7: 9.

31 *HD* Ex. 18: 23.

32 *HD* Num. 15: 33. Despite the anachronism, such is the term used by Neẓiv, and much of traditional Torah commentary, to refer to the group of elders assembled by Moshe to help him decide legal cases in the desert.

> that such is the case, for were it not so, the tree would be uprooted and would fall. And after [it takes root,] the tree emerges from the ground with a thick foundation, which is the foundation upon which the tree will stand [so as] not to be broken by the wind. Then it proceeds to grow narrowly. And [after] more of the tree [has grown], at the middle of its height, many branches spread out, and then it continues to grow narrowly, and then a few more branches spread out and then it continues to grow narrowly until it becomes a fully formed tree with countless branches along its width and with every branch carrying [additional] small branches.
>
> Such was the growth of *torat ha-pilpul* within [the people of] Israel. At the outset "that which the venerable student will, in the future, innovate" was engraved in the second tablets… and this was the root of *pilpul shel Torah*. And even though we have no understanding of how all of this could be contained within the tablets, nonetheless, we have to believe through the nuances of Scripture that it is so. And it is also logical, for if there was no Divine power in it [i.e., *pilpul shel Torah*] it would have already been uprooted and fallen by the harsh winds which have passed over this type of learning.[33]

Thus, it is the very fact that traditional Torah learning is part of an unbroken continuum dating back to Sinai—the fact that Moses learned it from God and along with Joshua practiced it proficiently, the fact that after a period of decay, the prophet Samuel along with Kings David and Solomon restored it to glory, the fact that later King Hezekiah immersed himself in it and after another dark period King Josiah ushered in its renaissance once again, and the fact that "from that point onward it has had unbridled growth"[34]—which proves the discipline's divine charac-

---

33 *HrD* Deut. 1: 3.

34 Ibid. Neẓiv's implication that Torah-learning today is at a more advanced stage than it was during earlier periods is consistent with his views on the matter expressed elsewhere in his writing and stands in striking contrast to the traditional conservative perspective which equates the passage of time with the "diminishing of the generations." See *HD* Num. 15:

ter and militates against succumbing to the "harsh winds" of changing times and intellectual milieus which have threatened to uproot it.

The older Neẓiv's world of the yeshivah is perhaps most dramatically reflected in the fact that he sees the book of Deuteronomy as dedicated almost completely to the theme of Torah study. By employing his interpretative technique which, based on a passage in *Sifre,* equates the biblical term "*ḥukim*" with rabbinic exegesis, and making use of his own equation of rabbinic exegesis with all traditional Torah study which preceded the talmudic age and all that continues to follow it, Neẓiv transforms Deuteronomy into the ultimate inspirational tract for the traditional yeshivah student. After all, each and every time Moses exhorts the people of Israel to follow God's "*ḥukim,*" he isn't reminding them to act in accordance with Divine law as most Bible commentators had previously assumed, but advocating the study of Talmud in exactly the manner practiced by the Lithuanian yeshivot of the nineteenth century. And it is precisely this dominant theme of Deuteronomy which, as Neẓiv explains in his introduction to the book, led the Sages to refer to it by the name *Mishneh Torah.*

> And since the general [nature] of this book and its essence comes to warn [the people] regarding the labor of Torah [that is,] to explain the nuances of Scripture—and this is known as *talmud*. And all the exhortation and the numerous admonitions of Moses our teacher, all of it comes for this purpose—so that they will accept upon themselves the yoke of Talmud…for this reason [the book] is called by its name *Mishneh Torah* from the language of *shinun shel Torah* (incisive learning of Torah)… the beginning and end of the exhortations in this book relate to the strengthening of *ḥukim u-mishpatim*—which is the Talmud—amongst [the people of] Israel. For from it flows the life of the nation and of Judaism in general. And in this regard the second covenant on the Plains of Moav and at the mountains of Gerizim and Eival was made, "to establish the words of the Torah, etc." And from it [comes] the stake and cornerstone for the ethics

23; *HrD* Ex. 19: 19, *EH* KH 1: 16.

> of prominent men, [both] those who merit the Torah and its labor, [and also] those who God blessed [with the financial resources] to strengthen it with upkeep and sustenance. For this reason the book is called *Mishneh Torah*. To sharpen [*le-shanen*] the sword and to bring forth the war of Torah. And with this we will have strength and light. Amen.[35]

### *The Salvific Power of Torah Study*

In addition to advocating for the antiquity of Torah study, Neẓiv in his *Ha'amek Davar* emphasizes that engaging in such study bears tangible salvific rewards. The attribution of salvific qualities to Torah study long predates Neẓiv; its roots can be traced back to aggadic statements of the Sages and early kabbalistic doctrines which were later emphasized by the Vilna Ga'on and popularized in Ḥayyim of Volozhin's *Nefesh ha-Ḥayyim*.[36] Drawing heavily on their own predisposition for mystical and kabbalistic thought, the Ga'on and Ḥayyim of Volozhin attribute universal cosmic significance to the act of Torah study—it is, in their view, the act which sustains the universe. Neẓiv, who though well-versed in traditional kabbalistic works was not predisposed to kabbalah study, takes a more practical approach to Torah's salvific power. In his view, the act of traditional Torah study, or *pilpulah shel Torah*, is what evokes the love of God[37] and represents the only means for a Jew to attain true happiness.[38] More importantly, it is traditional Torah study that ensures the survival of the Jewish people in the Diaspora,[39] and it is the only act capable of bringing the messianic redemption.[40]

In addition to the explicit expositions of Torah study's salvific nature found in *Ha'amek Davar*, Neẓiv repeatedly employs a number of related metaphors which reinforce the idea. The central metaphor used by Neẓiv in this vein is conveyed through the term *milḥemtah shel Torah*, which re-

35 *HD* Deut. Introduction.
36 See, e.g., *Nefesh ha-Ḥayyim*, 4: 11.
37 *HrD* Ex. 25: 20.
38 *HD* Deut. 4: 1; *HrD* Num. 10: 10.
39 *HD* Num. 14: 34.
40 *HD* Deut. 30: 2.

fers to the act of traditional Torah study as an act of war. In an act of war, one's life hangs in the balance. An act of war properly and thoroughly perpetrated results on the one hand in weariness and fatigue, but on the other hand in the perpetuation and sustenance of the life of the victor. Torah study, according to Neẓiv, does the same:

> For this reason it is called *milḥemtah shel Torah*—for just as those who go off to war [do so with the understanding] that some of them will be injured as a result and many of them will become weakened by the extreme caution and labor [it entails], so too [amongst] scholars of the Torah, some will struggle and become weak [as a result], but the one who emerges in peace from the battle receives his due reward.[41]

While the phrase *milḥemtah shel Torah* is of talmudic origin[42] and appears in other works from earlier in the nineteenth century,[43] the frequency with which it and its corollary metaphors are employed by Neẓiv is unparalleled.[44]

While the act of Torah study is an act of war, the sword one wields to perpetrate the act is the Torah itself. Here too, Neẓiv borrows a rabbinic metaphor (TB *Shabbat* 63a) and utilizes it in an unprecedented manner:

> And the Sages learned this meaning here from the [fact

---

41 *HD* Deut. 32: 3.

42 See TB *Megillah* 15b; *Ḥagigah* 14a; *Sanhedrin* 42a, 93b, 111b; TJ *Ta'anit* 4: 69b. It is also worth noting that this phrase, like the equation of "*ḥok*" with Midrash and the equation of "*ein davar reik*" with biblical omnisignificance, appears in *Sifre Ha'azinu piska* 16 (III: 336) as mentioned by Neẓiv in *HrD* Ex. 13: 16. As noted in Chapter 1, neither the printed edition nor the extant manuscript of '*Emek ha-Neẓiv* have Neẓiv's comments on *Sifre* Ha'azinu.

43 E.g., See the introduction by the sons of the Ga'on to *Beur ha-GRA* on *Shulḥan Arukh OH* (Shklov, 1803) as well as the introduction of Avraham Danzig to *Ḥayye Adam* [*ha-Menukad*] (Jerusalem, 1994), 6.

44 E.g., See *HD* Ex. 13: 16, Num. 20: 29, Deut. 32: 3; *HrD* Gen. 26: 5; Ex. 39: 37; Lev. 22: 42, Deut. 1: 3, 28: 10, 29: 12. Neẓiv also uses the term frequently in *Kidmat ha-'Emek* to *Ha'amek She'elah* and in his later responsa. See *HS KH* 1: 8; *HS KH* 1: 12; *HS KH* 1: 17; *HS KH* 1: 18; *HS KH* 2: 6, *HS KH* 3: 7; *HS KH* 3: 9; *HS KH* 3: 10; *HS KH* 3: 11 and *MD* 4: 80; *MD* 4: 83; *MD* 5: 13; *MD* 5: 19; *MD* 5: 68; *MD* 5: 75; *MD* 5: 99; *MD* 5: 102. See also his 1884 letter to Yisrael Yitzhak of Borowie, published as an introduction to *Revid ha-Zahav* (Warsaw, 1885). His frequent usage of the term was already noted by Meir Bar-Ilan (*Rabban*, 37) and its relation to the Ga'on's understanding of the Torah's salvific power was pointed out by Hannah Kats (*Mishnat ha-Naẓiv*, 79).

> that Scripture uses the word] "*mishmarti*" (my guard).[45] And delving into the logic of the Torah is referred to by Scripture with this name "*mishmarti*," because the study of Torah is not like [other] *miẓvot*. For all the *miẓvot* of the Torah are sustenance (lit., food) and repair of some world which was created for that purpose…[46] and because they are sustenance for the Heaven and Earth, every *miẓvah* has its proper time just as the food for every [living] thing has its proper time, with the exception of the study of Torah which is called a sword… for just as a sword comes to guard a person from someone who might harm him, so too the power of the Torah is as a guard from all evil.[47]

The evils from which the sword of Torah offers protection, according to Neẓiv, range from actual warfare[48] to medical maladies to the dangers posed by one's evil inclinations.[49] Thus it is the sword of Torah with which the Jewish people wage their metaphysical battle against the heavenly prosecutor on the Day of Judgment, Yom Kippur,[50] and the sword of Torah which helps fight the physical battles of the Jewish people as well.

---

45 The verse (Gen. 26: 5) explains that Abraham's descendants will merit the inheritance of the Land of Israel "because Abraham listened to my voice, and watched over my guard [*va-yishmor mishmarti*], my commandments, statutes, and laws."

46 Here we see that Neẓiv, like Ḥayyim of Volozhin and the Ga'on before him, was indeed well attuned to kabbalistic doctrine. While Allan Nadler correctly points to the fact that kabbalah study was central to Lithuanian Torah scholars of the eighteenth and early nineteenth century, he is incorrect in stating that Neẓiv abandoned such study. See his *The Faith of the Mithnagdim*, 29-49. For additional references by Neẓiv to kabbalistic material see *HS* Kidmat Ha-'Emek 1:1, 2:7, 2:12; *HS* Petaḥ Ha-'Emek 1:8; HS 8:6; *HD* Num. 1:42; *EH* Be-ha'alotekha 12 (I: 322); *EH* Shelaḥ 6 (II: 48); *HD* Ex. 19:6 *HD* Lev. 33 :29; *HD* Num. 3:41; *HD* Deut. 32:9; Metiv Shir 5:14.

47 *HrD* Gen. 26: 5.

48 Contemporary Israeli Orthodox society is probably most divided over the issue of whether or not to send their young men off to fight in the Israeli army. The Zionist *dati le'umi* camp, who look to Neẓiv as a founding father due to his support for the *Ḥibat Ẓion* movement and his role as a primary mentor of Avraham Yiẓḥak Kook, believe strongly that all young men should actively participate in army service. Their opposition in the *ḥaredi* camp maintain that young men would better protect the country by engaging in Torah study rather than shooting a machine gun or piloting an air force jet. It is ironic to note that, anachronisms aside, Neẓiv's writings seem to support, and are possibly the earliest thorough presentation of, the latter *ḥaredi* view and not that of the Zionist camp. See below for further support of this position.

49 *HrD* Gen. 36: 5; *HD* Gen. 12: 17.

50 *HD* Lev. 16: 16.

For example, it was the sword of Torah which brought Abraham success in his military campaigns,[51] the sword of Torah which protected the Jewish people from invasion in the Jubilee year,[52] and the sword of Torah which helped the Hasmoneans defeat their Greek oppressors.[53] For, even though there are "other things which help to bring victory in battle…the most effective means of protection in battle is the sword of the Torah."[54]

Even in his own times, writes Neẓiv, the Jewish people live and die by the sword of the Torah. The survival of a nation, after all, depends on three factors—the competent rule of the sovereign and faithful obedience of his subjects, the skillful leadership of the sovereign's officers and the willfulness of the people to follow their guidance, and the quality of the weaponry employed by those in service to the sovereign. Likewise the survival of the Jewish people "in the Land of Israel and, all the more so, in the Diaspora," depends on their acceptance of God's sovereignty, their acquiescence to the instructions of the rabbis, and their "weaponry, that is the Torah which is called the sword of Israel as I have written many times."[55]

Of course, not every male member of a given society is an active member of the armed forces. Only those who are qualified to fight do so, and they thus constitute an elite social class that engenders special treatment from the sovereign in return for their faithful service. It is the responsibility of others, though, to support the soldiers by seeing that their physical needs are met. This is true only in a time of peace, however. During a time of war, every able male becomes a member of the reserves and must do whatever they can to protect the nation. So too, writes Neẓiv, in the army of Torah. During times of peace, the ranks of the army are restricted to those particularly well-equipped for intense Torah study, while the remainder of society is required to support them. In times of war, though, when the existence of traditional Jewry is at stake, as it was perceived to be in the 1860s and 1870s, it is incumbent on everyone to join in the fight by learning Torah to the best of his ability.[56]

---

51 *HD* Gen. 12: 17.

52 When, according to Neẓiv, every male literally returned to his ancestral plot and spent the year engaged in Torah study. As a result, there was no standing army for that year but instead the people relied on the sword of Torah for their protection. See *HD* Lev. 25: 19.

53 See *HD* and *HrD* Ex. 39: 37.

54 Ibid., "*'Even ha-r'oshah ha-magen be-milḥamah hu' ḥarbah shel Torah.*"

55 *HD* Ex. 13: 2.

56 *HD* Deut. 29: 12. See also *HrD* Ex. 25: 20.

Similarly, Neẓiv notes that a sword is composed of two parts, the sword itself and the sheath within which it is carried. During times of peace, the sheath is a beautiful ornament worn by warriors, and the sword within it is there only to instill fear amongst the masses. There is no need to spend the energy required to draw the heavy sword at a time when no threat is present. In a time of war, however, the sheath's function is no longer ornamental but purely utilitarian, as a means of holding the sword until it has to be drawn. And, of course, in the face of danger one must spend whatever energy is necessary to draw one's sword and to fight with it as needed. So too, the Torah consists of two parts—the written Torah and the oral Torah. The former is the sheath whose words contain hints and references to the latter. During times of peace, one can and should gaze at the beauty which lies on Scripture's surface[57]—its prose and poetry, its history and ethics. And, as in the peaceful period of Neẓiv's youth, one might safely remark, as Neẓiv did in his commentary on *Sifre* through his constant identification of *'asmakhta'*, that the beauty of the sheath should not be clouded by the sharpness of the sword. During times of war, however, when traditional Jewry is threatened by a new class of scholars who seek only the sheath and not the sword which lies therein, it is the sharpness of the oral Torah's sword which takes precedence over all else.

### *Citation in* Ha'amek Davar

While we noted in Chapter Six that the reader of *Ha'amek Davar* is struck by the wide range of intellectual interests displayed by Neẓiv, the discerning reader may be equally struck by Neẓiv's nearly complete silence as to where he obtained such knowledge. Of course, the absence of such citations or references in *Ha'amek Davar* is all the more striking when set against the backdrop of *'Emek ha-Neẓiv,* which is filled with references to books which had been studied by the young Neẓiv.

It is certainly possible that Neẓiv, having grown wiser and more prudent in his older age, removed such citations as a cost-cutting measure. After all, every page of a printed text required the printer to reset the characters on his press. The fewer words a book contained, the fewer pages it would have, thus diminishing the labor and cost of publication.

57 *HrD* 13: 16.

However, the fact that the older Neẓiv consistently cites traditional rabbinic sources in *Ha'amek Davar*, from Rambam, Ramban, and Seforno to the Ga'on,[58] Reb 'Iẓele,[59] and Ḥayyim Berlin,[60] and even makes explicit mention of lesser known sources such as Elazar Moshe Hurwitz,[61] Yom-Tov Lipman Baslavsky,[62] and *Sefer Pa'aneaḥ Razei*,[63] makes it rather unlikely that Neẓiv excluded the sources of his extra-rabbinic knowledge to reduce the high cost of printing.

Insightful in this regard is an incident recorded by Barukh ha-Levi Epstein, Neẓiv's brother-in-law and nephew, in which Joshua Steinberg, a leading *maskil*, asked Neẓiv how he had acquired proficiency in grammar, rhetoric, Bible, and other literature. After all, it seemed to Steinberg as if Neẓiv devoted all of his time exclusively to the study of Talmud, its commentators, and the halakhic codes. According to Epstein, Neẓiv replied with a parable of a linen merchant who purchases linen in such large quantity that his suppliers are willing to throw in high-quality leather straps to hold it in transit for free. One who buys nothing from the suppliers, however, can only obtain the straps for a significant price. Thus, according to Epstein, Neẓiv explained that he was like the high volume linen merchant while Steinberg was like one who sought only the straps. Since Neẓiv devoted himself wholeheartedly to the study of Talmud he was able to acquire the other subjects "without effort and without a loss of time." Steinberg, on the other hand, could not.[64] While the historical veracity of many of the anecdotes and vignettes found in *Mekor Barukh* may well be questioned,[65] it is certainly true that this story

---

58 See Chapter 6, notes 36-40, above.

59 See Chapter 6, note 4, above.

60 See Chapter 6, note 5, above.

61 *HD* Num. 28: 31. Elazar Moshe Hurwitz (1817-1890) served as the *av bet din* in Pinsk from 1859 until his death in 1890. He is known for his Talmudic glosses, which were included in the Vilna edition of the Talmud Bavli, and for the fact that his daughter married Barukh ha-Levi Epstein.

62 *HD* Deut. 21: 16. Yom-Tov Lipman Baslavsky (Lippa Mirrer) (1821-1893) is best known for having served as the rabbi and Rosh Yeshivah in Mir beginning in 1874, and for his collection of responsa entitled *Malbushei Yom Tov*.

63 *HD* Lev. 16: 21; *HD* Lev. 25: 33; *HD* Num. 11: 15; *HD* Num. 12: 1; *HD* Num. 17: 27. *Pa'aneaḥ Razei* (or Raza) is a twelfth-century Torah commentary from the Tosafist circle.

64 Epstein (IV: 1825-1829).

65 See Dan Rabinowitz, "Rayna Batya and Other Learned Women: A Reevaluation of Rabbi Barukh Halevi Epstein's Sources," *Tradition* 35 (2001); Yehoshua Moondshine, "Mekor Barukh, Mekor ha-Kezavim," on Shturem.net, available at http://www.shturem.net/index.php?section=artdays&id=785.

captures the message implicitly conveyed by Neẓiv in his *Ha'amek Davar*. That is, his policy of citing only traditional texts leaves the reader with the impression that he acquired knowledge in a variety of extra-talmudic areas without seriously engaging extra-talmudic texts—an impression quickly dispelled by a glance into his earlier work on *Sifre.*

If, as *'Emek ha-Neẓiv* attests, Neẓiv acquired his breadth of knowledge by reading the likes of de' Rossi, Levita, Mendelssohn, and Wesseley, one is left to wonder why there is no mention of them, or the periodicals in which similar material was published, in Neẓiv's later commentary on Torah. The answer to this question may also lie in the changing realities of Lithuanian Jewish society during the middle decades of the nineteenth century.

### *The Hermeneutics of Traditionalism*

As noted above, although the young Neẓiv began the decade of the 1840s as one of many young talented Talmudists in Jewish Lithuania, by 1853 he had been thrust into a position of national communal leadership. Historians of nineteenth-century Russian Jewry have unanimously identified this very same period, the decades of the 1840s and 1850s, as a pivotal point in the emergence of the Eastern European Haskalah.[66] Neẓiv, therefore, transitions from the relatively carefree role of a *lamdan* and part-time lecturer to that of a communal leader charged with responsibility of training the traditional community's future leadership at precisely the same historical moment that the Haskalah begins to be perceived by the rabbinic establishment as a fierce challenge to the values of Lithuanian Jewish society. In the terms employed by Jacob Katz, the society in which the young Neẓiv developed, and the world from which his commentary on *Sifre* was borne, was a "traditional society," deriving its identity primarily from its inherited mores and values. The rabbinic society of *Ha'amek Davar,* with its self-identity largely impacted by the growing "other" composed of the *Maskilim*, was fast transitioning from "traditional" to "traditionalist." And, just as his new position in the

66 E.g., Mordekhai Zalkin, *Ba-'a lot Ha-Shaḥar: Ha-Haskalah ha-Yehudit be-'Imperiah ha-Rusit be-Me'ah ha-Tish'a 'Esreh* (Jerusalem: Magnes Press, 2000), 45, 102; See also Michael Stanislawski, *For Whom Do I Toil?: Judah Leib Gordon and The Crisis of Russian Jewry* (New York: Oxford University Press, 1988) and his *Tsar Nicholas I and the Jews: The Transformation of Jewish Society in Russia, 1825-1855* (Philadelphia: JPS, 1983).

developing world of the yeshivah accounts for shifts between the young Neẓiv's commentarial endeavors in *'Emek ha-Neziv* and that of *Ha'amek Davar*, so do his newfound responsibilities in a society now committed to warding off the challenge of Haskalah.

### *The 1840s: Tension without Fissure*

While a complete study of the emergence of Lithuanian Haskalah is beyond the scope of the present work, a brief look at the response of the Lithuanian rabbinate to what they perceived as a growing threat is germane to the present study. It is in the context of such responses and the concurrent rise of the yeshivah movement that the cultural milieu that characterized early-nineteenth-century midrash scholarship begins to fade. That is, the relative openness of intellectual inquiry which marked the world of Neẓiv's youth gradually became associated with the domain of Haskalah. As a result, the scholarly culture in which the mature Neẓiv composes his *Ha'amek Davar* differs significantly from the one in which he composed *'Emek ha-Neẓiv*.

Two events stand out in the course of the 1840s as having first piqued the interest and then inspired the fear of the Lithuanian rabbinic establishment with regard to the nascent movement for Haskalah. The first is Max Lilienthal's famous tour of the Pale of Settlement, in which he introduced the Tsar's intention of creating state-sponsored schools for Russian Jewry where a modern curriculum consisting of both Jewish and secular studies would supplant the traditional Talmud-only curriculum of the *ḥeder*.[67] The second event, and one which precipitated the opening of such state-sponsored primary schools, was the creation of state sponsored rabbinical seminaries in Vilna and Zhitomir in 1847. The new seminaries were charged with the responsibility of training modern rabbis, some of whom, it was hoped, would become the teachers and administrators of the new state-sponsored primary schools.[68]

When placed along the trajectory of the development of Eastern European Haskalah, these two events represent important milestones. They do not, however, signal an immediate fissure within Lithuanian

67 See Bruce L. Ruben, *Max Lilienthal: Rabbi, Educator, and Reformer in Nineteenth-Century America* (PhD dissertation, City University of New York, 1997), 55-59.

68 See Verena Dohrn, "The Rabbinical Seminaries as Institutions of Socialization in Tsarist Russia, 1847–1873," *Polin: Studies in Polish Jewry*, vol. 14 (2001).

Jewish society. Mordechai Zalkin has pointed out that the significance of these developments for the growth of Haskalah lies not in the numbers of young Jews influenced by Lilienthal or educated in these seminaries but in the confidence, financial support, and social structure they gave to the growing movement for Haskalah. The small group of individuals working to bring Haskalah to Russia now had greatly increased visibility within the community, a source of employment which could not be stripped away via excommunication by the more traditional elements of the community, and a social structure in which to interact with each other and in which to offer support in the pursuit of their cause.[69] All of these important contributions, though, developed over time and could hardly be discerned in the immediate context of the 1840s.

Furthermore, the foundational element of both Lilienthal's project and the rabbinical seminaries was a broadening of the traditional Jewish curriculum. As demonstrated above, the study of language, philosophy, and the natural sciences, while never standardized nor officially taught, had been embraced by prominent members of the rabbinic elite from the time of the Vilna Ga'on on through the first decades of the nineteenth century.[70] In fact, it seems that the notion of broadening the curriculum was one with which members of the traditional community, even beyond this small group of scholars, were quite comfortable. Such is precisely the attitude conveyed to Sir Moses Montefiore in his visit to the region in 1846, which he then documented in a report to Sergei Uvarov, Tsar Alexander's minister of education.

> With respect to the Talmud Tora schools, in which a knowledge of Hebrew language and its literature is exclusively taught, I beg leave to assert that there is not any school in the most distinguished Hebrew congregation in Europe that deserves to rank higher than those established in Warsaw and Wilna…I particularly inquired as to the reason why the Talmud Tora schools had no professors appointed for the Russian language and other branches of secular science and literature, this deficiency having struck me the more after having heard such pow-

69 See Zalkin's *"Ba-'a lot Ha-Shaḥar."*

70 See Chapter 2 above.

> erful arguments in favour of studying these, showing that knowledge of worldly science and literature, when combined with that of Hebrew and the observance of pure religion, was well adapted to improve an Israelite. The answer to my inquiry was, that they had not the means to procure such professors; that to have a master of that description would have given them the highest pleasure, but that having themselves to contend with innumerable difficulties in obtaining the ordinary and most urgent necessaries of life, they deemed it their first duty morally and religiously to procure, with the limited means they had, such instruction for their children as is essential for the enjoyment of their religion, leaving other kinds of learning for more favourable opportunities. Of their real feeling on this head the following incident is an example. I offered the means of procuring masters of the Russian language, geography, history, writing, and arithmetic in several schools, and my offer was most eagerly accepted, and the following day masters were engaged.[71]

Montefiore's contention that there were significant numbers of people in the 1840s who saw themselves as part and parcel of the traditional community yet were not opposed to the broadening of traditional Jewish education helps explain why certain prominent members of traditional Lithuanian Jewish society were less inclined to dismiss Lilienthal and his project. As alluded to earlier, Reb 'Iẓele of Volozhin is amongst those who accorded considerable respect to Lilienthal and the mission upon which he had embarked. While Jacob J. Schacter justly concludes that Reb 'Iẓele was probably not in favor of Lilienthal's reforms,[72] Pauline Wengeroff recounts that her father, a contemporary of Reb 'Iẓele, a fellow Lithuanian and member of the prominent Epstein rabbinical family, was rather excited by Lilienthal's initial proposition. She describes his reaction to the news as follows:

---

71 Moses Montefiore, *Diaries of Sir Moses and Lady Montefiore*, ed. Louis Loewe (London: Jewish Historical Society of England, 1983), 377.

72 See Jacob J. Schacter, "Haskalah, Secular Studies and the Close of the Yeshiva in Volozhin in 1892," *Torah u-Madda Journal* 2 (1990): 97-101.

> One day my father returned from *mincheh* with wonderful news: a Doctor of Philosophy named Lilienthal had been commissioned by the Ministry of Education (under the cultivated and humane Minister Uvarov) to travel throughout Russia and to investigate the competence of the *melamdim*, in whose hands rested the early education of Jewish youth. My father, a strictly observant Jew, was not too upset about the impending reforms; he himself had long been dissatisfied with the poor methods of instruction in the Jewish schools of Brest, and had been wishing for many improvements.[73]

While Lilienthal's mission is often portrayed as a failure due to the stiff opposition he encountered in staunchly traditional communities and due to his own subsequent emigration to the United States, much of that opposition may be attributed to the xenophobic reaction of Russia's conservative Jewish community to a German Jew employed by the Tsar who was suggesting sweeping reforms to one of their most hallowed institutions. It need not be synonymous, therefore, with a rejection of the early Haskalah's specific objectives of broadening Jewish education and modernizing Jewish cultural production. As such, from the vantage point of the mainstream traditional Lithuanian Jewish community, the 1840s might best be characterized as a time of roused suspicions, rather than outright opposition to the burgeoning Haskalah.

The opening of the state-sponsored Vilna seminary in 1847 seems to have elicited a similarly cautious yet mutedly positive response. In 1882, when a movement arose to re-open the then-defunct Vilna Seminary,[74] Mordecai Gimpel Jaffe, a contemporary of Neẓiv and a fellow student of Volozhin, warned the traditionalist community to learn from the miscalculation it made the first time the state opened its rabbinical seminaries in Vilna and Zhitomir in 1847. Then, he writes, it was assumed that these would be institutions of "*Torah ve-ḥokhmah, da'at u-madd'a.*" Only the prognosticators, the *zikne sha'ar*, cried, "these places will become houses

73 Pauline Wengeroff, *Rememberings: The World of a Russian-Jewish Woman in the Nineteenth Century*, trans. Henny Wenkart, ed. Bernard D. Cooperman (Bethesda: University of Maryland Press, 2000), 73.

74 The seminary was closed in 1873. For a history of the seminary see Israel Klausner, *Toldot Ha-Kehilah Ha-'ivrit bi-Vilnah* (Israel: 1969), 338-346.

of heresy!"[75] In fact, Jaffe writes that he had similarly high hopes for the Breslau Seminary headed by Zekhariah Frankel. In both cases, though, these seminaries proved to be grave disappointments to Jaffe due to the lack of fidelity to *Halakhah* and the lack of respect for the sages demonstrated by their graduates.[76] Nonetheless, it is clear that according to Jaffe's memory of the events, the initial reaction to the formation of the seminary in 1848 was cautious optimism by some and suspicion of the long-term results by others, but not widespread opposition.

The initial faculty of the Vilna Seminary similarly reflects its close ties to the traditional community. People like Yehudah Yudel Schershevski (1804-1866), Yehudah Behak (1820-1900), Ẓvi Hirsch Katzenellenbogen (1796-1868), and Shmuel Yosef Feunn (1818-1891) were all observant Jews steeped in traditional Jewish learning. In addition to his published *Kur la-Zahav* on talmudic aggadah (Vilna, 1858-1866), Schershevski left behind a notebook "with notes on *Moreh Nevukhim, Midrash Shoḥer Tov, Midrash Eikhah, Shir ha-Shirim, Kohelet, Esther, Torat ha-'Olah of the Rama, Neveh Shalom, Moreh Nevukhe Zemanienu, De'ot ha-Filosofim, ha-'Akeidah, Midrash Mishle, Midrash Tanḥuma, ha-Yuḥsin, Nishmat Ḥayyim,* [and] *Ḥazot Kasheh*"[77] Clearly, then, he was a man of impressive learning, and his interests were squarely in line with those of the world of early-nineteenth-century midrash commentary. Similarly, it is Behak who edits and annotates Ze'ev Wolf Einhorn's well known commentary on *Midrash Rabbah, Peirush MaHaRZU.*[78] As noted earlier, Katzenellenbogen's work on the thirty-two hermeneutical principles of aggadah is preceded by warm and personal approbations in which Sha'ul Katzenellenbogen, a father figure to Ẓvi Hirsch from whom he adopted the last name, refers to Ẓvi Hirsch as "*yedidi ha-ḥarif ve-shinun,*" "my sharp and insightful friend," and Avraham Abele (Poslover), the official rabbi of Vilna, notes that Ẓvi Hirsch "*kibel 'alav 'ol Torah u-parak me-'alav 'ol devarim 'aḥerim,*" "accepted upon himself the yoke of Torah and cast off the yoke of other things."[79] Likewise, both Meir Bar-Ilan and Barukh ha-Levi Epstein note that Feunn was a lifelong supporter of the Volozhin yeshivah[80] and that

75 Mordecai Gimpel Jaffe, "*Zikhronot Mordecai,*" *Mivḥar Ketavim* (Jerusalem: 1978), 29.
76 Ibid., 31
77 Steinschneider, vol. II, 92.
78 See *Midrash Rabbah* (Israel: Wagshal, 2001), 23.
79 *Netivot 'Olam* (Vilna: 1832).
80 Bar-Ilan, *Me-Volozhin*, 50.

Neẓiv purportedly remarked later in life that "the roots of Feunn's soul are in the *bet midrash* but he was mistakenly led to the *Maskilim*."[81] While Immanuel Etkes has pointed out that Yisrael Salanter turned down an invitation to join the seminary's faculty on seemingly ideological grounds, he also notes that Reb 'Iẓele supported his appointment, once again reflecting the mixed attitudes and general sense of uncertainty, rather than unified opposition, with which traditional Jewry viewed the state-sponsored Vilna seminary in the 1840s.[82]

The close ties between the seminary's faculty and the traditional Lithuanian community of the 1840s is further evidenced by Israel Klausner's description of the marked ideological shift which occurs in the 1860s as the original faculty, most members of which were raised and educated in the cultural milieu of early nineteenth-century Lithuania, is replaced by a younger and more radical generation of teachers.

> The teachers of the younger generation, most of whom were graduates of the seminary, took the place of the older Orthodox teachers. In place of Ẓvi Hirsch Katzenellenbogen, who stopped his work in 1866, came Ḥayyim Leib. In place of Adam Levinsohn came his son-in-law Joshua Steinberg, and in place of Idel (Yehudah) Sherishevski, came his son Eliyahu. The new generation of teachers were not masters of vast amounts of knowledge as were their predecessors, rather they had a mastery of Russian language, they shaved their beards and walked with their heads uncovered in their official capacities.[83]

Thus, while the Haskalah movement most certainly gained critical momentum during the 1840s from the endeavors of Lilienthal and the creation of the state seminaries, it was still in its infant stages. The *Maskilim* who increased their activities during those years were still a tiny and relatively insignificant percentage of the Lithuanian Jewish population. Such is the impression given by Michael Stanislawski's description of

---

81 Epstein (IV, 1834).

82 Etkes, *Salanter*, 148-149; See also Joshua M. Levisohn, *The Early Vilna Haskalah and the Search for a Modern Jewish Identity* (PhD dissertation, Harvard University, 1999), 68.

83 Klausner, 344.

Yehudah Leib Gordon's early years in Vilna,[84] and the impression given by Wengeroff in her description of the small maskilic circle to which her brothers-in-law belonged in Brest during the 1840s:

> These three young people, my brothers-in-law and their teacher, were probably the first in Brest to reach for the apple of knowledge that Lilienthal held out. To avoid scenes, they found a quiet little spot between two hills and away from our home, where they met with a like-minded group to debate literary questions and to decide burning cultural issues. But for all his exertions, my eldest brother-in-law never could find the spot on the apple where he could get a good bite. His "Asiatic" education resisted every assault from Europe, and he could have done much better for himself and for society with his Talmud learning. My younger brother-in-law enjoyed the apple, and in a short time became what was by the standards of that day an educated man. Reb Herschel the melammed grabbed for it with his plebian hands and took a great bite. Soon the "Orler" was transformed into an interesting, cultured Mr. Hermann Blumberg. In short, each youth of Brest enjoyed the apple of knowledge to a greater or lesser extent, but all tasted of it. The seed that Lilienthal sowed in Brest bore fruit in accordance with the soil upon which it chanced to fall. These young people were pioneers, although they themselves were condemned to cultural sterility. Though not a single outstanding personality emerges from among this early group in Brest, they smoothed the way from the next generation that would have an easier time getting an education, and would have much less prejudice to overcome.[85]

As pioneering as they were, the maskilic endeavors of the 1840s did not engender a full-scale reactionary shift from the more conservative el-

---

84 Stanislawski, *For Whom Do I Toil.*

85 Wengeroff, 79.

ements of Lithuanian society. As time progressed, however, the maskilic program began to make inroads farther into mainstream Jewish society; its leadership espoused a more radical position and a more concerted response from the traditionalist camp began to emerge.

*The 1860s: A Splintered Society*

While Pauline Wengeroff noted that in the 1840s her brothers-in-law were the only ones in Brest-Litovsk engaging the literature of the Haskalah, she also points out that a decade later the situation had changed dramatically.

> The Enlightenment movement would leave deep marks even in the orthodox circles among the poorer Jews. After just a single decade (1842-1852), one could see most children of the lower classes, even craftsmen, sitting in school, and European education became the common possession of the Jewish population.[86]

Yeḥezkel Kotik's (1847-1921) memories of his youth in Kamenets, a Lithuanian town approximately five miles from Brest-Litovsk, similarly demonstrate that by the late 1850s and the early 1860s, many within Lithuanian Jewish society were either taken by the program for Haskalah or, more often, were reacting to those who had joined their ranks.

> Young married fellows milled about the table. They were the married sons and sons-in-law who lived on *kest* with their more prosperous in-laws. They spent a good deal of their time prattling about mothers- and fathers-in-law and the tasty meals they had just had. The Talmud lay open in front of them as if they were about to begin studying, but chatting about one thing or another was more interesting.
>
> Every morning at ten o'clock, except Sundays, they went home for a bite and, for lack of anything better to do,

86 Ibid., 72.

> returned to the study house, pretending to continue their learning. Once again, they sat in front of their open tractates, but before long dropped all pretense of studying and started talking. When a particular topic was exhausted, they turned to chatting about the sins in the town, such as the reading of "*treyfe bikhlekh*" and about people that had turned heretic.[87]

The memoirs of Chaim Aronson (1825-1888) also provide important insight into the way in which Lithuanian Jewish society splintered through the late 1850s and early 1860s. Aaronson relates having received an invitation from a wealthy businessman named Raphael Munshevitz to come to his small town of Shvekshne on the Prussian frontier as a tutor for his boys. According to Aronson, Munshevitz, in the 1850s, desired a broader education for his children than that provided by the local *ḥeder*. He therefore extended the invitation to Aronson, not imagining there might be social implications of his actions. Aronson relates Munshevitz's initial feelings as follows:

> My boys are growing up without knowing anything about modern studies, for there is no teacher in this small town other than an ignorant melammed. I had thought of sending them to one of the big cities, either in Prussia or in this country, but they are too far away. In any case, their mother protests that no one will bother to look after them in a strange home. If I could find an enlightened teacher who is learned also in Torah, I would take him into my home and look after all his needs and pay him ninety rubles per half-year to teach my sons Torah and modern studies.[88]

Yet, a few months later, when Aronson decided to accept the invitation and word spread of his imminent arrival, a public outcry ensued, rallying the townsfolk against the introduction of Haskalah into their community.

---

87 Yeḥezkel Kotik, *Journey to a Nineteenth-Century Shtetl: The Memoirs of Yeḥezkel Kotik*, ed. David Assaf (Detroit: Wayne State University Press, 2002), 127.

88 Chaim Aronson, *A Jewish Life Under the Tsars: The Autobiography of Chaim Aronson 1825-1888*, trans. Norman Marsden (New Jersey: Allanheld, Osmun Publishers, 1983), 167.

> As soon as the word had spread in the city that the wealthy Raphael was bringing a new teacher into his house, the people led by the *melamedim* and the Rabbi had united against him saying: "Our city has been a kosher city from time immemorial. Our children are God-fearing and have never been tainted by the accursed Haskalah. Now you, of your own accord, seek to transgress, and to open our gates to defilement with all manner of heresy."[89]

Manushevitz, it seems, did not realize that by the late 1850s Lithuanian Jewry was being forced to take sides. One was either in favor of Haskalah or against it, and there could be no one in between. Bowing to the communal pressure and to the new realities of Lithuanian Jewish life, Manushevitz rescinded his offer to Aronson.

By the 1860s there are even more indications that the Lithuanian Jewish community was a fractured society. Mordechai Zalkin notes that traditionalists had begun to label "anyone who read secular books in foreign languages or poetry, science, and philosophy in Hebrew, an *apikorus* and a *min*."[90] Moshe Leib Lillienblum writes that when he arrived in Kovno in 1867 he immediately noticed two different sectors of society—the "new generation" whose "free-spiritedness" was even freer than his own, and an "old generation" of "clingers to the Torah." The new generation, according to Lilienblum, was no longer distinguished only by that which they thought and that which they said, but by the way in which they behaved as well. It was clear to Lilienblum, then a twenty-four-year-old Lithuanian raised in the world of traditional Torah study, that he had to choose one group or the other; the new generation or the old. For Lilienblum the answer was obvious: he belonged to the "new generation" of Lithuanian Jews.[91]

It was in the middle of the 1860s as well that Ya'akov Lifshitz, secretary to Yiẓḥak Elḥanan Spektor, prevailed upon Yeḥiel Brill to make the newspaper he published out of Paris an official organ of Eastern Europe's Orthodox community, thereby creating a traditionalist weapon

89 Ibid., 169.

90 Zalkin, 68.

91 Moshe Leib Lilienblum, *Ketavim Autobiografiyim*, Shlomo Breiman, ed. (Jerusalem: Mosad Bialik, 1970), 158.

against the maskilic press.[92] It was Lifshitz as well who, in reflecting on the period, identified the year 1840 as the moment in which the "light" of Eastern European Torah learning was first dimmed by the "spiritual assault" of the Haskalah, and in which was set in motion a new age of "severe servitude" and "depression" for the Lithuanian Orthodox community,[93] a development he devoted himself to combating.

Within the walls of the Lithuanian yeshivah, proponents of Haskalah began to emerge in the 1860s, as did the attempt by the traditionalist establishment to root them out. In her extensive work on the Lithuanian town of Eshyshok, Yaffa Eliach notes that "The Haskalah (the Jewish Enlightenment) finally reached the *shtetl* in the 1860s. It was not carried on the bayonets of Napoleon's soldiers, as happened in other towns, but rather was hidden between the Talmud pages of yeshivah students from larger cities."[94] She offers the following account, based on the memoirs of Eliezer Eliyahu Friedman, of the action taken by the traditionalist leaders of the town upon learning that members of their local yeshivah, the *kibbuẓ ha-Perushim*, were secretly delving into the literature of the Haskalah.

> All of Eshyshok's traditional leadership joined forces to fight the spread of the Haskalah among yeshivah students. The rooms of the prushim were searched for Haskalah books and newspapers, which were then turned to ashes in a public burning held in front of the rabbi's official dwelling on the shulhoyf. Afterward the prushim tried to evade the ever-searching eyes of the censors by tearing out the title page of forbidden books, but this tactic was soon discovered, and the vigilance merely increased.[95]

---

92 Ephraim Shimoff, *Rabbi Isaac Elchanan Spektor: Life and Letters* (Jerusalem: Sura Institute for Research, 1959), 48. On Lipschitz' see Israel Bartal's, "Zikhron Ya'akov' le-R. Ya'akov Lipschitz: Historiografia Ortodoksit?" (Hebrew) in *Milet* 2 (1984): 409–414; idem, " 'True Knowledge and Wisdom': On Orthodox Historiography," in *Studies in Contemporary Jewry* 10 (1994): 178–192; idem "Messianism and Nationalism: Liberal Optimism vs. Orthodox Anxiety" in *Jewish History*, 20, 1 (March, 2006): 5-17. On the related development of the Orthodox press in Galicia see Rachel Manekin's *The Growth and Development of Jewish Orthodoxy in Galicia, the "Machsike Hadas" Society, 1867-1883* (PhD Dissertation, Hebrew University, 2000).

93 Ya'akov Lipschitz, *Zikhron Ya'akov* (Kovno-Slobodka, 1924), vol 1, 84-86.

94 Yaffa Eliach, *There Once Was a World* (Boston: Little, Brown, and Co., 1998), 192.

95 Ibid.

If the administrators of the Eshyshok yeshivah were searching for and destroying maskilic works found amongst their students in the late 1860s, one can well assume that a similar, even if less extreme, wariness toward the recent inroads made by Haskalah pervaded the atmosphere of the yeshivah in Volozhin, under the direction of Neẓiv, at the same time.[96]

### *Lithuanian Torah Scholarship Responds*

Responses to the growth of the Haskalah movement were not only to be found in censorship and restrictive yeshivah policies. Within the intellectual work produced by the Torah scholars of Lithuania in the 1860s and 1870s a new awareness and fear of maskilic trends began to emerge. As the nineteenth century drew to a close and the twentieth century dawned, the staunchly conservative and parochial stance adopted by much of the Lithuanian rabbinic establishment stood in stark contrast to the cultural milieu of the Lithuanian midrash scholars of the century's early decades.[97]

A dramatic example of traditional Lithuanian Torah scholarship's response to the inroads made by the Haskalah over the decades of the 1850s and 1860s can be found in the work of Yehoshua Heller. Heller (1814-1880) served first as a *maggid* in the Lithuanian town of Grodno before being appointed as *av bet din* in the northern town of Polangen in Courland, after which he returned to Lithuania as *av bet din* of the town of Telz (Telshe).[98] As a member of Yisrael Salanter's new Mussar movement, Heller devoted his literary endeavors to works which emphasized proper behavior and the study of Torah in particular. His earliest work, published in Vilna in 1856 under the title *Divre Yehoshua*, focuses on the need for Mussar study as a complement to Torah study. In recounting "the situation of our times and its repercussions on the matter of Torah," Heller bemoans the fact that there are Torah learners who are not learning Mussar, and that there are learners of Mussar who do not study

96 See Stampfer, 157-160.

97 Again, it is important to note that Lithuanian scholars such as Yosef Rosen, Yaakov David Wilovsky, Yaakov Reines, and Avraham Yiẓḥak Kook, form a notable, though relatively small, exception to this trend.

98 For more on Heller, see Fuenn, *Keneset Yisrael*, 429.

enough Torah, thus becoming lax in their observance. Nowhere in the book, though, does he mention any heretical beliefs or practices which had pervaded his community. His second publication, titled *Ḥosen Yehoshua* (Vilna, 1862), is a manual which identifies the factors which can prevent the study of Torah and offers suggestions for mitigating them or removing them completely. Here too, the seduction of non-Torah literature, the espousal of non-Orthodox beliefs, or anything else of that nature does not even make it onto his list of detriments to Torah study.

Heller's last publication, however, is of a very different character. Composed during the 1860s and published in 1873, *Ma'oz ha-Dat* is dedicated completely to countering the heretical claims made by the *Maskilim* in regard to the nature and origin of the oral Torah as well as the normative status of rabbinic law. On the book's title page he describes the work as follows:

> In it is a discussion of the evidence found in the Written Torah for its companion, the [Oral] Tradition; of the foundations of exegetical *asmakhtot* in the Talmud and the obligation to obey rabbinic laws, their fences, their decrees, and their practices; of the praises of the Talmud and the story of its greatness; of the roots of our holy Torah from the first generation until the situation in our current generation. And on all of these it will put proofs and bring testimony [that] they will hear and say 'it is true!' The stragglers will gain strength, the youth will listen and will not stray from their paths, the wise will hear and will have what to answer those who spite them. Listen and let your souls live!

Clearly, by the 1860s questions regarding the authenticity and relevance of the oral Torah and rabbinic exegesis had emerged as a threat to the Lithuanian Talmud student, whereas it seems not even to have registered only a decade earlier.

Heller begins *Ma'oz ha-Dat* with a brilliant rhetorical maneuver intended to prove that the *Maskilim*, who had allied themselves with the Tsarist government of Alexander, as they had with Nicholas before him, were actually unfaithful allies of the Tsar, whereas the traditional community represented his true supporters. The body of Heller's work is styled in a format strikingly reminiscent of Samson Raphael Hirsch's *Nineteen Letters*, in that each chapter opens with a question from a fictitious student to his Orthodox teacher. Whereas Hirsch's German student is concerned with general questions regarding the relevance of traditional Judaism in the modern age, Heller's Lithuanian student, a well-versed Talmudist, is bothered by technical questions regarding the authenticity of the oral tradition, the validity of rabbinic exegesis, and the legal status of rabbinic laws versus those that are considered *me-de'orayt'a*.

Without fail, the answers given to Heller's student are staunchly conservative. Even the positions of traditional scholars with a slightly modern bent, such as Ẓvi Hirsch Chajes (1805-1855), are adamantly opposed.[99] Time and again, Heller mentions that the necessity for this work arises from the new challenges posed by the increasing number of "heretics" found in the Lithuanian community. For example, he notes that

> Since we have come to a time such as this [in which] those who cast off the yoke of Heaven have so multiplied, they are detaching themselves from the teachings of the religion, and they have grabbed onto the skirt of the sect of Saducees and are running with them. It is, therefore, our obligation, and it is good for us, and the hour demands it, that we shut the mouths of the liars and the haughty.[100]

Throughout the work one discerns the presence of two factions within the community, one in favor of traditional beliefs and one working to uproot them. And throughout the work Heller emphasizes the need

---

99 In a note on page 23, Heller takes issue with Chajes' contention that some of the *derashot* in the Talmud not labeled as *'asmakhta'* might actually be so. From the fact that the rabbis apply principles which emerge from such *derashot* to other laws, Heller concludes that they could not be *halakhah le-moshe mi-sinai* appended to the biblical text, as Chajes had contended, but rather reflect actual scriptural exegesis. Here again, Heller looks like Hirsch in ascribing almost all law to the biblical text itself. One's failure to see such laws arising from the text reflects only on the ignorant and degraded state of contemporary Jewish learning, not on the exegetical merit of the rabbinic methodology. See *Ma'oz ha-Dat*, 53-66. On Chajes, see Israel D. Bet-Halevi, *Rabbi Ẓvi Hirsch Chajes* (Tel Aviv: Achdut, 1955-56); Bruria Hutner David, *The Dual Role of Rabbi Ẓvi Hirsch Chajes: Traditionalist and Maskil* (PhD dissertation, Columbia University, 1971); Meir Herskovics, *Maharaẓ Chajes: Toldot Rabbi Ẓvi Hirsch Chajes u-Mishnatto* (Jerusalem: Mosad Harav Kook, 1972); Myles S. Brody, *A Time to Keep Silent and A Time to Speak: Judicial Activism and Passivity in the Thought of Rabbi TẒvi Hirsch Chajes* (A.B. Thesis, Harvard University, 2001).

100 Heller, 25.

for the traditionalist community to strike back. The following passage contains all of these elements in the most lucid manner and therefore deserves citation in full.

> And we, in the low state we are now in, have to stand guard in defending the protective measures, and the enactments, and the practices [of the Sages] more so than in the generations which preceded us, because due to our abundant iniquity the rays of the Torah have dwindled and become greatly weakened...and the more that a generation breaches, the more we say to it "repair!" so that the majority does not become breached.
>
> And all the more in these awful times, when due to our abundant iniquity civil war prevails amongst us, due to our brothers who hate us and banish us, whose hearts have followed their eyes to cast off the yoke of Heaven and to breach the fences of our Sages, may their memory be blessed, and to cut off the buds of the Tree of Life which is Torah, by saying that such is good for the tree. And they stand ready to uproot its roots as well and to turn it on its face as the men of the Reform [Movement] have already done in their places to their communities...
>
> And for this, those for whom the inheritance of their fathers is beautiful, and the flag of the Jew is a banner to be raised, should elevate their hearts in the ways of God and stand in the breach by acting according to the laws of exigent times as set forth in the Gemara and *Shulḥan Arukh*, [which is] to glorify the name of God by not letting go of any enactments or practices even a hair's breadth!
>
> And observance of this law obligates those who are wholesome in the religion of our holy Torah much more than it did during the planning stages before the horizons of nation-loving had become acceptable for us, for two reasons. The first is that then there was room to be lenient [in that] the rapist [*me'anes*] intended only

> for his own pleasure and not to violate religion...[101] But those who rebel against the light in our day, the men of Reform and their agents, pursue our trusted religion, and their intent is to level the walls of religion and to destroy its foundations. Second, then they were forced into this from others, and such a sin is not as severe... But such is not the case now, [when] thank God freedom has been granted by the king and officials in whose land we live for every man to walk in the name of his own God and to honor his religion. No one is forced, no one is compelled. No one protests and no one rebukes those who follow the laws of our Torah and observe its *mizṿot*—except our brothers, who banish us, who have divided us and who desire to bring us down into eternal ruin, to annul Torah!
>
> And for this we are obligated in this evil time to stand on guard of our religion and not to detract at all from that is written in the pure *Shulḥan Arukh*, which our great predecessors set out before us—even from the *minhagim* [we shall not detract the equivalent of a] strand of hair. And we shall not aspire and we shall not listen to the seducers and instigators who say that the religion is old and that old age has beset it, and that the old shall give way to the new.[102]

Such was the newly adopted sentiment of the *av bet din* of Telz, and he was not alone. Yiẓḥak Eliyahu Landau (1801-1876), who was appointed *maggid* of Vilna in 1868, similarly makes no reference to the presence of heretical beliefs or practices in the Lithuanian community in the numerous works he composed on midrash and aggadah throughout his prolific career. Yet, his last work, published in Vilna in 1876, which treats the talmudic *aggadot*, is prefaced by the following fierce denunciation of all who question the exegetical practices of the Sages:

---

101 The reference here is to the discussion in TB *Shabbat* 74b, which struggles to justify Esther's relationship with Aḥashverosh.

102 Ibid., 82-83.

And given that it is known that the words of the *aggadot* are founded on foundations of wisdom and truth and their peaks reach the heavens with the loftiest of matters; and all of their words are metaphoric riddles clothed in the mysteries of wisdom like a mask on the face of the radiant light of higher wisdom. And who will come upon their secrets in order to proceed inward in holiness? Not us who are of limited knowledge, who grasp on to the fleeting fringes of the time in order to ascend the summit of their holy intentions. Will the palace of the king be trampled by a provincial governor? Will the wingless one take flight through the heavens?...

How foolish are those who with haughtiness and contempt scorn the *aggadot* of the Sages. They are like the blind who were pulverized by the brilliance of the afternoon sun. Their vision has been plastered by the greatness of the Sages in every matter of every body of knowledge under the sun...

Pay attention men of mockery and hypocrisy! If someone would tell you from beginning to end what will be in the days to come, a detailed explanation of the things that will happen in the end of days, and then your eyes behold that not one word of his failed to be woven into the [fabric of] reality, you would certainly honor him! You would call him holy and say the word of God speaks through him for having revealed to you the mystery of progress, for who can say what will be after you? And, behold, the Sages of the Mishnah and the Talmud almost one thousand years ago envisioned a generation like yours who would be the last generation and with a nail of flint they engraved upon the talmudic tablet that in the footsteps of the Messiah impudence will prevail, the wisdom of the scribes will be spoiled, truth will be absent, the meet-

> ing place [of the sages] will be used for debauchery,[103] and many other [statements] like these...[104]

Likewise, Ḥayyim Berlin (1832-1912), Neẓiv's son, writing in 1895, dates the emergence of Haskalah as a threat to traditional Lithuanian Jewry to "the past generation," that is, the generation that came of age in the late 1850s and 1860s.

> And then, in the days of Noah, there were two generations—the generation of the Flood [who were] wicked (i.e., lustful) and the generation of the Dispersion [who were] deniers and heretics. But in this past generation, in the birth pangs of the Messiah, due to our numerous sins, both wicked hedonists as well as deniers and heretics have multiplied amongst us.[105]

Ḥayyim Berlin offers a similar description in a forceful letter he composed regarding the education of Jewish youth in 1902.[106] In this letter, which was signed by twenty-five of Lithuania's most prominent rabbinic figures, Berlin calls for increased vigilance in the education of Jewish children. He rails against modern pedagogic methods and aesthetic improvements which come at the expense of traditional Torah learning. He advocates teaching only that which is "proper and kosher" with an emphasis on that which promotes reverence for the sages. He also explicitly condones the start of Talmud study at as early an age as possible, at least for those children who can handle it.

A work written by Simḥah Kahana entitled *Magen Ha-Talmud*,[107] published the year before Berlin's letter, demonstrates just how different Lithuanian rabbinic society of the early twentieth century looked from that of the early nineteenth century. As we noted earlier, the scientific passages found in talmudic literature were the very first elements of aggadah to be systematically rejected by rabbinic authors. From the

103 TB Sot. 49b.

104 *Lishmo'a be-Limudim,* Petaḥ Davar (Vilna: 1876).

105 Ḥayyim Berlin, "Eulogy for Jacob Joseph Broide, 1895," *Sefer Nishmat Ḥayyim* (Jerusalem: 2003).

106 See Appendix C.

107 For more on Simcha Kahana and his anti-Zionist activity, see Yosef Salmon's *Religion and Zionism: First Encounters* (Jerusalem: Magnes Press, 2002).

Ge'onim to Rambam and well beyond, it was understood that the science of the fifth century need not govern the lives of medieval and early modern Jews. De' Rossi pushed the envelope further by advancing a similar stance regarding aggadic statements relating to geography, history and any other non-halakhic realm. While this position was vociferously opposed by some in the rabbinic establishment, we have shown that a group of early-nineteenth-century midrash scholars at the heart of Lithuania's rabbinic elite, a group which helped form the *weltanschauung* of the young Neẓiv, embraced this stance with open arms.

Kahana's book, however, represents a full-scale rejection of even the more moderate Maimonidean position. The work is an apologetic treatise defending the legitimacy of the Greek science found in the Mishnah and Talmud. And, whereas Ḥayyim Berlin gathered twenty-five signatories to his letter, Kahana, whose book was completed by 1893,[108] garnered letters from over fifty different leading Orthodox figures, many of whom were from culturally Lithuanian areas of the Russian Empire.[109] While it is clear from the content of these letters that few, if any, of these rabbis actually read Kahana's book, Kahana's intent in writing it was clear to them all. It is, after all, a "Defense of Talmud," an apologetic response to inroads made by the *Maskilim* and a project which met the overwhelming approval of the leading rabbis of the Lithuanian Jewish community at the turn of the twentieth century.[110]

Aside from the blatantly apologetic scholarship produced and approbated by late nineteenth-century Lithuanian rabbis, the mode of study which came to dominate the traditional Talmud study hall also bespeaks a clear shift from the trends of the earlier parts of the century. This style of learning, often referred to as the Brisker method, was popularized by Ḥayyim Soloveitchik, the husband of Neẓiv's granddaughter, along with his colleagues and students. While intellectually rigorous in its approach, and often bearing quite creative results, the Brisker method emphasized depth over breadth. It asked one to penetrate the recesses of one's own mind, not the recesses of a library or those of a printing

---

108 As evidenced by the dates in some of the approbatory letters.

109 Interestingly, included in the letters is one from Asher Ginzburg, the Zionist leader also known as "Ahad ha-Am." Amongst the rabbinic authors are Yeḥiel Mikhel Epstein, Ḥayyim Berlin, Yehudah Leib Rif, Eliyahu Feinstein, Ḥayyim Soloveitchik, and many others.

110 For another example of defensive Lithuanian commentary from the turn of the century, see *Nimuke ha-Ridbaz* (1904).

house, in order to resolve apparent difficulties in traditional texts. The midrashic literature, and certainly its aggadic portions, played little role in the process of Brisker study. The literature left by these scholars shows almost no interest in the disciplines of grammar, philosophy, or history. Likewise, the project of emending texts and the notion of ascribing contradictions in texts to human error are not to be found at all in the work of the Briskers.

Several explanations have been suggested for the success of the Brisker approach. These include its relative ease when compared to an approach which emphasized mastery of a broad canon of literature; the "safety" which some saw it offering those young men who might have otherwise been tempted by the intellectual pastures of Haskalah; and the atmosphere of collegial competitiveness its emphasis on innovation, or *ḥiddush,* created amongst those engaged in its study.[111] While more research in the field is still required, it seems clear that the decades which brought about the rise of Haskalah brought about a simultaneous retreat by the traditionalist elements from the world of broad intellectual engagement which characterized the methods of many early-nineteenth-century Lithuanian scholars, to a "safer" world of Talmud, Rambam, and the analytic power of their own minds.

We can return now to the fact that the young Neẓiv cited widely in his *`Emek ha-Neẓiv,* while in *Ha'amek Davar* citation is limited to works and authors deemed strictly traditional. In the intellectual milieu of early-nineteenth-century Torah scholarship, no stigmas were attached to the citation of de' Rossi and Levita, and one could study Mendelssohn and Wessely while remaining within the inner circles of the rabbinic elite. By the time Neẓiv composed his *Ha'amek Davar,* however, the culture of traditional Jewish Lithuania had changed significantly. These books were now the domain of the *Maskilim,* and exposure to them was seen by many as the first step toward apostasy. Thus, while Neẓiv never divorced himself from the content of such books, as is evident throughout *Ha'amek Davar,* in his position as *Rosh Yeshivah* of the `Eẓ Ḥayyim Yeshivah in Volozhin during the 1850s and 1860s, he could not in good conscience refer his impressionable readers to such sources. Indeed, this may also

111 Shlomo Tikochinski, *The Approach to Study in 19th Century Lithuanian Yeshivot* (Hebrew) (MA Thesis, Hebrew University, 2004). While his material on the Briskers is quite interesting, his section on Neẓiv's approach to study does not represent any new research.

explain why Neẓiv's commentary on *Sifre* was never published in his lifetime and was only first brought to press in 1958.

### Maskilim *in* Ha'amek Davar

Much as Neẓiv's acceptance of literal aggadic statements pertaining to Torah study in *Ha'amek Davar* is but one manifestation of the yeshivah ideology which runs throughout the work, so Neẓiv's reluctance to cite from non-traditional sources is but one example of his response to the rise of Haskalah found in *Ha'amek Davar*.

Viewed through this prism of the 1860s and 1870s, a period in which the fabric of Lithuanian mitnagdic society began to splinter, one begins to notice an uncanny concern with sectarianism which runs throughout *Ha'amek Davar*. The People of Israel during their sojourn in the desert were, in Neẓiv's conception, a people rife with sectarian conflict. While the majority of the people were initially faithful and loyal to God's command, a few vocal and influential minority groups, which Neẓiv refers to as "*katim*" or sects, often succeeded in swaying the masses toward their heretical agendas.[112] Time and again, particularly in the narrative sections of Exodus and Numbers, Neẓiv sees diverse factions and reads sectarian conflicts into the biblical account. Thus, for example, Neẓiv writes of a group who didn't believe God could rescue them from Egypt,[113] a group that believed God hated them and was marching them toward their deaths,[114] a group who did not want to live independent of the grace of God,[115] and groups who differed in their support of Korah and his men.[116] And, on a number of occasions, Neẓiv explicitly states that in these factions of the Desert Israelites he sees the heresies of contemporary Lithuania.

Above all, Neẓiv's Torah commentary repeatedly refers to one particularly prominent sect of Israelites who adhered to the belief that "Torah and *miẓvot* exist only in the Land of Israel."[117] It was this group that called

112 E.g., *HD* Ex. 13: 9; *HD* Lev. 9: 6; *HD* Lev. 26: 15; *HD* Lev. 36.

113 *HD* Ex. 13: 9.

114 *HD* Num. 14: 2; *HD* Num. 14: 39.

115 *HD* Num. 11: 6.

116 *HD* Num. 16: 19; *HD* Num. 16: 25-27; *HD* Num. 17: 6.

117 It is interesting to note that *Sifre* first raises this possibility and Neẓiv, in '*Emek ha-Neẓiv*, does not even comment (EH III: p. 81). Hence, we have another example of an idea which has its roots in *Sifre* but only becomes a polemical tool used by Neẓiv in his later Bible

for a return to Egypt, claiming that "the yoke of Torah and worship do not exist there." This fallacy, says Neẓiv, is just "like the mistake made by the last few generations" and those who subscribed to it were "worse than all the others in that they believed in the ability and will of God to bring them [there] in peace, but did not want to enter the Land of Israel since it necessitated bowing one's head under the yoke of Heaven."[118] In Neẓiv's account it was adherents to this ideology who had transformed the symbolic Golden Calf into full-fledged idolatry, it was people persuaded by such ideas who negatively influenced the masses upon the return of the spies,[119] it was they who persuaded the Jewish people to sin once they had settled into the Land of Israel, and they who were ultimately responsible for bringing about the present exile of the Jewish people from their land.[120] This sect continued to endure in the various lands of the Diaspora as well, as Jews again maintained that they were no longer constrained by God's law since they no longer lived in the land God had given them. This belief, then, along with the Divine wrath it incurs, is also responsible for the continuous persecution of the Jewish people in their various lands of exile.[121]

It is clear, then, that when Neẓiv the *Rosh Yeshivah* composed his *Ha'amek Davar* in the 1860s and 1870s he couldn't help but see the world around him and the heresies of "the last few generations"[122] which had become so prominent therein, leaping up at him from the biblical text. When he looked at the story of the Golden Calf, he might well have seen "the new generation of teachers" in the Vilna Seminary described by Klausner as having "shaved their beards and walked with their heads uncovered in their official capacities."[123] When he looked at the story of the spies, he might well have seen the same Lithuanian householders the young Talmud students of Yeḥezkel Kotik's memoir saw, who had committed "sins in the town, such as the reading of *treyfe bikhlekh*" and had thus "turned heretic."[124]

---

commentary.

118 *HD* Num. 14: 4.

119 *HD* Num. 14: 9; *HD* Num. 14: 39.

120 *HD* Ex. 32: 6. See also *HD* Lev. 26: 15; *HD* Lev. 26: 39; *HD* Lev. 26: 41.

121 *HD* Lev. 26: 36.

122 *HD* Num. 14: 4.

123 Klausner, 344.

124 Yeḥezkel Kotik, *Journey to a Nineteenth-Century Shtetl: The Memoirs of Yeḥezkel Kotik*, ed. David Assaf (Detroit: Wayne State University Press, 2002), 127.

Even in the non-narrative portions of the Bible, where there is no group of people upon whom such ideas and ideologies could be pinned, Neẓiv is often preoccupied with the notion of normative Jewish belief and the corrupting influence of heretics. Thus, for example, Neẓiv explains that leprosy of the head is a punishment for the sin of corrupt thoughts. These thoughts he categorizes into two general types. One type is faulty philosophical reasoning, in which one's own efforts to understand God and God's role in the world are led astray, resulting in the drawing of errant conclusions. Since great intellectual effort and contemplation are required to commit such a sin, Neẓiv concedes that it is rather rare and that it is generally considered a less stringent form of heresy. Neẓiv warns, though, that the select few who are guilty of this transgression pose a significant threat to the faithful masses, as they often feel the need to convince others that their own philosophical reasoning, and not the beliefs inherited via tradition, are in fact correct. The second type of iniquitous thought for which one received leprosy of the head is philosophical apathy, which Neẓiv notes is more common than faulty philosophical reasoning and constitutes a more severe transgression since it belies a complete lack of motivation to seek out God at all.[125]

Neẓiv is not only concerned with one's philosophical ruminations about the Divine, but also with the motivations which bring a person to Torah study. In a veiled criticism of those *Maskilim* interested in utilizing a *Wissenschaft* approach to Jewish text study as a means of justifying religious reform, Neẓiv warns that studying Torah with ulterior motives will, in turn, lead one to forsake its commandments.[126] Employing a slippery-slope argument reminiscent of Hungarian ultra-Orthodox ideologues, Neẓiv writes that one who stops observing the Torah's commandments will then come to mock those who are still observant. "And even though it is impossible to mock one who performs the commandments as explicitly stated in the Torah," such a person will instead attack "one who performs [*miẓvot*] according to the *ḥukim*, which are the *derashot* of the Sages, as we have written many times."[127] Then, the formerly observant Jew who approached Torah study with faulty motivations will go so far as to "pass a bill [of prohibition] on the *batei*

125 HD. Lev 13: 41. See also *HD* Num. 16: 1 and Deut. 29: 17.

126 *HD* Lev. 26: 14.

127 *HD* Lev 26: 15.

*midrashim* so that even one who wanted [to learn] can not do so."[128]

The specific danger perceived by Neẓiv in *Wissenschaft*-style study of the Torah is also made quite explicit in his *Ha'amek Davar*. He fears that one who views the biblical text with a historical lens will determine that certain laws and prohibitions were created for a particular historical context, and that the passage of time has rendered them obsolete. In rejecting such a position Neẓiv once again belies his own deeply rooted historical sensitivity. Instead of denying the correlation between the biblical law and its specific societal context and arguing for its timeless character as other traditionalists might have done, Neẓiv's historical sense forces him to accept the contextualization of the Torah's content. At the same time, his traditionalism leads him to argue that despite the fact that certain elements of the law clearly reflect the realities of an era long gone, nonetheless the Jewish people lack the jurisdiction to amend the laws accordingly. And, therefore, "even if it was written for a particular reason, once it is part of the Torah, it is worthy of *derashot* on very jot and tittle."

In fact, Neẓiv maintains that the Torah itself warns against the adoption of such an approach. At the end of Leviticus 19, whose laws Neẓiv writes were all composed "with good sense and reason according to the nature of the State and the times during the period of the giving of the Torah,"[129] Scripture warns, (Lev. 19:37) "and you shall guard all of my laws (*ḥukotai*) and all of my statutes (*mishpatai*) and you shall do them, I am God." Neẓiv explains this verse by stating that

> Scripture reiterated the warning so that one does not say that once the rationale [for the law] is nullified, the law [too] is nullified, God forbid, or so that one does not say that [due to the times] we should not expound (*ledrosh*) on this [law] according to the [exegetical] principles of the Torah (*ḥukei ha-Torah*), and [rather] we should only go according to its rationale alone. For this reason the Torah warns "and you shall guard all of my laws (*ḥukotai*) and all of my statutes (*mishpatai*)" [that is,] the *derashot* which

128 Ibid. See also Neẓiv's warning against those who misuse their Torah learning in *HrD* Num. 8: 15.

129 *HD* Lev. 19: 37.

> come by way of the principles (*ḥukim*) by which the Torah is expounded and the laws which emerge from them. For, after the Torah was legislated, we can't know the times and circumstances (*'ein lanu lada'at 'eit u-mishpat*), but [rather] the laws (*ḥukei*) of the Torah alone.[130]

In the beginning of Numbers, Neẓiv reiterates this position in less detail, but with the addition of the phrase *"le-dorot,"* suggesting that the problem of trivializing Torah law through historical contextualization was not only a problem of the past, but one that currently plagues the Jewish people. He writes that *"le-dorot kakh hu, she-gam be-batel ta'am ha-miẓvah lo batel ha-miẓvah el'a na'asah ḥok,"* "for all generations it is so, that even when the rationale of a *miẓvah* is nullified, the *miẓvah* is not nullified but becomes a *ḥok.*"[131]

By arguing that all *miẓvot* acquire the status of *"ḥok"* when the historical circumstances for which they were created have passed, a nexus emerges between Neẓiv's position regarding *ta'amei ha-miẓvot,* the ascription of rational reasons to the *miẓvot,* and his desire to root out contemporary maskilic heresies. That is, from the above passages we can extrapolate that every time Neẓiv reiterates in his *Ha'amek Davar* that the rationale behind the specific details of all Jewish laws are humanly unknowable[132] or that one must perform the *miẓvot* irrespective of their rationale,[133] he is similarly reminding his readers that historical contextualization of the biblical text, in which he freely dabbles, can have no bearing on halakhic norms. Thus, here too he is writing with an eye toward his own society and cautioning his readers against what he perceived to be the heretical position espoused by a growing number of *Maskilim*.

---

130 Ibid.

131 *HD* Num. 1: 19.

132 E.g., *HD* Ex. 21: 26; *HD* Lev. 27: 16; *HD* Num. 3: 47; *HD* Num. 15: 15; *HD* Deut. 22: 4; *HD* Deut. 22: 6; *HD* Deut. 22: 7. See also *MD* 5: 40; *MD* 5: 41; *MD* 5: 90. This class of laws whose rationale is unknown is referred to in rabbinic literature as *ḥukim*. It may not be coincidence that the same term that denotes the unknowability and therefore the immutability of Jewish laws is also the term which, for Neẓiv, refers to the process of rabbinic exegesis. Just as one cannot nullify the law itself by pretending to know its rationale and thereby making it dependent on its original historical context, so too one can not suggest that rabbinic exegesis is an obsolete relic of the past.

133 E.g; *HD* Gen. 50: 12; *HD* Ex. 12: 27; *HD* Ex. 18: 16; *HD* Deut. 22: 4; *HD* Deut. 22: 6; *HD* Deut. 22: 7.

Similarly, Neẓiv feels the need to iterate and reiterate to the readers of *Ha'amek Davar* that the oral Torah is no less essential to the life of a Jew than is its written counterpart. At times Neẓiv offers the traditional defense of the oral tradition, first articulated in the work of Sa'adya Gaon, which argues that the fact that certain verses are simply inexplicable in their written form, coupled with the fact that God would not have given His people a text which has no meaning, proves that God must have given Moses oral instructions as to what the verses meant.[134] On other occasions in *Ha'amek Davar*, Neẓiv conveys this message through the ascription of symbolic significance to biblical laws, such as the two components of the *tefillin*,[135] or the two Tamid sacrifices, both of which correspond to the two Torahs, one written and one oral. In a remarkably bold passage, Neẓiv writes that God instructed Moses to gather the entire nation to the gateway of the Tabernacle (Lev. 8:3) for the sole purpose of watching Moses perform a ritual act in a manner which contradicted the instructions which had explicitly been given by God beforehand. The purpose of this counterintuitive gathering was to teach "all of Israel the power of the Torah's Oral Tradition. For when they saw that Moses himself was doing it in a way contrary to that which was written, the entire nation would know the manner of the Torah" which is to follow the oral tradition given to Moses rather than the literal instructions offered by the Torah text itself.[136]

In addition to warning his readers about the dangers of heresy, Neẓiv also instructs them to stay away from those who have already turned to prohibited manners of thought. No one, writes Neẓiv, should argue with heretics,[137] not even an *adam gadol*,[138] a man of great stature. For one who "does not want to accept the yoke of Heaven," as was the case amongst some members of the new generation of Haskalah, or one who "nullifies the Torah by saying 'the Torah was only given to wean [us] off of idolatry,'" is more "evil and more bitter than one who worships idolatry."[139] Along the same lines, Neẓiv writes that "the Jewish soul is elevated according to the Torah mindset [*da'at Torah*] which is upon him, and when

134 E.g., *HD* Ex. 21: 1; *HD* Deut. 13: 1.
135 *HD* Ex. 13: 16; *HD* Num. 28: 4.
136 *HD* Lev. 3:8.
137 *HD* Num. 14: 6.
138 *HD* Lev. 13: 44.
139 *HD* Deut. 29: 17; *HD* Num. 15: 30.

he corrupts his Torah mindset his [soul] becomes worse than the soul of a person who does not have the mindset of Torah upon him." Therefore, such a person is willing to engage in acts which ordinary Gentiles would find abhorrent.[140]

In fact, Neẓiv was not only worried about exposure to wayward Jews, but comments in *Ha'amek Davar* reflect his general concern with what he perceived as a more general shift toward acculturation and assimilation in Lithuanian Jewish society in the 1860s and 1870s. As a result, from Genesis through Deuteronomy, Neẓiv emphasizes and reemphasizes the need for Jewish distinctiveness and the dangers of assimilation.[141]

From the very first time the children of Abraham are explicitly designated to develop into a great nation, the Torah, according to Neẓiv's interpretation, notes that these people are to remain apart from all others. Thus, when God says to Abraham (Gen. 15:13) "your children will be strangers in a land that is not theirs," the statement, in Neẓiv's view, is both a Divine promise that Abraham's descendents will be only temporary residents of the lands which host them, and a Divine direction "not to try and acculturate in a land which is not theirs in order to alleviate their status as strangers."[142]

The lesson of Jewish distinctiveness and cultural isolation is one that Jacob, Abraham's grandson, took to heart. Thus, when approaching the city of Shekhem on his return to Cana'an from 'Aram, Scripture records that Jacob set up camp (Gen. 33:18) "at the face of the city." Neẓiv there comments that

> according to the straightforward reading (*peshat*), he did not enter into the city but rather camped on the outskirts of the city which is referred to as "the face of the city." And this is in accordance with the character trait of Jacob to be a loner and not to mix with the nations of the world.[143]

---

140 *HD* Lev. 11: 44.

141 Neẓiv's anti-assimilationist agenda is mentioned by Eliakim (76-78), who contrasts Neẓiv's position with that of the Lithuanian maskilic poet Judah Leib Gordon's famous call to be "a man in the street and a Jew at home." Gordon, though, was advancing a bi-cultural model of Jewish life, not an assimilatory model.

142 *HrD* Gen. 15: 14.

143 *HD* Gen. 33: 18.

Later, Jacob similarly encamped on the outskirts of Hebron rather than entering the city "in order to be alone, as was his way."[144]

It is this character trait which, according to Neẓiv, explains Jacob's earlier decision not to remain with his brother Esau in the aftermath of their peaceful reunion.[145] Jacob's sons were also well acquainted with their father's desire that he, and they, should live apart from the other nations of the world. Therefore, in preparation for his father's arrival in Egypt, Joseph "removed all of the [Egyptian] residents of Goshen from their places" in order that Jacob "and his sons could live alone, not interspersed with the people of the land."[146]

Jewish cultural isolation was no less important when the Israelites exited the land of Goshen. Hence, when God redeemed his people from bondage in Egypt he intentionally took them through the wilderness "so that they would not mix with the nations of the world more than was necessary."[147] And, toward the end of their sojourn, when the Israelites did actively engage the people and culture of Midyan, they were led to sin and incurred the wrath of God.[148] Centuries later, the Jewish community of the Second Temple Period would again falter in this regard by "engaging in business with the nations of the world" which, in turn, contributed to God's decision to destroy the Temple.[149] And, in the period of Exile which ensued, and which ensues to this day, it is assimilationist and acculturationist trends which draw the Jewish people close to their host societies, thereby drawing their scrutiny and ultimately their hatred and persecution.[150]

The cultural and social isolation of the Jewish people advocated by Neẓiv in *Ha'amek Davar*, to which their salvation is closely bound, does not result simply from geographic separation from the Gentile community. Rather, writes Neẓiv, "these attributes are capable of being preserved only through Torah and Avodah (worship) which are the dividers between Israel and the nations."[151] Thus the newfound influences on Neẓiv

---

144 *HD* Gen. 37: 1.

145 *HD* Gen. 33: 15.

146 *HD* Gen. 45: 9. See also *HD* Gen. 46: 4 and *HD* Ex. 1: 7.

147 *HD* Deut. 32: 12. Also *HD* Ex. 13: 17.

148 *HD* Num. 20: 23.

149 *HD* Deut. 33: 28.

150 *HD* Lev. 26: 37. Much of Neẓiv's lengthy essay on anti-Semitism published at the end of his commentary on *Shir ha-Shirim* is devoted to this theme as well.

151 *HD* Gen. 46: 4.

of *Ha'amek Davar*—his rise to prominence in the burgeoning yeshivah movement and the concurrent rise of the movement for Haskalah—come together. One must be embraced and the other repelled for the Jewish people to survive. Both, however, make an unmistakable imprint on the way in which the older Neẓiv views the biblical text. It is this imprint which most definitively separates *Ha'amek Davar* from *'Emek ha-Neẓiv*.

# Afterword: Avenues for Further Research

From the preceding exploration of Neẓiv's work on *Sifre* and its cultural context, numerous new conclusions about the life of Naftali Ẓvi Yehudah Berlin and the world in which he lived can be drawn. As noted in the Introduction, however, more important than the specific arguments advanced above are the avenues which I hope it has opened for further research.

With regard to the personal life of Neẓiv, we have begun to draw a picture of a prodigious young man absorbed in the world of books during the third and fourth decades of the nineteenth century. His close relationship with David Luria served as a primary link to members of the scholarly circle in and around Vilna who had devoted themselves over the preceding three decades to the study of midrashic literature in unprecedented fashion. Their intellectual breadth, their penchant for textual emendation, and their search for *peshat* left a marked imprint on the intellectual development of the young Neẓiv, one that is most apparent in his work on *Sifre* but which is also foundational to his later work on *She'iltot* and his *Ha'amek Davar*. We have also suggested that this world, which witnesses a dramatic rise in the availability of Hebrew texts, played an important role in piquing the young Neẓiv's interest in the methods of the rabbinic sages and those of their medieval commentators. The related popularity of de' Rossi amongst the scholarly elite of this intellectual coterie clearly helped mold Neẓiv's hermeneutical approach as well.

In Chapter Seven, however, we noted that as the world around the young Neẓiv begins to change, so does Neẓiv's place within Lithuanian Jewish society. Adulthood, the emergence of the Mussar movement and of Haskalah, the burgeoning of the yeshivah movement, and Neẓiv's promotion to *Rosh Yeshivah* in Volozhin all occur during the decades of the 1850s and 1860s. And we demonstrated in Chapter Six that unlike his commentary on *Sifre*, Neẓiv's Torah commentary, *Ha'amek Davar*, dates to this period as well. We therefore suggested that this convergence of circumstances helps to explain much of the divergence in exegetical position and hermeneutical stance from *'Emek ha-Neẓiv* to *Ha'amek Davar*.

From Chapters One and Six as well as Appendix D, we can for the first time establish a definitive timeline of Neẓiv's intellectual products. His earliest major work is clearly his commentary on *Sifre*. It was started in the 1830s and seems to have neared completion prior to 1861. Not long after he began his work on *Sifre*, he also began his massive commentary on *She'iltot*, which he published in 1861. His work on Torah, however, as well as his printed work on *Mehilta'*, date from the 1850s into the next two decades.

Less definitive, however, was my brief sketch of the world of midrash study in the early decades of the nineteenth century. It was but a preliminary step to what I hope will be far greater research in this area. After all, the lives and work of Sha'ul Katzenellenbogen, Yehudah Leib Edel, Yeḥezkel Feivel, Ya'akov of Slonim, Ḥanokh Zundel ben Yosef, Avraham Schick, Yiẓḥak Eliyahu Landau, Ḥanokh Zundel Luria, Ẓvi Hirsch Katzenellenbogen, Ze'ev Wolf Einhorn, Shmuel Strashun, Ẓvi Hirsch ha-Kohen Rappaport, Radal, and Yoel Dober ha-Kohen Perski have all yet to receive serious scholarly attention. While my research led me to begin studying quite a few of their printed works, it was but a dent in their voluminous ouvre. A systematic study of their commentaries and notes promises to reveal much more about their scholarly coterie and its impact on Lithuanian Jewish culture. Such revelations promise to add significantly to questions of great import to Jewish historiography. For example, their unapologetic foray beyond the traditional rabbinic cannon might well encourage scholars of Eastern European Haskalah to return once again to the question of the degree to which the movement for Haskalah, particularly in and around Vilna, was a product imported and adapted from the Jews of Western Europe, or whether it deserves to be seen more as an organic outgrowth of the scholarly rabbinic culture of Jewish Lithuania. And, as I began to demonstrate, a study of this circle of scholars might also add significantly to the debate over the intellectual impact and legacy of the Vilna Ga'on and his work. Likewise, further research into the sudden growth of the Eastern European Hebrew print industry during the late eighteenth and early nineteenth centuries, as well as its impact on this group of scholars and beyond, promises to enrich our understanding of Jewish intellectual, political, religious, and social history of this period.

In Chapter Seven we suggested that the ideology of the yeshivah, with its emphasis on the study of Torah and its salvific power, largely influenced the way in which the Neẓiv approached and understood the biblical text. Undoubtedly, Neẓiv is not the only one whose intellectual endeavors were shaped by the growth of the Yeshivah movement or by a need to respond to the Mussar movement. Hence, this too offers a promising avenue of research. Indeed, there has been no systematic study to date of the ideology of Torah study beyond Ḥayyim of Volozhin's *Nefesh ha-Ḥayyim*. It goes without saying that such a study is a scholarly desideratum.

In addition to being influenced by the ideology of the yeshivah, we suggested that Neẓiv was part of a larger movement amongst the Lithuanian rabbinate to distance itself from the perceived dangers of the growing Haskalah. While this move toward traditionalism has been studied extensively in the context of nineteenth-century Germany, Hungary, and Galicia by Katz, Samet, Silber, and others, this facet of Jewish Lithuania has received far less attention, and its impact upon Torah scholarship in particular has yet to be treated in a sophisticated manner.

It is my hope that this brief window into the world of Neẓiv will inspire others, as it has inspired me, to pursue these related areas of research in the years to come.

# APPENDICES

## Appendix A: The Unattributed Influence of Radal on *Ha'amek Davar*

The commentaries of Radal might well have played an important role in the Neẓiv's later commentarial work. The following is one example in which the content of a novel, unattributed comment by Neẓiv in his *Ha'amek Davar* seems to be based on Radal's notes to *Midrash Rabbah*. There may, in fact, be many others, and a close comparison of the content of the two works may prove rather fruitful.

The passage in *Bereishit Rabbah* cites the Bible's description of God conveying to Noah his intent to destroy the world, which reads (Gen. 7:17) "to destroy all flesh...everything on Earth will perish (*yigva'*)."[1] In order to clarify the meaning of the rather strange verb used to convey the meaning "perish," "*yigva'*," the midrash writes "*yiẓmok*" indicating that the remains of living animals would become dried out and wrinkled as a result of the impending flood. On this midrashic statement Radal writes as follows:

> See *Matanot Kehunah*.[2] And it is because the verse initially says "to destroy all flesh" that it is [further] explained that "perish" which is written later [means] to be dried up after the destruction and the death. (And it is possible that it is the hardening into stone of the bodies and bones of animals which scientists agree were from the days of the Flood due to the fact that they are generally found in

---

1 Translation follows the JPS Bible.

2 The passage in *Matanot Kehunah*, a sixteenth-century *Midrash Rabbah* commentary composed by Issachar Ber ben Naftali ha-Kohen, to which Radal refers the reader, distinguishes between two different usages of the word "*yigva'*." One is in the context of cooking and describes the process of food becoming dry and hardened by lengthy exposure to the fire. The second is in the context of the Bible's account of Ya'akov's death due to old age. He states as follows:

> "*Yigva', yiẓmok*": It is the language of "*miẓtamek ve-yafeh lo,*" *Perek Kirah* (TB *Shabbat* 37b). And it comes to teach us that the meaning of the word "*yigva'*" is not like (Gen. 49: 33) "*va-yigva' va-ye'esaf 'el 'amav*" which is death of a kiss and restricted only to the righteous.

> places which have climates in which such animals could not have lived at all, like in the northern lands).[3]

Neẓiv's first comments on the word *"yigva'"* note, as did Radal in his explanation of *Midrash Rabbah,* that the verse contains the verbs *"le-shaḥet"* and *"yigva'"* in order to indicate two different actions which would be carried out against the living beings outside of the ark during the Flood. Neẓiv agrees with Radal that the first verb indicates the onset of death, but whereas Radal elaborates on the interpretation of the midrash of *"yigva'"* as *"yiẓmok,"* and thus he understands the second verb to indicate a drying up or petrifying of the bones following death, Neẓiv understands *"yigva'"* as indicating the disintegration of the flesh as a result of the rushing water.[4]

Furthermore, the second half of Neẓiv's comments on *"yigva'"* note the fact that the term has two different meanings. "And the root *gva'* is at times used to indicate an easy death that is free of illness and pain, and therefore it is used in reference to the death of the righteous, and at times it refers to water's wiping out the flesh of a body, and therefore the *mabul*[5] was of water." This distinction is an unmistakable response to the comments found in *Matanot Kehunah* referred to by Radal.[6] There too one finds two meanings ascribed to the word *yigva,* one of which indicates a painless death. However, whereas *Matanot Kehunah* explains the second usage of *"yigva'"* in line with the interpretation of *Midrash Rabbah,* Neẓiv offers a different explanation in line with his position that the bodies of the dead animals were completely annihilated by the floodwaters. Thus Neẓiv clarifies, precisely as Radal did, that without the verb *"le-shaḥet"* one would not have known which usage of *"yigva'"* was intended. With the inclusion of *"le-shaḥet,"* however, one understands that *"yigva'"* could not be intended to mean an act of death, and hence it is understood that the second usage is the proper one in this context.

While this type of exegetical move is a fairly standard feature of rabbinic commentary, there is one more point which Neẓiv makes in this passage which clearly testifies to the prominence of Radal's comments in his mind as he composed this text. While Neẓiv does not believe that

3 David Luria, *Midrash Rabbah* (Israel: Wagshal, 2001), 31: 12 (314-315).
4 *HD* Gen. 6: 17.
5 Generally translated as "flood."
6 See n. 2 above.

*"yigva'"* alludes to the petrification of antediluvian animals, as Radal did, he finds another nuance of the very same verse which does in fact allude to the discovery of prediluvian fossils beneath the Earth's surface. He writes that the intended implication of the verse's phrase "everything on Earth" is that only animals who were above ground and thus exposed to the raging waters were completely destroyed. The bones of those animals which were beneath the Earth's surface, however, remained intact.[7] Neẓiv then calls the reader's attention to his comments later on when the Bible again reiterates that (Gen. 7:23) "All existence on the face of the Earth was wiped out." There Neẓiv not only mentions the discovery of fossils as did Radal, but also mentions the fact that the fossils are found in climates in which such animals do not currently live, as Radal did as well.

> "On Earth:" Specifically those that were resting on the face of the Earth. But there remained a few bodies upon which a great deal of soil had fallen due to the pouring waters and they remained intact. And they are the bones which Earth diggers find...And even though they are found in climates in which [such animals] do not live, that is because they changed their 'way upon the land'[8] prior to the flood and traveled to foreign places.[9]

Thus, if we return to the words of Radal, we note that every point made by Neẓiv on this topic corresponds to a point made by Radal. Radal first called on the reader to see *Matanot Kehunah.* Neẓiv included the distinction of *Matanot Kehunah,* but changed it slightly to suit his purposes. Radal then explains the necessity for both of the verse's verbs, as does Neẓiv. Radal goes on to suggest a connection between the verse and the discovery of petrified fossils of ancient animals. Neẓiv's understanding of the word *"yigva'"* does not permit him to draw that same connection, but he draws another connection between the verse and the discovery of fossils. Lastly, Radal notes that some scientists explain the appearance of these fossils in climates inhospitable to such animals as a result of the

7 Ibid.
8 A reference to Gen. 6: 12.
9 *HD* Gen. 7: 23.

bones having been carried there by the flood. Neẓiv, who understands the verse as indicating that the raging waters of the flood left no bones intact, could not adopt the theory Radal cites in the name of science. In its place, Neẓiv offers the theory that the corruption of the world prior to the flood had ecological ramifications and led to the wandering of animals out of their natural habitats. These animals, who died before the flood and whose bones were covered by the Earth, explain, according to Neziv, the scientific mystery refered to by Radal.

It seems, then, that the influence of Radal is to be found not only in Neẓiv's early work on *Sifre* and *She'iltot* but in his later works and in passages that do not mention Radal's name as well. To gauge the full extent of Radal's influence on Neẓiv, therefore, a close critical comparison of the complete works of both men is required. Such an endeavor, however, exceeds the scope of the present project.

# Appendix B: Emendations to *Sifre ʻEkev* According to the Ga'on and Neẓiv

| Reason For Neziv's Emendation | Citation | Parallel | (Sulzbach, 1802) | Neziv (Jerusalem, 1958) | GRA (Vilna, 1866) | Finkelstein (New York, 1969) |
|---|---|---|---|---|---|---|
| Attempts to improve syntax / grammar | Ekev 1 (III: p. 44) | | וחברון שבע שנים נבנתה לפני צוען מצרים, מפני מה, שהיתה מקום מלכות | וחברון שבע שנים נבנתה לפני צוען מצרים, וצוען מה היתה, מקום מלכות | וחברון שבע שנים נבנתה לפני צוען מצרים, שהיתה מקום מלכות | פיסקא לז<br>וחברון שבע שנים נבנתה לפני צוען מצרים, צוען מה היה, מקום מלכות |
| | Ekev 1 (III: p. 45) | Yalkut | נמצא קרוי שתי שמות | נמצא קרוי שלשה שמות | נמצא קרוי שלשה שמות | פיסקא לז<br>נמצא קרוי שלשה שמות |
| | Ekev 1 (III: p. 46) | Yalkut | או מה שור זה פסול מכל קרניו | אי מה שור זה אין בו פסולת אלא קרניו | או מה שור זה פסול מכל שבו מקרניו | פיסקא לז<br>או מה שור זה אין בו פסולת מקרניו |
| | Ekev 2 (III: p. 48) | | מה כלכול האמור להלן בשני רעבון הכתוב מדבר אף כלכול האמור כאן בשני רעבון הכתוב מדבר | מה כלכול האמור להלן לא בשני רעבון הכתוב מדבר אף כלכול האמור כאן לא בשני רעבון הכתוב מדבר | מה כלכול האמור להלן בשני רעבון הכתוב מדבר אף כלכול האמור כאן בשני רעבון הכתוב מדבר | פיסקא לח<br>מה כלכול האמור להלן בשני רעבון הכתוב מדבר אף כלכול האמור כאן בשני רעבון הכתוב מדבר |
| | Ekev 3 (III: p. 50) | | ועוד שנותן טעם | ועוד שנותנת טעם | ועוד שנותן טעם | פיסקא לט<br>ועוד שנותן טעם |
| | Ekev 3 (III: p. 51) | | יכול יהיו מים גורשים את העפר ממקום בקעה | יכול יהיו מים גורשים את העפר למקום בקעה | יכול יהיו מים גורשים את העפר ממקום הר למקום בקעה | פיסקא לט<br>יכול יהיו מים גורשים את העפר למקום בקעה |
| | Ekev 4 (III: p. 53) | | שלא הפרשתם תרומה ומעשרות מכם את הגשמים | שלא הפרשתם תרומה ומעשרות מנעו מכם את הגשמים | שלא הפרשתם תרומה ומעשרות יגזלו מכם את הגשמים | פיסקא מ<br>שלא הפרשתם תרומה ומעשרות מנעו מכם את הגשמים |
| | Ekev 4 (III: p. 54) | | הם ברשותי ליתן בהם ברכה, כשם שאני נותן בהם ברכה בשדה | הם ברשותי ליתן בהם ברכה בבית, כשם שאני נותן בהם ברכה בשדה | deleted entire line | פיסקא מ<br>הם ברשותי ליתן בהם ברכה בבית, כשם שאני נותן בהם ברכה בשדה |
| | Ekev 5 (III: p. 56) | | ולמדתם אותם ושמרתם לעשותם, מגיד שמעשה תלוי בתלמוד | אם כן, למה נאמרה ולמדתם אותם ושמרתם לעשותם, מגיד שמעשה תלוי בתלמוד | אם כן, מה תלמוד לאמר ולמדתם אותם ושמרתם לעשותם, מגיד שמעשה תלוי בתלמוד | פיסקא מא<br>ולמדתם אותם ושמרתם לעשותם, מגיד שמעשה תלוי בתלמוד |

| Reason For Neziv's Emendation | Citation | Parallel | (Sulzbach, 1802) | Neziv (Jerusalem, 1958) | GRA (Vilna, 1866) | Finkelstein (New York, 1969) |
|---|---|---|---|---|---|---|
| Attempts to improve syntax / grammar | Ekev 1 (III: p. 44) | | וחברון שבע שנים נבנתה לפני צוען מצרים, מפני מה, שהיתה מקום מלכות | וחברון שבע שנים נבנתה לפני צוען מצרים, וצוען מה היתה, מקום מלכות | וחברון שבע שנים נבנתה לפני צוען מצרים, שהיתה מקום מלכות | <u>פיסקא לז</u><br>וחברון שבע שנים נבנתה לפני צוען מצרים, צוען מה היה, מקום מלכות |
| | Ekev 1 (III: p. 45) | Yalkut | נמצא קרוי שתי שמות | נמצא קרוי שלשה שמות | נמצא קרוי שלשה שמות | <u>פיסקא לז</u><br>נמצא קרוי שלשה שמות |
| | Ekev 1 (III: p. 46) | Yalkut | או מה שור זה פסול מכל קרניו | אי מה שור זה אין בו פסולת אלא קרניו | או מה שור זה פסול מכל שבו מקרניו | <u>פיסקא לז</u><br>או מה שור זה אין בו פסולת מקרניו |
| | Ekev 2 (III: p. 48) | | מה כלכול האמור להלן בשני רעבון הכתוב מדבר אף כלכול האמור כאן בשני רעבון הכתוב מדבר | מה כלכול האמור להלן לא בשני רעבון הכתוב מדבר אף כלכול האמור כאן לא בשני רעבון הכתוב מדבר | מה כלכול האמור להלן בשני רעבון הכתוב מדבר אף כלכול האמור כאן בשני רעבון הכתוב מדבר | <u>פיסקא לח</u><br>מה כלכול האמור להלן בשני רעבון הכתוב מדבר אף כלכול האמור כאן בשני רעבון הכתוב מדבר |
| | Ekev 3 (III: p. 50) | | ועוד שנותן טעם | ועוד שנותנת טעם | ועוד שנותן טעם | <u>פיסקא לט</u><br>ועוד שנותן טעם |
| | Ekev 3 (III: p. 51) | | יכול יהיו מים גורשים את העפר ממקום בקעה | יכול יהיו מים גורשים את העפר למקום בקעה | יכול יהיו מים גורשים את העפר ממקום הר למקום בקעה | <u>פיסקא לט</u><br>יכול יהיו מים גורשים את העפר למקום בקעה |
| | Ekev 4 (III: p. 53) | | שלא הפרשתם תרומה ומעשרות מכם את הגשמים | שלא הפרשתם תרומה ומעשרות מנעו מכם את הגשמים | שלא הפרשתם תרומה ומעשרות יגזלו מכם את הגשמים | <u>פיסקא מ</u><br>שלא הפרשתם תרומה ומעשרות מנעו מכם את הגשמים |
| | Ekev 4 (III: p. 54) | | הם ברשותי ליתן בהם ברכה, כשם שאני נותן בהם ברכה בשדה | הם ברשותי ליתן בהם ברכה בבית, כשם שאני נותן בהם ברכה בשדה | deleted entire line | <u>פיסקא מ</u><br>הם ברשותי ליתן בהם ברכה בבית, כשם שאני נותן בהם ברכה בשדה |
| | Ekev 5 (III: p. 56) | | ולמדתם אותם ושמרתם לעשותם, מגיד שמעשה תלוי בתלמוד | אם כן, למה נאמרה ולמדתם אותם ושמרתם לעשותם, מגיד שמעשה תלוי בתלמוד | אם כן, מה תלמוד לאמר ולמדתם אותם ושמרתם לעשותם, מגיד שמעשה תלוי בתלמוד | <u>פיסקא מא</u><br>ולמדתם אותם ושמרתם לעשותם, מגיד שמעשה תלוי בתלמוד |

| Reason For Neziv's Emendation | Citation | Parallel | (Sulzbach, 1802) | Neziv (Jerusalem, 1958) | GRA (Vilna, 1866) | Finkelstein (New York, 1969) |
|---|---|---|---|---|---|---|
| | Ekev 5 (III: p. 57) | Yalkut | אשר אנכי מצוה אתכם היום, מנין אתה אומר שאם שמע אדם דבר מפי קטן כשומע מפי חכם | מנין אתה אומר שאם שמע אדם דבר מפי קטן כשומע מפי גדול, תלמוד לאמר אשר אנכי מצוה אתכם היום | אשר אנכי מצוה אתכם היום, מנין אתה אומר שאם מע אדם דבר מפי ש קטן כשומע מפי חכם | פיסקא מא<br>אשר אנכי מצוה אתכם היום, מנין אתה אומר שאם שמע אדם דבר מפי קטן שבישראל יהא בעיניו כשומע מפי חכם |
| | Ekev 5 (III: p. 58) | Yalkut | ועוד הרי הוא אומר | הרי הוא אומר | וכן הוא אומר | פיסקא מא<br>הרי הוא אומר |
| | Ekev 5 (III: p. 58) | | על שער בת רבים, וכן הוא אומר (שה"ש ז:ה) אפך כמגדל הלבנון צופה פני דמשק | על שער בת רבים, (שה"ש ז:ה) אפך כמגדל הלבנון צופה פני דמשק | על שער בת רבים, מהו אומר (שה"ש ז:ה) אפך כמגדל הלבנון צופה פני דמשק | פיסקא מא<br>על שער בת רבים, מה הוא אומר (שה"ש ז: ה) אפך כמגדל הלבנון צופה פני דמשק |
| | Ekev 6 (III: p. 61) | | או ואספת דגנך תירושך ויצהרך ממעיט הפירות | או אינו אלא ממיעוט הפירות | או ואספת דגנך תירושך ויצהרך ממעוט הפירות | פיסקא מב<br>או ואספת דגנך תירושך ויצהרך מפני מיעוט הפירות |
| | Ekev 7 (III: p. 63) | | יבלו ימיהם בטוב ושנותם בנעימים. היא גרמה להם | יבלו בטוב ימיהם. היא גרמה | יבלו בטוב ימיהם וברגע שאול יחתו. היא גרמה להם | פיסקא מג<br>יבלו בטוב ימיהם וגו' היא גרמה להם |
| | Ekev 7 (III: p. 65) | | אילו הן נקראים על שמם | אילו הם נקראים על שמו | ילו הן נקראים על א שמו | פיסקא מג<br>אילו נקראו על שמו |
| | Ekev 7 (III: p. 67) | Yalkut | מה חרי אף האמור להלן עצירת גשמים וגלות אף חרי אף האמור כאן עצירת גשמים וגלות | מה חרי אף האמור כאן עצירת גשמים וגלות אף חרי אף האמור להלן עצירת גשמים וגלות | מה חרי אף האמור להלן עצירת גשמים וגלות אף חרי אף האמור כאן עצירת גשמים וגלות | פיסקא מג<br>מה חרי אף האמור כאן עצירת גשמים וגלות אף חרי אף האמור להלן עצירת גשמים וגלות |
| | Ekev 12 (III: p. 74) | | וקנה כרם ולא עמל בהם | וקנה כרם לא אעמל בהם | וקנה כרם ולא עמל בהם | פיסקא מח<br>וקנה כרם ולא עמל בהם |
| | Ekev 12 (III: p. 74) ki-lomar = kol mar | Yalkut | זה תלמיד שלא למד מתחלתו ונפש רעבה כלומר מתוק לא היה אלא מה שלמד | זה תלמיד שלמד מתחלתו ונפש רעבה כל מר מתוק שלא היה לו אלא מה שלמד | זה תלמיד שלא למד מתחלתו ונפש רעבה כל מר מתוק זה מי שלמד מתחלתו | פיסקא מח<br>תלמיד מתחלתו לא למד כל דבר לא היה אלא מה שלמד |

| Reason For Neziv's Emendation | Citation | Parallel | (Sulzbach, 1802) | Neziv (Jerusalem, 1958) | GRA (Vilna, 1866) | Finkelstein (New York, 1969) |
|---|---|---|---|---|---|---|
| | Ekev 12 (III: p. 75) | Yalkut | מה מים אין להם דמים | אי מים אין להם דמים | [אי] מה מים אין להם דמים | <u>פיסקא מח</u><br>מה מים אין להם דמים |
| | Ekev 12 (III: p. 75) | yslkut | שנאמר | תלמוד לאמר | שנאמר [נ"א תלמוד לאמר] | <u>פיסקא מח</u><br>שנאמר |
| | Ekev 12 (III: p. 75) | Yalkut | או אינו אלא לפי ששונה ראשונים ומשכחם | ומנין למי ששונה ראשונים ומשכחם | או אינו אלא לפי ששונה ראשונים ומשכחם | <u>פיסקא מח</u><br>ומנין שאם שומע ראשון ראשון ומשכחו |
| | Ekev 12 (III: p. 75) | Yalkut | אם בעיניו אינה חמודה כיצד בא ליטול נכסיו ובהמתו | אם בעיניו אינו חומדה כיצד בא ליטול נכסים ובהמה | אם בעיניו אינה חמודה כיצד בא ליטול נכסיו ובהמתו | <u>ספרי דברים</u><br><u>פיסקא נב</u><br>אם בעיניו אינה חומדה כיצד בא ליטול נכסים ובהמה |
| | | | | | | |
| Editor didn't know that two passages from same verse | Ekev 1 (III: p. 44) | | שנאמר +משלי ח כב+ ה' קנני ראשית דרכו קדם מפעליו מאז, ואומר +שם /משלי/ ח כג+ מעולם נסכתי מראש | שנאמר +משלי ח כב+ ה' קנני ראשית דרכו קדם מפעליו מאז, +שם /משלי/ ח כג+ מעולם נסכתי מראש | שנאמר +משלי ח ב+ ה' קנני ראשית כ דרכו קדם מפעליו מאז, ואומר +שם /משלי/ ח כג+ מעולם נסכתי מראש | <u>פיסקא לז</u><br>שנאמר +משלי ח כב+ ה' קנני ראשית דרכו קדם מפעליו מאז, ואומר +שם /משלי/ ח כג+ מעולם נסכתי מראש |
| | | | | | | |
| Misspelled foreign word | Ekev 1 (III: p. 45) | TB | ואני מוליכך בגלגוטיקא | ואני מוליכך בגלוטיקא | ואני מוליכך בגלגוטיקא | <u>פיסקא לז</u><br>ואני מוליכך בגלגטיקא |
| | | | | | | |
| Editor / copyist misread word | Ekev 2 (III: p. 47): r' Yitzhak = r' tzadok Daled / vav read as het | TB | אמר להם רבי יצחק | אמר להם רבי צדוק | אמר להם רבי צדוק | <u>פיסקא לח</u><br>אמר להם רבי צדוק |

| Reason For Neziv's Emendation | Citation | Parallel | (Sulzbach, 1802) | Neziv (Jerusalem, 1958) | GRA (Vilna, 1866) | Finkelstein (New York, 1969) |
|---|---|---|---|---|---|---|
| | Ekev 2 (III: p. 48) Changes shivre to bishvil based on accepted understanding of II Samuel | | ומה ארון שלא נעשה לא לשכר ולא להפסד אלא לשברי לוחות שבו | ומה ארון שלא נעשה לא לשכר ולא להפסד אלא בשביל לוחות שבו | ומה ארון שלא נעשה לא לשכר ולא להפסד אלא לשברי לוחות שבו | פיסקא לח<br><br>ומה ארון שלא נעשה לא לשכר ולא להפסד אלא לשברי לוחות שבו |
| | Ekev 7 (III: p. 68) kofato = komato | Yalkut | קצר קופתו | קצר קמתו | קצר (קופתו) [קמתו] | פיסקא מג<br><br>קצר קופתו |
| | Ekev 7 (III: p. 69) kofato = komato | Yalkut | שגדש קמתו | שגדש קופתו | שגדש (קמתו) [קופתו] | פיסקא מג<br><br>שגדש בקופתו |
| | Ekev 12 (III: p. 74) ki-lomar = kol mar | Yalkut | זה תלמיד שלא למד מתחלתו ונפש רעבה כלומר מתוק לא היה אלא מה שלמד | זה תלמיד שלמד מתחלתו ונפש רעבה כל מר מתוק שלא היה לו אלא מה שלמד | זה תלמיד שלא למד מתחלתו ונפש רעבה כל מר מתוק זה מי שלמד מתחלתו | פיסקא מח<br><br>תלמיד מתחלתו לא למד כל דבר לא היה אלא מה שלמד |
| | Ekev 12 (III: p. 75) din = dayo, she-shanah = she-manah | | זה שהוא אומר דין ששנה לו רבו | זה שהוא אומר דיו שמנה לו רבו | זה שאומר דיי מה ששנה לי רבי | פיסקא מח<br><br>זה שאומר דיי מה ששנה לי רבי |
| | Ekev 12 (III: p. 75) she-bi-borkha = shel bor'akha | Yalkut | רבי שמעון בן יוחי אומר הרי הוא אומר (משלי ה :טו) שתה ממים שבבורך ואל תשתה מים עכורים ותמשך עם דברי מינים.<br><br>homeoteleuton | רבי שמעון בן יוחי אומר הרי הוא אומר (משלי ה :טו) שתה ממים של בוראך ואל תשתה מים עכורים ותמשך עם דברי מינים. | רבי שמעון בן יוחי אומר הרי הוא אומר (משלי ה :טו) שתה מים שבבורך [ממי שעמך בעיר אחר כך פורש בכל ו מקום וכן הוא אומר היתה כאניות סוחר ממרחק תביא לחמה. רבי שמעון בן מנסיא אומר שתה מים מבורך ממים של בוראך] ואל תשתה [מים] עכורים ותמשך עם דברי מינים. | פיסקא מח<br><br>רבי שמעון בן יוחי אומר הרי הוא אומר (משלי ה :טו) שתה מים מבורך וגו' שנה ממי שעמך בעיר ואחר כך הפרש בכל מקום וכן הוא אומר (שם /משלי/ לא יד) היתה כאניות סוחר. רבי שמעון בן מנסיא אומר הרי הוא אומר שתה מים מבורך שתה מימיו שבראך ואל תשתה מים עכורים ותמשך עם דברי מינים. |

| Reason For Neziv's Emendation | Citation | Parallel | (Sulzbach, 1802) | Neziv (Jerusalem, 1958) | GRA (Vilna, 1866) | Finkelstein (New York, 1969) |
|---|---|---|---|---|---|---|
| | Ekev 12 (III: p. 75) she-lamad = shel adam | | מה מים אין<br>משמחים לבו שלמד | מה מים אין<br>משמחים לבו של<br>אדם | מה מים אין<br>משמחים לבו<br>שלמד | פיסקא מח<br>מה מים אין<br>משמחים את הלב |
| | Ekev 12 (III: p. 78) pe'ulatam = pa'alam | Yalkut TB | רבי אלעזר ברבי<br>צדוק אומר עשה<br>דברים לשם<br>פעולתם דבר בהם<br>לשמן | רבי אלעזר ברבי<br>צדוק אומר עשה<br>דברים לשם פעלם<br>דבר בהם לשמם | רבי אלעזר ברבי<br>צדוק אומר עשה<br>דברים לשם פעלם<br>דבר בהם לשמן | פיסקא מח<br>רבי אלעזר ברבי<br>צדוק אומר עשה<br>דברים לשם<br>פעולתם דבר בהם<br>לשמם |
| | | | | | | |
| Converts passage to same format as previous or following statement | Ekev 2 (III: p. 47) | | גמליאל ברבי לא<br>ישמשנו | רבן גמליאל ברבי<br>לא ישמשנו | גמליאל לא<br>ישמשנו | פיסקא לח<br>גמליאל ברבי לא<br>ישמשנו |
| | Ekev 4 (III: p. 54) | Yalkut | כשם שאני נותן<br>בהם מארה בשדה,<br>ורקבובית בפירות<br>ויין מחמיץ ושמן<br>מבאיש | כשם שאני נותן<br>בהם מארה בשדה,<br>כנימה ורקבובית<br>בפירות ויין מחמיץ<br>ושמן מבאיש | deleted entire line | פיסקא מ<br>כשם שאני נותן<br>בהם מארה בשדה,<br>כינה ורקבובית<br>בפירות ויין מחמיץ<br>ושמן מבאיש |
| | Ekev 12 (III: p. 74) | | היום אני לומד היום<br>אני שונה למחר אני<br>שונה | היום אני לומד<br>למחר אני לומד<br>היום אני שונה<br>למחר אני שונה | היום אני לומד<br>[למחר אני לומד]<br>היום אני שונה<br>למחר אני שונה | פיסקא מח<br>היום אני למד למחר<br>אני למד היום אני<br>שונה למחר אני<br>שונה |
| | Ekev 12 (III: p. 78) | Yalkut | אורך ימים בימינה<br>ובשמאלה עושר<br>וכבוד בעולם הזה | אורך ימים בימינה<br>לעולם הבא<br>ובשמאלה עושר<br>וכבוד בעולם הזה | deleted entire line | פיסקא מח<br>אורך ימים בימינה<br>לעולם הבא<br>בשמאלה עושר<br>וכבוד בעולם הזה |

| Reason For Neziv's Emendation | Citation | Parallel | (Sulzbach, 1802) | Neziv (Jerusalem, 1958) | GRA (Vilna, 1866) | Finkelstein (New York, 1969) |
|---|---|---|---|---|---|---|
| | Ekev 15 (III: p. 82) | Yalkut | ומנין שכנגדו בים<br>הרי הוא שלהם<br>תלמוד לומר מן<br>המדבר והלבנון הזה<br>עד הנהר הגדול נהר<br>פרת ועד הים הגדול<br>מבוא השמש יהיה<br>גבולכם, והמדבר<br>גבולכם, מן הנהר<br>הגדול, נהר פרת. מן<br>הנהר גבולכם ואין<br>הנהר גבולכם אם<br>כיבשתם את הנהר<br>יהיה גבולכם והנהר<br>גבולכם: ועד הים<br>הגדול מבוא השמש.<br>עד הים גבולכם<br>ואין הים גבולכם<br>אם כבשתם יהיה<br>גבולכם | ומנין שכנגדו בים<br>הרי הוא שלהם<br>תלמוד לומר מן<br>המדבר והלבנון הזה<br>עד הנהר הגדול נהר<br>פרת ועד הים הגדול<br>יהיה גבולכם מן<br>המדבר ואין המדבר<br>גבולכם אם<br>כיבשתם המדבר,<br>מדבר גבולכם. מן<br>הנהר הגדול, נהר<br>פרת. מן הנהר<br>הגדול, נהר פרת<br>ואין הנהר גבולכם<br>אם כיבשתם הנהר<br>גבולכם.. ועד הים<br>האחרון ואין הים<br>גבולכם אם כבשתם<br>גבולכם | ומנין שכנגדו בים<br>הרי הוא שלהם<br>תלמוד לומר מן<br>המדבר והלבנון מן<br>הנהר נהר פרת ועד<br>הים האחרון יהיה<br>גבולכם. מן<br>המדבר ואין<br>מדבר גבולכם אם<br>ה<br>בשתם אף המדבר<br>כ<br>גבולכם. מן הנהר,<br>ואין הנהר גבולכם<br>אם כבשתם אף<br>הנהר יהיה<br>גבולכם. ועד הים<br>ואין הים גבולכם<br>אם כבשתם יהיה<br>גבולכם | <u>ספרי דברים</u><br><u>פיסקא נא</u><br><br>ומנין שכנגדו בים<br>הרי הוא שלהם<br>תלמוד לומר מן<br>המדבר והלבנון מן<br>המדבר גבולכם ואין<br>המדבר גבולכם<br>ואם כבשתם יהי<br>גבולכם והמדבר<br>גבולכם, מן הנהר,<br>נהר פרת, מן הנהר<br>גבולכם ואין הנהר<br>גבולכם ואם<br>כבשתם יהי גבולכם<br>והנהר גבולכם, ועד<br>הים גבולכם ואין<br>הים גבולכם ואם<br>כבשתם יהי גבולכם |
| | | | | | | |
| Substitutes synonym | Ekev 3 (III: p. 51) | Yalkut | או לפי ששותה מי<br>גשמים אבל אינו<br>שותה מי שלחים...<br>או לפי ששותה מי<br>שלחים אבל אינה<br>שותה מי שלגים | או לפי ששותה מי<br>גשמים אבל אינו<br>שותה מי נחלים... או<br>לפי ששותה מי<br>נחלים אבל אינה<br>שותה מי שלגים | או לפי ששותה מי<br>גשמים אבל אינו<br>שותה מי שלחים...<br>או לפי ששותה מי<br>שלחים אבל אינה<br>שותה מי שלגים | <u>פיסקא לט</u><br><br>או לפי ששותה מי<br>גשמים אבל אינו<br>שותה מי שלוחים...<br>או לפי ששותה מי<br>שלוחים אבל אינה<br>שותה מי שלגים |
| | | | | | | |
| Removes extraneous words | Ekev 2 (III: p. 47) | | אלא למגונה<br>ולמשובח שבה | אלא למגונה שבה | אלא למגונה שבה | <u>פיסקא לח</u><br><br>אלא למגונה שבה |
| | Ekev 2 (III: p. 49) | | רבי שמעון בן יוחאי<br>אומר הרי בורות<br>חצובים אשר לא<br>חצבת, והלא בור<br>אשר לא חצבת,<br>כרמים אשר לא<br>נטעת שעכשו באת<br>בארץ | רבי שמעון בן יוחאי<br>אומר, והלא בידוע<br>אשר לא חצבת,<br>שעכשו באת לארץ. | רבי שמעון בן<br>יוחאי אומר אם<br>נאמר בתים מלאים<br>ורות חצובים למה<br>ב<br>נאמר אשר לא<br>חצבת, אשר לא<br>נטעת,ץ | <u>פיסקא לח</u><br><br>רבי שמעון בן יוחי<br>אומר, והלא בידוע<br>שלא מלאתה,<br>שעכשו באת לארץ,<br>ובורות חצובים<br>אשר לא חצבת,<br>והלא בידוע שלא<br>חצבת, שעכשו באת<br>לארץ |
| | Ekev 3 (III: p. 50) | | בית כור מלמעלה<br>בית כור מלמטה<br>נמצא חמשה<br>מכופלות | בית כור מלמעלה<br>נמצא חמשה<br>מכופלות | בית כור מלמעלה<br>בית כור נמצא<br>חמשה מכופלות | <u>פיסקא לט</u><br><br>בית כור מלמעלה<br>ונמצא חמשה<br>מכופלות |

| Reason For Neziv's Emendation | Citation | Parallel | (Sulzbach, 1802) | Neziv (Jerusalem, 1958) | GRA (Vilna, 1866) | Finkelstein (New York, 1969) |
|---|---|---|---|---|---|---|
| | Ekev 7 (III: p. 66) | Yalkut | ה' מיני פורעניות הם | מיני פורעניות הם | ה' מיני פורעניות הם | פיסקא מג<br>מיני פורעניות הם |
| | Ekev 7 (III: p. 67) | | נאמר כאן אף ונאמר להלן אף חרי | נאמר כאן אף ונאמר להלן אף | נאמר כאן [חרון] אף ונאמר להלן חרי אף | פיסקא מג<br>נאמר כאן חרי אף ונאמר להלן חרי אף |
| | Ekev 7 (III: p. 67) | | חרב וחיה רעה ורעב ודבר ועצירת גשמים וגלות | חרב וחיה רעה ודבר ועצירת גשמים וגלות | חרב וחיה רעה ודבר ועצירת גשמים וגלות | פיסקא מג<br>חרב ודבר וחיה רעה ועצירת גשמים וגלות |
| | Ekev 7 (III: p. 67) | Yalkut | שיהיו אומות העולם אומרים הם שרוים בטובה | שיהיו הם שרוים בטובה | שיהיו בבליים אומרים הם שרוים בטובה | פיסקא מג<br>שיהיו אומות העולם שרוים בטובה |
| | Ekev 7 (III: p. 69) | Yalkut | כיוצא בה אתה אומר | כיוצא בה | deleted entire passage | פיסקא מג<br>כיוצא בה |
| | Ekev 12 (III: p. 73) | TB ADRN | הוי זהיר בצפור זו לבני אם | הוי זהיר בצפור זו אם | הוי זהיר בצפור זו לבני אם | פיסקא מח<br>הוי זהיר בצפור זו לבני אם |
| | Ekev 12 (III: p. 77) | | הוא חייכם ואורך ימיכם שלא תאמר | הוא חייכם שלא תאמר<br>(טעות הדפוס) | הוא חייכם ואורך ימיכם שלא תאמר | פיסקא מח<br>הוא חייכם שלא תאמר |
| | | | | | | |
| | | | | | | |
| Based on the syntax of other similar *derashot* | Ekev 3 (III: p. 50) | | ואלו הם כי ארץ אשר אתם עברים שמה לרשתה | ואלו הם כי הארץ אשר אתה בא שמה לרשתה, והארץ אשר אתם עברים שמה לרשתה | ואלו הם כי הארץ שר אתה בא שמה א לרשתה, והארץ אשר אתם עברים שמה לרשתה | פיסקא לט<br>ואלו הם כי הארץ אשר אתה בא שמה לרשתה, והארץ אשר אתם עברים שמה לרשתה |
| | | | | | | |
| Changes verse of the *derashah* | Ekev 5 (III: p. 59) | TB | תלמוד לומר בכל לבבך ובכל נפשך ובכל מאדך. וכי יש עבודה בלב | תלמוד לומר בכל לבבכם. וכי יש עבודה בלב | תלמוד לומר בכל לבבכם. וכי יש עבודה בלב | פיסקא מא<br>תלמוד לומר בכל לבבכם ובכל נפשכם. וכי יש עבודה בלב |

| Reason For Neziv's Emendation | Citation | Parallel | (Sulzbach, 1802) | Neziv<br>(Jerusalem, 1958) | GRA<br>(Vilna, 1866) | Finkelstein<br>(New York, 1969) |
|---|---|---|---|---|---|---|
| | Ekev 7 (III: p. 66) | Yalkut<br>TB | אלא מה תלמוד<br>לומר אלהים אחרים<br>מלמד שעשו להם<br>עגלים הרבה | אלא מה תלמוד<br>לומר אלה אלקיך<br>מלמד שעשו להם<br>עגלים הרבה<br>או אשר העלוך | אלא מה תלמוד<br>לומר אלה אשר<br>עלוך מלמד שעשו<br>ה<br>להם עגלים הרבה | פיסקא מג<br>מה תלמוד לומר<br>אלהים אחרים<br>מלמד שעשו להם<br>עגלים הרבה |
| | Ekev 7 (III: p. 66) | | למה נאמר לפי<br>שנאמר תשמרון את<br>מצות ה' אלהיכם<br>מגיד הכתוב שכשם<br>שאדם צריך להזהר<br>בסלעו שלא תאבד<br>כך צריך להזהר<br>בתלמודו שלא יאבד | למה נאמר לפי<br>שנאמר לשמור את<br>מצות ה' אלהיכם<br>מגיד הכתוב שכשם<br>שאדם צריך להזהר<br>בסלעו שלא תאבד<br>כך צריך להזהר<br>בתלמודו שלא יאבד | למה נאמר שמור<br>תשמרון מגיד<br>הכתוב שכשם<br>שאדם צריך להזהר<br>בסלעו שלא תאבד<br>כך צריך להזהר<br>בתלמודו שלא<br>יאבד | פיסקא מח<br>למה נאמר<br>לפי שנאמר והיה<br>אם שמוע תשמעו<br>אל מצותי שומע אני<br>כיון ששמע אדם<br>דברי תורה ישב לו<br>ולא ישנה תלמוד<br>לומר כי אם שמור<br>תשמרון מגיד<br>שכשם שאדם צריך<br>להזהר בסלעו שלא<br>תאבד כך צריך<br>להזהר בתלמודו<br>שלא יאבד |
| | | | | | | |
| Adds extra word or prefix | Ekev 3 (III: p. 50) | Mishnah | רבי יוסי המשולם<br>אומר | רבי יוסי בן<br>המשולם אומר | רבי יוסי המשולם<br>אומר | פיסקא לט<br>רבי יוסי בן<br>המשולם אומר |
| | Ekev 4 (III: p. 55) | Yalkut | אין לי אלא שאר<br>צות עד שלא כבשו<br>מ | אין לי אלא שאר<br>מצות שעד שלא<br>כבשו | אין לי אלא שאר<br>מצות עד שלא<br>כבשו | פיסקא מא<br>אין לי אלא עד שלא<br>כבשו |
| | Ekev 5 (III: p. 57) | Yalkut | וכשענש על<br>התלמוד יותר מן<br>המעשה | וכשם שענש, ענש<br>על התלמוד יותר מן<br>המעשה | וכשם שתלמוד<br>גדול ממעשה כך<br>נשה גדול ממעשה<br>ע | פיסקא מא<br>וכשם שענש על<br>התלמוד יותר מן<br>המעשה |
| | Ekev 7 (III: p. 68) | Yalkut | וכן אתה מוצא<br>בשבט בנימן | וכן אתה מוצא<br>שבט יהודא ובנימן<br>ב | וכן אתה מוצא<br>בשבט [יהודה]<br>ובנימן | פיסקא מג<br>וכן אתה מוצא<br>בשבט יהודה ובנימן |
| | Ekev 11 (III: p. 71) | Yalkut | לשובע שמחות | רבי שמעון בן יוחי<br>אומר לשבע שמחות | [רבי שמעון בן יוחי<br>אומר] לשבע<br>שמחות | פיסקא מז<br>רבי שמעון בן יוחי<br>אומר לשבע שמחות |

| Reason For Neziv's Emendation | Citation | Parallel | (Sulzbach, 1802) | Neziv<br>(Jerusalem, 1958) | GRA<br>(Vilna, 1866) | Finkelstein<br>(New York, 1969) |
|---|---|---|---|---|---|---|
| | Ekev 11<br>(III: p. 72) | Yalkut | מה כוכבים פעמים<br>נגלים פעמים נכסים | מה כוכבים פעמים<br>נגלים פעמים נכסים<br>כך הצדיקים | מה כוכבים פעמים<br>נגלים פעמים<br>נכסים אף צדיקים<br>כן | פיסקא מז<br><br>מה כוכבים פעמים<br>נכסים פעמים נגלים<br>כך הצדיקים |
| | Ekev 12<br>(III: p. 74) | Yalkut | שתים שלש פרשיות | שתים שלש פרשיות<br>בחודש | שתים שלש<br>פרשיות [בחודש] | פיסקא מח<br><br>שתים שלש פרשיות<br>בחדש |
| | Ekev 12<br>(III: p. 75) | Yalkut | לא היה אלא מה<br>שבתוכו | לא היה בו אלא מה<br>שנותנים בתוכו | ואין בו אלא מה<br>שנותן בתוכו | פיסקא מח<br><br>לא היה אלא מה<br>שבתוכו |
| | Ekev 12<br>(III: p. 76) | Yalkut | מנין אתה אומר<br>שאם שמע אדם<br>מדברי תורה | מנין אתה אומר<br>שאם שמע אדם<br>דבר מדברי תורה | מנין אתה אומר<br>שאם שמע אדם<br>[דבר] מדברי תורה | פיסקא מח<br><br>מנין אתה אומר<br>שאם שמע אדם<br>דבר מדברי תורה |
| | | | | | | |
| Factually incorrect | Ekev 5 (III: p. 56) | Yalkut | גדול תלמוד שקודם<br>לחלה ארבעים שנה<br>ולמעשרות חמשים<br>וארבע שנה<br>וליובלות מאה<br>ושלש | גדול תלמוד שקודם<br>לחלה ארבעים שנה<br>ולמעשרות ששים<br>ואחת שנה וליובלות<br>מאה ושלש | גדול תלמוד<br>שקודם לחלה<br>ארבעים שנה<br>ותרומות<br>ולמעשרות חמשים<br>וארבע שנה<br>ולשמטים ששים<br>ואחת וליובלות<br>מאה ושלש | פיסקא מא<br><br>גדול תלמוד שקודם<br>לחלה ארבעים שנה<br>ולמעשרות חמשים<br>וארבע ולשמטים<br>ששים ואחת<br>וליובלות מאה<br>ושלש |
| | | | | | | |
| Text as is does not make sense | Ekev 6 (III: p. 60) | Yalkut | ומנין שנתנה ברכה<br>אחת לישראל שכל<br>הכללות כלולות בה | ומנין שנתנה ברכה<br>אחת לישראל שכל<br>הברכות כלולות בה | ומנין שנתנה ברכה<br>אחת לישראל שכל<br>ברכות כלולות בה<br>ה | פיסקא מב<br><br>ומנין שנתנה ברכה<br>אחת לישראל שכל<br>הברכות כלולות בה |
| | Ekev 7 (III: p. 66) | Yalkut mekhilta | רבי יצחק אומר<br>אילו נפרע שמה | רבי יצחק אומר<br>אילו נפרט שמה | רבי יצחק אומר<br>אילו נפרט שמה | פיסקא מג<br><br>רבי יצחק אומר<br>אילו נפרט שמה |
| | Ekev 7 (III: p. 66) | Yalkut mekhilta | רבי אומר למה<br>נקרא שמן אחרים<br>שהם אחרים<br>שבמעשיהם שמי<br>שהם אחרים<br>במעשיהם קראם<br>אלהות. | רבי אומר למה<br>נקרא שמם אלהים<br>אחרים שהם<br>אחרונים לאחרון<br>שבמעשים שמי<br>שהם אחרונים<br>שבמעשים קראם<br>אלהות. | רבי אומר למה<br>נקרא שמן אחרים<br>שהם אחרים<br>לאחרונים<br>שבמעשים העושה<br>והקוראם אלהות<br>(בהע"א לאחרונים<br>שבמעשים שמי<br>שהם אחרונים<br>שבמעשיהם קראם<br>אלהות.) | פיסקא מג<br><br>רבי אומר למה<br>נקרא שמם אלהים<br>אחרים שהם אחרים<br>לאחרון שבמעשים<br>שמי שהוא אחרון<br>במעשים קראם<br>אלהות. |

| Reason For Neziv's Emendation | Citation | Parallel | (Sulzbach, 1802) | Neziv (Jerusalem, 1958) | GRA (Vilna, 1866) | Finkelstein (New York, 1969) |
|---|---|---|---|---|---|---|
| | Ekev 12 (III: p. 77) | doesn't use Yalkut, TB, or tosefta | דבר התיר שהולכים מעיר לעיר | זו דבר הלכה שהולכים מעיר לעיר | כמו תייר שהולך מעיר לעיר | פיסקא מח<br><br>'רבותינו התירו שהולכים מעיר לעיר |
| | Ekev 14 (III: p. 80) | Yalkut | מנין לרבות מסעיהם | מנין לרבות מסיעיהם | מנין לרבות מסייעיהם | פיסקא נ<br><br>מנין לרבות את מסייעיהם |
| | Ekev 14 (III: p. 80) | | מלמד שאמורי משבעה עממים | מלמד שאחד משבעה עממים | מלמד שאחד משבעה עממים | ספרי דברים פיסקא נ<br><br>מלמד שאחד משבעה עממים |
| | | | | | | |
| | | | | | | |
| Acknowledges variant but does not emend | Ekev 3 (III: p. 50) | | תלמוד לומר ארץ הרים ובקעות | תלמוד לומר ארץ הרים ובקעות | תלמוד לומר ארץ הרים ובקעות | פיסקא לט<br><br>תלמוד לומר ארץ הרים ובקעות |
| | Ekev 12 (III: p. 76) | Yalkut | וכתוב במגילת חסידים | וכתוב במגילת חסידים<br><br>י"ש: סתרים | וכתוב במגילת חסידים [נ"א סתרים] | פיסקא מח<br><br>וכתוב במגילת חריסים |
| | Ekev 12 (III: p. 77) | doesn't use Yalkut, TB, or tosefta | דבר התיר שהולכים מעיר לעיר | זו דבר הלכה שהולכים מעיר לעיר | כמו תייר שהולך מעיר לעיר | פיסקא מח<br><br>'רבותינו התירו שהולכים מעיר לעיר |

# Appendix C: Selections from Ḥayyim Berlin's "Letter on Education, 1902"

Printed in *Sefer Nishmat Ḥayyim* (Jerusalem, 2003), 91-95

But to our heart's dismay, in the previous generation there emerged from amongst us pretenders who deceive us into killing, heaven forbid, the Torah of life which is in our possession with a venomous kiss. At first they craftily praised, lauded, and elevated the rhetoric and poetry of the Bible and brought about an appreciation of the simple reading of Scripture to the point that the received Oral Torah upon which God covenanted with us was cast off of it… And so, in walking their path of *peshat*, they trampled on the portion of *derash* and aggadah of our holy rabbis to the point that they became words of nonsense and fiction in the eyes of children.

And so they went and distorted minds and ruined the taste of Torah in the palates of innumerable fathers and sons to the point that they advocated making [the study of our] holy language, which is but a vehicle for the understanding of Torah, into the principle objective; and the objective of studying Torah for the sake of Torah they made into a mere vehicle for the "Knowledge of the Hebrew Language [*yedi'at sefat 'ever*]." And since the entire point of studying Torah is only for the purpose of knowing the Hebrew language, they made the study of Torah secondary and books of methodology primary. Some of them began to teach Torah to young children in the manner that one teaches secular history.

And the book of Vayikra and all of the sacrifices about which our Sages said "let the pure ones (i.e., children) come and be engrossed in matters of purity" they skip completely and don't teach. And likewise they skip certain portions which they find inappropriate to teach at all to children, yet our fathers and sages never dreamt that young children would come to an errant heart from portions of the holy Torah…

And these people who prevent their children from [studying] certain portions of the Torah because of the far fetched concern that they might be unfit for young souls such as these, they themselves offer them up to excessive reading in which their minds and hearts are saturated in stories of lust which imbues in them a poison which destroys their body and soul. And could the study of the holy language in such a manner possibly be called a *miẓvah*?!

Let us look at how far we have strayed these days from the path of our fathers before [us]. In the previous generation our fathers themselves would speak amongst themselves in order to choose a teacher for their children who was a scholar and an educator and careful to engage in the work of God faithfully, [and who] was known to be fearful of Heaven…

Now many fathers have been swept away by the flow of distorted ideas which has found itself agents who toll her bells [saying] 'a youth need only know the language of his people and her history and in them all of Judaism rests,' and the blessings which the father makes at the moment in which he enters his son into the covenant of Abraham our forefather (i.e., the circumcision) [which states] 'that he should merit to grow into Torah, marriage, and good deeds,' is but a manner of speech from the generation that has passed and [has now] been annulled. And since the Torah according to the new fashion is nothing but holy language learned from methodologies and secular poetry, the teachers are forced to compete with each other in [excelling] in the path of the new pedagogy, and the one who replaces more of the old in face of the new, is praised and lauded for their prodigious acts…

The education which emerges from the Path of Life has been abandoned to instructors and teachers who are fascinated most by the sound of their words. And, due to the fact that Torah has fallen in their hands to teach it in a secular fashion and to make it secondary to the methodologies or to annul them completely, Heaven forbid, and to base the education of the progeny of Israel almost completely on Hebrew language in the manner in which vernacular languages [are taught], we find teachers of falsehood who are free in their thoughts and perverted in their paths, who themselves impose upon the hearts of the students the poison of denying the Divine holiness of the written and received Torah and the miracles and Providence of God. And it is the mothers who have the upper hand in choosing teachers such as these, because most fathers are preoccupied, and one follows the next in falling captive to the [new] fashions. Today we are most concerned that the classroom should be well organized and pleasant, with fresh air, [and] an education reformed and articulated in accordance with modern tastes, so that everyone can praise the magnificence of the teacher and the classroom, but there is no concern for the essence and the foundation—that in it should be learned Torah in its true purity and that in it children should be educated in religion and ethics, and that they should fulfill the *mizvot* in actuality…

As such, we see it as a *mizvah* and an obligation upon us now to act for [the sake] of our holy Torah (for we have no remnant but her) and for [the sake] of the world of Judaism which stands and is sustained by the breath of the young children of the Rabbi's house, in order to enlighten and awaken all those who truly wish to educate their children in Torah and *mizvot* and good deeds. But because they are mired in preoccupations, the education of their children has led and been dragged along the new paths which pervert according to the manner of the times, due to a lack of a discerning eye and [insufficient] attention... And they [i.e., the parents] must all open their eyes and devote their attention to the following things which we consider a *miẓvah* and an obligation to publicize:

1. That every Jew is obligated to teach his sons the Five Books of the Torah, Nevi'im, and Ketuvim according to the *peshat* which is straight and kosher, together with the commentary of Rashi, z"l, and the commentaries of the other Rishonim, in a manner that agrees and fits with the traditions of the Sages...
2. To seek *melamdim* who are known as experts in their faith[10] and as fearers of Heaven, [who are] careful in [observance] of *miẓvot* and matters of the Sages...
3. Just as there is a *miẓvah* on every person to set aside time for learning Torah, to observe the times of *Kri'at Shem`a* and *tefilah be-ẓibur*, and to engage in and fulfill all the *miẓvot* performed by both the community and the individual, so too there is an even greater *miẓvah* and obligation on every individual to set aside time from his schedule to oversee and guide the education of his children, [to make sure] that they are educated on the path which our fathers and rabbis traversed from time immemorial...
4. It is also a *miẓvah* to explain these matters well to the women and masses, for the Judaism of the children is dependent on a proper and kosher education...

And the merit of the great *miẓvah* of "and you shall teach to your children" will protect all those who guide their children in the path of Torah...

Signed,
Ḥayyim Berlin, Elizavetgrad

10 "'*Emunatam*." It is possible that the original word was "'*umanutam*" meaning their craft.

Signatories:

Eliyahu Feinstein, Pruzin
Eliezer Gordon, Telz
Eliezer Rabinowitz, Minsk
Ephraim Shelomoh Zalman, Lipna
Benzion [Sternfeld], Bielsk
Eliakim Shelomoh Shapira, Grodno
Avraham ben Moshe, Grodno
Gavriel Ze'ev Margoliot, Grodno
Zerah ben ha-Ga'on Binyamin
Ḥayyim Meir Noah Levin, Vilna
Yehiel Mihel Epstein, Novardok
Yiẓḥak Blazer, previously of Petersburg
Yehoshuah, Zarik
Yiẓḥak Ya'akov Rabonowitz, Ponevezh
Yehuda Ha-Levi Lifshitz, Meremsh
Yosef Zundel, Esheshok
Yiẓḥak ha-Kohen Feigenbaum, Warsaw
Yehudah Leib Rif, New Zhagory
Moshe Danishevsky, Slobodka
Moshe ben ha-Ga'on Yehoshuah Eizik, Riga
Meir Atlas, Kobrin
Moshe Shmuel Shapira, Babroisk
Ẓvi Hirsch Broide, Old Zhagory
Raphael Shapira, Volozhin
Shimon Ber, Shedliz

## Appendix D: *Birkat ha-Neẓiv* and the Question of Genre

As noted earlier, one might be inclined to attribute the disparity between Neẓiv's work on *Sifre* and his commentary on Torah to the differing nature of the books upon which the respective commentaries are based. *Sifre,* after all, is a highly technical text whose study is generally restricted to the scholarly elite, while the Torah contains a large degree of narrative and even its technical portions are often well known and frequently studied by the general Jewish populace. While there is certainly some truth to this contention, the fact that Neẓiv's work on *Mekhilta'* contains many of the elements present in *Ha'amek Davar* yet absent in *'Emek ha-Neẓiv* suggests that the differences between *'Emek ha-Neẓiv* and *Ha'amek Davar* have less to do with genre and more to do with the time period within which they were written.

While Neẓiv's work on *Mekhilta'*, first published in 1970 under the title *Birkat ha-Neẓiv,*[11] shares certain elements with his work on *Sifre,* such as constant emendation of the rabbinic texts,[12] in many significant areas it differs greatly. The starkest difference between *'Emek ha-Neẓiv* and *Birkat ha-Neẓiv* is probably with regard to citation. Unlike his commentary on *Sifre,* but much like his commentary on Torah, *Birkat ha-Neẓiv* contains no references to books outside the pale of traditionalist Jewish learning.[13]

---

11 *Mekhilta de-Rabi Yishma'el* (Tel Aviv: ha-Ṿa'ad le-Hotsa'at Kitve ha-Natsiv, 1970)

12 E.g., BH Bo, 7; *BH* Bo, 9; *BH* Bo, 10; *BH* Bo, 14; *BH* Bo, 18; *BH* Bo, 19; *BH* Bo, 27; *BH* Bo, 31; *BH* Bo, 34; *BH* Bo, 37; *BH* Bo, 62 BH Bo, 65; *BH* Bo, 66; *BH* Bo, 67; *BH* Bo, 73; *BH* Bo, 74; *BH* Bo, 75; *BH* Bo, 84; *BH* Bo, 85; *BH* Bo, 93; *BH* Bo, 97; *BH* Bo, 97; *BH* be-Shalah, 110; *BH* be-Shalah, 111; *BH* be-Shalah, 113; *BH* be-Shalah, 114; *BH* be-Shalah, 115; *BH* be-Shalah, 117; *BH* be-Shalah, 118; *BH* be-Shalah, 119; *BH* be-Shalah, 120; *BH* be-Shalah, 121; *BH* be-Shalah, 126; *BH* be-Shalah, 127; *BH* be-Shalah, 131; *BH* be-Shalah, 139; *BH* be-Shalah, 140; *BH* be-Shalah, 141; *BH* be-Shalah, 145; *BH* be-Shalah, 147; *BH* be-Shalah, 148; *BH* be-Shalah, 149; *BH* be-Shalah, 151; *BH* be-Shalah, 152; *BH* be-Shalah, 153; *BH* be-Shalah, 154; *BH* be-Shalah, 155; *BH* be-Shalah, 156; *BH* be-Shalah, 158; *BH* be-Shalah, 163; *BH* be-Shalah, 164; *BH* be-Shalah, 166; *BH* be-Shalah, 171; *BH* be-Shalah, 173; *BH* be-Shalah, 174; *BH* be-Shalah, 176; *BH* be-Shalah, 179; *BH* be-Shalah, 185; *BH* be-Shalah, 189; *BH* be-Shalah, 190; *BH* be-Shalah, 191; *BH* be-Shalah, 193; *BH* be-Shalah, 199; *BH* Yitro, 201; *BH* Yitro, 209; *BH* Yitro, 210; *BH* Yitro, 211; *BH* Yitro, 218; *BH* Yitro, 223; *BH* Yitro, 224; *BH* Yitro, 225; *BH* Yitro, 229; *BH* Yitro, 236; *BH* Yitro, 246; *BH* Yitro, 247; *BH* Yitro, 252; *BH* Yitro, 253; *BH* Mishpatim, 255; *BH* Mishpatim, 258; *BH* Mishpatim, 260; *BH* Mishpatim, 261; *BH* Mishpatim, 265; *BH* Mishpatim, 270; *BH* Mishpatim, 271; *BH* Mishpatim, 278, etc.

13 The reference to de' Rossi's *Me'or 'Einayim* found in *Birkat ha-Neẓiv* (be-Shalah, 148) is a

The other feature of the *Sifre* commentary which is noticeably diminished in *Birkat ha-Neẓiv,* as it is in *Ha'amek Davar,* is the project of identifying *'asmakhta'*. There are only five occasions in the lengthy work in which a statement of the rabbis is identified as such.[14]

On the other hand, a number of the features central to *Ha'amek Davar,* yet absent from *'Emek ha-Neẓiv,* do appear in Neẓiv's commentary on *Mekhilta'*. Thus, for example, in *Birkat ha-Neẓiv* one finds Neẓiv employing his understanding of "*ḥukim*" as a reference to the thirteen hermeneutical principles of Rabbi Ishmael.[15] There one finds repeated emphasis on the antiquity of the oral Law[16] and on the importance of Torah study.[17] There, too, one finds an elaborate discussion of Neẓiv's approach to *ta'amei ha-mizvot*.[18] As such, the absence of these elements from Neẓiv's work on *Sifre* cannot be attributed to the fact that *Sifre* is a work of *midrash halakhah,* for *Mekhilta'* is also a work of *midrash halakhah* and there, as in his commentary on Torah, these elements are to be found.

In fact, Neẓiv's work on *Mekhilta'* not only diminishes the role of genre in explaining the differences between *'Emek ha-Neẓiv* and *Ha'amek Davar,* but solidifies the claim that the difference between the two works lies in their period of composition. For, while often assumed to be a product of Neẓiv's youth akin to his work on *Sifre,* the printed edition of Neẓiv's commentary on *Mekhilta'* is probably more accurately dated to his later years.

The association of *Birkat ha-Neẓiv* with Neẓiv's youth stems from the passage found in the introduction to his commentary in *She'iltot,* which

---

verbatim replication of his comments in his *Sifre* commentary, *EH* Be-ha'alotekha 26 (I: 268), and should not be treated as part of the work composed by Neẓiv on *Mekhilta'*. See below on the nature of the printed edition of *Birkat ha-Neẓiv*. The fact that he cites Yeḥezkel Feivel, *Toldot Adam* (BH Yitro, 219), is historically significant in light of Edward Breuer's work, which displayed the broad learning which is evident in Yeḥezkel Feivel's book. See his "The Haskalah in Vilna: R. Yeḥezkel Feivel's *'Toldot Adam'*," *Torah u-Madda Journal* 7 (1997): 15-40. Given the prominent stature of Yeḥezkel Feivel amongst the rabbinic elite of Jewish Lithuanian during the first decades of the nineteenth century, and given the fact that his knowledge of non-traditional sources remains unreferenced in *Toldot Adam,* it is not similar to the works of de' Rossi, Wessely, and Mendelssohn which Neẓiv cites in his commentary on *Sifre.*

14 *BH* Bo, 80; *BH* Bo, 83; *BH* Yitro, 241; *BH* Mishpatim, 267; *BH* Mishpatim, 325.

15 *BH* be-Shalah, 167; *BH* be-Shalah, 168.

16 *BH* be-Shalah, 172; *BH* be-Shalah, 173; *BH* Yitro, 217.

17 *BH* be-Shalah, 113; *BH* be-Shalah, 130, *BH* be-Shalah, 161; *BH* Yitro, 226; *BH* Yitro, 237; *BH* Yitro, 250.

18 *BH* Yitro, 209-210.

was first published in 1861. There he writes:

> And I, of meager stature (*he-'ani*), in my innocence pursued during my youth an investigation of the exegesis of our Rabbis of Blessed Memory which are scattered amongst the Talmud [and] which are not understood upon first glance at the Bible. And I pored over the *Mekhilta'* and *Torat Kohanim,* the primary books of source material, and from there explained positions of the sages of the Talmud, who are the true warriors, until I discovered explanations with the help of He Who Grants [Knowledge] even to the unworthy. And I wrote in a book a composition on *Sifre Midrash Bamidbar* and *ve-'Eleh ha-Devarim,* in which the ways of the Tanna' are brief, and from there explained some *beraiytot* in *Mekhilta'* and *Torat Kohanim* which have not been addressed by the commentators. Yet, it[19] is hidden with me until I find the time, with the help of He Who Formed the Luminaries, to bring it to press and to distribute it (*le-hakhnis le-she'arim*).[20]

Based on this passage one might assume that the commentary printed under the name *Birkat ha-Neẓiv* is synonymous with the "*beraiytot* in *Mekhilta,'*" which Neẓiv "explained" during his "youth." While such is certainly the assumption which the editors of *Birkat ha-Neẓiv* have made, or the assumption they wish their readers to make, by virtue of their having cited the above passage from *Ha'amek She'elah* in their preface to *Birkat ha-Neẓiv,* a critical analysis of the text suggests otherwise.

An analysis of *Birkat ha-Neẓiv* must begin by noting that, from an historical perspective, the printed text is not a very reliable document. The editors themselves note that they have filled in lacunae in the commentary with comments made by Neẓiv elsewhere which pertain to the *Mekhilta'* text at hand. Yet such editorial insertions are not identified in the text. Also, the parenthetical remarks found in the body of the commentary are at times clearly the words of Neẓiv himself,[21] and at other

19 The *Sifre* commentary.

20 *HS Kidmat ha-'Emek* 1: 17.

21 As in *BH* Bo Yitro, 27, where Neẓiv parenthetically notes that only after having written his original comments did the Vilna edition of the Talmud containing the emendations of

times clearly the words of a later editor.[22] Nonetheless, there is no reason to believe that the commentary as a whole does not represent the work of Neẓiv. And there is sufficient reliable evidence to date the bulk of that work to the later years of Neẓiv's life.

The first clue which suggests that the commentary printed as *Birkat ha-Neẓiv* is not synonymous with the early work of Neẓiv on *Mekhilta'* comes from the sheer size of the commentary. The printed commentary is roughly one-third of the size of the printed edition of *'Emek ha-Neẓiv*. However, the latter commentary contains both *Sifre* Numbers and *Sifre* Deuteronomy, whereas *Birkat ha-Neẓiv* treats only the halakhic midrash on the book of Exodus. As such, the size of the *Mekhilta'* commentary is roughly equivalent to that of his commentary on *Sifre*—shorter than his work on Numbers, but longer than his work on Deuteronomy.[23] On the other hand, the printed edition of Neẓiv's comments on *Torat Kohanim*, the compilation of halakhic midrash to the book of Leviticus, is far smaller then either *Birkat ha-Neẓiv* or *'Emek ha-Neẓiv*. In fact, the terse comments therein resemble *hagahot* or notes to a text rather than a full-fledged commentary.

If we return to the passage from *Kidmat ha-'Emek* cited above, Neẓiv's description of his work on *Torat Kohanim* seems to be accurately portrayed by the printed text in that he describes his endeavor as merely explaining "a few *beraiytot*." Similarly, his description of his work on *Sifre* as a "composition" which he "wrote in a book" reflects the printed form of *'Emek ha-Neẓiv*. His description of his work to date on *Mekhilta'*, however, does not seem to reflect the commentary printed as *Birkat ha-Neẓiv*. After all, Neẓiv equates his work on *Mekhilta'* with his work on *Torat Kohanim*. Both are merely explanations of a few *beraiytot*, and it is only on *Sifre* that Neẓiv has composed a genuine commentary. Thus, we might well imagine that the work on *Mekhilta'* to which Neẓiv was referring in the

---

Yeḥezkel Landau (*Mar'eh Yeḥezkel*) come to press.

22 As in *BH* be-Shalah, 172, where a reference is given to the fifth volume of *Meshiv Davar*. As attested to by Neẓiv in a statement printed in the beginning of *Meshiv Davar*, this work, a collection of his responsa, only came into being during the last year of Neẓiv's life, and was published a year after his death. Furthermore, the fifth volume is a collection of various letters, responsa, and other short writings of Neẓiv published for the first time in 1993. Thus, the parenthetical reference must have been inserted by the editor.

23 For the moment, I am not factoring in my earlier suggestion that part of the *Sifre* commentary was lost since the editors of *Birkat ha-Neẓiv* make a similar suggestion regarding the *Mekhilta'* commentary, and, although a discovery of the texts might prove us wrong, at present we can consider each of the missing pieces to factor each other out.

1861 passage found in *Ha'amek She'elah* looked much like the brief notes found in the printed edition of *Torat Kohanim*. The lengthy commentary on *Mekhilta'* printed under the name *Birkat ha-Neẓiv*, however, is, in great measure, the product of Neẓiv's later years.

The notion that the printed text of *Birkat ha-Neẓiv* is not the same as the work mentioned by Neẓiv as a product of his youth is further solidified by the editors of the printed text themselves. For, over the length of the commentary, they make reference to three different versions of the commentary which they have before them. One is the source of the core text, one they refer to as "*mahadurah tinyana*'" or the second edition,[24] and one is referred to by the acronym "*mem-heh-daled-vav-aleph*" meaning either "last edition" or "another edition."[25] Unfortunately, the editors provide no indication as to whether the printed text includes everything found in all three editions or whether they only chose to include a few passages from the earlier editions, but it is sufficiently clear that what is printed in *Birkat ha-Neẓiv* is not simply the explanations of "a few *beraiytot*" composed in Neẓiv's youth and referred to in *Ha'amek She'elah*.

Another indicator of *Birkat ha-Neẓiv*'s late composition are its references to Neẓiv's other works. With great consistency throughout the work, Neẓiv refers the readers of his *Mekhilta'* commentary to his commentary on *Sifre*.[26] While we noted above that not all of the references found in the printed text can be safely attributed to Neẓiv, there is no question that comments such as "I already wrote in *Sifre* "[27] or "In *Sifre* Be-ha'alotekha *piska'* 34 it expounds *'al ha-mizbeaḥ'*...and there I explained the matter with the help of Heaven" most certainly stem from the hand of Neẓiv himself. Since *'Emek ha-Neẓiv* contains numerous citations of *Mekhilta'* yet no references to Neẓiv's commentary thereon, we can safely assume that the composition of *Birkat ha-Neẓiv* followed that of *'Emek ha-Neẓiv*.

A similar argument can be made from the references in *Birkat ha-*

---

24 *BH* Bo, 19; *BH* Bo, 25; *BH* Bo, 64; *BH* Bo, 72; *BH* Bo, 89; *BH* Bo, 97; *BH* be-Shalah, 102; *BH* be-Shalah 114; *BH* be-Shalah 127; *BH* be-Shalah 156; *BH* be-Shalah 164; *BH* be-Shalah 180; *BH* be-Shalah 183; *BH* Yitro, 221.

25 *BH* be-Shalah, 188; *BH* Yitro, 246.

26 *BH* Bo, 4; *BH* Bo 9; *BH* Bo 14; *BH* Bo 18; *BH* Bo 29; *BH* Bo 39; *BH* Bo 46; *BH* Bo 51; *BH* Bo 55; *BH* Bo 58; *BH* Bo 69; *BH* Bo 71; *BH* Bo 92; *BH* Bo 97; *BH* be-Shalah, 135; *BH* be-Shalah, 157; *BH* be-Shalah, 172; *BH* be-Shalah, 176; *BH* be-Shalah, 177; *BH* be-Shalah, 197; *BH* Yitro, 201; *BH* Yitro 211; *BH* Yitro 214; *BH* Yitro 223; *BH* Yitro 225; *BH* Yitro 228; *BH* Yitro 229; *BH* Yitro 232; *BH* Yitro 233; *BH* Yitro 244; *BH* Yitro 252; *BH* Mishpatim, 263; *BH* Mishpatim 279; *BH* Mishpatim 293; *BH* Mishpatim 299; *BH* Mishpatim 317; *BH* Mishpatim 319; *BH* Yitro, 252.

27 *BH* Bo, 39.

*Neẓiv* to *Ha'amek She'elah*.[28] Once again, comments such as "I have already settled [the matter] in *Ha'amek She'elah* in the additions to the third volume, paragraph 111"[29] clearly come from Neẓiv and most probably date later than the 1867 publication of the third volume of *Ha'amek She'elah*. It is also worth noting that while Neẓiv does refer to his commentary on *She'iltot* in *'Emek ha-Neẓiv*, it is always referred to there as "my commentary on *She'iltot*" whereas in *Birkat ha-Neẓiv* it is almost always referred to by its proper name, *Ha'amek She'elah*.[30] In all probability, in the 1830s and 1840s as Neẓiv was composing both his *Sifre* commentary and beginning work on his *She'iltot* commentary, the latter work did not have a proper name. The name *Ha'amek She'elah* was probably given shortly before publication in 1861, and thus its citation in *Birkat ha-Neẓiv* as such further supports the late period of composition we are suggesting.

In fact, unlike *'Emek ha-Neẓiv* and *Ha'amek She'elah*, *Birkat ha-Neẓiv* even contains numerous references to *Ha'amek Davar*.[31] Here too, comments the likes of "as I wrote in *Ha'amek Davar* on many occasions"[32] and "as we already explained in *Ha'amek Davar*"[33] which come within the context of a larger discussion, cannot be attributed to later editorial insertions. By contrast, in the printed work of Neẓiv on *Torat Kohanim* there are only five references to *Ha'amek Davar*, all of which either stand alone as the only comment on a given passage or appear as an afterthought following a discussion.[34] Likewise, none of them are written in first person and thus one might well assume that they were inserted later by an editor. The references in the *Mekhilta'* commentary, on the other hand, seem

28 *BH* Bo, 25; *BH* Bo 30; *BH* Bo 42; *BH* Bo 48; *BH* Bo 50; *BH* Bo 51; *BH* Bo 54; *BH* Bo 60; *BH* Bo 65; *BH* Bo 80; *BH* Bo 91; *BH* be-Shalah, 124; *BH* be-Shalah 128; *BH* be-Shalah 144; *BH* be-Shalah 166; *BH* be-Shalah 171; *BH* be-Shalah 172; *BH* be-Shalah 173; *BH* be-Shalah 188; *BH* be-Shalah 192; *BH* Yitro, 203; *BH* Yitro 233; *BH* Yitro 237; *BH* Yitro 240; *BH* Yitro 241; *BH* Yitro 242; *BH* Yitro 247; *BH* Yitro 249; *BH* Mishpatim, 267; *BH* Mishpatim 269; *BH* Mishpatim 275; *BH* Mishpatim 290; *BH* Mishpatim 299; *BH* Mishpatim 311; *BH* Mishpatim 327; *BH* Mishpatim 333.

29 *BH* Mishpatim, 299.

30 *BH* Bo, 76, is an exception and may signify a vestige of Neẓiv's earlier work on *Mekhilta'*.

31 E.g., *BH* Bo, 2; *BH* Bo, 3; *BH* Bo, 13; *BH* Bo, 14; *BH* Bo, 24; *BH* Bo, 36; *BH* Bo, 37; *BH* Bo, 54; *BH* Bo, 56; *BH* Bo, 60; *BH* Bo, 79; *BH* Bo, 81; *BH* be-Shalah, 113; *BH* be-Shalah, 128; *BH* be-Shalah, 160 (HrD, HD); *BH* be-Shalah, 162; *BH* be-Shalah, 167; *BH* be-Shalah, 169 (HD; HrD); *BH* be-Shalah, 172; *BH* Yitro, 209; *BH* Yitro, 216; *BH* Yitro, 217 (*Kidmat ha-'Emek*); *BH* Yitro, 220; *BH* Yitro, 236; *BH* Mishpatim, 315.

32 *BH* Bo, 2.

33 *BH* Bo, 81.

34 Neẓiv's work on *Torat Kohanim* is printed in the back of *Birkat ha-Neẓiv* (Jerusalem, 1997). See *Shemini Mekhilta' de-Milu'im* 6 (17), 35 (18); *Shemini* 2: 2, 3: 6 (20); *'Emor* 4: 3 (35).

to be part of Neẓiv's own composition. While we need not go so far as to date *Birkat ha-Neẓiv* after the 1879 publication of *Ha'amek Davar,* these references do suggest that much of *Birkat ha-Neẓiv* was composed once a core text of *Ha'amek Davar* had been created and named, which leads us again to the 1860s and 1870s.

Dating *Birkat ha-Neẓiv* to the 1860s and 1870s makes it contemporaneous with *Ha'amek Davar*, thereby returning us to where we began. Despite the significant ways in which the commentary on *Sifre* which Neẓiv penned in his youth prepares the way for his later Torah commentary, in certain areas *Ha'amek Davar* represents a striking shift from the project of his youth. Many of the elements which set the Torah commentary apart from the *Sifre* commentary can be found in *Birkat ha-Neẓiv* as well, thus suggesting that the difference between the works is not attributable to a change in genre alone, but is in large part a testament to the general shift in exegetical approach and intellectual endeavor which Neẓiv underwent as he matured from the young student who composed *'Emek ha-Neẓiv* into the older *Rosh Yeshivah* who composed *Ha'amek Davar*.

# Bibliography


Alon, Menachem. *Jewish Law: History, Sources, Principles.* Translated by Bernard Auerbach and Melvin J. Sykes. Philadelphia: JPS, 1993.

Aronson, Chaim. *A Jewish Life Under the Tsars: The Autobiography of Chaim Aronson 1825-1888.* Translated by Norman Marsden. New Jersey: Allanheld, Osmun Publishers, 1983.

Asher, ha-Kohen. *Sefer Birkat Rosh.* Warsaw: Ts. Y. Bamberg, 1855.

Ashkenazi, David Mosheh Avraham ish Trevish. *Sefer Mirkevet ha-Mishnah.* Brooklyn, New York: Hayim Alter Lerner, 5673 [2003].

Ashkenazi, Moshe David. *Sifre 'im Perush Toldot Adam.* Jerusalem: Mosad ha-Rav Kook, 1972-1974.

Assaf Simḥah. *Mekorot le-Toldot ha-Ḥinukh be-Yisrael.* New York: Bet ha-Midrash le-Rabbanim be-Amerikah, 2001.

------. "*Sifriyot Batei Midrash,*" *Yad la-Kore* 1:7-9 (Nov./Dec. 1946-Jan. 1947): 170-172.

------. *Be-Ohalei Ya'akov.* Jerusalem: Mosad ha-Rav Kook, 1943.

Avraham ben Eliyahu of Vilna. *Be'er Avraham.* Warsaw: 1887.

------. *Midrash Agadat Bereshit.* Vilna: 1802.

------. *Rav Pe'alim: Meḥkar 'al kol Midreshe* HaZaL. Warsaw: 1884.

Avraham ben Eliyahu of Vilna. *Targum Avraham.* Jerusalem: 1896.

Bacon, Brenda. "Reflections on the Suffering of Rayna Batya and the Success of the Daughters of Zelophehad." *Nashim* 3 (2000):249-256.

Baḥya ben Asher. *Sefer Rabenu Baḥya: Be'ur 'al ha-Torah.* Korets, 1823-1827.

Bar Ilan, Meir. "Introduction to Ha'amek Davar." In *Ha'amek Davar*, edited by Hillel Cooperman. Jerusalem: 1981.

------. *Fun Volozhin biz Jerusalem.* New York: Oryom Press, 1933.

------. *Rabban Shel Yisrael.* New York: Histadrut ha-Mizrahi beAmerikah, 1943.

Bar-Ilan, Naftali. "Peirush Ha'amek Davar le-ha-Neẓiv z"l." *Afikei Neḥalim* III (1971): 119-125.

Baron, Salo W. *The Russian Jew Under Tsars and Soviets.* New York: The Macmillan Company, 1964.

------. "Azariah de' Rossi: A Biographical Sketch." In *History and Jewish Historians*, edited by Arthur Hertzberg and Leon Feldman, 167-173. Philadelphia: JPS, 1964.

Bartal, Israel. "Mordechai Aaron Gunzberg: A Lithuanian Maskil Faces Modernity." In *Profiles in Diversity*, edited by Frances Malino and David Sorkin. Detroit: Wayne State University Press, 1998.

------. "'True Knowledge and Wisdom': On Orthodox Historiography." *Studies in Contemporary Jewry* 10 (1994): 178–192.

------. The *Jews of Eastern Europe, 1772-1881.* Translated by Chaya Naor. Philadelphia: University of Pennsylvania Press, 2005.

------. "Messianism and Nationalism: Liberal Optimism vs. Orthodox Anxiety." *Jewish History* 20:1 (March, 2006): 5-17.

------. "Zikhron Ya'akov' le-R. Ya'akov Lipschitz: Historiografia Ortodoksit?" *Milet* 2 (1984): 409–414. (Hebrew)

Basser, Herbert W. *In the Margins of the Midrash: Sifre Ha'azinu Texts, Commentaries, and Reflections.* Atlanta: Scholars Press, 1990.

-------, ed. *Pseudo-Rabad: Commentary to Sifre Deuteronomy Edited and Annotated According to Manuscripts and Citations*. Atlanta: Scholars Press, 1994.

Behak, Yehudah. *Be'ur Ma'amar Ḥazal.* Brooklyn: 1993.

------. *Midrash Rabbah Esther.* Israel: 1964.

------. *Midrash Rabbah.* Vilna: 1855.

Ben Ezra, Akiva. *R' Pinḥas Mikha'el.* New York: Mokire Rabanan, 1953.

Benayahu, M. "The Polemic Regarding the *Me'or 'Einayim* of Azariah de' Rossi." *Asufot* 5 (Jerusalem, 1991): 213-265.

Ben-Sasson Ḥayyim Hillel, "Ishiyuto shel HaGRA ve-Hashpa'ato Ha-Historit." *Zion* 31 (1966).

Berdichevsky, Micah Yosef. "Bar Bei Rav." *Hameliz* 19 (1888).

------. "Olam HaAzilut." *Ha-Kerem* (Nov., 1887).

------. "'Megilat Shir HaShirim' shel HaNeẓiv." *Ha-Ẓefirah* (25 Tevet 5648 [1888]).

------. "Toldot Yeshivat Eẓ HaḤayyim." *He-'Asif* (1887).

Berlin, Ḥayyim. "Shikekhah u-Peah." *Bet Midrash* I (1888).

------. *Nishmat Ḥayyim:Ma'amarim u-Mikhtavim.* Jerusalem: Yeshivat Ḥayyim Berlin and Bet Midrash Paḥad Yiẓḥak, 2003.

Berlin, Isaiah ben Yehudah Loeb. *Mine targuma*, Vilna, 1836.

Berlin, Naftali Ẓvi Yehudah. *Iggerot ha-Neẓiv.* Jerusalem, 2003.

------. *Imrei Shefer.* Tel Aviv, 1960.

------. *Kidmat Ha'emek.* Jerusalem: Mosad Harav Kook, 1999.

------. *Meromei Sadeh.* Jerusalem: 1953-1959.

------. *Meshiv Davar.* Jerusalem: 1993.

------. *Oẓarot ha-Neẓiv*. Jerusalem: Ben Arzah, 2002.

------. *Rinah Shel Torah.* Jerusalem: Yeshivat Volozhin, 1999.

------. *She'ar Yisrael.* Jerusalem: Yeshivat Volozhin, 1999.

------. *Birkat ha-Neẓiv.* Jerusalem: Yeshivat Volozhin, 1997.

------. *Derashot ha-Neẓiv.* Jerusalem: Yeshivat Be'er Ya'akov, 1993.

------. *Emek HaNeẓiv.* Jerusalem: Va'ad li-Hotza'at Kitve Ha-Neẓiv, 1959-1961.

------. *Ha'amek Davar.* Jerusalem: Yeshivat Volozhin, 1999.

------. *Ha'amek She'elah.* Jerusalem: Mosad Harav Kook, 1999.

------. *Ḥiddushei ha-Neẓiv mi-Volozhin: Ḥiddushim u-Bi'urim 'al ha-Torat Kohanim.* Jerusalem: 1969.

Bet-Halevi, Israel D. *Rabbi Ẓvi Hirsch Chajes.* Tel Aviv: Achdut, 1955-56.

Bialik, Hayim Nahman. *Igrot Ḥayim Naḥman Bialik.* Tel Aviv: Devir, 1937-39.

Bialoblocki, Samuel. *'Em la-Masoret.* Tel Aviv: Bar Ilan University, 1971.

*The Bibliography of the Hebrew Book 1473-1960.* The Institute for Hebrew Bibliography. Yeshiva University Gottesman Library, New York. http://www.yu.edu/

Libraries/page.asp?id=246

Blau, Yosef, ed. *Lomdus: The Conceptual Approach to Jewish Learning*. Jersey City: Ktav Publishing House, 2006.

Bleich, Judith. *Jacob Ettlinger, His Life and Works the Emergence of Modern Orthodoxy in Germany*. Ph.D Thesis, New York University, 1974.

Blumenthal, Nachman, ed. *Sefer Mir*. Jerusalem: Encyclopedia of the Diaspora, 1962.

Bonfil, Robert, ed. *Kitvei Azariah min ha-'Adomim*. Jerusalem: The Bialik Institute, 1991.

Breuer, Edward. "Between Haskalah and Orthodoxy: The Writings of R. Ya'akov Ẓvi Meklenburg." *Hebrew Union College Annual* 66 (1995): 259-287.

------. "The Haskalah in Vilna: R' Yeḥezkel Feivel's Toldot Adam." *The Torah U'Maddah Journal*, vol. 7 (1997).

Breuer, Mordechai. *Ohole Torah: ha-Yeshivah, Tavnitah ve-Toldoteha*. Jerusalem: The Zalman Shazar Center, 2003.

Broda, Avraham. *Bayit ha-Gadol*. Vilna, 1838.

Brody, Myles S. *A Time to Keep Silent and A Time to Speak: Judicial Activism and Passivity in the Thought of Rabbi Ẓvi Hirsch Chajes*. A.B. Thesis, Harvard University, 2001.

Brody, Robert. *The Ge'onim of Babylonia and the Shaping of Medieval Jewish Culture*. New Haven: Yale University Press, 1998.

Brzezinski, A.J. *Rabi Eliyahu Ḥayyim Meisel*. Tel Aviv: 1957.

Budick, Sanford, and Geoffrey H. Hartman, eds. *Midrash and Literature*. New Haven: Yale University Press, 1986.

Bunimovitsh, David. *Mikhtav me-Eliyahu: Parashat Gedulat ha-Rav Eliyahu Levinzohn me-Kratingen*. Vilna: Sheraga Faivel Garber, 1901.

Canpanton, Isaac ben Jacob. *Darkhe ha-Gemara*. Petaḥ-Tikvah: Y. Kohen, 1964.

Chajes, Ẓvi Hirsch. *Igeret bikoret*. Pressburg: 1853.

------. *Kol Sifre Mahariẓ Ḥayyut*. Jerusalem: Divre Hakhamim, 1958.

Christman, Miriam Usher. *Lay Culture Learned Culture: Books and Social Change in Strasbourg*. New Haven: Yale University Press, 1982.

Clanchy, Michael T. "Looking Back from the Invention of Printing." In *Literacy in Historical Perspective*, edited by Daniel P. Resnick, 7-22. Washington, DC: Library of Congress, 1983.

Cohen, Chester G. *Shtetl Finder: Jewish communities in the 19th and early 20th centuries in the Pale of Settlement of Russia and Poland, and in Lithuania, Latvia, Galicia, and Bukovina, With Names of Residents*. Bowie, MD: Heritage Books, 1989.

Cohen, Israel. *Vilna*, 2nd ed. Philadelphia: JPS, 1992.

Cooperman, Hillel. *Mafteaḥ Inyanim le-Peirush Ha'amek Davar 'Al ha-Torah*. Jerusalem: 1981.

David ben Moshe of Novogroduk, *Galya Masekhet*. Vilna, 1844.

David, Bruria Hutner. *The Dual Role of Rabbi Ẓvi Hirsch Chajes: Traditionalist and Maskil*, Ph.D Thesis, Columbia University, 1971.

de' Rossi, Azariah. *Kitvei Azariah min ha'Adomim*. Edited by Robert Bonfil. Jerusalem: The Bialik Institute, 1991.

------. *The Light of the Eyes*. Translated and edited by Joanna Weinberg. New Haven: Yale University Press, 2001.
Dembitzer, Ḥayyim Nathan. *Sefer Kelilat Yofi*. Jerusalem: 1989.
Druk, D. "Ha-Ga'on R' Yaakov Ẓvi Mecklenberg." *Horev* 7-8 (1938).
Dubnow, Simon. *History of the Jews in Russia and Poland From the Earliest Times Until the Present Day*. Philadelphia: JPS, 1918.

Edel, Yehudah Leib. *'Afike Yehudah*. Lemburg: 1802.
------. *Kuntrus ha-Pe'alim be-Shem Safah le-Ne'emanim*. Lemberg: 1793.
------. *Mayyim Tehorim*. Bialystok: 1817.
------. *Mei Niftoaḥ*. Bialystok: 1816.
Edelman, S.R. *Ha-Tirosh*. Warsaw: 1881.
Einhorn, Ze'ev Wolf ben Israel Isser. "Perush haMeharzo." In *Midrash Rabbah*. Vilna: 1855.
------ *Baraita de-Sheloshim u-Shetayim Middot de-Rabbi Eliezer beno Shel Rabbi Yosi ha-Galili*. Tel Aviv: Zion, 1969.
------. *Midrash pesikta rabati de-Rav Kahana*. Breslau: 1831.
------. *Midrash Tana'im*. Vilna: 1838.
Eisenstadt, Benzion. *Rabane Minsk ve-Ḥakhameha*. Israel: 1969.
Eisenstein, Elizabeth. *The Printing Press as an Agent of Change*. New York: Cambridge University Press, 1979.
Eisenthal, A. "Mishnat HaNeẓiv." *Ereẓ Ẓvi* (1989): 71-89.
Elboim, Yaakov. *Le-Havin Divre Ḥakhamim : Mivḥar Divre Mavo le-Agadah u-le-Midrash, mi-shel Ḥakhme Yeme ha-Benayim*. Jerusalem: Mosad Bialik, 2000.
Eliach, Yaffa. *There Once Was a World*. Boston: Little, Brown, and Co., 1998.
Eliakh, Dov ben David Ẓvi. *Avi Ha-Yeshivot*. Jersualem: Mekhon Moreshet Ha-Yeshivot, 1990.
------ . *Sefer Ha-Ga'on*. Jerusalem: Moreshet HaYeshivot, 2001.
Eliakim, Nissim. *Ha'amek Davar la-Neẓiv*. Moreshet Yaakov, 2003.
Eliasberg, Mordecai. *Ha-Rav Mordekhai Eliasberg*. Tel Aviv: 1947.
Eliyahu ben Shelomoh of Vilna. *Aderet Eliyahu*. Dubrovno: 1804.
------. *Avot de-Rabbi Natan*. Vilna: 1833.
------. *Be'urei ha-GRA* on *Shulḥan Arukh, OH*. Shklov: 1803.
------. *Be'urei ha-GRA* on *Shulkḥan Arukh, EH*. Vilna: 1819.
------. *Be'urei ha-GRA* on *Shulkḥan Arukh, YD*. Grodno: 1806.
------. *Divre ha-Yamim*. Grodno: 1820.
------. *Eliyahu Rabba*. Brno: 1802.
------. *Hagahot* on *Mishanyot*. Grodno: 1818.
------. *Mekhilta 'im Hagahot ha-Gera*. Vilna: 1844.
------. *Shenot Eliyahu*. Lemburg: 1799.
------. *Sifre: Ba-midbar, Devarim 'im Hagahot Meyuḥasot le-Eliyahu mi-Vilna*. Jerusalem: 1974.
------. *Sifre: Bamidbar, Devarim 'im Hagahot Meyuḥasot le-Eliyahu mi-Vilna*. Jerusalem: 1974.

------. *Taharat ha-Kodesh*. Zholkva: 1804.

Epstein J.N. *Introduction to Tannaitic Literature: Mishna, Tosephta and Halakhic Midrashim* (Hebrew). Edited by E.Z. Melamed. Jerusalem: Magnes Press, 1957.

Epstein, Barukh ha-Levi. *Mekor Barukh*. Vilna: 1928.

Epstein, Yehudah Yudil ha-Levi. *Minḥat Yehudah*. Jerusalem: H. Wagshal, 1989.

Epstein, Zalman. *Kitve Zalman Epshtayn*. St. Petersburg: Joseph Luria, 1904.

Etkes, Immanuel. "Le-She'elat Mevasrei ha-Haskalah be-Mizrah Europah." *Tarbiẓ* 57 (1987):95-114. [Reprinted in *Ha-Dat ve-ha-Ḥayyim: Tenu'at ha-Haskalah ha-Yehudit be-Mizraḥ Eropah*. Edited by Immanuel Etkes, 25-44. Jerusalem, 1993.]

-------. "Shitato u-Pa'alo shel R' Ḥayyim mi-Volozhin ke-Teguvat ha-Hevrah ha-Mitnagdit la-Hasidut." *PAAJR* XXXVIII-XXXIX (1972): 1-45.

------. "Immanent Factors and External Influences in the Development of the Haskalah Movement in Russia." In *Toward Modernity: The European Jewish Model*, edited by Jacob Katz, 13-32. New Brunswick: Transaction Publishers, 1987.

------. "Introduction To Photographic Reprint." *Te'udah be-Yisrael*. Jerusalem: 1977.

------. *Lita be-Yerushalayim*. Jerusalem: Yad Yitshak ben Ẓvi, 1991.

------. "Marriage and Torah Study among the Lomdim in Lithuania in the Nineteenth-century." In *The Jewish Family: Metaphor and Memory*, edited by David Kramer, 153-178. Oxford: Oxford University Press.

------. *Rabbi Israel Salanter and the Mussar Movement: Seeking the Torah of Truth*. Philadelphia: JPS, 1993.

------. *The Ga'on of Vilna: The Man and His Image*. Translated by Jeffrey M. Green. Berkeley: University of California Press, 2002.

------, ed. *Mosad Ha-Yeshivah*. Jerusalem: 1989.

------, ed. *Ha-Dat Ve-ha-Ḥayyim: Tenu'at ha-Haskalah be-Mizrah Eiropa*. Jerusalem: The Zalman Shazar Center, 1993.

Etkes, Immanuel, and Shlomo Tikochinsky, eds. *Yeshivot Lita: Pirkei Zikhronot*, Jerusalem: The Zalman Shazar Center, 2004.

Ezekiel Feivel ben Ze'ev Wolf, *Toldot 'Adam*. St. Louis: N. Rubinson, 1926.

------. *Biur Maharif* in *Midrash Rabbah*. Vilna: 1885.

Febvre, Lucien. *The Coming of the Book: The Impact of Printing 1450-1800*. Translated by David Gerard. London: Verso, 1990.

Feigenson, Shmuel Shraga. "Le-Toldot Defus Romm." In *Yahadut Lita*, Vol. 1. Tel Aviv: 'Am Ha-Sefer, 1959.

Feiner, Shmuel. *The Jewish Enlightenment*. Translated by Chaya Naor. Philadelphia: University of Pennsylvania Press, 2002.

Feinstein, Aryeh Loeb. *'Ir Tehilah: ha-Korot le-'Adat Yisrael she-be-'Ir Brisk*. Warsaw, 1886.

Finkelstein, Louis. *Sifra on Leviticus*, vol. 1. New York: Jewish Theological Seminary, 1989.

Fishbane, Michael A. *The Exegetical Imagination: On Jewish Thought and Theology*. Cambridge, MA: Harvard University Press, 1998.

Fishman, David E., *Russia's First Modern Jews: The Jews of Shklov*. New York: New York University Press, 1995.

Fraade, Steven D. *From Tradition to Commentary: Torah and its Interpretation in the Midrash Sifre to Deuteronomy*. Albany: State University of New York Press, 1991.

Frank, Tanhum. *Toldot Bet ha-Shem be-Volozhin*. Jerusalem: 2001.

Friedberg, Ch. B. *Bet Eked Sepharim*, 2nd ed. Tel Aviv: 1952.

------. *Ha-Defus ha-'Ivri be-Polaniyah*. Tel Aviv: 1950.

Friedenstein, Shimon Eliezer. *Sefer 'Ir Giborim: Korot 'Ir Hor'odna'*. Israel: 1969.

Fuenn, S. J. "Dor dor ve-dorshav" in *Hakarmel* 4 (1879).

------. *Keneset Yisrael*. Warsaw: 1886.

------. *Me-Haskalah Loḥemet le-Haskalah Meshameret*. Edited by Shmuel Feiner. Jerusalem: Merkaz Dinur, 1993.

------. *Kiriah Ne'emanah*. Vilna: 1915.

Ginzberg, Louis. *Students, Scholars and Saints*. Philadelphia: JPS, 1928.

Glenn, Menahem G., *Israel Salanter, Religious-Ethical Thinker: The Story of a Religious-Ethical Current in Nineteenth-century Judaism*. New York: Bloch Publishing Co., 1953.

Goitein, Barukh. *Kesef Nivḥar*. Jerusalem: 1997.

Gold, Leonard Singer, ed. *A Sign and a Witness*. New York: New York Public Library and Oxford University Press, 1988.

Goldberg, Jacob. *Jewish Privileges in the Polish Commonwealth*, vol. I. Jerusalem: The Israel Academy of Sciences and Humanities, 1985.

Goldberg, Hillel, *Israel Salanter: Text, Structure, and Idea*. New York: Ktav Publishing House, 1982.

Goldin, Judah. *Studies in Midrash and Related Literature*. Edited by Barry L. Eichler and Jeffrey H. Tigay. Philadelphia: JPS, 1988.

Gotlober, A.B. *Zikhronot u-Masa'ot*. Edited by R. Goldberg. Jerusalem: 1976.

Grafton, Anthony T. "The Importance of Being Printed." *Journal of Interdisciplinary History* 11 (1980): 265-86.

------. *Defenders of the Text: The Traditions of Scholarship in an Age of Science, 1450-1800*. Cambridge, MA: Harvard University Press, 1991.

Gries, Ze'ev. *Sefer Sofer, ve-Sipur bi-Reishit ha-Ḥasidut*. Israel: ha-Kibutz ha-meyuhad, 1992.

------. *Sifrut ha-Hanhagot*. Jerusalem: Mosad Bialik, 1989.

Guenzburg, Mordecai Aaron. *Aviezer: Sefer Toldot 'Ish Ram ha-Ma'alah*. Vilna: Sh. Y. Fin [ve-] T. Rozenkrants, 1863.

------. *Devir*. Vilna: M. Man, 1844-1864.

*Haggadah shel Pesah 'im Peirushim Yikarim ve-Neḥmadim me-Rabanei Geonei k"k Vilna*. Vilna, 1877.

Halamish, Moshe, et al, eds. *Ha-GRA u-Bet Midrasho*. Ramat Gan: Bar Ilan University Press, 2003.

Halbertal, Moshe. *Mahapekhot Parshaniyot be-Hithavutan*. Jerusalem: Magnes Press, 1997.

Halevi, Aharon. *Sefer Mateh Aharon*. Saloniki: Betsalel ha-Levi Ashkenazi, 1820.

Halperin, Israel, ed. *Pinkas Va'ad 'Arba' 'Araẓot*. Jerusalem: Bialik Institute, 1945.
------. "The Council of Four Lands and the Hebrew Book." *Kiryat Sefer* 9 (1932).
------. "*Va'ad 'Arba' 'Araẓot be-Polin ve-ha-sefer ha-'Ivri*," in *Yehudim ve-Yahadut be-Mizrah Eiropah*. Jerusalem: 1968.
*Ha-Maggid*. Lyck. Sept. 12, 1861-May 20, 1863.
Ḥanokh Zundel ben Yosef. "'Eẓ Yosef, 'Anaf Yosef." In *Midrash Tanḥuma*. Vilna: 1833.
------. "Eẓ Yosef", "'Anaf Yosef," "Yad Yosef." In *Midrash Rabbah* vol. 1. Israel: Wagshal, 2001.
------. *Commentary on Midrash Tanḥuma*. Stettin: 1833.
------. *Commentary on Midrash Shmuel*. Stettin: 1860.
------. *Commentary on Seder 'Olam*. Stettin: 1845.
------. *Midrash Rabbah of the Five Megillot*. Vilna and Grodno, 1829-34; 2nd ed. Vilna: 1845.
------. *Mivḥar Mi-Peninim*. Warsaw: 1870.
Harris, Jay M. *How Do We Know This Midrash and the Fragmentation of Modern Judaism*. Albany: SUNY Press, 1995.
------. *Nachman Krochmal: Guiding the Perplexed of the Modern Age*. New York: New York University Press, 1991.
Hayes, Christine Elizabeth. *Between the Babylonian and Palestinian Talmuds*. New York: Oxford University Press, 1997.
Ḥayyim Avraham ben Aryeh Leib. "Pat Leḥem." In *Ḥovot ha-Levavot*. Shklov: 1803.
Herskovics, Meir. *Maharatz Chajes: Toldot Rabbi Ẓvi Hirsch Chajes u-Mishnatto*. Jerusalem: Mosad Harav Kook, 1972.
Hoffmann, David Ẓvi. *Zur Enleitung in die halachischen Midraschim*. Berlin: M. Driesner, 1886–87. [Translated as "Le-heker Midrashei ha-Tana`im," in *Mesilot le-Torat ha-Tanaim*. Edited by A.Z. Rabinowitz. Tel Aviv: 1928.]
Horovitz, Saul. *Siphre D'be Rab*. Leipzig: 1917.
Horowitz Rivka, *Controversies Surrounding the Life, Work and Legacy of Rabbi Yisrael Salanter*. MA thesis, Touro College, 1993.
Hundert, Gershon David. "The Library of the Study Hall in Volozhin, 1762; Some Notes on the Basis of a Newly Discovered Manuscript." *Jewish History* 14:2 (2000): 225-244.
------. *Jews in Poland Lithuania in the Eighteenth-century: A Genealogy of Modernity*. Berkeley: University of California Press, 2004.
Hurvits, E. L., and S. J. Feunn. *Pirhei Ẓafon*. Vilna: 1841 and 1844.

Ibn Ḥayyim, Aaron. *Sefer Korban Aharon*. Desoya: 1742.
Ibn Nagrela, Samuel. *Mevo ha-Talmud*. Bat-Yam: Sh. Kohen-Duras, 1992.
Isaacs, M., "Ha-Ẓava ve-ha-Milhamah be-Mishnat ha-Neẓiv." *MiZohar LaZohar* (1984): 9-21.
Ish Shalom, Meir. *Sifre de-ve Rav: 'Im tosafot Me'ir 'Ayin; ḥelek rishon*. Vienna: 1864.

Jacobs, Irving. *The Midrashic Process: Tradition and Interpretation in Rabbinic Judaism*. Cambridge: Cambridge University Press, 1995.

Jacobs, Louis. *Studies in Talmudic Logic and Methodology*. London: Vallentine, Mitchell, 1961.

Jaffe, Mordecai Gimpel. *Zikhronot Mordecai* in *Mivḥar Ketavim*. Jerusalem: 1978.

-------. *Beur ha-Ram me-iti Aharon Mosheh Padoa mi-Karlin; ve-nilveh elav tosefet beurim ve-hagahot me-et Mordekhai Gimpel*. Jerusalem: H. Wagshal, 1986.

Jaffe, Mordecai Gimpel. *Tikhelet Mordekhai*. Jerusalem: 1954.

*Jewish Encyclopedia*. New York: 1901-1906.

Joseph, Howard. "'As Swords Thrust Through the Body': Neẓiv's Rejection of Separatism." *Edah Journal* 1:1 (2000).

------. *Why Anti-Semitism: A Translation of "The Remnant of Israel"* New Jersey: Jason Aronson, 1996.

Jung, Leo, ed. *Jewish Leaders 1750-1940*. New York: Bloch Publishing, 1953.

------. *Guardians of Our Heritage*, 1724-1953. New York: Bloch Publishing, 1958.

Kagan, Israel Meir Ha-Kohen. *Torat Kohanim*. Piotrkow: M. Tsederboim, 1911.

Kamelhar, Moshe. *Rabi Dov Ber Maizelsh*. Jerusalem: Mosad Ha-Rav Kook, 1970.

Kaplan, Ẓvi . "Le-Darko shel rabi Ḥayyim mi-Volozhin ba-halakhah." In *Me-Olamah Shel Torah*, 9-43. Jerusalem: 1974.

Karlinski, Ḥayyim. *Ha-Rishon Le-Shoshelet Brisk*. Jerusalem: Mekhon Yerushalayim, 1984.

Kats, Hannah. *Mishnat ha-Neẓiv*. Israel, 1990.

Katz, Dov. *Rabbi Yisrael me-Salant*. Jerusalem: ha-Histadrut ha-Tsiyonit ha-Olamit, 1974.

Katz, Jacob."Jewish Civilization as Reflected in the Yeshivot: Jewish Centers of Higher Learning." *JWH* 10 (1967): 674-704.

Katz, Maidi. "Secular Studies at the Volozhin Yeshiva." In *Jewish Legal Writings by Women*, edited by Micah D. Halpern and Chana Safrai. Jerusalem: Urim Publications, 1998.

Katzenellenbogen, Ẓvi Hirsch. *Netivot 'Olam*. Vilna, 1832.

Klausner, Israel. *Vilna: Yerushalayim de-Lita*. Israel: Ghetto Fighter's House, 1988.

------. *Toldot Ha-Kehilah Ha-'ivrit bi-Vilnah*. Israel: 1969.

Kluger, Yehudah Aaron. *Toldot Shelomoh*. Jerusalem: Ma'ayan ha-Hokhmah, 1955.

Kobrin, Rebecca and Don Seeman. "'Like One of the Whole Men': Learning, Gender and Autobiography in R. Barukh Epstein's *Mekor Barukh*." *Nashim* 2 (1999): 52-94.

Kook, Avraham Yiẓḥak. "*Rosh Yeshivat Eẓ Ḥayyim*." In *Kenesset Yisrael*, edited by S.J. Finn, 138-147. Warsaw, 1888.

------. "*Ẓvi La-Ẓadik*." *Maḥzike Ha-Das* 8 (1886).

Kotik, Yeḥezkel. *Journey to a Nineteenth-Century Shtetl: The Memoirs of Yeḥezkel Kotik*. Edited by David Assaf. Detroit: Wayne State University Press, 2002.

Kupman, Y. "'Et Milhamah le'umat 'Et Shalom al pi ha-Neẓiv." *Merhavim* 1 (1990): 285-297.

Lamm, Norman. *Torah Lishmah: Torah for Torah's Sake in the Works of Rabbi Ḥayyim of Volozhin and his Contemporaries*. New York: Yeshiva University Press, 1989.

Landau, Yiẓḥak Eliyahu. *Aḥarit ha-Shalom*. Vilna: 1871.
------. *Derekh Ḥayyim*. Vilna: 1872.
------. *Derushim le-Kol Ḥefzehem*. Vilna: 1871-77.
------. *Dover Shalom*. Warsaw: 1863.
------. *Evel Kaved*. Eydtkuhnen: 1873.
------. *Kiflayim le-Toshiyyah* [Joel]. Jitomir: 1865.
------. *Kiflayim le-Toshiyyah* [Psalms]. Warsaw: 1866.
------. *Kol Sha'on*. Vilna: 1872.
------. *Lishmo'a ba-Limudim*. Vilna: 1876.
------. *Ma'aneh Eliyahu*. Vilna: 1840.
------. *Mekhilta 'im Be'ur Berurei ha-Middot*. Vilna: 1844.
------. *Mikra' Soferim*. Suvalk: 1862.
------. *Patshegen ha-Dat*. Vilna: 1870.
------. *Patshegen*. Vilna: 1858.
Leoni, Eliezer, *Sifra shel ha-'Ir ve-Shel Yeshivat "Eẓ Ḥayyim."* Tel Aviv: Ha-Irgun shel bene Volozin be-Medinat Yisrael u-ve-'Araẓot ha-Berit, 1970.
Levin, Yehoshua Heschel. *Haggahot on the Midrash Rabbah*. Vilna: 1843.
------. *Ma'ayne Yehoshu'a*. Vilna: 1858.
Levin, Yehudah Leib. *Rabi Ayyzel Ḥarif*. Jerusalem: Mosad Harim Levin, 1982.
------. "Zikhronot ve-Ra'ayanot." In *Sefer ha-yovel huval le-shai Nahum Sokolow*, 354-367. Warsaw: 1934.
Levinsohn, Yiẓḥak Baer. *Bet Yehudah*. Vilna: 1839.
Levisohn, Joshua M. *The Early Vilna Haskalah and the Search for a Modern Jewish Identity*. PhD Thesis, Harvard University, 1999.
Lewin-Epstein, Elias Wolf. *Zikhronotai*. Tel Aviv: Ha-'Aḥim Levin Epshtain, 1932.
Lichtstein, Abraham Yekutiel Zalman ben Moses Joseph. *Zera' Avraham*. Dyhernfurth: 1811 and 1819.
Lifshitz, H. "HaNeẓiv ViYehuso LiYeshuv Erez Yisrael." *Kotleinu* 13 (1990): 559-563.
Lifshitz, Yaakov Ha-Levi. *Sefer Toldot Yiẓḥak*. Warsaw: 1896.
------. *Zikhron Ya'akov*. Kovno: 1924.
Lilienblum, M.L. *Ḥata'ot Ne'urim*. Jerusalem: 1970.
------. *Ketavim Autobiografiyim*. Edited by Shlomo Breiman. Jerusalem: Mosad Bialik, 1970.
Lilienthal, Max. *Max Lilienthal, American Rabbi: Life and Writings*. Edited by David Philipson. New York: The Bloch Publishing Company, 1915.
Lincoln W. Bruce. *Nicholas I: Emperor and Autocrat of All the Russias*. DeKalb, IL: Northern Illinois University Press, 1989.
Lipman, David Matityahu. *Toldot he-'Arim Kovna' ve-Slabodka' ve-Gedolehen*. Israel: 1968.
Litvin, Joseph. "Naphtali Tzevi Berlin (the NEẓiv)." In *Men of the Spirit*, edited by Leo Jung. New York: Kymson Publishing Co., 1964.
Livni, David. *Jerusalem de-Lita*. Tel Aviv, 1929.
Lowenstein, Leopold. Index Approbationum. Frankfurt am Main: J. Kauffmann, 1923.
Luria, David ben Yehudah. *Sefer She'elot u-teshuvot Radal*. Tel Aviv: Y. A. Landa, 1967.

------. *Teshuvot ha-Ge'onim*. Leipzig: 1868.
------. "Peirush Radal." *Midrash Rabbah*. Vilna: 1843-45.
------. "Peirush Radal." *Pesikta Rabbati*. Warsaw: 1893.
------. *Agadot Shmuel*. Warsaw: 1851.
------. *Kadmut Sefer Ha-Zohar*. Koenigsberg: 1856.
------. *Midrash Pesikta Rabati de-Rav Kahana*. Warsaw: 1893.
------. *Sefer Kitve ha-Ga'on R. David Luria, zaẓal*. Jerusalem: 1990.
------. *Sefer Pirke De-Rabbi Eliezer*. Warsaw: 1852.
Luria, Ḥanokh Zundel ben Yeshayahu. *Kenaf Renanim*. Kratashin: 1842.

Maggid, Shelomoh Zev. *Mussar ve-Da'at*. Vilna: 1868.
Maimon, Yehudah Leib. *Toldot Ha-Gera*. Jerusalem: Mosad Ha-Rav Kook, 2000.
Malachi ben Ya'akov, ha-Kohen. *Sefer Yad Malakhi*. New York: Hotsa'at Sifre Kodesh "Mishor", 2001.
Malakhi, A.R. "Pa'alo ha-Safruti shel R. Naftali Ẓvi Yehudah Berlin." *Jewish Book Annual* 25 (1967-68): 233-238.
Malbim, Meir Leibush. *Ha-Torah ve-ha-Miẓvah*. Warsaw: 1874-80.
Malbim, Meir Leibush. *Mikra'e Kodesh*. Warsaw: 1874.
Margolies, Morris B. *Samuel David Luzzatto, Traditionalist Scholar*. New York: Ktav Publishing House, 1979.
Margoliot, Ḥayyim Zalman. *Dubna' Rabati: Toldot Ha-'ir Dubna'*. Israel: 1968.
Mark, Jacob. *Bi-Meḥitẓatam shel Gidolei Yisrael* [Gegoylim fun unzere Zayt]. Translated by Shmuel Hagi. Jerusaelm: Gevil, 1968.
Maskilieson, Avraham. *Be'er Avraham*. Vilna: 1844.
Melamed, Ben-Zion. *Vilna*. Tel Aviv: Moreshet, 1983.
Menkes, Mordekhai. *Sefer Tekhelet Mordekhai*. Jerusalem: 1903.
Me-Slonim, Avraham. *Be'er Avraham* [Mekhilta' de-Rabi Yishma'el]. Jerusalem: Yeshivat Bet Avraham--Slonim, 1985.
Miller, Israel David. *Sefer Toldot Menakhem*. New York: 1954.
Mirsky, Samuel Kalman, ed. *Mosdot Torah be-Eropah be-Vinyanam u-ve-Ḥurbanam*. New York: Ogen, 1956.
Mohilever, Samuel. *Sefer Shmuel*. Edited by Judah Leib Fishman (Maimon). Jerusalem: 1923.
Montefiore, Moses. *Diaries of Sir Moses and Lady Montefiore*. Edited by Louis Loewe. London: Jewish Historical Society of England, 1983.

Nadav, Mordekhai. *Pinkas Patuaḥ*. Tel Aviv: Goldstein-Goren Center, 2003.
Nadler, Allan. *The Faith of the Mithnagdim*. Baltimore: Johns Hopkins University Press, 1997.
Nathanson, Marcus. *Kontres Ayyelet ha-Shaḥar* in "Pirhe Zafon," ii. 165-180.
Neriah, Moshe Ẓvi. *Toldot HaNeẓiv*. Tel Aviv: Yedide Bet Volozhin, 1943.
------. *Pirkei Volozhin*. Jerusalem: 1964.
Neugroschel, Z.A. "Behirat Am Yisrael BiMishnat HaNeẓiv MiVolozhin." *Talelei Orot* 6 (1995): 144-156.

Neusner, Jacob. *Sifre to Deuteronomy: An Analytical Translation*. Atlanta: Scholars Press, 1987.
------. *Sifre to Deuteronomy: An Introduction to the Rhetorical, Logical, and Topical Program*. Atlanta: Scholars Press, 1987.
------. *Sifre to Numbers: An American Translation and Explanation*. Atlanta: Scholars Press, 1986.

Olishinski, Moshe Zev. *Mi-Boker 'ad 'Erev: Autobiographiah*. Tel Aviv: Mizapeh, 1937.

Padua, Ya'akov Meir, *Mekor Mayyim Ḥayyim*. Sudlikov: 1836.
------. *Ketonet Pasim*. Koenigsburg: 1840.
Paperna, A.I. *Zikhroynes*. Warsaw: 1923.
Pelli, Moshe. *The Age of Haskalah: Studies in Hebrew Literature of the Enlightenment in Germany*. Leiden: E.J. Brill, 1979.
Perl, Gil S. "No Two Minds are Alike: Pluralism and Tolerance in the Work of Neẓiv." *Torah u-Madda Journal* 12 (2004): 74-98.
Perski, Yoel Dober Ha-Kohen me-Volozhin. *Bate Kehunah*. Vilna: 1871.
------. *Ḥayye Asaf*. Warsaw: 1858.
------. *Kevod Melakhim*. Books i, ii, Königsberg: 1851; books iii-xxi, Vilna: 1853.
------. *Shemen Ra'anan, Heikhal Ra'anan on Zayit Ra'anan*. Koenigsburg: 1857.
Pines, Y.M. *Kitve Yehiel Pines*. Jerusalem: 1934-38.
*Pirke Volozhin: Matayim Shanah le-Yisud 'Em ha-Yeshivot, Yeshivat Volozhin be-Shenat 563 'al Yede 'Avi ha-Yeshivot, Rabi Hayim me-Volozhin*. Efrat: Kolel Efrat shele-yad Bet ha-keneset Magen Avraham, 2003.
Posner, Raphael, and Israel Ta-Shema, eds. *The Hebrew Book: An Historical Survey*. New York: Leon Amiel, 1975.

Rabiner, Ze'ev Aryeh. "Mi-Pihem U-Mi-Pi Kitavam shel Talmidei HaNeẓiv." In *Or Mufla: Maran Ha-Rav Kook Zaẓal*. Tel Aviv: 1972.
------. *Sefer Ha-Rav Yaakov Mazeh*. Tel Aviv: Moreshet, 1958.
------. *Ha-Ga'on Rabi Eliezer Gordon* Zatsal. Tel Aviv: Z.A. Rabiner, 1968.
------. *Maran Rabenu Me'ir Simḥah Kohen*. Tel Aviv: 1963.
------. *Talile Orot*. Tel Aviv: Moreshet, 1955.
Rabinowitz, Dan. "Rayna Batya and Other Learned Women: A Reevaluation of Rabbi Barukh Halevi Epstein's Sources." *Tradition* 35:1 (Summer 2001): 55-69.
Rabinowitz-Teomim, Eliyahu David ben Benjamin. *Seder Eliyahu*. Jerusalem: Mosad Ha-Rav Kook, 1983.
Rappaport, Ẓvi Hirsch ha-Hohen. *'Ezrat Kohanim, Tosefet ha-'Azarah*. Vol.1, Vilna: 1845; Vol. 2, Zhitomir: 1866.
Reiner, Elhanan. "Temurot be-Yeshivot Polin ve-Ashkenz be-Meot ha-16-17 ve-Havikuah 'al ha-Pilpul." In *Ke-minhag Ashkenaz ve-Polin*, edited by Yisrael Bartal, et al. Jerusalem: Merkaz Zalman Shazar le-toldot Yisrael, 1993.
------. "The Ashkenazi Elite at the Beginning of the Modern Era: Manuscript Versus Printed Book." *Polin* 10 (1997): 85-98.
------. "The Attitude of Ashkenazi Society to the New Science in the Sixteenth

Century." *Science in Context* 10, 4 (1997): 589-603.
Reines, Moshe. *Sefer Dor ve-Ḥokhamav*. Cracow: Fischer, 1890.
Reines, Yiẓḥak Ya'akov.'*Urim Gedolim*. Vilna: Y.L. Mats, 1886.
*Reshimah shel Shemot Ha-ḥaverim li-Ḥevrat Mekiẓe Nirdamim 1865*-66. Lyck, 1866.
Riasanovsky, Nicholas. *Nicholas I and Official Nationality in Russia*. University of California Press, 1959.
Rivkind, Yiẓḥak. *Iggerot Ẓion*. Jerusalem: Hebrew Press, 1923.
Rosenfeld, B.Z. "Ben Ish le-Ishto al pi Peirush ha-Neẓiv BiParhsat Yiẓḥak ve-Rivkah." *Talelei Orot* 6 (1995): 216-236.
Rosenfeld, Moshe. *Ha-Defus ha-Ivri me-Reishito Ad Shenat 1948*. Jerusalem, 1992.
Rosenstein, Neil. *The Unbroken Chain*. New York: CIS Publishers, 1990.
Rosman, M.J. *The Lord's Jews: Magnate-Jewish Relations in the Polish-Lithuanian Commonwealth during the 18th Century*. Cambridge, MA: Harvard University Press, 1990.
Ruben, Bruce L. *Max Lilienthal: Rabbi, Educator, and Reformer in Nineteenth-Century America*. Ph.D Thesis, City University of New York, 1997.

Saiman, Chaim, "Legal Theology: The Turn to Conceptualism in Nineteenth-Century Jewish Law." *Journal of Law and Religion* 21 (2005-2006): 39-103.
Salmon, Yosef. *Religion and Zionism: First Encounters*. Jerusalem: Magnes Press, 2002.
Samson ben Isaac, of Chinon. *Sefer keritut*. Brooklyn: Y. Ts. H. Rothenberg, 1961.
Saperstein, Marc. "The Earliest Commentary on the Midrash Rabba." In *Studies in Medieval Jewish History and Literature*, edited by Isadore Twersky. Cambridge, MA: Harvard University Press, 1979.
------. *Decoding the Rabbis: A Thirteenth-Century Commentary on the Aggadah*. London: Harvard University Press, 1980.
Schacter, Jacob J. "Haskalah, Secular Studies and the Close of the Yeshiva in Volozhin in 1892." *Torah u-Madda Journal* 2 (1990): 76-133.
Scharfstein, Zevi. *Toldot HaḤinukh be-Yisrael Be-Dorot ha-Aḥronim*. New York: Ogen, 1945.
Scheinberger, Yosef. *Sefer 'Amudei 'Esh*. Jerusalem: 1954.
Scherschevski, Yehudah Yudel. *Kur la-Zahav*. Vilna: 1858-1866.
Schick, Avraham Ben Aryeh Löb. *'En Avraham*. Königsberg: 1848.
------. *'Eshed ha-Neḥalim*. Vilna: 1843.
------. "*Tahalukhot ha-Midrash*." In *Midrash Rabbah*. Vilna: 1843.
------. *Maḥazeh ha-Shir*. Warsaw: 1840.
------. *Zera' Avraham*. Vilna-Grodno: 1833.
------. *Tanna de-Bei Eliyahu, Rabba Zuta 'im Meore Esh*. Sudilkov: 1834.
Schick, Eliyahu Ben Benjamin. *'En 'Eliyahu on En Ya'akov*. Vilna: 1869-74.
Seeman, Don. "The Silence of Rayna Batya: Torah, Suffering, and Rabbi Barukh Epstein's 'Wisdom of Women'." *Torah u-Madda Journal* 6 (1995-1996): 91-128.
*Sefer Ma'aseh Gedolim*. Hotza'at Yosef Weiss, 1979.
Shabad, Avraham Ḥayyim. *Sefer Toldot Ha-Yamim*: *Ha-'ir Minsk vi-gidoleha*. Israel, 1968.
Shabtai of Horodok. *Sefer 'Emek Shaveh*. Brooklyn, NY: Ahim Goldenberg, 1998.

Shapira, Moshe Samuel. *Har-Rav Moshe Shmuel ve-Doro*. New York: 1964.
-----. *Toldot Rabenu Ḥayim mi-Volozhin*. Jerusalem: 1967.
------. *Ha-Rav Moshe Samuel ve-Doro*. New York: 1964.
Sharlo, Smadar. *Polmos ha-Mussar ha-Sheni:Ben Shitat ha-Mussar Shel ha-Rav Kook le-Shitato Shel R. Yisra'el mi-Salant*. MA thesis, Touro College, 1996.
*Shemuel David Lusato: Matayim Shanah le-Huladeto*. Edited by Reuven Bonfil, et al. Jerusalem: Magnes Press: 2004.
Shimoff, Ephraim. *Rabbi Yizḥak Elchanan Spektor: Life and Letters*. Jerusalem: Sura Institute for Research, 1959.
Shmuel ben Yosef ha-Levi of Bialostok. *Shut Bigdei Yesha'*. Vilna: 1844.
Shochat, Azriel. *'Im Ḥilufei Tekufot*. Jerusalem: 1960.
Shulvass, Moshe Avigdor. "Ha-Torah ve-Limudeha bi-Polin ve-Lita." In *Bet Yisrael Bi-Polin*, volume II, edited by Yehiel Halperin, 13-35. Jerusalem: 1954.
Siegel, Lester. *Historical Consciousness and Religious Tradition in Azariah de' Rossi's Me'or 'Einayim*. Philadelphia: JPS, 1989.
*Sifra de-ve Rav hu' Sefer Torat Kohanim*. Vienna: Y.H. Shlosberg, 1862.
*Sifra hu Torat Kohanim*. Warsaw: S. Orgelbrand, 1866.
Slutski, Avraham Yaakov. *Shivat Ẓion*. Be'er Shev'a: Ben Gurion University, 1988.
Solomon, Norman. *The Analytic Movement: Ḥayyim Soloveitchik and His Circle*. Atlanta: Scholars Press, 1993.
Soloveitchik, Haym. "Rupture and Reconstruction: The Transformation of Contemporary Orthodoxy." *Tradition* 28, 4 (1994): 90.
Sosland, Henry Adler. "Discovering the Neẓiv and his Ha'amaik Davar." *Judaism* 51:3 (2002):315-327.
Spero, Schubert. "The Neẓiv of Volozhin and the Mission of Israel." *Morasha* 2, 2 (1986): 1-14.
Spiegel, Ya'akov Samuel. *'Amudim be-Toldot ha-Sefer ha-'Ivri*, 2nd ed. Ramat Gan: Bar Ilan University Press, 2005.
Stampfer, Shaul. *Ha-Yeshivah ha-Lita'it be-Hithavhutah ba-Me'ah ha-Tesh'a-'Esreh*. Jerusalem: The Zalman Shazar Center, 1995.
------. *Shalosh yeshivot Lita'iyot ba-me'ah ha-tesh'a-'esreh*. PhD dissertation, Hebrew University, 1981.
Stanislawski, Michael. *For Whom Do I Toil? Judah Leib Gordon and the Crisis of Russian Jewry*. New York: Oxford University Press, 1988.
-----. *Tsar Nicholas I and the Jews: The Transformation of Jewish Society in Russia, 1825-1855*. Philadelphia: JPS, 1983.
Steinschneider, Hillel Noah Maggid.*'Ir Vilna*, Vol. I. Vilna: Ha-almanah veha-aḥim Rom, 1900.
------.*'Ir Vilna*, Vol. II. Edited by Mordechai Zalkin. Jerusalem: Magnes Press, 2002.
Stern, David. *Parables in Midrash: Narrative and Exegesis in Rabbinic Literature*. Cambridge, MA: Harvard University Press, 1991.
Strack, Hermann Leberecht. *Introduction to the Talmud and Midrash*. Translated by Markus Bockmuehl. Minneapolis: Fortress Press, 1992.
Strashun, Shmuel. "Peirush RaShaSh." In *Midrash Rabbah*. Vilna, 1843-45.

Ta-Shema, Israel, "Seder Hadpasatam Shel Ḥiddushei ha-Rishonim le-Talmud." *Kiryat Sefer* 50 (1975): 325-336.

------. "Peirush Ashkenazi-Zarfati Kadum le-Midrashei Bereishit ve-Vayikra Rabba Mekhilta ve-Sifre, be-Ketav Yad," *Tarbiz* 55, 1 (1985-89): 61-76

Tauber Aryeh, *Meḥkarim Bibliografiim*. Jerusalem: Hebrew University, 1932.

Tchernowitz, Ḥayyim. *Pirke Ḥayyim*. New York: 1953.

Tevil, David. *Naḥal 'Eitan*. Vilna: 1855.

------. *Naḥalat David*. Vilna: 1864.

------. *Bet David*. Warsaw: 1854.

Tikochinski , Shlomo, *The Approach to Study in 19th Century Lithuanian Yeshivot* (Hebrew). MA Thesis, Hebrew University, 2004.

Tosefa'ah, Samuel Abigdor. *Tana Tosfa'ah*. Vilna: 1837-1849.

Tsuriel, Moshe. *Oẓarot ha-Rav Neẓiv*. Bene Brak: Yahadut haTorah, 1996.

Twerski, Yohanan, and Yiẓḥak Zilbershlag, eds. *Sefer Turov*. Boston: Bet ha-Midrash le-Morim, 1938.

Twersky, Isadore. *Introduction to the Code of Maimonides*. New Haven: Yale University Press, 1980.

Tzinovitz, Moshe. *Eẓ Ḥayyim: Toldot Yeshivat Volozhin, Moreha, Ḥayyeha, Talmideha, v'Torateha*. Tel Aviv: Hotsa'at Mor, 1972.

Urbach, E.E. "Hevrat Mekize Nirdamim 1864-1964." In *Meḥkarim be-Ma'adei ha-Yahadut*, vol. 2 (1998): 816-828.

Vinograd, Yeshayahu. *Oẓar Sifre ha-GRA*. Jerusalem, 2003.

Volozhiner, Ḥayyim ben Yiẓḥak. *Nefesh HaḤayyim*. Edited by Binyamin Yehoshua Zilber. Jerusalem: 1983.

------. *She'elot u-Teshuvot Ḥut ha-Meshulash*. Vilna: Y. L. Lipman Mets, 5642, 1882.

Volozhiner, Samson. *Zikhron Shimshon*. Vilna, 1879.

Weiner, Y. "Mavet Moḥi—Da'at ha-Neẓiv me-Volozhin." *Asya*, 13 (3-4), 1996.

Weiss Halivni, David. *Peshat and Derash: Plain and Applied Meaning in Rabbinic Exegesis*. New York: Oxford University Press, 1991.

Weiss, Yiẓḥak Hirsch. *Mekhilta' 'im Perush Middat Soferim*. Vienna: Y.H. Shlosberg, 1865.

Wengeroff, Pauline. *Rememberings: The World of a Russian-Jewish Woman in the Nineteenth Century*. Translated by Henny Wenkart, edited by Bernard D. Cooperman. Bethesda: University of Maryland Press, 2000.

Wildmann, Yiẓḥak Eisik. *Magen ve-tsinah: Kadmut sefer ha-Zohar me-et David Lurya*. Bene Brak: Netsah, 1985.

Ya'akov of Karlin. *Kehilat Ya'akov*. Vilna: 1847.

------. *Mishkenot Ya'akov*. Vilna: 1837.

*Yahadut Lita*, eds. A Ya'ari et al. Tel Aviv: Hotza'at 'Am Ha-Sefer, 1984.

Yehiel Mihkel ben Ẓvi Hirsch. *Le-Zekher Yisrael*. Vilna: 1834.
Yehudah Loew ben Bezalel. *Sefer Be'er ha-Golah*. New York: Judaica Press, 1969.
Yiẓḥak of Karlin. *Keren Orah*. Vilna: 1851.

Zabludowski, Jehiel Michael Ben Ḥayyim. *Me Mikal*. Vilna: 1872.
------. *Mish'an Mayyim*. Vilna: 1861.
Zalkin, Mordekhai. *Ba-'alot ha-Shaḥar: ha-Haskalah ha-Yehudit be-'Imperiah ha-Rusit be-Me'ah ha-Tish'a 'Esreh*. Jerusalem: Magnes Press, 2000.
------. *Haskalat Vilna*. Jerusalem: Hebrew University, 1992.
------. *Me-Ginze Vilna: Te'udot Historiyot le-Toldot Yehude Lita'*. Be'er Sheva: Ben Gurion University, 2001.
Zevin Shelomoh Yosef, *Ishim Ve-Shitot*. Tel Aviv: Bitan Ha-sefer, 1952.
Zinsberg, Israel. *A History of Jewish Literature*, vols. VI-VIII. Edited and Translated by Bernard Martin. New York: Ktav Publishing House, 1976.
Zitron, Samuel Leib. "Milhemet dinastiyut be-yishvat Volozhin" in *Reshumot*, I (1925) 123-135.
Zunz, Leopold. *Ha-Derashot be-Yisrael ve-Hishtalshelutan ha-Historit*. Jerusalem: Mosad Bialik, 1954.

## Index

*'Agunot*, 103
*'Anaf Yosef*, 51, 93
*'asmakhta'*, 101-104, 188n87, 193, 206, 222n99, 263
Aaron ibn Ḥayyim, 43
Abraham, 123n84, 185, 192, 195, 196, 197-199, 204n45, 205, 235, 258
Abraham Schwadron collection, 19
*Aderet Eliyahu*, 131, 137-138, 139, 179
*Aesop's Fables*, 55, 88
*Afike Yehudah*, 50n41, 109
aggadic, 44, 45, 47, 49, 51, 52, 53, 85, 95, 101, 106, 107, 132, 146, 149, 159, 184, 192-193, 195-196, 202, 227, 228
*aggadot*, 46, 50n39, 62, 67, 95, 101, 115, 116, 119, 132, 192, 196, 224-225
Agus, Ḥayyim Yehudah, 29
*Akeidat Yiẓḥak*, 90, 157, 163, 164
Albo, Joseph, 84, 89, 156, 157
Alshekh, Moshe, 107, 108
amoraic, 42, 44, 46, 49, 97, 196
Aquinas, Thomas, 107
Aramah, Isaac, 84, 90, 148, 156
*Arba'ah Turim*, 142
Aronson, Chaim, 217-218
*Arukh ha-Shulḥan*, 14, 129, 130, 130n14
*Aseifat Zekeinim*, 163
Asheri, 142
Ashkenazi, Shmuel Yaffe (Yefeh To'ar), 43
Assaf, Simḥah, 20n48, 155
Augustine, 107, 165
*Les Aventures de Télémaque*, 54, 55n65, 88
*Avodat ha-Kodesh*, 162-164
*Avot de-Rabbi Natan*, 118, 138
Avraham ben David of Posquieres, 91
Avraham ben Eliyahu, 44
Azulai, Ḥayyim David, 107
Azulai, Yosef David, 80n103, 89

Baḥya ben Asher ben Ḥalāwah (Rabbeinu Bahya), 161-162, 164
Baḥya Ibn Paquda, 84
Bar-Ilan, Meir (son of subject), 11n4, 16n26, 20, 20n48-49, 21n51, 57, 174, 194, 203n44, 213
Baslavsky, Yom-Tov Lipman, 171, 207
*batei midrash*, 155, 158n107
*Bayit Ḥadash*, 142
*Be'er ha-Golah*, 108n41
Be-ha'alotekha, 95, 117, 118
Behak, Yehuda, 213
*Ben Aryeh*, 144
Benveniste, Yehoshua, 143
*Berayta*, 49, 77, 104n32, 141
*Berayta of the 32 Middot*, 36, 90
Berdyczewski, Mikha Yosef, 17
Berlin, Ḥayyim, 13, 20n48, 57, 207, 226, 227, 257-260
*Berurei ha-Middot*, 93, 131
*Bet Middot*, 156
*bet midrash*, 136-137, 155-156, 167, 214
Betu'el, 185
*Bet Yehudah*, 109
*Bet Yosef*, 142,
Bezalel ha-Kohen, 55, 171
Bil'am, 177
*Birkat ha-Neẓiv*, 19n47, 24, 29, 190n1, 262-268
The *Biur*, 85, 89, 175
Böhmer, Yisrael, 179
Böhmer, Yosef, 179
Bonfil, Robert, 108, 109, 126
Breuer, Edward, 110, 263n13
Brill, Yeḥiel, 218
Bunim, Simḥah, 60, 135

Caro, Yosef, 91, 107, 140, 142
Chajes, Ẓvi Hirsch, 222
Charlop, Zevulun, 33
Chmielnicki, Bogdan, 151
Claudius Ptolemaeus, 110

Danaan, Sa'adiah ibn, 81
Defour, Peter, 154
*de-rabbanan*, 100, 102, 103, 104, 125
de'Rossi, Azariah, 89, 105-111, 112-120, 121-126, 148, 161, 177, 178, 179, 180, 192, 193, 195, 208, 227, 228, 239
*de-'orayyta*, 100, 102, 103, 104n32, 125, 180n64
*derashah/derashot*, 99, 102, 103, 104, 115, 125, 126, 172, 181n67, 189, 222n99, 231, 232
*Derekh Ereẓ Zuta*, 94, 130
*Derekh Ḥayyim*, 94
*Divre Yehoshua*, 220
*Divre Yosef*, 32
Dubno, 45-47, 50, 53, 91n158, 135, 148

Edel, Yehudah Leib, 50, 51n41, 53, 88, 95, 109, 110, 128, 132, 141, 146, 148, 240
Edelman, Simḥah, 55, 88
Edels, Samuel, 98
Edels, Yehudah, 111
*Eifat Ẓedek*, 130, 135, 137
Einhorn, Ze'ev Wolf ben Yisrael Isser, 44-45, 49n36, 52, 53, 54, 55, 57, 67-68, 70, 90, 101, 132, 141, 213, 240
Eisenstein, Elizabeth, 164-165
Eliach, Yaffa, 219
Eliakim, Nissim, 21, 74n63, 174-175, 235n141
Eliezer, Rabbi, 183
Eliyahu ha-Kohen, 143
*Eliyahu Rabba*, 95, 138, 179
*Eliyahu Zuta*, 95
Emden, Yaakov, 89
*'Emek ha-Neẓiv*, 19, 23-24, 27-40, 71, 78, 79, 104, 105n36, 161, 168-171, 175, 181n67, 203n42, 228, 265-268; *Ha'amek Davar* and, 173-174, 190, 191, 206, 209, 237, 239, 262, 263; influences; 23, 97, 111, 112, 125, 127, 167, 208; text of, 59, 63-66, 91, 94, 96, 102, 113, 115n63, 189; treatment of, 20, 21, 24-25, 42
*Emek Halakhah*, 30, 35
'Emunot ve-De'ot, 88, 157
*En Avraham*, 50
*En Ya'akov*, 46, 50, 52, 156
Epstein, Barukh ha-Levi (nephew of subject), 14, 15, 16n24, 20, 57, 136, 171, 207, 213
Epstein, Moshe Mordekhai, 17
Epstein, Yeḥiel Mikhel ha-Levi, 14, 129, 130n14
*'Eshed Neḥalim*, 50, 53, 55, 67, 101
Etkes, Immanuel, 21, 128, 137, 141, 214
Eupatoria (Black Sea port city, Ukraine), 89
Eusebius, 178
Eẓ Ḥayyim Yeshivah, 9, 15, 17, 54, 55, 228
*Ezrat Kohanim*, 47, 94

Falk, Joshua, 92n161, 98
Feivel, Yeḥezkel, maggid of Vilna, 47-48, 49, 53, 67, 90, 110, 128, 146, 147, 240, 263n13
Feunn, Shmuel Yosef, 110-111, 112n55, 213, 214
François Fénelon, 54, 54n65
Frank, Tanhum, 14n18, 22n57
Frankel, David, 92n161, 143, 144
Frankel, Zekhariah, 103n30, 213
Fried, Eliezer Yiẓḥak, 16, 147n75, 194
Friedman, Eliezer Eliyahu, 219

Gallico, Elishah, 107
*Gan Naul*, 89, 175
geonic, 17, 82n109, 106, 107, 145, 157, 168, 187

Gombiner, Avraham Abele (*Magen Avraham*), 43, 54, 94, 111
Gordon, Eliezer, 127
Gordon, Yehudah Leib, 215, 235n141
Gries, Ze'ev, 155

*Ha'amek Davar*, 18, 34n29, 74n63, 174-179, 185, 187-188, 190-197, 202, 206-209, 229-230, 232-237, 242; dating, 105n36, 169-171; reception of, 21, 33n23, 104; relation to Neẓiv's other works, 23-25, 39, 173, 180-182, 189, 228, 239, 262-263, 267-268
*Ha'amek Davar la-Neziv* (Nissim Eliakim), 21
*Ha'amek She'elah*, 17-18, 18n37, 28-32, 39, 48, 65, 71n52, 103n30, 157, 160, 168-171 264, 266-267
Habiba, Yosef, 80
Hadasi, Yehudah, 88, 90, 175
*Haderat Zekeinim*, 106
*Hagahot ve-Ḥidushei ha-Rashash*, 47
haggadah, 19, 46, 51, 86, 132
Hai Ga'on, 106, 119, 145
halakhah, 18, 91, 96, 99, 103, 116, 117, 143, 144, 176, 193, 213
halakhic, 10, 13, 14, 17-19, 29, 42, 44, 46, 55, 58, 64, 65, 89, 91, 92, 96, 98, 125, 127n3, 129, 139, 140, 142-146, 160-162, 168-169, 187, 196, 207, 233, 265
*halakhot*, 115, 180-181, 187, 188, 198
*Halakhot Gedolot*, 81
*ha-Ketav ve-ha-Kabbalah*, 55
*ha-Levanon*, 171
*ha-Maggid*, 32, 57n74, 81n105, 157
Ḥanokh Zundel ben Yosef , 51, 53, 61, 69, 71, 86, 93, 132, 146, 166, 240
*Harḥev Davar*, 34n29, 39, 172, 173, 178, 178n52, 193
Harkavy, Avraham, 17, 145
Harris, Jay, 7, 22, 102, 115, 179
*Hasagot*, 91
Haskalah, 12, 22, 24, 85, 86, 90, 105n36, 109, 110, 165, 208-210, 212, 214, 216-220, 226, 228, 229, 234, 237, 239, 240, 241
*Ḥayye Asaf*, 55
Ḥayyim Avraham ben Aryeh Leib, 148
Ḥayyim of Volozhin, 9, 12, 15, 22, 66n29, 126, 129, 156n102, 179, 194, 197, 202, 241
Heidenheim, Zev Wolf, 175
*Heikhal Ra'anan*, 94
Heller, Yehoshua, 220-222
Herzfeld, Aharon Yosha Eliyahu, 83
Hillel ben Elyakim, 42
Hirsch, Samson Raphael, 38n41, 222
*Ḥosen Yehoshua*, 221
*Ḥovot ha-Levavot*, 156
*ḥukim*, 181-182, 191, 196, 201, 231, 233, 263
Hume, David, 165
Hundert, Gershon, 149, 153, 155, 156
Hurwitz, Elazar Moshe, 171, 207

*Iggeret ha-Neḥamah*, 171
*Iggrot ha-Neẓiv*, 19
*'Ikkarim*, 157
Illya, Menashe, 86
Imperial Library of St. Petersburg, 17n33, 145
*'Imrei Binah*, 106, 112, 114, 115n63, 119, 125
Isaac of Corbiel, 161
Isaachar Ber ben Naftali ha-Kohen (*Matanot Kehunah*), 43, 61, 242, 243,
Isaiah of Trani, 121, 123
*Ishim ve-Shitot* (Shelomoh Yosef Zevin), 21
Ishmael, Rabbi, 182, 183, 191, 199, 263
Isserles, Moshe, 91
*'Ittur Soferim*, 62, 94
*Iyye ha-Yam*, 51, 132

Jaffe, Mordecai Gimpel, 55, 88, 212-213
Jerome, 107, 119
Jossipon, 119

Judah Ha-Levi, 84

*Kadmut Sefer ha-Zohar*, 48
Kahana, Simḥah, 226-227
Karelitz, Avraham Yeshayahu, 10n2
Katzenellenbogen, Aryeh Leib (av bet din of Brisk), 84
Katzenellenbogen, Sha'ul, 48, 49, 53, 128, 141, 213, 240
Katzenellenbogen, Ẓvi Hirsch, 36, 47, 49, 52-53, 57, 85-86, 101, 131, 132, 137, 213, 214, 24o
Kayara, Shimon, 81, 169
*Kenaf Renanim*, 47, 83, 148, 176
*Kevod Elohim*, 54
*Kidmat Ha-'Emek*, 18, 27, 28, 65, 265
*Kiriyah Ne'emanah*, 110-111
*Kol Elohim*, 106
Kook, Avraham Yiẓḥak, 10n2, 17, 39, 204, 220n97
*Korban ha-'Edah*, 92n161, 143
Kotik, Yeḥezkel, 216, 230
Kranz, Ya'akov ben Wolf, 148
*Kur la-Zahav*, 213
*Kuzari*, 89, 119, 163

Lampornati, Yiẓḥak, 111
Landau, Yiẓḥak Eliyahu, 45-46, 49, 51, 52, 53, 62, 68, 86, 91, 93, 95, 130, 132, 134, 137, 146, 147, 159, 176, 224, 240
Lebowitz, Baruch Ber, 10n1
Levin, Yehoshua Heschel, 55, 146
Levinsohn, Adam, 214
Levinsohn, Isaac Baer, 12, 109, 178
Levita, Eliyahu (ha-Baḥur), 89, 161, 175
Lichtenstein, Avraham Yekutiel, 79, 94, 156
Lifshitz, Ya'akov, 218-219
Lillienblum, Moshe Leib, 218
Lilienthal, Max, 15, 16, 193, 209-212, 214, 215
Lincoln, W. Bruce, 12n6
Lipkin, Zev Wolf, 144
Luria, David (Radal), 16n26, 47, 48, 49, 51, 53, 54, 55, 57-60, 59n81, 63, 67, 70, 84, 85, 86, 90, 91, 92, 101, 126, 131, 135, 136, 137, 141, 146, 145, 176, 239, 240, 242-245
Luria, Ḥanokh Zundel ben Yeshaya, 47, 49, 53, 63, 83-84, 86, 90, 146, 148, 175, 176, 240
Luria, Shmuel, 135
Luria, Solomon, 98
Luria, Yehudah Yidel, 48
Lyady, 154, 161

*Magen Ha-Talmud*, 226
Maggid, 23, 45, 47, 48, 50, 53, 83, 84, 86, 88, 91n158, 109, 110, 146-149, 160, 163, 167, 186, 220, 224
Maggid, Shelomoh Zev, 47n27, 147, 147n75
Maharal, 107, 108, 113, 120
Maharshal, 48
*Maḥazeh ha-Shir*, 50
*Maḥazik Berakhah*, 107
Malbim, Meir Leibush, 77, 147
*Ma'oz ha-Dat*, 221
*Mar'eh Penim*, 143
Margoliot, Yehudah Leib, 156
Margoliot, Ẓvi Hirsch ben Aryeh, 156
Margolioth, Moshe, 92n161, 143, 144
Marshalkovitz, Ẓadok, 46
Martyr, Justin, 107

*Masekhet Kallah*, 46
*Masekhet Shekalim*, 143
*Masekhet Soferim*, 62, 68, 86n135, 94, 130
*Masekhet Yevamot*, 103, 193
*Masekhet Zera'im*, 143
maskilic, 81n105, 90, 108, 110, 215, 216, 219, 220, 233, 235
*Masoret ha-Masoret*, 89, 175
Meir ha-Kohen, 54
Meir Simḥah of Dvinsk, 10n2, 127
Meiri, 81
*Mekhilta'*, 19, 24, 27, 28, 45, 52, 55, 68,

69, 76, 91, 93, 95, 115, 130, 131, 135, 137, 139, 140, 144n62, 156, 158, 165, 167, 170n3, 172, 175, 190n1, 262-267
*Mekiẓe Nirdamim*, 157
Meklenburg, Ya'akov Ẓvi, 55
*Mekor Barukh*, 16n24, 32n23, 136, 207
Meltzer, Issar Zalman, 10n1
Mendelssohn, Moses, 37, 84, 85, 86n135, 89, 90, 108, 148, 175, 177, 193, 208, 228, 263n13
*Menorat ha-Ma'or*, 113
*Me'or 'Einayim*, 89, 105-111, 112, 114, 115, 118, 119, 120, 122, 126, 142, 161, 178
*Me'ore ha-'Esh*, 50
*Meromei Sadeh*, 19
*Meshiv Davar*, 19, 130n14, 178n52, 265n22
*Meshiv Nefesh*, 51
*Midrash Aggadat Bereishit*, 44, 52, 90
*midrash halakhah*, 7, 45, 91n158, 116, 125, 138, 146, 158, 172, 187, 189, 263
*Midrash Rabbah*, 43, 45, 47, 48, 50-53, 55, 58, 61, 67, 69, 70, 71, 76, 79, 84, 86, 88, 90, 101, 131, 132, 144n62, 146, 156, 159, 166, 167, 172, 192, 213, 242, 243
*Midrash Shoḥer Tov*, 52, 55, 90, 213
*Midrash Tana'im*, 45
*Midrash Yelamedeinu*, 118
Miezeles, Dov Baer, 55
*Mishnat ha-Neziv* (Hanah Kats), 21
*Mikra' Soferim*, 62, 94
mitnagdic, 10n2, 18, 19, 128, 229
*Miẓuy ha-Middot*, 93
Mohilev, 147, 148
*Moreh Nevukhim*, 88, 89, 163, 164, 213
Montefiore, Sir Moses, 210-211
Moshe Ben Ya'akov, 109n49, 142, 161
Mussar, 9, 13, 194, 195, 220, 239, 241

Nahmanides, 98, 162
Nathanson, Yosef Sha'ul, 50
*Nefesh David*, 48
*Nefesh ha-Ḥayyim*, 9, 15, 129, 130, 194, 197, 202, 241
*Netivot 'Olam*, 36, 49, 53
Novhardok, 83, 84
Novogroduk, 47, 96n180, 146, 148

Onkelos, 173
oral Torah, 115, 117, 126, 180, 181, 188, 190, 191, 206, 221, 234, 257
*Orḥot Ḥayyim*, 94
Origen, 107

*parashah* (no cap), 38, 39, 71, 78, 92, 95, 124, 174
*Parashat* (cap), 35, 38, 40, 72n53, 78, 95, 112, 123, 125
*Peirush ha-Maharif*, 47
*Peirush MaHarZU*, 45, 213
*Pene Moshe*, 92n161, 143
*Perek ha-Shirah*, 47, 63
Perlow, Yeruḥam, 145
Perski, Yoel Dober ha-Kohen, 54-55, 70, 88, 90, 94, 240
*Pesikta' de-Rabbi Eliezer*, 90
*Pesikta' de-Rav Kahana*, 48, 90, 156
*Pesikta' Rabbati*, 44-45, 52-53, 67-68, 90
*Petaḥ ha-Emek*, 82
Philo, 178
Phoebus, Uri, 152
*Pirkei de-Rabbi Eliezer*, 48, 84, 91, 112-113, 131, 136, 159
*piska'*, 38-40, 77-79, 112, 113, 115, 117, 118n71, 119, 121, 122, 125, 266

Rabad of Posquières, 42-43
Rabbeinu Asher, 142
Rabinowitz, Binyamin David, 86
Rambam, 11n3, 51, 58, 63, 79, 84, 85, 88, 89, 91, 100, 102, 103, 106, 109, 116, 125, 127, 142, 148, 156, 157, 163, 167, 171, 174n22, 180, 207, 227, 228
Rappaport, Yisrael, 48
Rappaport, Ẓvi Hirsch ha-Kohen, 46,

53, 57, 91, 94, 136, 146, 240
*Rav Pe'alim*, 44
Reb 'Iẓele, 15-16, 22n57, 30-31, 35, 126, 137n30, 176, 193-194, 207, 211, 214
Rebecca, 185-186
Recanati, Menachem, 116
Riasanovsky, Nicholas, 12n6
Rif, 79, 82, 173
Rosen, Yosef of Dvinsk, 10, 127, 220n97
Rosh Yeshivah, 15-17, 21, 59n82, 193-195, 207n62, 228, 230, 239, 268
*Ruaḥ Ḥen*, 89

Sa'adya Ga'on, 81, 84, 85, 88, 102, 116, 145, 156, 157, 234
Salanter, Yisrael, 9, 12, 13n9, 136, 144, 194, 214, 220
Samson ben Isaac of Chinon, 89
Samson of Chinon, 161
Satanow, Isaac, 83n111, 161
Schacter, Jacob J., 7, 211
Schershevski, Yehudah Yudel, 213
Schick, Avraham, 50, 51, 53, 55, 62, 67, 87-88, 90, 95, 100n18, 101, 176, 240
Schwarz, Yehosef, 32
*Sedeh Yehoshua*, 143
*Seder Olam*, 52, 132
*Seder Olam Rabba*, 179
*Sefer Eshkol ha-Kofer*, 89, 175
*Sefer ha-Ḥinukh*, 109
*Sefer ha-Keritut*, 89, 161, 164
*Sefer ha-Miẓvot*, 145
*Sefer Halakhot Gedolot*, 144-145
*Sefer 'Ikkarim*, 89
*Sefer Me'irat 'Einayim*, 142
*Sefer Me'or 'Einayim*, 89, 105-107, 108n41, 110, 111, 119, 126, 178
*Sefer Miẓvot Gadol*, 109n49, 161
*Sefer Miẓvot ha-Katan*, 161
*Sefer Pa'aneaḥ Razei*, 207
Seforno, 207
*Sha'ar ha-Gemul*, 162
Shapira family of Jerusalem, 24, 30, 32, 33, 35n30, 36, 37n36, 40n50
Shapira, Raphael, 30, 57, 63
*She'iltot*, 17, 18, 27, 28, 31, 47n29, 48, 57-58, 71n52, 81-82, 105n36, 137n30, 145-146, 160-162, 164, 167, 168-170, 187, 239, 240, 245, 263, 267
*She'iltot of Rav Aḥai Ga'on*, 17, 58, 145, 160
*Shelaḥ*, 30, 31n20, 35, 40, 72, 124
*Shemen Ra'anan*, 94
*Shenot Eliyahu*, 138
Sherira Ga'on, 106, 113
Sherishevski, Eliyahu, 214
Sherishevski, Idel (Yehudah), 214
*Shiyare Korban*, 143
Shkop, Shimon, 17
Shmuel ben Hofni, 106, 145
Shmuel ha-Naggid, 145
*Shulḥan Arukh*, 37n36, 43, 50n40, 107, 139, 140-142, 179, 223, 224; *Oraḥ Ḥayyim*, 54n64, 138, 140; *Yoreh De'ah*, 138; *'Even ha-'Ezer*, 138
*Sifre*, 42, 43, 47, 58-60, 71-80, 90-92, 94, 97-105, 111-115, 119-126, 139-141, 164, 172-176, 206, 262-268; publications, 39, 109, 118n71, 135, 156, 158, 167, 229; text of, 35, 38, 117, 144, 180-182, 190-191, 201; work of Neẓiv on, 16n26, 19, 23, 28, 29-31, 55, 61, 63-65, 95-96, 131, 137-138, 160, 161, 163, 168-170, 179, 187, 188, 193, 208, 239-240, 245
*Sifte Kohen*, 142
Solomon ibn Aderet (Rashba), 81n107, 92n161, 116, 162, 164
Soloveitchik, Ḥayyim, 9, 16n24, 63, 98, 127, 171, 227
Soloveitchik, Yosef Baer, 15n24, 54, 63n13, 147n75, 179n55, 194,
Spektor, Yiẓḥak Elḥanan, 50n39, 179n55, 218
Stampfer, Shaul, 7, 21, 128, 129-131, 133, 134n24, 137, 141, 158
Stanislav August Poniatowski, King, 154

Stanislawski, Michael, 22, 214
Steinberg, Joshua, 207, 214
Steinschneider, Hillel Noah Maggid, 49n35, 50n39, 85, 146
Stern, Yosef Zekhariah, 145
Strashun, Matityahu, 55-56, 70, 110-111
Strashun, Shmuel, 47, 49, 53, 55, 57, 70, 90, 101, 240
*sugyot*, 99

*ta' shema'*, 25
"Tahalukhot ha-Midrash", 100n18, 101
*Taharat ha-Kodesh*, 138
Talmi, 88
Talmud, 77, 96, 126, 142, 172-174, 180-181, 199, 216, 219, 225-228; commentary, 13, 19, 31n20, 42, 52, 80, 95, 97, 101-104, 127; publications, 47, 109, 132, 264n21; study of, 9-10, 148, 161, 195, 201, 207, 209, 210, 215, 230; text of, 18, 25, 27, 63, 65, 99, 110, 193, 122-123, 221, 264
Talmud Bavli, 47, 48, 49n34, 51, 56, 76, 79, 95, 104n32, 121, 140, 143n54, 165, 207n61
Talmud Yerushalmi, 18, 48, 50n40, 76, 79, 109, 140, 143, 157, 161, 167
Talmudic, 12, 44, 46, 50, 62, 66, 77, 82, 89, 92, 96n180, 98-99, 102, 104, 123, 132, 139, 142, 156, 161, 162, 173, 178, 184, 185, 189, 191, 201, 203, 207n61, 213, 224, 225, 226
Talmudist, 15, 84, 193, 208, 222
Tam, Jacob Meir, 98
tanaitic, 42, 44, 46, 49, 97, 122, 144, 196
*Tanḥuma*, 51, 69, 90, 93, 132, 156, 159, 167, 213
*Tanna de-Bei Eliyahu*, 50, 62, 87, 90, 95, 100n18, 159, 176
*Tana de-ve Rabbi Yishmael*, 182
*Targum Onkelos*, 37
*Tazri'a*, 29
*Telemaque*, see *Les Aventures de Telemaque*
*Teshuvot Geonim*, 145
*Te'udah be-Yisrael*, 12n8
Tiktin, Solomon, 67
*Tishbi*, 89, 161, 164, 175
*Torah she-Be'al Peh*, 169
*Torat ha-'Adam*, 162, 164
*Torat Kohanim*, 19, 27, 28, 29, 46, 55, 79, 109, 113, 264-267
*Tosefet ha-'Azarah*, 47, 94, 136
Tosfa'ah, Shmuel Avigdor, 52n54, 132
Traub, Avraham Shimon, 145
Tsar Nicholas, 12, 22, 221
*Ture Zahav*, 142

Uvarov, Sergei, 210, 212

*Va'ad 'Arba' 'Arazot*, 151, 153
*Va'ad le-Hoza'at Kitve ha-Neziv*, 30
*Va'ad Lita*, 153
Volozhin, 9, 10, 14-18, 21, 24, 32n23, 54, 58, 90, 147, 155-157, 167, 176, 194, 212, 213, 220, 228, 239
Volozhin Circle, 54-56, 66, 70, 88, 110, 146

Wasserman, Elhanan, 10n1
Weinberg, Joanna, 107-108
Wengeroff, Pauline, 211, 215, 216
Wessely, Naftali Herz, 86, 89, 90, 108, 175, 228
Western, 32, 57, 197; Europe, 12, 55, 86n135, 92n161, 108, 142, 156, 158, 240
written Torah, 97, 115, 117, 181n67, 197, 206, 221

Ya'akov ibn Habib, 50, 156
Ya'akov of Slonim, 44, 45, 49-53, 69, 90, 91n158, 110, 128, 130, 135, 137, 140-141, 240
*Yalkut Shim'oni*, 43, 52, 54, 55, 70, 76, 90, 159
*Yede Moshe*, 61
*Yefeih Mar'eh*, 109

Yehonatan ben David ha-Kohen, 80
Yehuda ha-Levi, 89, 163
Yehuda Loew ben Beẓalel, 107
*yeshivah*, 9, 10, 12, 15-18, 21, 54, 147n75, 192, 194, 196, 201, 209, 213, 219-220, 229, 237, 239-241
Yiẓḥak ben Yedaya, 43
Yokheved, 123
Yosef, Ya'akov, 147
*Yossipun*, 89, 177

Zalkin, Mordechai, 210, 218
*Zayit Ra'anan*, 43, 54, 94
*Zera' Avraham*, 50, 61, 71n52, 79, 94, 156
Zev Wolf ben Yehudah Ha-Levi, 30, 35
*Zikkaron la-Rishonim ve-Gam la-Aḥaronim*, 145
Zilberman, Eliezer Lipman, 157
Zunz, Leopold, 108, 111